REPUBLICANISM AND
BOURGEOIS RADICALISM

Isaac Kramnick

Republicanism and Bourgeois Radicalism

POLITICAL IDEOLOGY IN LATE EIGHTEENTH-CENTURY ENGLAND AND AMERICA

Cornell University Press

ITHACA AND LONDON

First published 1990 by Cornell University Press.

International Standard Book Number 0–8014–2337-6 (cloth)
International Standard Book Number 0–8014–9589–X (paper)
Library of Congress Catalog Card Number 90–55133
Printed in the United States of America
Librarians: Library of Congress cataloging information
appears on the last page of the book.

⊗The paper used in this book meets the minimum requirements
of American National Standard for Information Sciences—
Permanence of Paper for Printed Library Materials, ANSI Z39.48–1984.

For my mother,
Helen Mael Spiro

Contents

Preface

I N A TIME when theories of postmodernism abound and history is said to have come to an end, it is well to acknowledge the eighteenth century as a decisive battleground on which modernity won great victories over the past in a war that had begun three centuries before. My earlier writings have concentrated on figures who resisted the social and intellectual dimensions of modernity. Bolingbroke and Burke bridge the century with their nay-saying. In this book I turn to apostles of modernity.

I have been interested in English radicalism of the late eighteenth century for thirty years, ever since my senior year in college, when I had the good fortune to be directed in an honors thesis on William Godwin by the incomparable Judith Shklar. In the years since then I have written primarily on conservatism, to be sure, but all the while I have recognized that behind the conservatives' nostalgia lies a nightmarish fear of radical change.

For Edmund Burke that specter was given reality by a group of radical conspirators whom he caricatured as "literary caballers," "intriguing philosophers," "political theologians," and "theological politicians." Burke was writing about Richard Price and other nonconformist pests such as Joseph Priestley and Thomas Paine, who, according to Burke, were "unacquainted with the world in which they are so fond of meddling and inexperienced in all its affairs on which they pronounce with so much confidence." This book is about that meddling and those pronouncements.

Parts of the argument presented here were tried out at various academic colloquia. I learned much from stimulating interchanges with faculty and students at UCLA, Columbia, Rochester, Syracuse, Geneseo, Lehigh, Pennsylvania, Yale, Clark, Cambridge, Edinburgh, Sussex, Exeter, and University College, London. Parts of several chapters have also appeared as articles and I am deeply appreciative of the permission to use them and for the helpful correspondence they generated. Parts of chapter 2 appeared as "Religion and Radicalism: English Political Theory in the Age of Revolution," in *Political Theory* 5, no. 4 (1977): 505–34, copyright © 1977 by Sage Publications, Inc.; used by permission of Sage Publications, Inc. Parts of chapter 3 appeared as "Eighteenth-Century Science and Radical Social Theory: The Case of Joseph Priestley's Scientific Liberalism," in *Journal of British Studies* 25 (January 1986): 1–30, published by the University of Chicago Press, copyright © 1986 by the North American Conference on British Studies. Parts of chapter 4 appeared as "Children's Literature and Bourgeois Ideology: Observations on Culture and Industrial Capitalism in the Later Eighteenth Century," in *Culture and Politics from Puritanism to the Enlightenment*, edited by Perez Zagorin (Berkeley: University of California Press, 1980), pp. 203–40. Parts of chapter 5 appeared as an introduction to *The Thomas Paine Reader* (Harmondsworth: Penguin, 1987). Parts of chapter 6 appeared as "Republican Revisionism Revisited," in the *American Historical Review* 87, no. 3 (June 1982): 629–64. Parts of chapter 8 appeared as "'The Great National Discussion': The Discourse of Politics in 1787," in *William and Mary Quarterly*, 3d ser., 45 (January 1988): 3–33.

Two dear people deserve special thanks. My wife, Miriam Brody, has shared with me love, friendship, and intellectual companionship for over a quarter of a century. She and our children are the true prizes in "the race of life." The benign intervention of my mother, Helen Mael Spiro, in my early years made the course of my life possible, with whatever combination of virtue and self-interest it has contained. I dedicate this book to her with all my love.

ISAAC KRAMNICK

Ithaca, New York

REPUBLICANISM AND
BOURGEOIS RADICALISM

CHAPTER 1

Liberalism, the Middle Class, and Republican Revisionism

REPUBLICANISM is historically an ideology of leisure. Its conception of citizenship privileges people who need not work, who have the time to devote themselves to civic life. In this commitment to public duty independent landowners realize their essence as human beings. No one has expressed this republican ideal better than Aristotle in his *Politics:*

> In the state with the finest constitution, which possesses just men who are just absolutely and not relatively to the assumed situation, the citizen must not live a mechanical or commercial life. Such a life is not noble, and it militates against virtue. Nor must those who are to be citizens be agricultural workers, for they must have leisure to develop their virtue, and for the activities of a citizen.[1]

Liberalism, at its origin, is an ideology of work. It attributes virtue to people who are industrious and diligent and condemns as corrupt privileged aristocrats and leisured gentlefolk. The essence of humanity is the obligation to work. The classic articulation of this valuation of work is found in chapter five, "Of Property," in Locke's *Second Treatise of Government.* God has commanded his creature "to subdue the earth, i.e. improve it for the benefit of life, and therein lay out something upon it that was his own, his labour." God has given property to the "industrious" and "labour was to be his title to it." The fact that indi-

---

[1]Aristotle, *Politics,* bk. 7, chap. 9. There is, of course, the republican warrior ideal, which emphasizes exertion, but not work. The mythos of hardworking Cincinnatus leaving his plow to defend his country is also much less characteristic of true republican iconography than is the Roman senator or the gentry-statesman whose properties are worked by slaves, tenants, or wage laborers.

viduals have "different degrees of industry" explains and legitimates differential possessions, since that is justly one's own property which one "has mixed his labor with and joined to it something that is his own." Compacts, laws, and governments derive their origins from this "property which labor and industry began."[2] Locke's God is a very Protestant God, and indeed, behind liberal social theory looms the world view of Protestantism.

In the general scholarly preoccupation with liberalism as a political theory of individual rights, consent, and a limited state, and inversely with republicanism as a communitarian theory of participation and civic obligation, too little attention is paid to social and economic ideology. A fundamental shift occurred in the seventeenth and eighteenth centuries in attitudes toward leisure and work. A culture that from time immemorial had privileged leisure and disparaged work was turned upside down; now work became the cultural ideal and leisure the less worthy other. This reversal was to have profound implications for conceptualizations of society and the polity. Behind it was Protestantism, a development too often neglected in recent political scholarship.

This book takes for its center this transvaluation of leisure and work and explores its impact on social and political theory. It does so by examining a particularly formative moment in the history of liberalism, its Anglo-American articulation in the late eighteenth century. With this assumption of profound change and discontinuity the book challenges a fairly entrenched scholarly concensus that sees continuity, or even an outright longing for the past, as the all-pervasive characteristic of the political discourse of the period.

Of Chains and Races

Radicals as reactionaries: that is the received wisdom on reform in late eighteenth-century Britain. Bernard Bailyn describes "eighteenth-century English radicals" as concerned "not with the need to recast the social order nor with the problems of economic inequality and the injustices of stratified societies but with the need to purify a corrupt constitution." This reactionary reading of radicalism received its imprimatur in the post–World War II work of Herbert Butterfield and Ian Christie, both of whom read the reform movements of the 1770s, 1780s, and 1790s as preoccupied with the restoration of lost Anglo-Saxon political rights and uninterested in social questions. In the writ-

---

[2]John Locke, *Second Treatise of Government*, chap. 5, paras. 32, 33, 34, 27, 45.

ings of J. G. A. Pocock and Gordon Wood the radical zeal of Richard Price, Joseph Priestley, James Burgh, even John Thelwall reflects the "dread of modernity" or an unwillingness "to accept the developments of the eighteenth century." For Pocock "radical demands for Parliamentary and franchise reform" were informed by "classical republican values."[3]

The consensus among scholars is impressive. Colin Bonwick describes English radicals as "at one with the society in which they lived. They . . . accepted the normality of a stratified society." They were unwilling "to examine the problems flowing from social inequality . . . in this respect they were incurably conservative." For Forrest McDonald and Lance Banning all radicalism, from *Cato's Letters* to Burgh, "from the Restoration to the French Revolution," was "without exception" in opposition to the new financial order and interested only in restoring lost rights and proper constitutional balance. This orthodox reading of eighteenth-century radicalism is best captured by Carla Hay, who writes of "the fundamentally conservative aspiration of English radicals . . . to restore some mythic yesteryears when virtue flourished and an harmonious equilibrium governed men's social and political relationships."[4]

Now there is nothing unusual in uncovering the seemingly paradoxical presence of reactionary elements in overtly radical ideology. There is, in fact, a good deal of backward-looking nostalgia or lament for a lost golden age in most radical thought. Radical movements, as well, often invoke the past as they chart new futures. Gerrard Winstanley's Diggers and other millenarians looked back to the shared fellowship of early Christianity. Marx, according to some interpreters, saw the paradigm of unalienated communal existence in ancient Greece. Others have stressed how crucial the anthropologist Lewis Henry Morgan's work on the Iroquois was for the vision held by Marx and Engels of some archetypal lost stage of primitive communism. Jean-Jacques

---

[3]Bernard Bailyn, *The Ideological Origins of the American Revolution* (Cambridge, Mass., 1976), p. 283; see Herbert Butterfield, *George III, Lord North, and the People, 1779–1780* (London, 1949), esp. pp. 229–56, 337–52; the following works by Ian Christie: *Myth and Reality in Late Eighteenth-Century British Politics and Other Papers* (London, 1970); Introduction to G. S. Vetch, *The Genesis of Parliamentary Reform* (London, 1964); and *Wilkes, Wyvill, and Reform* (London, 1962); Gordon Wood, *The Creation of the American Republic* (New York, 1972), passim; J. G. A. Pocock, *The Machiavellian Moment: Florentine Political Thought and the Atlantic Republican Tradition* (Princeton, N.J., 1975), pp. 567, 547, and "Virtue and Commerce in the Eighteenth Century," *Journal of Interdisciplinary History* 3 (1972): 133, 122.

[4]Colin Bonwick, *English Radicals and the American Revolution* (Chapel Hill, N.C., 1977), pp. 18, 260; Forrest McDonald, "A Founding Father's Library," in *Literature of Liberty* 1 (January–March 1978): 13; Lance Banning, *The Jeffersonian Persuasion* (Ithaca, 1978), pp. 61, 62; Carla Hay, *James Burgh, Spokesman for Reform in Hanoverian England* (Washington, D.C., 1979), pp. 104, 105.

Rousseau's democratic future is developed through the lenses of the Spartan past. Many French and American revolutionaries saw themselves as reviving the republicanism of antiquity. Pëtr Kropotkin's anarchist followers could find in his writings lyrical praise for the lost medieval commune as well as his conviction that the destruction of the nation-state would revive older ideals of "mutual aid." Syndicalists and guild socialists were often motivated in part by a longing for aspects of the corporate past. Luddites, food rioters, and other early critics of industrial capitalism were much more likely to be looking backward to the paternalist world they sensed passing than to the future creation of a new Jerusalem.

What is questionable about the scholarly consensus on English late eighteenth-century radicalism is not, then, the simple assumption that some part of it was backward-looking, but the assumption that at its core it was reactionary. Such a reading is fundamentally flawed. English radicals, especially after 1760, were in fact, much more likely to frame their arguments in terms of natural rights than of historical rights and much more likely to invoke Lockean than republican themes. They were less concerned with nostalgic country concerns than with modern middle-class socioeconomic grievances. In fact, what gives English eighteenth-century radicalism its coherence is its very desire "to destroy the existing order and create anew." English radicalism sought to topple the social order of rank and privilege, the static stratified society of ascription. It would replace that society with a new liberal ideal, a society of achievement, a social order of competitive individualism, in which social mobility was possible and the rightful reward for ingenious people of talent and hard work.

Central and enduring in liberalism is this unique conception of liberty and equality, rooted principally in attitudes toward work and the marketplace, toward achievement and talent. This revolutionary liberal ideal is best expressed in two famous cultural documents. The first, Beaumarchais's *Marriage of Figaro*, was written in 1783, just before the French Revolution. The play, of course, was the basis of Mozart's opera. The plot, though complicated, is for our purposes quite simple. It is built around the competition between the great aristocrat Count Almaviva and a commoner, the hard-working, industrious Figaro, for the hand of Susannah. When the Count seems almost to have outwitted Figaro in Act V, Figaro delivers his famous denunciation: "Just because you're a great Lord, you think you're a genius. Nobility, fortune, rank, position—you're so proud of those things. What have you done to deserve so many rewards? You went to the trouble of being born, and no more."[5] So subversive were these sentiments that the

---

[5]P. A. C. de Beaumarchais, *The Marriage of Figaro* (New York, 1966), Act V, p. 90.

play was banned and surfaced again in France only after the Revolution had dealt even more definitively with the Almavivas.

The second document is from Thomas Mann, part of whose genius consisted in his ability to describe with meticulous accuracy European bourgeois civilization. In *Buddenbrooks* Mann gives a much more vivid summary of these basic liberal beliefs than did Beaumarchais: his nineteenth-century liberal revolutionary Morten Schwartzkopf is speaking, criticizing a friend who has just spoken well of an aristocratic acquaintance:

> They need only to be born to be the pick of everything, and look down on all the rest of us. While we, however hard we strive, cannot climb to their level. We, the bourgeoisie—the Third Estate as we have been called—we recognize only that nobility which consists of merit; we refuse to admit any longer the rights of the indolent aristocracy, we repudiate the class distinctions of the present day, we desire that all men should be free and equal. . . . So that all men, without distinction, shall be able to strive together and receive their reward according to their merit.[6]

Writing early in the twentieth century—a century when these values would be assaulted on the left and right (as he so beautifully depicted in his *Magic Mountain*)—Mann expressed the same sense of liberalism as Beaumarchais. Basic to the dreams of both Figaro and Schwartzkopf is a vision of society in which the rule of privilege is replaced by equal opportunity and in which individuals, now masters of their destiny, are no longer the slaves of history, tradition, or birth.

Figaro's and Schwartzkopf's liberal vision of an ideal society is not some timeless, eternal ideal of humanity, however, or found, like so much else of our culture, in the antique world of Greece or Rome or the Judeo-Christian tradition. It has a distinct history. It emerged at a specific historical moment, for specific reasons, and with specific intellectual justifications. That moment came in the grand transformation wrought in the Europe of the sixteenth, seventeenth, and eighteenth centuries by the rise of Protestantism and capitalism. The traditional hierarchical world was replaced in Western Europe by the modern liberal world as we know it.

Fundamental to this profound confrontation between the aristocratic ideal and its challenger, the ideal of equal opportunity emblazoned on the banners of the middle class, are certain recurring metaphorical notions. The ideological struggle is expressed in images of chains, motion, and races.

Thanks to Arthur O. Lovejoy, we know well that the hierarchical political ideal of Christian and aristocratic Europe was part of the larger

<hr>

[6]Thomas Mann, *Buddenbrooks* (New York, 1961), p. 106.

cosmological ideal of God's great chain of being, in which all creatures were held together, linked in given ranks to the great plenitude that was God's universe. This metaphor of the chain serves two functions. It describes infinite interconnectedness, the continuous linkage of each gradation in creation. It also described the fixity of God's creation. Social ranks are held in place; they are chained to their assigned place. It is God who fixes this place and, according to Viscount Bolingbroke, one must offer thanks, "O my creator! that I am placed in a rank . . . to which I belong." Robert Walpole's upstart moneymen and the calculators and economists despised by Burke refused to be chained to the place to which they belonged. They were Alexander Pope's prideful men who "quit their sphere," who in their pride broke "the chain alike."[7] Such men rejected the wisdom of James Nelson, who in 1756 described "the whole body of the people" in England as linked, "as it were, in one continued chain," and of the Tory moralist who wrote in 1746 that

> it has pleased the almighty Governor of the world to make a difference in the outward condition of his subjects here below, and though high and low; rich and poor, one with another are all his servants, yet in the course of his Providence he has thought good to appoint various orders and degrees of men here upon earth. Some of these are placed by him in a high, others in a low estate. Some are born to rule, others to obey. Hence arises the necessity that some should be Masters, others Servants: and this constitutes a mutual relation and duty between them.[8]

The decline in use of the metaphor of the chain is one benchmark of the triumph of modernity. As John Stuart Mill asked in his essay "On the Subjection of Women," "What is the peculiar character of the modern world, that which chiefly distinguishes modern institutions, modern social ideas, modern life itself, from those of times long past? It is that human beings are no longer born to their place in life and chained down by an inexorable bond to the place they are born to."[9] If chains and immobility are the metaphoric embodiment of the hierarchical ideal, we should not be surprised that its liberal replacement was captured in talk of motion, mobility, and races.

The ideology of English social radicalism begins, then, with Thomas

---

[7]Arthur O. Lovejoy, *The Great Chain of Being* (New York, 1960); Henry St. John, Lord Bolingbroke, *Works* (Philadelphia, 1841), 4:339; Alexander Pope, *Essay on Man*, epistle 1, ll. 124, 246.

[8]James Nelson, *An Essay on the Government of Children* (London, 1756), p. 317; Tory moralist quoted in R. W. Malcolmson, *Life and Labour in England, 1700–1780* (New York, 1981), p. 44.

[9]John Stuart Mill, "The Subjection of Women," in *Essays on Sexual Equality*, ed. Alice S. Rossi (Chicago, 1970), pp. 142–43.

Hobbes. This chronicler of "masterless men" saw the defining feature of freedom as unimpeded movement. Freedom is "the absence of opposition . . . external impediments of motion." Individuals who are not stopped from doing whatever is their "will, desire, or inclination to do" experience "freedom from chains and prison." Hobbes provides us a brilliant model of individualistic society in which all persons are freed from chains. As self-moving, self-directing independent machines, they constantly compete with one another for power, wealth, and glory. People know their value or worth by comparing themselves with one another, by looking at their worth in the market of shared life. Free individuals do not cooperate, they compete constantly to outdo one another. Hobbes was the first to offer a new metaphor that enshrines freedom understood as motion and competition as the key to human nature. Life is a race. In *The Elements of Law* he suggests that "the comparison of the life of man to a race . . . holdeth so well for this our purpose. . . . This race we must suppose to have no other goal, nor other garland, but being foremost."[10] In his use of the metaphor of "the race of life" Hobbes anticipated brilliantly the psychology of the modern bourgeois individual. It was Adam Smith who refined it for the ideological uses of the eighteenth century. But before Smith there was John Locke.

Locke's suggestion that unlimited acquisition of money and wealth was neither unjust nor morally wrong was a move absolutely essential for the late eighteenth-century liberal agenda of competitive individualism and equal opportunity. Locke's very Protestant God commands us to work the earth, and in return the hardworking and industrious have the right to what they produce by their work. Since God has given people "different degrees of industry," some have more talent and work harder than others.[11] It is just and ethical, then, for them to have as many possessions as they want. This logic is crucial to the emerging ideology. If individuals are to define themselves in terms of what they achieve in the race of life, and if this sense of achievement is seen increasingly in terms of work and victory in a market society where talent and industry have their play, then the traditional Christian and moral economy barriers to unlimited accumulation have to fall. How else can achievement and sense of self be known if not by economic success?

An utterly new understanding of the individual and society was emerging. Ascription, the assignment to some preordained rank in life, came more and more to be replaced by achievement as the major de-

[10]Thomas Hobbes, *Leviathan*, chap. 21, and *The Elements of Law*, chap. 9.
[11]Locke, *Second Treatise*, chap. 5, para. 27.

finer of personal identity. Individuals increasingly came to define themselves as active subjects. They no longer tended to see their place in life as part of some natural, inevitable, and eternal plan. Their own enterprise and ability mattered; they possessed the opportunity (a key word) to determine their place through their own voluntary actions in this life and in this world.

Now—and this is the truly critical step—what one did in this world came soon to be understood primarily as what one did economically, what one did in terms of work. In the world of work one was the author of self. Individuality became an internal subjective quality; work became a concrete test and property a material extension of self. Inherent in this development is the birth of the market society, where the allocation and distribution of such valuable things as power, wealth, and fame came to be seen as the result of countless individual decisions, not of some authoritative norms set by custom, God, or ruling-class decree. Who has more, who has less, whether some get any—such things are decided less by a social or moral consensus than by the free action of individual actors seeking their own gain in a context of continuous competition. What one has or gets, and therefore who one is, is no longer the reward appropriate to one's prescribed place; it is what one can get, the product of what one does in the competitive market.

The new theory of individuality had far-reaching political implications. To be free, truly self-defining, master of the self, the individual had to eliminate all barriers to that individuality. So war was declared against religious restraint on free thought and against economic restraint on a free market. What I am describing is, of course, the gradual liquidation of the aristocratic world and its replacement by the liberal capitalist order. It is the crusade of Figaro and Schwartzkopf.

Adam Smith's contribution was to reinforce Hobbes's reading of human nature. All men are ambitious, he writes. Each man constantly strives "to better his own condition." This ambition, he tells us in *The Wealth of Nations*, is "a desire which comes with us from the womb and never leaves us till we go into the grave." He returns to Hobbes's metaphor. Life, Smith writes in *The Theory of Moral Sentiments*, is "a race for wealth and honour and preferments." Government, alas, unfairly interferes in the race. It sets aside offices and power for the privileged, rendering as winners the idle aristocracy who lack any talent or merit. Government thus interferes in the natural freedom to "outstrip all competitors."[12]

---

[12]Adam Smith, *The Wealth of Nations*, ed. Andrew Skinner (Baltimore, 1970), p. 441, and *The Theory of Moral Sentiments* (Edinburgh, 1813), 1:188.

Smith posits two archvillains in *The Wealth of Nations*. First is the "corporate spirit," the institutional relics of the feudal past which in the poor laws and apprentice laws, for example, violate individual freedom of movement and choice and therefore handicap some runners in the race of life. Smith turns on what he takes to be the hypocrisy in the bourgeois camp, for that corporate spirit, he contends, lingers on in businessmen and manufacturers who call upon legislative power to interfere in their behalf with special privileges and favors— again to the detriment of a fair and equitable race. The second villain is the idle, unproductive, wasteful, and prodigal aristocracy. Some readers have noted that Marx's *Kapital* reads like a morality play with its Mr. Moneybags and Mr. Collective Worker; chapter 3, book 2, of *The Wealth of Nations* reads just as poignantly. There is good man and there is evil man. "Every prodigal appears to be a public enemy, and every frugal man a public benefactor." Smith makes it quite clear who it is that represents the evils of idleness, unproductivity, and prodigality, and with this assessment sets forth a theme central to bourgeois radicalism.

> The labour of some of the most respectable orders in the society is, like that of menial servants, unproductive of any value, and does not fix or realize itself in any permanent subject, or vendible commodity, which endures after the labour is past, and for which an equal quantity of labour could afterwards be procured. The sovereign, for example, with all the officers both of justice and war who serve under him, the whole army and navy, are unproductive labourers. They are the servants of the public and are maintained by a part of the annual produce of the industry of other people. In the same class must be ranked, some of the gravest and most important, and some of the most frivolous professions: churchmen, lawyers, physicians, men of letters of all kinds; players, buffoons, musicians, opera-singers, opera-dancers, etc.[13]

Smith shares Figaro's reading of the aristocracy. Not only are they profligate and idle but they lack talent and intrinsic merit. They have what they have only by virtue of birth. In his *Theory of Moral Sentiments* Smith asks:

> By what important accomplishments is the young nobleman instructed to support the dignity of his rank, and to render himself worthy of that superiority over his fellow citizens? . . . Is it by knowledge, by industry, by patience, by self-denial, or by virtue of any kind . . . what were the talents and virtues by which he acquired this great reputation? Was it by the scrupulous and inflexible justice of all his undertaking, by the immense dangers and difficulties with which they were attended, or by the

[13]Smith, *Wealth of Nations*, pp. 441, 430–31.

unwearied and unrelenting application with which he pursued them? Was it by his extensive knowledge, by his exquisite judgment, or by his heroic valour? It was by none of these qualities.[14]

He had merely gone to the trouble of being born.

For the liberal theorist government itself is always a potential tyrant, waiting to interpose itself arbitrarily in the citizen's restless pursuit of wealth and happiness. Aristocratic government imposes another burden on its people, however: it is also expensive. The taxes it raises from the productive middle class in order to fund its hordes of privileged retainers constitute the real essence of tyranny, according to Smith.

> In the midst of all the exactions of government, this capital has been silently and gradually accumulated by the private frugality and good conduct of individuals, by their universal, continual, and uninterrupted effort to better their own condition. It is this effort, protected by law and allowed by liberty to exert itself in the manner that is most advantageous, which has maintained the progress of England towards opulence and improvement. . . . It is the highest impertinence and presumption, therefore, in kings and ministers, to pretend to watch over the economy of private people, and to restrain their expense. They are themselves always, and without any exception, the greatest spendthrifts in the society. Let them look well after their own expense, and they may safely trust private people with theirs. If their own extravagance does not ruin the state, that of their subjects will.[15]

Were administration simplified, taxes cut, retainers dropped, and wars ended, were government simply an inexpensive and impartial umpire over the "race for wealth and honours," then the middle class would win the laurels, Smith writes, for the runners in the race of life are urged on by the "uniform, constant, and uninterrupted effort of every man to better his condition."[16]

Smith has few illusions, however. He knows that even if the expensive and unproductive aristocratic social order were eliminated and the race run with equal opportunity for all the runners, only some would win. Obvious differentials would remain in people's ability to "better [their] own condition." An unexpected note of Christian pessimism intrudes with Smith's acknowledgment that seldom does the race provide "real satisfaction," and that it is often really "contemptible and trifling." Equally seldom, however, does anyone look at the race in such an "abstract and philosophical light," and a good thing, too. The

[14]Smith, *Theory of Moral Sentiments*, 1:116, 117.
[15]Smith, *Wealth of Nations*, p. 446.
[16]Ibid., pp. 441–42.

race, the competition, the illusion that everyone can win, and the alleged pleasures of victory are all necessary and worthwhile deceptions. It is because of these fictions that progress is possible. In a remarkable moment of candor Smith attributes the wondrous progress of capitalist civilization to deception.

> And it is well that nature imposes upon us in this manner. It is this deception which rouses and keeps in continual motion the industry of mankind. It is this which first prompted them to cultivate the ground, to build houses, to found cities and commonwealths, and to invent and improve all the sciences and arts, which enable and embellish human life; which have entirely changed the whole face of the globe, have turned the rude forests of nature into agreeable and fertile plains, and made the trackless and barren ocean a new fund of subsistence, and the great road of communication to the different nations of the earth. The earth, by these labours of mankind, has been obliged to redouble her natural fertility, and to maintain a greater multitude of inhabitants.[17]

The central importance of the metaphor of the "race of life" in Anglo-American ideology owes less to Smith than to the Protestant Dissenters, who used it constantly in the last third of the eighteenth century. These men and women, epitomized by the great chemist Joseph Priestley, were, as we shall see, at the forefront of virtually every middle-class political, social, economic, and cultural reform movement of the period. The Dissenters' invocation of the "race of life" emerged in the great cause that propelled many of them into reform politics, the long campaign to repeal the Test and Corporation Acts. These legislative relics of seventeenth-century anti-Catholic frenzy prohibited the talented and highly successful Dissenter merchants, industrialists, scientists, intellectuals, teachers, and professionals from holding important public offices because they did not subscribe to the creed of the Church of England.

Much of Dissenter pamphleteering attacked the acts for violating the natural rights of individuals to practice their religion without state interference. But in addition to their demands for freedom of religion, they insisted that the discriminating legislation unjustly intruded the state into the free competitive market of careers and rewards due talented and industrious individuals, by reserving public offices for Anglicans. One after another of their pamphlets claimed, as we shall see, that the Test and Corporation Acts violated the fundamental social principles "let all mankind start fair in the race of life."[18]

---

[17]Smith, *Theory of Moral Sentiments*, 1:417–18.
[18]Thomas Walker, *A Review of Some of the Political Events Which Have Occurred in Manchester during the Last Five Years* (London, 1794), pp. 46–47.

The reality of social mobility and its prerequisite, the ability to compete fairly for society's valuable things, not a quest for lost historical rights, was at the heart of the Dissenters' radical agenda. Priestley insisted that since "every individual wishes to rise above his neighbors," the society had to ensure "free access to honors and employments, free scope to abilities." James Burgh, the great dissenting schoolmaster of Newington Green, demanded for all "an equal chance to rise to honours." David Williams, the dissenting minister, radical follower of Priestley, and friend of Benjamin Franklin and Thomas Jefferson, repeated the theme in 1789: "All men should start from equal situations and with equal advantages, as horses do on the turf. Afterwards everything is to depend on ability and merit." Even William Godwin called for equal opportunity, not leveling. In his *Enquiry Concerning Political Justice* he, too, invoked the metaphor of the race: "let us start fair; render all the advantages and honours of social institution accessible to every man in proportion to his talents and exertions."[19]

What particularly distressed his wife, Mary Wollstonecraft, was not only that in this race the winners were always men but that women did not even bother to run. She lamented their socially conditioned lack of ambition. "Woman," she wrote in her *Vindication*, was just like Smith's useless aristocrat, "in her self complete," possessed of "all those frivolous accomplishments." Unlike bourgeois man, she lacked any desire to improve herself. Women were socialized to avoid the race, to avoid the ambitious individual scramble for the rewards due to talent and merit. Wollstonecraft's message was that women should become more like the assertive men of the middle class. Women were "always on the watch to please." Instead of "laudable ambitions," they were ruled by "romantic wavering feelings." Only education and political rights could fit them for the race. "There must be more equality established in Society, or morality will never gain ground, and the virtuous equally will not rest firmly even when founded on a rock, if one half of mankind be chained to its bottom by fate."[20]

For Priestley's circle the winners in the race were self-made men and women who literally created themselves, who gave birth to themselves. They were, in the vernacular of Ben Franklin and Tom Paine, ingenious. Clever, to be sure, as we now use the word, but to the radical mentality of the late eighteenth century the ingenious winners

[19]Joseph Priestley, *Lectures on History and General Policy*, 4th ed. (London, 1826), lecture 18, p. 337; James Burgh, *Crito; or, Essays on Various Subjects*, 2 vols. (London, 1766, 1767), 2:68; David Williams, *Lectures on Education* (London, 1789), 4:64; William Godwin, *Enquiry Concerning Political Justice*, ed. Isaac Kramnick (Baltimore, 1976), p. 470.

[20]Mary Wollstonecraft, *Vindication of the Rights of Woman*, ed. Miriam Brody Kramnick (New York, 1975), pp. 150–53, 252.

of the race were those who were authors of themselves, those who generated themselves, in contrast to men of breeding, born to rule, bred to win.

It's important to remember that Priestley, Burgh, Godwin, and Williams were or had been dissenting ministers, and many of their radical colleagues were equally familiar with the Scriptures. They could easily have found Christian legitimacy for their description of life as a race. Several times Paul refers to having "finished the race," "running the race," "having reached the finish line." Indeed, in 1 Corinthians 9:24 Paul makes clear that "while all the runners in the stadium take part in the race, the award goes to one man. In that case, run so as to win."[21] The inevitability of Paul's mission, its irresistible fulfillment of God's plan, is rendered by the repeated references to the course of life, life as a race. So it is with its very Protestant rendering in the language of the dissenting radicals. Humankind follows a fixed course or path like the heavenly bodies. The virtuous person is irresistibly urged to run the course of life as a race in which he seeks "to rise above his neighbor." He is obsessive and anxious in his desire to "better his own condition," which runs the course of his life, as Smith described it, "from the womb . . . till we go into the grave."

Despite its optimism, assertiveness, and self-confidence, then, liberalism has another face, a frightened and fearful view of market society and the race of life as fraught with dangers, the most horrible of which is the possibility of losing. A convincing case can be made that liberal social theorists of the seventeenth and eighteenth centuries presumed fear to be the basic human motive that first sets people running—or, in Smith's words, "rouses and keeps in continual motion the industry of mankind." The religious interpretation of this linkage is familiar from the writings of Max Weber and R. H. Tawney, but we are less familiar with the explicit claims of the early liberals themselves. Locke, for example, held in his *Essay on Human Understanding* that "the chief, if not the only spur to human industry and action is uneasiness." This feeling of uneasiness, a desire for "some absent good," drives us to enterprise. But we are ever fearful; once driven to the race, we never lose our uneasiness. We are permanently cursed, wrote Locke, with "an itch after honour, power, and riches," which in turn unleashes more "fantastical uneasiness."[22]

Anxiety forever haunts the bourgeois. "Fear and anxiety," Smith wrote, are the "two great tormentors of the human breast." They persist because the race of life has winners and losers, and above all else

---

[21]See also Phil. 3:12–14; Heb. 12:1; 2 Tim. 4:7–8.
[22]John Locke, *An Essay on Human Understanding*, ed. A. C. Fraser (Oxford, 1894), bk. 20, sec. 6.

the bourgeois fears failure. For Smith the possibility of losing ground was "worse than death." Runners in the race of life fear losing what they have, or losing simply because to lose is to become a nonperson. Only success in the marketplace brings the notice and valuation of others. These early liberal theorists knew very well what insecurity often lurks in the heart of the bourgeois. To be a loser is to be invisible, according to Smith:

> What are the advantages which we propose by that great purpose of human life which we call bettering our condition? To be observed, to be attended to, to be taken notice of . . . the poor man, on the contrary, is ashamed of his poverty. He feels that it . . . places him out of the sight of mankind. . . . To feel that we are taken no notice of, necessarily damps the most agreeable hope, and disappoints the most ardent desire, of human nature. The poor man goes out and comes in unheeded, and when in the midst of a crowd is in the same obscurity as if shut up in his own house. . . . They turn away their eyes from him.[23]

No one in the eighteenth century perceived the obsessive quality of the liberal vision of competitive individualism and "the race of life" better than Rousseau, the great antagonist of that ideal. It was for him a nightmarish vision of a person "always moving, sweating, toiling, and racking his brains to find still more laborious occupations." Rousseau saw that "universal competition and rivalry" end up "making so many aspirants who run the same course." Like Smith, Rousseau recognized that even if few win, the race "excites and multiplies our passions," but he could not ultimately share Smith's view that the deception is worthwhile. Indeed, the irresistibility and mindlessness of the competition between runners who constantly compare their performances and measure themselves against the efforts of the other runners forged a new set of chains that bound people everywhere—people who were, in fact, born free.[24]

Rousseau sensed what we now know. The ideal of equality of opportunity and its rendition in the metaphor of life as a fairly run race was at its origins in the eighteenth century an effort both to reduce inequality and to perpetuate it. It was egalitarian at its birth because it lashed out at the exclusiveness of aristocratic privilege, but it sought to replace an aristocratic elite with a new elite, albeit one based more broadly on talent and merit. Equality of opportunity is a theory not really of equality but of justified and morally acceptable inequality.

[23]Smith, *Theory of Moral Sentiments*, 1:108, 109.
[24]Jean-Jacques Rousseau, *Discourse of the Origin of Inequality*, in *The Social Contract and Discourses*, ed. G. H. D. Cole (New York, 1950), pp. 270, 266, and *Social Contract*, in ibid., p. 3. See also Jean-Paul Marat, *The Chains of Slavery* (London, 1774).

What can legitimate a system in which some people have more than others? Only the requirement that all have an equal opportunity to get more. Equality for liberals really means fairness. Let the race be fair, let all have an equal chance to win.

Equality of opportunity presumes a noncooperative vision of society. It encompasses no ideal of community or quest for the common good. Individuals compete on an equal footing, and as in any race, some win, others lose. According to the theory, those that win do so because they are more talented and work harder than the losers. Equality of opportunity presumes that people have different abilities and talents. This basic human inequality in talents will, in a free society, legitimize status differentials. The society is free if the race is fair. The race is not fair, there is no equality of opportunity, when freedom to realize oneself through success and achievement is impaired. Such freedom is impaired whenever ethical, religious, or social limitations are placed on economic activity, whenever governments interfere in the race by favoring some privileged class whose members could not win on their own. Equality of opportunity, then, is historically the ideal of the revolutionary middle class, perhaps the most powerful weapon in its successful battle to end the rule of aristocratic privilege.

Radicalism in the eighteenth century did invoke themes of the past, to be sure; it spoke on occasion of the Witenagemot, the ancient parliament, and of the Norman yoke and lost Saxon rights. But it also spoke of a much more ambitious enterprise, the creation of a new social order. English radicalism demanded political reform in order to destroy forever the aristocratic world of ascribed status. Equality of opportunity was a social ideal that assumed that the have-nots were the truly skilled and industrious. Given a freely competitive race of life, these talents would move them to the front, a victory for virtue as well as for merit.

No surprise, then, that the enemies of English bourgeois radicalism reacted with horror to this threat to the principle of hierarchy and returned to the imagery of chains. The writings of Josiah Tucker, Edward Tatham, Matthew Goodenough, William Paley, Richard Hey, and Soame Jenyns in the last three decades of the century are replete with invocations of a social order of "regular gradations and distinctions." God has decreed "servitude and dependencies . . . from the meanest peasant or mechanic through all the ranks and orders of society up to the king upon the throne in whom the chain of subordination terminates." Tatham wrote in 1791 of "a great chain of subordination to the king." Soame Jenyns praised the "wonderful chain of Beings . . . from the senseless clod to the brightest Genius of Human Kind." Burke, of course, knew better than latter-day Namierites, knew better than

Christie, Butterfield, and their Tory historian follower Jonathan Clarke, knew better than Bailyn and Pocock and the republican school that an ideology lay at the heart of radicalism, and he detested it. He hated it because, as he told the House of Commons on February 9, 1790, it sought "to break all those connexions, natural and civil, that regulate and hold together the community by a chain of subordination."[25]

Burke, like John Stuart Mill, saw as the defining feature of modern politics the replacement of the chain by the race as the structuring metaphor of society. Mill gloried in the new ideal that saw individual men—and, he hoped, some women, too—"free to employ their faculties and such favourable chances, as offer" in the competitive race, "to achieve the lot which may appear to them most desirable." Burke, however, lamented the passing of "the age of chivalry" and saw "the glory of Europe extinguished forever."[26]

No small part of the blame or credit for breaking the "chain of subordination" must go to British bourgeois radicalism of the late eighteenth century. It helped introduce and popularize the metaphorical language of liberal politics and modernity. That language would take hold in America as well. It would be used by the Founding Fathers. Jefferson and Franklin knew Price and Priestley personally. Benjamin Rush and John Adams were longtime correspondents with Richard Price. Adams and his fellow colonists knew Burgh's writing as well as they knew the works of Price and Priestley. Paine and then Priestley would, in fact, come to America.

But the language of the race had its own American Protestant roots as well. Boston's Society for Encouraging Industry and Employing the Poor proclaimed in the 1750s the need to stimulate a "spirit of industry and frugality" among the poor. Americans and all humanity "were made for business." The virtuous person was an active person, for it was "a shameful thing for any to eat the bred of idleness." No one deployed this language better than Franklin, who in those same 1750s offered Americans the wisdom of *Poor Richard's Almanack*. "Idleness," he wrote, "is the Dead Sea that swallows all values: Be active in Busi-

---

[25]Edward Tatham, *Letters to Edmund Burke on Politics* (Oxford, 1791), p. 77; Soame Jenyns, *Disquisitions on Several Subjects* (1782), in *The Works of Soame Jenyns, Esq.*, ed. C. N. Cole (London, 1790), 3:179; *Parliamentary History* 28 (1790–1791): 359. See also Josiah Tucker, *Selections from His Economic and Political Writings*, ed. R. L. Schuyler (New York, 1931); Matthew Goodenough, *Plain Thoughts by a Plain Citizen of London* (London, 1792); William Paley, *Reasons for Contentment Addressed to the Labouring Part of the British Public* (Carlisle, 1792); Richard Hey, *Happiness and Rights: A Dissertation upon Several Subjects Relative to the Rights of Man and His Happiness* (York, 1792); *Works of Joseph de Maistre*, ed. Jack Lively (New York, 1971), p. 212: "We are bound to the throne of God by a pliant chain."

[26]Mill, "Subjection of Women," p. 143; *XXVIII Proceedings*, p. 359.

ness that temptation may miss her aim. The bird that sits is easily shot." Father Abraham's message in the *Almanack* is clear: the "genteel who live of extravagancies . . . are reduced to poverty, and forced to borrow of those . . . who through industry and frugality have maintained their standing."[27]

Action instead of indolence, constant restlessness and work instead of enjoyment and luxury are the marks of the virtuous American. No surprise, then, that Benjamin Colman of the Brattle Street Church compared Christian life "to a Race, a Warfare; Watching, Running, Fighting; all which imply Activity, Earnestness, Speed, etc; and we are bid to labour and strive." Nathaniel Henchman, another Massachusetts preacher, told his congregation that this race required "the utmost striving of the whole man." By 1773 an American observer would, indeed, note in terms much like Smith's that his countrymen were involved "in one continued Race: in which everyone is endeavoring to distance all behind him; and to overtake or pass by, all before him."[28]

America in time became the natural home of liberal ideology. Its creed is competitive individualism and the metaphor of the "race of life" is repeatedly invoked. Its presidents are particularly fond of using it. In Abraham Lincoln's words one hears easily the moral conviction that hard work is the way to better one's condition. For Lincoln, indeed, the metaphor embodied the fundamental values of American life.

I happen temporarily, to occupy this White House. I am a living witness that any one of your children may look to come here as my father's child has. It is in order that each of you may have, through this free government which we have enjoyed, an open field and a fair chance for your industry, enterprise, and intelligence; that you may all have equal privileges in the race of life, with all its desireable human aspirations. It is for this that the struggle should be maintained, that we may not lose our birthright—not only for one, but for two or three years. The nation is worth fighting for, to secure such an inestimable jewel.[29]

[27]*Industry and Frugality Proposed as a Means to Make Us a Rich and Flourishing People* (Boston, 1753), p. 10; Charles Chauncey, *The Idle-Poor Secluded from the Bread of Charity by the Christian Law* (Boston, 1752), pp. 7, 11–12; Benjamin Franklin, "Poor Richard Improved" (1756), in *The Papers of Benjamin Franklin*, ed. L. W. Labaree (New Haven, Conn., 1959), 7:83, 341, 346.

[28]Benjamin Colman, *A Sermon at the Lecture in Boston after the Funerals* (Boston, 1717), p. 14; Nathaniel Henchman, *A Holy and Useful Life, Ending in Happy and Joyful Death* (Boston, 1721), p. 8; *Charleston* [*S.C.*] *Gazette*, March 1, 1773, quoted in Carl Bridenbaugh, *Myths and Realities of the Colonial South* (New York, 1963), p. 115.

[29]Abraham Lincoln, "Address to the 166th Ohio Regiment, August 22, 1864," in *Lincoln's Speeches, Letters, and Miscellaneous Writings*, ed. Don E. Fehrenbacher (New York, 1989), pp. 398–99.

The metaphor could also be used in the morally complacent and self-righteous defense of those who had made it in American bourgeois society, as it was by Herbert Hoover:

> It is as if we set a race. We through free and universal education provide the training of the runners; we give to them an equal start; we provide in the government the umpire of fairness in the race. The winner is he who shows the most conscientious training, the greatest ability, and the greatest character.[30]

Even deep into the twentieth century the metaphors of the race and chains could be enlisted in efforts to secure a fairer competition for people traditionally excluded from the race. They are heard in the words chosen by President Lyndon Johnson in his 1965 commencement address at Howard University to announce the policy of affirmative action, a unique late twentieth-century American adaptation of the core liberal ideal of equal opportunity: "You do not take a person, who for years has been hobbled by chains and liberate him, bring him up to the starting line of a race and then say 'you are free to compete with all the others,' and still justly believe that you have been completely fair."[31]

Class and Ideology

On the question of class in England in the eighteenth century the scholarly consensus prevailing in recent years is also quite at odds with the view I offer here. E. P. Thompson, for example, is much more interested in the development of what he calls "plebeian radicalism" in the England of that period than in describing the emergence of a middle-class radicalism. Thompson tends to see England in the eighteenth century as characterized by what he labels "essential polarities." He writes of the "poor" and the "great," the "popular" and the "polite," the "plebs" and the "patricians." Occasionally he equates these categories with nonpropertied and propertied, or lower class and upper class. Thompson says little about a third group, a middle class of propertied people who saw themselves as by no means allied with the great, the polite, or the patrician. Thompson is preoccupied by "the polarization

---

[30]Herbert Hoover, quoted in Donald J. Boorstin and B. M. Kelley, *A History of the United States* (Lexington, Mass., 1983), p. 488.

[31]Lyndon B. Johnson, "The Howard University Address," in *The Moynihan Report and the Politics of Controversy*, ed. Lee Rainwater and W. L. Yancey (Cambridge, Mass., 1969), p. 126.

of antagonistic interests and the corresponding dialectic of culture." It is in this light that his splendid resurrection of working-class and popular ideology must be read. It is there that Thompson finds "resistance to the ruling ideas and institutions of society." It was in the direct, turbulent actions of the popular crowd that hegemonic control was challenged.[32]

In the last half of the eighteenth century, however, we find antagonistic interests and conflicting ideologies that require more than the dichotomy of plebeian and patrician. A self-conscious third group asserted their interests as quite different from those of the ruling aristocracy and gentry at the same time that they sought eagerly to differentiate themselves from what they considered to be the less virtuous poor beneath them. This middle class also repudiated the ruling ideas and institutions of aristocratic England. Thompson may well be right when he argues that by the 1790s and Pitt's repression, middle-class interests were frightened by the vogue of Paine and revolutionary sentiment among the poor (although I shall argue that this break was less dramatic than Thompson assumes) and turned to an alliance with the gentry and aristocracy through the Napoleonic period. But such an alliance should not be seen as negating the very real class antagonism that existed from 1760 on between the middle class and the aristocratic-gentry ruling class. And to grant this antagonism is to abandon Thompson's bipolar view of eighteenth-century English society.

In reality, Thompson's analysis and mine differ only in emphasis. His sense of "gentry-pleb" relations, captured in his vivid metaphor borrowed from school physics, does acknowledge at least the existence of a third force.

> This is very much how I see eighteenth-century society, with, for many purposes, the crowd at one pole, the aristocracy and gentry at the other, and until late in the century, the professional and merchant groups bound down by lines of magnetic dependency to the rulers, or on occasion hiding their faces in common action with the crowd.[33]

Just when is "late in the century"? In noting the hold of paternalist assumptions over all segments of society, Thompson insists that one cannot exclude the middle class. But he rejects the view "that this parasitism was curbed, or jealously watched, by a purposive, cohesive, growing middle class of professional men and of the manufacturing

---

[32]E. P. Thompson, "Patrician Society, Plebeian Culture," in *Journal of Social History* 7 (Summer 1974): 395, and "Eighteenth-Century English Society: Class Struggle without Class," in *Social History* 3 (1978): 150.

[33]Thompson, "Eighteenth-Century English Society," p. 151.

middle class." Such a class, he adds, "did not begin to discover itself until the last three decades of the century." He assumes that for most of the century the middle class "submitted to a client relationship" with the great; tradesmen, attorneys, and intellectuals were deferential and dependent on their betters. Thompson is willing, however, to be more precise on the timing of this break. He suggests that the gentry-aristocratic hegemony went unchallenged until the "intellectual radicalism of the early 1790's." He grants that when the ideological break from paternalism occurred "in the 1790s it came in the first place less from the plebeian culture than from the intellectual culture of the dissenting middle class."[34] The emphasis of Thompson's work has been on the ideology of plebeian radicalism; my concern here is the rejection of paternalism and patronage by bourgeois radicalism, the "intellectual culture of the dissenting middle class."

We differ, then, on the timing and the intensity of this bourgeois assault on the "ruling ideas and institutions of society," and, of course, in our basic interest in it. Still, we agree on its central credo, for Thompson notes that what most infuriated this professional and merchant group about aristocratic and gentry hegemony was "its attendant humiliations and its impediments to the career open to talents." My objective is not unlike Thompson's. His work in articles and books (and that of his students) has provided a powerful eighteenth-century first chapter to what most scholars have previously considered the wholly nineteenth-century story of the "making of the English working class." My intention is similarly to develop an eighteenth-century first chapter for what is conventionally seen as a nineteenth-century story—the tale of the making of a "purposive, cohesive, growing middle class of professional men and of the manufacturing middle class."[35]

A very different version of this story is offered in Harold Perkin's influential *Origins of Modern English Society.* His is a profoundly different reading of the middle class and its place in English political and social life. Far from seeing it as in any way cohesive, purposive, or assertive in the eighteenth century, he finds it reluctant "to abandon paternalism and be provoked into class antagonism." The "birth of the middle class" occurs only in 1815, when, according to Perkin, the northern manufacturers, who had hitherto been uninterested in meddling in politics and who had been "loyal and quiescent" during wartime, turned against Britain's ancien régime. In 1815, Perkin contends, the middle class resolved to "assert its own power through its own representatives." It turned then for the first time against the "old soci-

---

[34]Ibid., pp. 142, 143, 163, 164.
[35]Ibid., pp. 143, 142.

ety compact by which the landed interest ruled on behalf of all the rest." Proof of its "birth" is that "for the first time" the middle class gave an appreciative audience and positions of leadership to such emancipated and alienated intellectuals as Jeremy Bentham, David Ricardo, and James Mill.[36]

That for three decades before the war and even for some time during the war important segments of the manufacturing community were politically active and usually critical of the old order and that they patronized and eagerly read the works of such intellectuals as Burgh, Priestley, and Price are not part of Perkin's story. He ignores these prenatal signs of middle-class vitality because they point to an assertive revolutionary class that is very far from his sense of the period. According to Perkin, the middle class reluctantly came into existence in 1815 only because of the corn law of that year, which convinced them that the landowning aristocracy governed only in its own interest. In this Tory reading of British history there would never have been an assertive middle class but for the ineptitude of the ruling class. Historical change is produced not by rebellious classes on the make but by the mistakes of the elite and privileged classes. It was, Perkin concludes, "irresponsible use of aristocratic power, then, [that] provoked the middle class into existence."[37]

Class does not figure in British society in the eighteenth century for Perkin because the bonds of patronage and dependency prevented any class feelings from emerging, or, as he puts it, any "vertical antagonism between a small number of horizontal groups." The old order with its ruling principles of patronage and connection was characterized by "horizontal antagonism between vertical interest pyramids," which for Perkin means interest politics. Not class but competing interests, the various estates, corporate, geographical, and religious interests, the connections and factions of court and country, "ins" and "outs," was the stuff of English politics until 1815. The agitation for parliamentary reform which began in the 1760s and rose to crescendo in the 1790s is written off as "characteristic of the old society." The reformers were merely an interest group of "outs," seeking office or at best lost rights. These reformers were neither interested in nor responsible for the industrialization of England. It was, in fact, Britain's landed aristocracy, its "extraordinary elite," that took the initiative here and "used it to create all the preconditions of an industrial revolution," which would ultimately radically disrupt the very traditional order over which it presided.[38]

---

[36]Harold Perkin, *The Origins of Modern English Society* (London, 1969), pp. 192, 214.
[37]Ibid., p. 214.
[38]Ibid., pp. 176, 30, 45, 177, 192, 194, 347, 183.

It is for making this latter case that Perkin's book is most often cited. And it is a fascinating case he makes, documenting the aristocracy's involvement with banking, commerce, transport, and manufacturing. The aristocracy's role in the abandonment of wage fixing and apprenticeship clauses as bearers of a new laissez-faire ideology is also an argument well made. Perhaps less valuable is the suggestion that the elite deserve the credit for the Industrial Revolution because, after all, their landed policy of enclosure drove the workers into the factories. Of similarly questionable value is Perkin's suggestion that the aristocracy helped bring about the Industrial Revolution because their dominance in politics and the church "helped to divert the energies of the Dissenters away from politics and towards labouring in their vocations of industry and trade." The modernizing aristocracy is still for the most part a well-made case, and a necessary and useful corrective to an account (such as mine) that tends perhaps too much to the other extreme. But surely revisionism has run riot in Perkin's Tory version of a modernizing, innovative, cohesive aristocracy and an utterly irrelevant and quiescent bourgeoisie that played little if any role in "the breakdown of the old order." To be sure, Perkin sees some place in the story for disenchantment with patronage and dependency on the part of the "middle and lower ranks or orders." Still, he is convinced that this disenchantment was "indeed provoked by a rejection on the part of the higher ranks" of their paternal and protective responsibilities. Like Thomas Carlyle, Michael Sadler, and Benjamin Disraeli, Perkin is convinced that the old order was done in by "abdication on the part of the governors."[39]

Though they differ radically in their visions of historical change, Perkin and Thompson see eye to eye on the virtual irrelevance of the middle class in the social structure of the eighteenth century. Both tend to see it as too submerged in the complex world of deference and connection to play any critical (in both senses of the word) role. Both are preoccupied by a polarity of gentry/aristocratic ruling class and all the rest. The one sees one pole as vital and innovative while the other sees it as regressive and the agent of hegemonic control. The one sees no class feelings in the century at all, the other sees plebeian radicalism in a culture and politics of rebellion. But both are convinced of the unimportance of a class-conscious third force, a radical bourgeoisie.

It may well be that Perkin's very concern to answer Thompson forces him to duplicate Thompson's oversight of any important middle-class consciousness. Thompson was wrong, Perkin contends, in labeling Paine, Thomas Hardy, and the English Jacobins of the 1790s as class

[39]Ibid., pp. 12, 56, 66–68, 71–76, 182.

spokesmen. "Were they a class," he asks, "were they emancipated from the system of dependency?" No, he answers, because they were self-evidently not "consciously proletarian," and the workers clearly did not flock to their tents. But this argument assumes the only options are privilege and proletariat. They were indeed out "to apply the axe to the old society" and they were indeed spokesmen for a class, but for a radical middle class. In fact, this is why not all workers flocked to the tents of Paine, Priestley, and the others. They sensed this problem perhaps better than both Thompson or Perkin. Like Thompson, Perkin tends to see class and class consciousness as meaningful concepts in the eighteenth century only in regard to the working class; the middle class does not count. How else does one explain a passage in which Perkin dismisses the agitation of John Cartwright and Christopher Wyvill as "highly respectable—that is, they did not assume the character of a class attack upon the aristocracy."[40] Can it not be both? Can a class attack on the aristocracy not be respectable? It must be considered unrespectable only if one's reading of class is constrained within a polarity of respectable notables and revolutionary workers. A third force was at work, highly respectable men and women out to destroy the world of patronage and paternalism.

To his credit, Perkin does recognize and properly describe a middle-class assault on the old order when he turns to the "entrepreneurial ideal" that he sees emerge in the nineteenth century. The idealization of competition, hard work, talent, and frugality, the condemnation of idleness, patronage, aristocratic corruption, and jobbing are vividly depicted in the rhetoric of Henry Brougham and James Mill. But this glorification of the middle class as the nation, "the glory of England," the "wealth and glory of the British name," is not new.[41] Nor is the antagonism of that class to the ruling ideas and institutions of aristocratic England. The roots of that class and its consciousness lie deep in the previous century, in the Midlands factories, the provincial philosophical societies, and the dissenting schools and chapels of Warrington, Hackney, and Stoke Newington.

Another divergent view is found in Albert Hirschman's equally influential *Passions and the Interests*. To be sure, his vivid account of the moral acceptability of the private acquisitive drive and of commerce, banking, and industry as virtuous enterprises is important for my purposes. But Hirschman is also outspoken in his insistence that the abandonment of antimoneymaking, anticommerical ideals and the decline of the heroic ethos of honor and glory were neither sudden nor unan-

[40]Ibid., pp. 193–94, 209.
[41]Ibid., pp. 221–31, 276, 294.

ticipated. The most important divergence of his views from mine, however, lies in his conviction that "this enormous change did not result
from any single victory of one fully armed ideology over another."
Those who destroyed the traditional values were not, he suggests,
offering new ones that "corresponded to the interests or needs of a
new class." They were not advocates "of a new bourgeois ethos." The
intellectual promoters of an expanded commerce and industry in the
seventeenth and eighteenth centuries were, according to Hirschman,
not spokesmen for "marginal social groups" or "an insurgent ideology." Their ideas emerged at the centers of power, among notables
and intellectuals grappling with affairs of state who sought new principles to curb chaos and constrain passion.[42]

Hirschman's argument is most appealing, especially in his suggestive critique of Weber by his linkage of the rise of capitalism to
intended consequences. It is also a position not seriously at odds with
mine. Even if one grants that the intellectuals he cites were not class
spokesmen, what they articulated became the moral and theoretical
arsenal that later ideologists could and would call upon. When men of
industry in Birmingham, Sheffield, and Manchester legitimated avarice
and commercialism in their efforts to redistribute power in late eighteenth-century English society, it has become an insurgent ideology.
When Dissenters opposed the Test and Corporation Acts for the redistributive goal of opening careers to the talented and morally superi-
or virtuous men of commercial success, the arsenal was being used by
a restless and assertive marginal social group. One can grant the non-
bourgeois origin of these ideas, grant their genesis in "the industrial,
managerial and administrative elite," without denying that their political impact became essentially ideological in the hands of an eighteenth-
century insurgent group that used them to justify a new ideal of middle-class consciousness and solidarity and to claim a new distribution
of political power in society.[43]

A final reading of this period which differs from mine is R. S. Neale's.
Like Perkin, Neale sees landed and aristocratic wealth and power as
much more critical in the modernization of Britain in the eighteenth and
nineteenth centuries "than any activity by a bourgeoisie." The big
bourgeois made no effort to question the political power of the landed
aristocracy during the period of industrialization, Neale argues, and he
offers the familiar reading of the reform movements as nondistributive
in intent but simply fueled "by a sense of loss of liberties and political
rights." Neale does provide an extremely important and useful docu-

[42]Albert O. Hirschman, *The Passions and the Interest: Political Arguments for Capitalism
before Its Triumph* (Princeton, 1977), pp. 12, 129.
[43]Ibid., p. 129.

mentation of the role of landowners and the aristocracy in making possible eighteenth-century industrialization through his depiction of the way their changing needs led to significant adaptations in property and business law, all of which were essential preconditions for both capitalism and industrialism. But like Perkin, Neale goes beyond redressing historiographic imbalance to write off the bourgeoisie entirely. All traces of the middle class, of a bourgeoisie playing "a most revolutionary part," are removed from "the crucial period of industrialisation" in the eighteenth and early nineteenth centuries.

> As a class for itself it certainly did not exist. English industrial capitalists or entrepreneurs (we must call them something) were either too busy making their economic fortunes, or spending them to gain entrée to the landowning and aristocratic class, to be conscious of themselves as a class in opposition to their rulers. As a class in itself it is also unlikely that it existed.[44]

Like much of the anticlass revisionism at work in the scholarship on this period, Neale has taken a useful and significant contribution and applied it with a vengeance. On the contrary, the bourgeois did indeed exist and they played "a most revolutionary part." In this formative period the bourgeois were very much "conscious of themselves as a class in opposition to their rulers." A full-fledged sense of class consciousness did emerge among the industrial and intellectual figures in Priestley's circle. The canonical criteria for such consciousness offered by Marx lend authority to this claim. In *The Eighteenth Brumaire* he denied the smallholding peasants of France the status of a class. They were numerous, to be sure, and they lived in similar circumstances. Their objective "economic conditions of existence" placed them, "their mode of life," and "their interests" in opposition to other groups in the community. If class were a thing, a definitional category, a static structural corollary deducible from a process of production, then surely this peasantry qualified. But class for Marx was an experiential category, a relationship among human beings within history. These peasants, he wrote, had "no wealth of social relationships." They were isolated from one another. Though they shared an identity of interests, they lacked a shared consciousness of that identity. Insofar as they experienced "no community, no national bond, and no political organisation among them, they do not form a class." They were incapable of "enforcing their class interests in their own name." For Marx, then, class

---

[44]R. S. Neale, *Class and Ideology in the Nineteenth Century* (London, 1972) and "The Bourgeoisie, Historically, Has Played a Most Revolutionary Part," in *Feudalism, Capitalism, and Beyond*, ed. Eugene Kamenka and R. S. Neale (Canberra, 1975), pp. 90–91.

struggle is a political and social struggle, and groups without political and cultural solidarity do not exist as classes. It is around the relational reality of a shared struggle that a class is organized, a struggle that is "a political one directed against the whole present system."[45] This, we shall see, was indeed the case with Priestley and his industrial and intellectual friends.

E. P. Thompson offers a useful contemporary gloss on this perspective on class. Class for Thompson is a "historical category," based on observation of the way people have lived and behaved over time. Class cannot be isolated as a static entity—so many people who at such-and-such a time occupy this or that place in the productive process. One cannot make it emerge automatically by plugging history into a "prior theoretical model of a structural totality." It becomes visible only when one looks at the lives of people and their relationships. Class is "something which in fact happens . . . in human relationships." Within a specific historical context it is a relationship "embodied in real people and in a real context." What is critical to Thompson in this relational reading of class is exactly what Marx emphasized, "the wealth of social relationships," the shared consciousness of community, culture, and political struggle.

> Class happens when some men, as a result of common experiences . . . feel and articulate the identity of their interests as between themselves, and as against other men whose interests are different from [and usually opposed to] theirs. . . . Class consciousness is the way in which these experiences are handled in cultural terms: embodied in traditional value systems, ideas and institutional forms.[46]

Like Marx, Thompson sees the emergence of class as a development involving common struggle. This struggle precedes class. "Classes do not exist as separate entities, look around, find an enemy class, and then start to struggle."[47] People who find they share a common interest in resisting exploitation or asserting and defending a sense of superiority struggle against others and in this process come to forge their existence as a class.

It is in class consciousness and class solidarity, the shared social sense of hostilities, sympathies, and superiority, that one finds class in this experiential approach, not in the mathematical or theoretical charts

---

[45]Karl Marx, *The Eighteenth Brumaire of Louis Bonaparte* (Moscow, 1963), pp. 123–24, and *The German Ideology* (London, 1965), p. 405.

[46]Thompson, "Eighteenth-Century English Society," pp. 146–49. See also E. P. Thompson, *The Making of the English Working Class* (New York, 1963).

[47]Thompson, "Eighteenth-Century English Society," pp. 148–49.

of reifiers who search out the thing that is class which must be present. Eric Hobsbawm puts the case succinctly: "Class in the full sense only comes into existence at the historical moment when classes begin to acquire consciousness of themselves as such."[48] But equally important, as it was for Marx, is the political and organizational articulation of that consciousness. Thus Thompson writes that the emergence of the working class was

> revealed first in the growth of class consciousness: the consciousness of an identity of interests as between all these diverse groups of working people and as against the interests of other classes. And, second, in the growth of corresponding forms of political and industrial organisation. . . . The making of the working class is a fact of political and cultural, as much as of economic history. It was not the spontaneous generation of the factory system. . . . The working class made itself as much as it was made.[49]

This reading of class, though shaped primarily to explain and document the emergence and the making of the proletariat, is just as appropriately applied to the earlier emergence of a middle class and bourgeois consciousness in late eighteenth-century England. When we use the criteria and reasoning set forth by this line of analysis, it should become clear that a bourgeoisie did exist, not because it had to but because we can reconstruct the shared experiences of real people, industrialists and intellectuals. Their behavior (part of which is writing) reveals a patterned sense of common interests against and superiority to a class above and a class below. They shared "a wealth of social relationships," a sense of community, a national bond, and, as we shall see, political and industrial organization. The bourgeois figures in Priestley's circle developed in the last four decades of the eighteenth century a full-blown class consciousness, and they articulated their common experience and interest in a wide variety of cultural expressions and a hegemonic value system. The bourgeois made themselves into a class through political and cultural struggle with a system in which they saw talent and merit achieve little. They knew what they were doing and said what they were doing.

Bourgeois radicalism was the politics of Figaro's kinsmen in Britain. It was the political program of middle-class men and women who were convinced that they had done more than the aristocracy, and that they more than anyone else deserved social and political rewards. Bourgeois radicalism was the ideological vision of industrialists, scientists,

---

[48]Eric Hobsbawm, "Class Consciousness in History," in *Aspects of History and Class Consciousness*, ed. István Mészáros (London, 1971).
[49]Thompson, *Making of the English Working Class*, p. 194.

and their intellectual spokesmen who set out in late eighteenth-century Britain to destroy the political, social, and cultural hegemony of people who had merely gone to the trouble of being born.

Long before Marx, eighteenth-century observers assumed the interdependence of the economy and the polity. The likes of Priestley, Anna Barbauld, Josiah Wedgwood, Price, and Paine saw themselves as harbingers of political as well as economic change. Contemporaries had numerous concrete symbols of this linkage even within the same family. Not the least impressive were, of course, the Cartwright brothers, Edward, the inventor of the power loom, and John, the indefatigable campaigner for adult male suffrage, annual Parliaments, payment for MPs, and equal electoral districts. Conventional wisdom, in fact, had it that economic change naturally begat political change. David Hume and Adam Smith shared Montesquieu's conviction that commercial societies had more political liberty. Economic determinism was a common feature of Scottish historical analysis, and it, too, presumed the liberalizing tendencies of economic growth. Sir James Steuart wrote:

> In countries where the government is vested in the hands of the great Lords, as is the case in all aristocracies, as was the case under the feudal government, and as it still is the case in many countries in Europe, where trade, however, and industry are daily gaining ground, the statesman who sets the new system of political economy on foot, may depend upon it, that either his attempt will fail, or the constitution of the government will change. If he destroys all arbitrary dependence between individuals, the wealth of the industrious will share, if not totally root out the power of the grandees.[50]

Henry Fielding, though not the scholar Steuart was, nevertheless was, as a novelist and a government official, an astute observer of his times. For him, too, it was beyond doubt that economic change would produce political change. "Trade," he wrote, "hath given a new face to the whole nation, hath in great measure subverted the former state of affairs." Only the ignorant and the socially blind could not see the political consequences of this transformation, Fielding wrote in a letter to the *Public Advertiser*:

> To conceive that so great a change as this in the people should produce no change in the constitution is to discover, I think, as great ignorance as would appear in the physician who should assert that the whole state of the blood may be entirely altered from poor to rich, from cool to inflamed, without producing any alteration in the constitution of man.[51]

[50]Sir James Steuart, *An Inquiry into the Principles of Political Economy* (1767), ed. Andrew Skinner (Chicago, 1966), 1:214.
[51]Henry Fielding, in *The Public Advertiser*, September 11, 1760.

The middle-class men and women in Priestley's circle organized and worked hard to further their common interests. They persisted in campaigning for parliamentary reform and for repeal of the Test and Corporation Acts. They were responsible for the new organizational structure that grew up around economic issues in which political and class interests met. Wedgwood and Matthew Boulton's creation of the General Chamber of Manufacturers in 1785 is a moment of profound significance, which, as Asa Briggs has noted, "marked an important landmark in changing social consciousness."[52] Manufacturers saw that their vital interests were at stake in trade treaties, in patent regulations, and in legislation that protected labor. As a result, they organized to influence public outcomes. Because of this organization for what Marx would later describe as "enforcing their class interests in their own name," they were able to chip away steadily at the paternalist legislation involving apprenticeship, wage regulation, and general conditions in industry which had evolved over the centuries to protect workers. Keenly aware of their middle-class interests, they interpreted Pitt's income tax as an assault on their class, and it, too, served only to further their development of a sense of class unity.[53]

The articulation of this common experience, this shared consciousness, is what I take to be the ideology of bourgeois radicalism. Existence as a unified class presumes, as Marx noted, the existence of an "appeal to their [class] right."[54] The absence of such an ideology was, indeed, another reason for his reluctance to see the smallholding French peasantry qualify as a class. No such lack can be attributed to the English bourgeoisie. Theirs was a full-fledged defense of class right, middle-class right, inspired by a felt consciousness of shared interests. In its historical context their ideology was unabashedly radical and progressive.

By labeling the ideas and politics of a Wedgwood, a Priestley, or a Wollstonecraft as ideological I enter, albeit reluctantly, the methodological thicket that surrounds the term "ideology." Others have already expended much energy in efforts to cut through to some definitive and true meaning of ideology. It is, to be sure, an elusive concept, but one that can be used with wide latitude, for it is also a rich concept, with numerous dimensions and facets that need not exclude others. I am less worried than others that the term is too comprehensive, so all-

---

[52]Asa Briggs, *From Iron Bridge to Crystal Palace* (London, 1979), p. 114. See also his "Language of Class in Early Nineteenth-Century Britain," in *Essays in Labour History in Memory of G. D. K. Cole*, ed. Asa Briggs and John Saville (London, 1967), and P. J. Corfield's excellent "Class by Name and Number in Eighteenth-Century Britain," *History* 72 (February 1987).

[53]B. E. V. Sabine, *A History of the Income Tax* (London, 1973), chap. 2.

[54]Marx, *German Ideology*, p. 350.

inclusive as to lack discriminating power or empirical relevance. I am also less worried about the merging of ideology with such concepts as idea, belief, opinion, creed, myth, utopia, and ethos.[55] None of these concepts is irrelevant, however, if it is amplified by function and organization. Ideas and values, beliefs and attitudes are not themselves ideological; they become so when they are put in the service of politicized interests involved in a struggle to affect the distribution of power and the outcomes of public policy.

Much of the literature captures some facet of this process, and we need not isolate one defining quality as truly exclusive. We can be eclectic in our use of "ideology." Karl Mannheim's insight that social or political ideas are not disembodied products of abstract thought but are "always bound up with the existing life situation of the thinker" is just as useful as the approach that sees these ideas as reflecting and expressing class and economic interests. Similarly one need not exclude from the concept of ideology the notion that it is in some sense historically a response to stress, uncertainty, or social strain. It is in such periods, after all, that the distribution of power is in question and up for grabs and that interests accordingly articulate visions and programs for redistribution. Nor is Clifford Geertz's conception of ideology as a set of metaphorical cultural symbols that provide road maps to give meaning and pattern to public life incompatible with the reading of ideology as an expression of interest or strain. One needs a road map, as Geertz notes, not only when one is lost but also when one seeks to get somewhere; with a map one can choose one path over another. Geertz correctly sensed, in fact, that it was in late eighteenth-century England and France, not in nineteenth-century Europe, that the use of road maps began in earnest. But these insights are not enough. Ideology has a final critical dimension that by no means excludes any of the others but complements them. These ideas born in social strain and articulated by organized interests must ultimately, as Norman Birnbaum has noted, "contain . . . evaluations of the distribution of power in the society in which these assertions are developed and propagated."[56] Life is not literally a race, but what a magnificent metaphor the radical bourgeoisie seized upon! Power and prizes were there to be won and the old rules proclaiming winners and losers were under tremendous strain. How better to arrange that the new victors would be the class of talent and hard work than to offer this new powerful

---

[55]See, e.g., Giovanni Sartori, *Democratic Theory* (Detroit, 1962), pp. 51–60.

[56]Karl Mannheim, *Ideology and Utopia* (New York, n.d.), p. 59; Clifford Geertz, "Ideology as a Cultural System," in *Ideology and Discontent*, ed. David Apter (New York, 1964), pp. 47–76; Norman Birnbaum, "The Sociological Study of Ideology," *Current Sociology* 9 (1960): 91.

symbol, the race? It is ideology at work in all its richness as interest, as strain, as cultural system.

The seedbed for this ideology in late eighteenth-century England consisted of the provincial scientific, philosophical, literary, and constitutional societies that sprang up everywhere—in Manchester, Derby, Birmingham, Sheffield, Norwich, London. Here and in the dissenting academies and in the burgeoning associations of manufacturers could be found the "wealth of interacting social relations" that produced family intermarriage as well as solidarity and class consciousness. In these institutions the capitalist, intellectual, and bourgeois businessman, the political activist, and the religious dissenter came together. While such industrialists as Wedgwood, Thomas Cooper, James Watt, John Wilkinson, and Jedediah Strutt will be part of our concern, we shall also concentrate on the thinkers of this class, "its active conceptualizing ideologists," who, according to Marx, "develop and perfect the illusions of the class about itself." It was this group that articulated the ideology's sense of representing "the common interest of all members of society." It conceived the formulas that sought "to give its ideas the form of universally valid ones." These people sought, as James Mill saw that all classes seek, "to get up a system of morality for themselves, that is conformable to their own interests, and to urge it upon other men." These efforts would ultimately prove successful and they would fulfill John Stuart Mill's similar prediction that "wherever there is an ascendant class, a large portion of the morality of the country emanates from its class interest and its feelings of class superiority."[57] But that sense of moral superiority would emerge not in the nineteenth century, as it is conventionally dated, but in the crucial early years of political struggle in the late eighteenth century. It is that new consciousness born of shared interests and common social relationships and the symbols used to represent it which is our subject.

The writings of Priestley's circle represent a vivid consciousness of the mission of the middle class in English society. Several decades before James Mill and numerous other Victorian spokesmen for the bourgeoisie proclaimed the moral superiority of the industrious middle ranks, the radicals of the 1770s, 1780s, and 1790s were doing so. There emerged a unique middle-class pride that would later be expressed as a special mission to fill what was felt to be the void between "an ignorant labouring population and a needy and profligate nobility."[58]

The special trait of the middle class was its usefulness, its abhorrence

---

[57]Marx, *German Ideology,* pp. 79–80; James Mill, in *Westminster Review* 6 (1826): 255; John Stuart Mill, quoted in Perkin, *Origins of Modern English Society,* p. 273.
[58]"The Church of England and the Dissenters," *Blackwoods* 15 (1824): 397.

of idleness. The middle-class industrialists and intellectuals saw themselves as a people set apart, adrift in a sea of the great and the poor. Their chapels, their clothes, their hard work, and often their provincialism literally set them apart as much as the Test and Corporation Acts did. They responded with a conviction of unabashed superiority and a vigorous embrace of modernity. They ushered in new notions of time and discipline, and several among them even sought to restructure the English language to rid it of its aristocratic and feudal qualities. Thomas Spence and Horne Tooke's ventures into alphabetic and grammatical reform, though far ahead of their day, were symptomatic of the ideological imperialism at work. Nothing would stand in the way of Priestley's middle-class colleagues in their effort to take over and transform English life. Their mission was to clear away the thick underbrush of outdated and useless institutions, to simplify and reform government, to expose prejudice, mystery, and fiction to the glare of light. In them the crusade of the philosophes is joined to the interests of the middle class. Simplicity—the rejection of the arcane, the mysterious, the complex—becomes their creed; and it is this creed that Burke so eloquently attacked in his writings of the 1790s.

The commitment of these radicals to an intellectual and social transformation of English life and attitudes as well as their conviction of moral superiority was ridiculed in Francis Jeffrey's review of Priestley's *Memoirs* in the *Edinburgh Review* of 1806. Jeffrey had observed "a succession of authors who seem to have fancied that they were born to effect some mighty revolution in the different departments to which they have applied themselves," and who operated principally "in the west of England." They are not to be listened to, however, for "Dr. Priestley and his associates," like all provincials, "took no cognizance of any sort of excellence or distinction but their own." When, on the other hand, Priestley himself sought modernity and reform in America, he was welcomed by its philosophe, Jefferson, who wrote to him, "Yours is one of the few lives precious to mankind."[59]

Organized in and by their wealth of social relationships to a consciousness of community and shared interests, the ideologues of middle-class radicalism in Priestley's circle were by no means nostalgic defenders of the past, set against modernity and commerce, as they are conventionally depicted. They were, as we shall see, ardent believers in progress and change. But their ideas were not totally new. Many of the themes we will encounter in their ideology had their antecedents.

---

[59]Francis Jeffrey, "Memoirs of Dr. Priestley," *Edinburgh Review* 9 (1806): 147; Jefferson to Priestley, March 21, 1805, in *The Works of Thomas Jefferson*, ed. P. L. Ford (New York, 1908), p. 216.

Its millenial fervor, for example—infinitely more secularized, to be sure—was still a lineal descendant of the seventeenth-century saintly ancestors of many of the Dissenters. Praise of thrift, industry, self-reliance, and time management and condemnation of idleness and profligacy were also themes writ large in the earlier Puritan preachings of a Thomas Stanley in the sixteenth century and a Richard Baxter in the seventeenth. On the politico-economic level, much of the ideology of this middle-class radicalism is, as we shall note, borrowed from and developed on the writings of Locke. These ideologues relied heavily on Locke's theory of property, of work, of individualism and political rights. His vision of the relation between religion and the state and his doctrines of contractual and limited government play important roles in the writings of these late eighteenth-century liberals.

A final important antecedent of middle-class radical ideology is to be found in the seventeenth-century writings (including Locke's) on the free-market economy. The school of Thomas Mun, Josiah Child, Nicholas Barbon, and Charles Davenant, so skillfully and sensitively recreated in the writings of Joyce Appleby, provided many intellectual themes developed by these late eighteenth-century middle-class theorists. They had earlier developed the idea of a harmonious social order organized around voluntary and natural interactions of individuals. They accepted the legitimacy of private profit-seeking, and saw ambition and self-interest as proper human activities in a social order where market behavior and economic freedom were the norm. They also contributed to a general climate of increasing political liberty, for as Appleby notes, "the belief in natural economic laws served as a solvent of political authority based upon will or sovereignty."[60]

These linkages to the past notwithstanding, there is something unmistakably new about the bourgeois radicalism of Priestley's circle. It is the politicization of these ideas and values, their championship by an organized insurgent class that used them in a political struggle against both the ruling class and ruling institutions, that is new. The early years of industrialization were producing a greatly expanded middle level of English society, a section of the population whose leadership dramatically repudiated the traditional structure of privilege and rank. The ideology expressed by its thinkers as part of this struggle contained middle-class values and themes that were not always new, but the articulation of these themes in political consciousness—middle-class consciousness—was decidedly new and explosive.

That radical consciousness contained contradictory tendencies, as

---

[60]Joyce Appleby, *Economic Thought and Ideology in Seventeenth-Century England* (Princeton, N.J., 1978), p. 279.

we shall see. On the one hand, it sought to liberate men and women from all forms of restraint, political, economic, and religious. On the other hand, bourgeois radicalism preached order, discipline, and subordination, whether in the workhouse, factory, prison, or hospital. Bourgeois radicalism directed its emancipatory message to the aristocracy, its authoritarian one to the poor.

Less consciously contradictory but potentially even more so was the ideology's position on power. Its fundamental thrust was against power, against the decentralized power that restrained individuality. It attacked the paternalistic restraints of the moral economy in the countryside as well as the feudal and guild restrictions of local corporate and parish regulations. It removed parliamentary barriers to a free market while attacking church restrictions on both profit and free religious expression. Yet in the course of this assault it left one sole source of legitimate power, the state, whose ultimate, now unchecked power could prove infinitely more awesome and frightening to individuality than its predecessors.

In addition to internal contradictions, bourgeois radicalism, like all other ideologies and especially radical ones, contained much that exaggerated, distorted, or falsified. Much of its rhetoric was inconsistent and many of the beliefs it articulated were inaccurate or beyond empirical proof. While it glorified the ascetic Dissenter as the cultural ideal, some of its bearers, such as the Cartwrights, were Anglicans. English society was far from the rigidly immobile structure the radicals decried. England made room for a good deal of social mobility (especially in comparison with other European nations) and not all jobs and careers were the preserves of privilege and birth. At the same time, the image of legions of self-reliant, self-made, "ingenious" men and women of humble origins climbing the entrepreneurial ladder of success was also part myth. Aristocrats were by no means all idle and lazy profligates. Some of them were as enterprising and industrious as their middle-class inferiors. Nor, of curse, did the landed aristocrats roll over in surrender before the assertive bourgeois. They kept the main positions of power in local and central government well into the last decades of the nineteenth century. For that matter, it was never altogether clear how deeply the bourgeois really hated the aristocrats. With the rarest of exceptions, they never attacked the system of land tenure or the laws of inheritance. Their failure to do so may reflect their own envy of and desire to ape the aristocracy, as well as an ultimate ideological commitment to certain similar values in the face of what would eventually evolve as other ideological challengers.

But accuracy and verifiability are not the stuff of ideology. They are more the domain of disinterested science. In this latter enterprise,

Geertz suggests, the "style is restrained, spare—resolutely analytic." The bourgeois radicals were less interested in intellectual clarity than in commitment. Their style, like that of all ideologists, is "ornate, vivid, deliberately suggestive."[61] They were engaged in action and struggle. Such metaphors as "the race of life" and such symbolic constructs as "the self-made man" are far removed from the technique of the scientific analyst, but they cut to the quick the older ideology of status and patronage, revealing its distortions and myths while legitimizing the struggle to bury it. My interest is less in the scientific diagnosis of the period than in recreating and understanding the ideology of bourgeois radicalism on its own terms, as its adherents saw it and the world. My objective is to capture and recreate the expression of that ornate, vivid, and deliberately suggestive consciousness.

Republicanism, Neo-Lockeanism, and the Politics of Scholarship

The countersuggestion that an ideology of individualistic Lockean liberalism was alive and well in late eighteenth-century Britain, as well as in America, has received mixed reviews from the scholarly community. Gordon Wood has dubbed Joyce Appleby, John Diggins, and me "neo-Lockean" for our insistence on the significance of liberal ideas in late eighteenth-century Anglo-American ideology.[62] The term is suggestive, for it highlights the extent to which this position is a reassertion of what used to be historical orthodoxy.

The *ricorso* of neo-Lockeanism has evolved in reaction to the shift that has occurred in the reading of the history of political thought. Until the mid-1970s the orthodox view shaped on the right by Leo Strauss, on the left by Harold Laski and C. B. Macpherson, and in the center by two hundred years of Whig history, personified in America by Carl Becker and Louis Hartz, had John Locke's liberalism, for better or for worse, as the dominant ideology from the seventeenth century through the nineteenth in the English-speaking world. Liberalism has been toppled in recent years and replaced by a new hegemonic ideology, republicanism. A modern self-interested, competitive, individualistic ideology emphasizing private rights has been replaced at the center of eighteenth-century political discourse by a classical-Renaissance ideology emphasizing selfless duty-based participation in the communal pursuit of the virtuous public good. At the center of this

[61]Geertz, *Ideology,* pp. 71–72.
[62]Gordon Wood, "Hell Fire Politics," *New York Review of Books,* February 28, 1985, p. 30.

upheaval has been the work of J. G. A. Pocock and his writings on "civic humanism" and "classical republicanism." Pocock has not been alone in the assault on Lockean liberalism, and this assault has as often been fueled by partisan passion as by disinterested scholarship.

Republican revisionism and the debunking of the influence of Locke have come principally from the right. Bailyn's *Ideological Origins of the American Revolution* was, in part, a rereading of the American Revolution intended to free it from decades of progressive scholarship. Walter Nicgorski, however, best captures the animus that often motivates the Locke debunkers. In a 1976 piece for the Natural Law Institute of the Notre Dame Law School he suggested that "being Locke's country at once constricts America's aspirations and paradoxically so over-simplifies them at times as to create a threat similar to that posed by the millenialism of totalitarian democracy." We are given not the conventional Rousseau as the source of this dreaded modern affliction but Locke with his "constriction of moral-political discourse to the terms of individual liberty and equality." To read the Declaration of Independence as Lockean leads to the civil rights movement, feminism, and "the right of revolution," according to Nicgorski. He concludes that

> the restoration of an effective public philosophy can be aided by being reminded that the American moral-political tradition does not simply add up to Locke writ large and that the Declaration of Independence did not suggest to all Americans a heady and vigorous individualism. Sacrifice, restraint, virtue and justice, were hallmarks of other authentic American traditions that joined in the Revolution and entered the stream of American life.[63]

Two years later the Catholic Garry Wills offered Francis Hutcheson and the Scottish Enlightenment to replace Locke as the intellectual influence on Jefferson's Declaration and with them also a tradition for America that was less egoistic, more communal, moral, and public-spirited.

Donald Winch's book *Adam Smith's Politics* (1978) reaffirmed the new wisdom. Republican historiography resulted in "a major casualty"; Locke and "liberal or bourgeois individualism" were proved to be "of strictly limited significance" in eighteenth-century political thought and ideology. Winch took particular pleasure in this "remarkable historiographic upheaval" because it did in "political theorists and historians" whose trumpeting of Locke's influence allegedly sprang from partisan political motives, not from scholarly integrity. Locke's defen-

[63]Walter Nicgorski, "The Significance of the Non-Lockean Heritage of the Declaration of Independence," *American Journal of Jurisprudence* 21 (1976): 176, 158, 177.

ders, according to Winch, believed in"heroes or evil geniuses" more than "the historical facts of the case might allow." They had "present-minded reasons" for their falsely asserting the importance of Lockean liberalism. Winch sees the specter of Marx behind historians who misguidedly cling to Locke. Smith's politics were those of civic humanism, he proclaims,

> not an episode—however crucial—that occurred some way along a road which runs from Locke to Marx. Smith was not in the grip of some hidden historical force which destined him to work out in more detail or more frankly the ramifications of a set of problems posed by Locke, the true and sinister import of which was only discerned by Marx.[64]

Pocock, too, sees the dead hand of Marx behind neo-Lockean scholarship. Especially suspect for him is anyone who suggests that political theory took on a liberal cast in the seventeenth century. Such scholars, be they liberals or antiliberals, Straussians or Marxists, are vilified for writing "as if the liberalism which they define had held the field . . . from the days of Hobbes and Locke." It is not even liberals themselves who set up and hold to this erroneous notion of liberal hegemony, he suggests. Pride of villainous place, according to Pocock, goes to Marxists, for liberalism is more an invention of "those who would attack then . . . those who would practice it." Pocock sees liberalism as a mere popular front for Marxism. He is "prepared to entertain" the idea that liberal ideology was "perfected less by its proponents than by its opponents, who did so with the intention of destroying it."[65] Any mention of the bourgeoisie, of the middle class—indeed, any claim for the significance of Locke in eighteenth-century ideology—is according to Pocock, a stalking horse for systematic Marxism.

Pocock is reduced to name-calling, for those who "attack the republican interpretation" are "bent on maintaining the Lockean and liberal-capitalist interpretation." He wrote in the *Journal of the History of Ideas* in 1987: "Diggins is some kind of Calvinist, Kramnick some kind of Marxist, and Appleby is a neo-Jeffersonian." Two years earlier, in his *Virtue, Commerce, and History,* he had written that for "Kramnick . . . every diminution of the role of Locke is an implicit attack on Marx," a strange verdict on one who had never written a word on Marx. Surely, in any case, there is a difference between claiming, quite accurately, that one cannot have Marx without Locke and claiming that to find Locke is necessarily to opt for Marx. Pocock is clear as to where he stands on eighteenth-century radicalism. Whereas misguided "Marxist

---

[64]Donald Winch, *Adam Smith's Politics* (Cambridge, Eng., 1978), pp. 29, 180.
[65]J. G. A. Pocock, *Virtue, Commerce, and History* (Cambridge, Eng., 1985), pp. 61, 59, 71.

and Marxisant historians . . . feel obliged to explain all social opposition or radical thought in pre-industrial eighteenth century Britain as the ideology of a bourgeoisie," the truth is that "radicalism in the eighteenth century . . . was conducted largely in the name of classical-republican and agrarian-military values."[66]

In the chorus of criticism of neo-Lockeanism, the current darling of English Tory historiography is Jonathan Clark. His resurrection of a hegemonic "monarchical, aristocratic, Anglican regime" from 1688 to 1832 requires ruthless exposition of the errors of all non-Tory readings of eighteenth-century British history. Like Winch, Clark holds that the use (even in hindsight) of such terms as "bourgeois radicalism," "Lockean liberalism," and "middle-class radicals" is proleptic and anachronistic. On the last page of his revisionist history he singles out an example of all that is wrong in eighteenth-century scholarship. The erroneous tradition, which he sees as beginning with Caroline Robbins' *Eighteenth-Century Commonwealthman*, "yields, by extrapolation, an interpretation of late eighteenth century 'radicalism' which was perfectly captured by an article of Professor Kramnick's."[67] To Clark's credit, he does not suggest a Marxist agenda; neo-Lockeans, it seems, can be dupes in their own right.

Winch and Pocock notwithstanding, the left is not altogether happy with the central claim of neo-Lockeanism, the importance of individualistic liberalism in late eighteenth-century Anglo-American ideology. Take, for example, Marx and Engels themselves. Though they were convinced that "the bourgeoisie, historically, has played a most revolutionary part," especially in Britain, their narrative emphasizes seventeenth- and nineteenth-century events and thinkers. In *The German Ideology* Marx moves from Hobbes and Locke to Bentham and Mill in his description of utilitarianism. Engels, in his discussion of the "British bourgeoisie" in *On Historical Materialism*, moves directly from 1640 and "the compromise of 1689" to the events of the 1830s and 1848. The compromise settlement of the Glorious Revolution, which, according to Engels, reserved political and social power for the aristocracy as long as "the economic interests of the financial, manufacturing, and commercial middle class were sufficiently attended to," remained in place, he suggests, until the Reform Bill and anti–corn Law agitation. Only then, deep in the nineteenth century, does Engels see a politically assertive middle class.[68]

---

[66] J. G. A. Pocock, "Between Gog and Magog: The Republican Thesis and the *Ideologia Americana*," in *Journal of the History of Ideas* (1987): 339; *Virtue*, p. 242.

[67] J. C. D. Clark, *English Society, 1688–1832* (Cambridge, Eng., 1985), p. 424. The reference is to an earlier version of chap. 2, below.

[68] Karl Marx and Friedrich Engels, *The Communist Manifesto*, in *Marx and Engels' Basic Writings on Politics and Philosophy*, ed. Lewis S. Feuer (New York, 1959); Marx, *German Ideology*, pp. 109–13; Friedrich Engels, *"On Historical Materialism,"* in *Basic Writings*, pp. 57–61.

As indicated earlier, the writings of the contemporary Marxist E. P. Thompson are also at odds with the neo-Lockean reading of eighteenth-century English ideology. Pocock, interestingly enough, is seemingly not concerned with Thompson's quite significantly different reading of eighteenth-century class dynamics. Pocock insists on linking the erroneous Kramnick with the evil Thompson.[69]

In this sketch of the politics of eighteenth-century scholarship lies a final irony. Republican civic humanism and the debunking of Locke, initiated on the right partly to expose the Marxism allegedly lurking in Lockean or neo-Lockean scholarship, have found their most recent vocal champions on or near the left, among communitarian critics of liberal individualism and in the critical legal studies movement with its rejection of "liberal constitutionalism." Michael Sandel articulates the premise of both camps in his claim that "the debate about the meaning of our past carries consequences for the debate about present political possibilities." For him an American with republican origins holds out the prospect of "revitalizing our public life and restoring a sense of community." For Morton Horwitz, America's republican tradition, derived in part from "eighteenth-century English oppositionist thought," the Scottish Enlightenment, Montesquieu, and Rousseau, provides a profound insight into the non-neutral, "normative and constitutive character of law." Frank Michelman sees the civic humanism of English and American seventeenth- and eighteenth-century thought as a "counter ideology," a "visionary opposite," which, despite its "sometime historical connection with an obnoxiously solidaristic social doctrine," provides an exaltation of a community and regime truly of laws and not of men.[70]

These legal scholars and communitarians, whatever one may think of their political prescriptions, are absolutely correct in their reading of an America where liberalism has been hegemonic—the neutral state triumphant over the normative state for Horwitz; the Federalists triumphant over the Anti-Federalists for Frank Michelman, Cass Sunstein, and Mark Tushnet; Rawlsian calculating individuals triumphant over Rousseauean seekers of the general will for Sandel. In the debates between those of us who see Locke alive and well in the eighteenth century and those who see the unitary sway of civic humanism these writers perceive a conflict between a hegemonic ideology and potentially preferable alternatives. As they touch base with republicanism for their alternative, whatever their politics, they must, like J. H. Hex-

---

[69]Pocock, *Virtue, Commerce, and History,* pp. 242, 292.

[70]Michael Sandel, "The State and the Soul," *New Republic,* June 10, 1985, pp. 39–40; Morton Horwitz, "Republicanism and Liberalism in American Constitutional Thought," 29 *William and Mary Law Review* 53 (1986): 69–73; Frank Michelman, "The Supreme Court, 1985 Term," 100 *Harvard Law Review* 4 (1986): 18.

ter, wonder at Pocock's persistence in construing the history of modern political thought as devoid of the influence of liberalism.[71]

Liberalism there was in late eighteenth-century England and America alongside the older ideal of republicanism, a progressive liberalism still subversive of the status quo. (It would not always be so.) That radical ideology and the tensions created by its confrontations with republicanism are the burden of the pages that follow.

[71]See the textbook by Geoffrey R. Stone, L. M. Seidman, Cass Sunstein, and Mark Tushnet, *Constitutional Law* (Boston, 1986); 97 *Yale Law Journal* 8 (1988) (devoted entirely to a symposium, "The Republican Civic Tradition"); J. H. Hexter, "Republic, Virtue, Liberty, and the Political Universe of J. G. A. Pocock," in *On Historians* (Cambridge, Mass., 1979), pp. 293–303.

PART ONE

BOURGEOIS RADICALISM
AND ENGLISH DISSENT

CHAPTER 2

Religion and Radicalism:
The Political Theory of Dissent

I N HIS *Reflections on the Revolution in France*, Burke lamented the great transformation that he sensed taking place in European civilization. "The age of chivalry is gone," he wrote, "that of sophisters, economists and calculators has succeeded. The glory of Europe is extinguished for ever."[1] Throughout most of his career, even in the *Reflections*, Burke was convinced that England was the principal evidence of this most unfortunate transition. He singled out one group as the major modernizing agent in his England—the sectarian Protestant Dissenters. He was right. While many strands of English life—even parts of the aristocracy itself—contributed to the modernity that enveloped the ancien régime, the strongest strands were the Dissenters. Theirs were the boldest voices attacking the traditional order; they were the secular prophets, the vanguard, of a new social order. These talented and industrious Protestant Dissenters played the decisive role in transforming England into the first bourgeois civilization.

In the course of this ambitious enterprise the Dissenters developed a radical ideology complete with notions of government, of society, and of virtue. One finds here the articulation of inherited ideas of Lockean liberalism with a progressive and revolutionary fervor that sought to topple all aspects of the aristocratic world—of Burke's beloved age of chivalry. The major force behind this radicalization of Lockean liberalism was its capture in the early stages of the Industrial Revolution by these Protestant Dissenters, the embodiment of the entrepreneurial spirit.

[1] *Reflections on the Revolution in France*, ed. Edmund Burke, Conor Cruise O'Brien (Baltimore, 1969), p. 170.

This spirit was a transatlantic radicalism. The radicals in America and England shared many things: a common enemy, a common nonconformist religious heritage, and a common sense of alienation—of being outsiders, albeit superior outsiders, in the closed world of rank, privilege, and power. We all know that the spirit of James Harrington, Locke, and the Baron de Montesquieu hovered over American social and political thought in the 1760s, 1770s, and 1780s. Colonial professors, preachers, and presses might also cite Algernon Sidney, even Bolingbroke, and *Cato's Letters* of an earlier day. But what absorbed Americans in the decades around the revolution were John Wilkes and the writings of the Reverends Price, Priestley, and Burgh.[2] These were the radical kinsmen of the American patriots, holding the eastern flank in the battle against tyranny, corruption, and unrepresentative government.

Protestant Dissent: The Making of Bourgeois Civilization

By the 1760s and 1770s large numbers of English Dissenters, the subdued and rather quiescent descendants of the nonconformist sects that had waged revolution under Cromwell, had already emigrated to the American colonies. Those Baptists, Presbyterians, Independents (Congregationalists), Unitarians, and Quakers who remained in England constituted about 7 percent of the population. But those 7 percent nearly destroyed aristocratic England and its traditional values. They were at the heart of the progressive and innovative nexus that linked scientific, political, cultural, and industrial radicalism. The Dissenters played an innovative role vastly disproportionate to their numbers. One study reveals that while they made up 7 percent of the population (90 percent were Anglican), these nonconformists contributed some 41 percent of the important entrepreneurs between 1760 and 1830. The Anglicans who made up virtually all the remaining population contributed only 58 percent. In relation to their numbers, then, the nonconformists produced some nine times as many entrepreneurs as the Anglicans. The findings are even more interesting when manufacturing is distinguished from agriculture, transport, and mining: in manufacturing, which in this period involved and symbolized the most innovative activity, the nonconformists contributed fourteen times as many entrepreneurs as the Anglicans did. The reality

2See Pauline Maier, "John Wilkes and American Disillusionment with Britain," *William and Mary Quarterly* 20 (1963): 373–95; *From Resistance to Revolution* (New York, 1974); Bernard Bailyn, *The Ideological Origins of the American Revolution* (Cambridge, Mass., 1967); Staughton Lynd, *The Intellectual Origins of American Radicalism* (New York, 1968).

is more dramatic still. The names that conventionally symbolize the Industrial Revolution virtually *all* belong to Dissenters. The men memorialized in the mnemonic scheme used by generations of English schoolchildren to personalize the Industrial Revolution—the three W's, Watt, Wilkinson, and Wedgwood—were Dissenters to a man. Each of the new manufacturing industries was presided over by a Dissenter. In cotton textiles Samuel Oldknow and Jedediah Strutt became the partners of the Arkwrights; in Manchester we find Thomas Walker and Thomas Cooper. Steel was the domain of the Quaker Darby family, the Unitarian John Wilkinson, and the Presbyterian James Watt. The potteries had Wedgwood.[3]

An equally strong case can be made for the central and crucial role played by Dissenters in scientific and political innovation. Among these Dissenters Joseph Priestley best qualifies as the principal architect of bourgeois radicalism. Radical in politics, laissez-faire theorist in economics, innovator in science and technology, founder of the modern Unitarian movement, Priestley schooled England's new men of business in the series of dissenting academies at which he taught while personally serving as the critical link between virtually all aspects of the progressive and innovative bourgeois nexus. Brother-in-law to Wilkinson, friend of Price and Wollstonecraft, "guide, philosopher, and friend to Boulton, Watt and Wedgwood at Birmingham,"[4] he was "Gunpowder Joe" to Burke and the church-and-king mob that burned his laboratory and home in 1791 and sent him to finish his days in Dissenter paradise—America.

The Dissenters were proud of their achievements and unafraid to note their wealth. Self-congratulations, in fact, was often paired with threats to leave, should Anglican and aristocratic England bear down too hard on dissent. In his *Rights of Man* the Quaker Tom Paine noted that the leading manufacturers in England were the Dissenters of Man-

---

[3]Everet E. Hagan, *On the Theory of Social Change* (Homewood, Ill., 1962), pp. 261–309. See also Witt Bowden, *Industrial Society in England towards the End of the Eighteenth Century* (New York, 1925); T. S. Ashton, *Iron and Steel in the Industrial Revolution* (Manchester, 1924); George Unwin, *Samuel Oldknow and the Arkwrights* (Manchester, 1924); A. E. Musson and Eric Robinson, *Science and Technology in the Industrial Revolution* (Manchester, 1969); D. G. C. Allen, *William Shipley: Founder of the Royal Society of Arts* (London, 1968); Raymond V. Holt, *The Unitarian Contribution to Social Progress in England* (London, 1938); Duncan Coomer, *English Dissent under the Early Hanoverians* (London, 1946); Betsy Rodgers, *Georgian Chronicle: Mrs. Barbauld and Her Family* (London, 1958); C. M. Elliot, "The Political Economy of English Dissent, 1780–1840," in *The Industrial Revolution*, ed. R. M. Hartwell (Oxford, 1970); Neil McKendrick, "Josiah Wedgwood and Factory Discipline," *Historical Journal* 4 (1961); R. B. Rose, "The Priestley Riots of 1791," *Past and Present* 18 (November 1960); E. P. Thompson, "Time, Work-Discipline, and Industrial Capitalism," *Past and Present* 38 (December 1967): 56–97.

[4]Quoted in Robert E. Schofield, *The Lunar Society of Birmingham* (Oxford, 1963), p. 353.

chester, Birmingham, and Sheffield. He quoted "one of the richest manufacturers in England" who said in his hearing that "England, sir, is not a country for a Dissenter to live in—we must go to France." Paine warned his readers that it was the Dissenters who carried the English economy to its heights and that the same men had the power to "carry it away." According to Priestley, "one-half of the wealth of the nation has been the acquisition of Dissenters." Their secret was one that, he argued, would guarantee success for anyone. "The habits of industry and frugality which prevail among them will not fail to make any set of men rich."[5] Priestley also held out the possibility that if pushed too far the Dissenters would leave, as of course he himself would do in 1794. The irony is that it was just such a sense of potential mobility and lack of identification with the soil and traditions of England that encouraged the very hostility against them which Priestley warned against.

> I shall just mention three other men now living, and all of them Dissenters, whose spirit has so much improved, they may be almost said to have created, their several manufactures, from which this country already derives the greatest honour and advantage. Mr. Wedgwood, Mr. Wilkinson and Mr. Parker. Such MEN AS THESE ARE THE MAKERS OF COUNTRIES; and yet such men as these, if not these men themselves, would the mad bigotry of this country exult in seeing depart for France, America, or Ireland.[6]

Why the Dissenters played this crucial role in the development of bourgeois England in the late eighteenth century is difficult to say, and any explanation must be tentative. The school of Max Weber and R. H. Tawney throws some light on the question, though neither Weber nor Tawney applied his argument to this crucial eighteenth-century link between Protestant nonconformity and capitalism. According to this by now familiar interpretation, the Protestants' preoccupation with industry and hence with innovation in the eighteenth century is associated with religious doctrine, as popularized by Richard Baxter and John Bunyan. Through labor and successful enterprise the Protestant comes to terms with the burdensome anxiety over salvation, in the process developing an ethic of effort, thrift, and industry—an ethic marvelously matched to the requirements of a growing industrial economy.[7]

Though this argument is of some explanatory value, it does not

---

[5]Tom Paine, *The Rights of Man* (Baltimore, 1969), p. 110; Joseph Priestley, *An Appeal to the Public on the Subject of the Riots in Birmingham* (Birmingham, 1792), p. 104, and *Proper Objects of Education in the Present State of the World* (London, 1791), p. 12.

[6]Priestley, *Appeal to the Public*, p. 103.

[7]See Max Weber, *The Protestant Ethic and the Rise of Capitalism* (New York, 1958); R. H. Tawney, *Religion and the Rise of Capitalism* (New York, 1958).

address directly the Dissenters' receptivity to innovation. To account for it we may have to stress sociological factors, particularly marginality, as some Dissenters themselves did. One of the earliest theorists to suggest the influence of marginality (though he did not use the term itself) was the nineteenth-century economic historian Werner Sombart, who stressed exclusion from public offices and the state church as historically critical in turning the energy of Protestant Nonconformists and Jews into commercial and industrial channels. These newer realms of activity, too recent and too low in status to be monopolized by the established privileged class, were open to them. In short, as Sombart argued in regard to the medieval Jew, eighteenth-century society offered the Dissenter few other means to prosper.[8]

Perhaps even more significant was the Dissenters' psychological marginality, for very basic to their self-consciousness was their sense of difference, of separateness, of alienation from the mainstream of English life and orthodoxy. They belonged to two communities, the broader English Protestant community and the narrower minority of the sects. Lucy Aikin, a member of Priestley's circle, has poignantly described in her memoirs the sense of what it was like to grow up a Dissenter in the late eighteenth century.

> I should scarcely be believed were I to recount the bitter persecution we poor children underwent in the children's parties we frequented, for the offence of denying ourselves *on principle* the dainties which children most delight in. But how were these hostilities aggravated by the agitation of the repeal of the Test Act? . . . What was the lot of us poor little ones? Children persecuted by children for words, for names, of the meaning of which none of them had the slightest conception. I have sat a whole evening while others were dancing, because nobody would dance with a Presbyterian. I have been pushed, hunted, even struck, as I stood silent and helpless to the cry of Presbyterian.[9]

Even the dress and appearance of the most successful of Dissenters was a sign of their separateness. When a group of manufacturers that included Wedgwood, Watt, and Wilkinson traveled to London in 1785 to petition members of Parliament on trade legislation, a contemporary noted: "Messrs. Watt, Reynolds, Wilkinson, etc. have knowledge and fortune which their dress don't indicate and therefore will too probably be treated slightly." And of course the Dissenters in Priestley's circle were always perceived as geographically and culturally marginal. They were provincials whose domain was the values of the West Country and the Midlands. As Francis Jeffrey noted in the *Edinburgh Review*, exposure to the mainstream of London society would cool their pretensions.[10]

Thorstein Veblen argued that exclusion from the benefits and values of an establishment, be it political or intellectual, produces both a psychological disposition to innovation and reform and a unique tolerance of novelty and change. Veblen was writing in 1919 about ghetto Jewry, insisting that an independent Jewish state with a Jewish establishment and Jewish orthodoxy would end the innovative and creative role played by marginal Jews in central and eastern Europe in the nineteenth and early twentieth centuries.[11]

When Robert E. Park introduced the phrase "marginal man" into the sociological literature in 1928, he, too, had in mind the European Jew who sought to leave the ghetto and was rebuffed by the majority culture and society. The marginal man in Park's writings and as elaborated by Everett Stonequist in 1937 lived on the border of two societies, societies that made incompatible demands on him. Park and Stonequist, like Veblen, were intrigued by the personality characteristics that seemed to flow from this existence on the margins. Such people tended to be ambitious and concerned with upward mobility, to strive to move from the status associated with the minority group to that associated with the majority. This urge to acquire the rewards and privileges associated with membership in the broader community coexisted with the desire to be true in some way to at least some of the unique features of the minority group. Park and Stonequist also suggested, as had Veblen, that marginal people were the great questioners and innovators in any particular period, that they saw as relative what others saw as absolute. They were predisposed to question and criticize received truths because they were involved in two ways of thought. They were thus not so limited as the ordinary culture-bound individual.[12]

It is not difficult to hypothesize, then, a similar receptivity to innovation and an ability to question the existing order, economic, intellectual, scientific, or political, among the English Dissenters of the eighteenth century. We see in them the ambitious striving for upward mobility found in people who have no stake in orthodoxy, for in fact they were excluded from the traditional rewards available to the members and defenders of the Church of England.

[10]Quoted in Schofield, *Lunar Society of Birmingham*, p. 353; Francis Jeffrey, "Memoirs of Dr. Priestley," *Edinburgh Review* 9 (1806).
[11]Thornstein Veblen, "The Intellectual Pre-eminence of Jews in Modern Europe," *Political Science Quarterly*, March 1919.
[12]Robert E. Park, "Human Migration and the Marginal Man," *American Journal of Sociology* 32 (May 1928): 881–93; Everett Stonequist, *The Marginal Man* (New York, 1937). See also R. H. Turner, *The Social Context of Ambition* (San Francisco, 1964), pp. 4–18.

Their sense of alienation, their existence on the margins was by no means contrived self-indulgence or cultivated paranoia. It had concrete foundations in the objective world. For most of the eighteenth century it was technically illegal, for example, to carry on a Unitarian service. But much more onerous were the Test and Corporation Acts, the most humiliating of the badges the Dissenters had to wear to indicate their difference. This legislation, dating from the Restoration and originally directed against Catholics, required all holders of offices under the crown to receive the sacrament according to the rites of the Anglican church. The acts also excluded nonsubscribers to the Anglican creed from any office in an incorporated municipality. In addition, only Anglicans could matriculate at Oxford and Cambridge. Exclusion from public jobs was the most serious effect of the acts, however, for legions of these talented Dissenters were denied one of the most important means a society has to reward its successful: public office in the military or civil establishment.

The radical and innovative role that the Dissenters played in the decades after 1760 was directly related to their marginality, and the Dissenters themselves sensed that their creative role in English life was related to their exclusion from its mainstream. Anna Barbauld, children's writer and one of the female radicals in Priestley's circle whom Walpole lampooned as the "Amazonian allies" of Jacobinism, made the connection clear in her *Address to Opposers of the Repeal of the Corporation and Test Acts* (1790). You have disqualified us, branded us, and kept us separate, she shouts at the establishment. "You have set a mark of separation upon us, and it is not in our power to take it off." But in doing so the Anglicans had also carved out the unique mission of the dissenters, she hastens to add.

> You have rendered us quick frighted to encroachment and abuses of all kinds. We have the feelings of men. We have no favours to blind us, no golden padlock to our tongues, and therefore it is probable enough that, if cause is given, we shall cry aloud and spare not. . . . It is perfectly agreeable to a jealous spirit of a free constitution that there should be some who will season the mass with the wholesome spirit of opposition.[13]

The Dissenter not blinded by establishment rewards and not silenced by the financial advantages of mouthing orthodox truth is uniquely capable of seeing the appeal of novelty and speaking words of criticism. Some two decades earlier Priestley had made the same point. "We Dissenters," he wrote, "consider it as our singular privilege, that our situation, how unfavourable soever in other respects, is

[13]Anna Barbauld, *Address to Opposers of the Repeal of the Corporation and Test Acts* (London, 1790), p. 25.

favourable to free inquiry; and that we have no such bias upon our minds, in favour of established opinions." Even after his laboratory had been destroyed by a mob in 1791, Priestley proudly asserted his dissenting nature. "I bless God," he wrote to his friends in Birmingham, "that I was born a Dissenter, not manacled by the chains of so debasing a system as that of the Church of England and that I was not educated at Oxford or Cambridge." To one of Priestley's friends, the minister and radical Richard Price, the Dissenters indeed owed their innovative and radical disposition to the fact that they had been spared Oxford and Cambridge. The ancient universities, he wrote, were "fortresses erected for the security and preservation of the Church of England and defended by Tests and Subscriptions." Free from this training in orthodoxy, the Dissenters did not believe that truth had been found 200 years earlier. They were not bound to "vile dogmatism," they were not given to "notions of sacredness in disputable doctrines and stuffing the mind with prejudices." Dissenters, Price concluded, had a peculiar calling made easier by their exclusion; it was "to suspect our public creeds and forms."[14]

In his *Reflections on the Revolution in France*, Burke proudly proclaimed the English a people who cherished ancient and sacred doctrines, or prejudices, as he called them. Ideas were worthy simply by virtue of dogged persistence over time. Dissenters such as Price had no truck with the self-evident truth of ancient ideas, however; they saw themselves as engaged in a messianic mission to, as Barbauld put it, "destroy the empire of prejudices, that empire of gigantic shadows." Like the Hebrews, they had been chosen by God for this task, and the oppression they suffered for their difference was proof of their selection.

> It is to speculative people, fond of novel doctrines, and who by accustoming themselves to make the most fundamental truths the subject of discussion, have divested their minds of the reverence which is generally felt for opinions and practices long standing, that the world is ever to look for its improvement or reformation.[15]

[14]Joseph Priestley, *A View of the Principles and Conduct of the Protestant Dissenters with Respect to the Civil and Ecclesiastical Constitution of England* (London, 1769), p. 5, and *Familiar Letters Addressed to the Inhabitants of the Town of Birmingham in Refutation of Several Charges Advanced against the Dissenters* (Birmingham, 1790–1792), letter 4, p. 6; Richard Price, *Evidence for a Future Period of Improvement in the State of Mankind with the Means and Duty of Promoting It* (London, 1787), pp. 41–44.

[15]Barbauld, *Address to Opposers*, p. 37; see also her "On Prejudice," in *The Works of Anna Barbauld* (London, 1825), 1:321, and her "Thoughts on the Devotional Taste and on Sects and Establishments" (1775), where she wrote: "The faults of an establishment grow venerable from length of time; the improvements of a sect appear whimsical from their novelty. Ancient families, fond of rank, and of that order which secures it to them, are on the side of the former. Traders incline to the latter; and so do generally men of genius, as it favors their originality of thinking" (ibid., p. 252).

Self-consciously, then, the Dissenters saw themselves not only as patrons of scientific and industrial modernity but as enemies of established opinions, vile dogmatism, public creeds, and the empire of prejudice. Freed from restraining golden padlocks on their tongues, they were a people "fond of novel doctrines." The weapons most effective in their assault on the empire of prejudice were their schools. The dissenting academy is a critical factor in any explanation of their innovative inclinations and performance. It provided a preparation peculiarly appropriate for the new age. The leaders of bourgeois England did not come from Oxford and Cambridge, where classical and clerical education still dominated the preparation of gentlemen. Adam Smith noted their irrelevance. They were, he wrote, "sanctuaries in which exploded systems and obsolete prejudices found shelter and protection, after they had been hunted out of every other corner of the world."[16] The schools where learning flourished in the eighteenth century were the academies set up by the sects in response to their exclusion from Oxford and Cambridge. And it was a particular kind of learning that flowered there, perfectly matching the needs of an emerging bourgeois civilization. These academies provided the middle class with a practical education.

The central figure in the development of this bourgeois education was Joseph Priestley, both through his writings and in the example of his many years as teacher in dissenting academies. Priestley's goal was a worldly education in the affairs of society—economic, political, and scientific. "Why," he wrote, "should youths be trained to be ministers, lawyers, and doctors, and not be trained to be merchants, clerks, and tradesmen?" His concern, as he described it in his *Essays on a Course of Liberal Education for Civil and Active Life*, was to remedy the defect of traditional education, which neglected students "who were not designed for any of the learned professions." These young people needed "a set of lectures equally useful for any department of life, such as has a nearer connection with their conduct in it."[17]

Priestley's influence was most directly felt in his years as the guiding spirit behind Warrington Academy, the most influential of all the eighteenth-century dissenting academies, which from 1757 to 1786 "made a mark on the intellectual life of the country comparable only to that of a great university like Oxford or Cambridge at a later period." Located

---

[16]Quoted in Bowden, *Industrial Society in England*, p. 61.
[17]Joseph Priestley, *Essays on a Course of Liberal Education for Civil and Active Life* (London, 1765), pp. 7, 9. See also his *Proper Objects of Education*. For background on the dissenting academies, see Irene Parker, *Dissenting Academies in England* (Cambridge, Eng., 1914); Herbert McLachlan, *Warrington Academy, Its History and Influences* (Manchester, 1943), and *English Education under the Test Acts* (Manchester, 1931); Anthony Lincoln, *Some Political and Social Ideas of English Dissent, 1763–1800* (Cambridge, Eng., 1938).

between Manchester and Liverpool, Warrington was the financial fruit of dissenting churchmen and Midlands manufacturers. In turn, it produced three decades of educated sons of the middle class. Here a young French doctor destined for fame and martyrdom in the French Revolution was supposed to have taught foreign languages in the 1770s. Though definitive proof is lacking, friends of Jean-Paul Marat often spoke of the time he spent at Warrington during the early English phase of his radical career. It is Priestley, however, who is definitively identified with Warrington. In his years as head tutor there (1761–1767) Priestley conducted all classes in English. He added history, geography, and chemistry to the curriculum. He introduced the study of English grammar and simple arithmetic. He taught the history and laws of England and the commercial laws and policies of England and its neighbors. Bookkeeping and other commercial arts were stressed. All of these subjects, he wrote, were necessary "because a different and better furniture of mind is requisite to be brought into the business of life."[18] A full 50 percent of Warrington's graduates went into business, another 25 percent into law and medicine, and the rest into the ministry.

Priestley and his educational reforms, which soon spread to all the academies, not only produced businessmen and ministers who themselves preached to businessmen but, as one might suspect, also produced middle-class radicals in politics, restless in the face of restrictions in a political and social order still very much dominated by the aristocracy and aristocratic principles.

After the decline of Warrington, the leading dissenting academy in the 1780s and 1790s was Hackney in London. Here Priestley occasionally lectured and Richard Price worked full-time. Burke described the academy at Hackney in 1792 as "the new arsenal" in which subversive doctrines and arguments were forged.[19] It was not an exaggerated assessment of the general role of the dissenting academy, which did in fact train the bourgeoisie to undermine Burke's England. The ancient universities, like Burke, stood fast against the spread of radical ideals. At Oxford in 1792 the university chaplain attacked from his pulpit the doctrines of original contract, power derived from the people, the lawfulness of resistance—all venerable Lockean notions but now rendered suspect and subversive by their currency in the Dissenters' curriculum.

Such wild, visionary, enthusiastic notions, have always been counteracted, and opposed by the examples and instructions of this university,

---

[18]McLachlan, *Warrington Academy*, p. 209; Louis R. Gottschalk, *Jean Paul Marat: A Study in Radicalism* (Chicago, 1967), pp. 6–7; Priestley, *Essays on a Course*, p. 2.

[19]Edmund Burke, "An Appeal from the New to the Old Whigs," in *The Works of the Right Honourable Edmund Burke*, ed. Henry Bohn (London, 1877–1884), 3:91.

which may, without vanity boast, that it has been steadier in its principles, and suffered more for its consistency, in the support of regal government, than perhaps any place of the like nature in the Christian world.[20]

The dissenting academies did, in fact, arm the children of the bourgeoisie with a new learning and with new anti-aristocratic political ideals. Priestley was quite outspoken in his belief that only the educated youth of the middle class could perpetuate the wondrous potential of the new bourgeois civilization. This is the message of his lecture to the parents and supporters of the academy at Hackney in 1791. It is a marvelous catalogue of bourgeois radical ideals and principles.

Train our youth to the new light which is now almost everywhere bursting out in favor of the civil rights of men, and the great objects and uses of civil government. While so favourable a wind is abroad, let every young mind expand itself, catch the rising gale, and partake of the glorious enthusiasm, the great objects of which are the flourishing state of science, arts, manufactures, and commerce, the extinction of wars, with the calamities incident to mankind for them, the abolishing of all useless distinctions, which were an offspring of a barbarous age, (producing an absurd haughtiness in some, and a base servility in others) and a general release from all such taxes and burdens of every kind, as the public good does not require. In short, to make government as beneficial and as little expensive and burdensome as possible. . . . Let them be taught that the chief objects of their instruction are the young, and especially those in the middle classes of life, such as those of whom the converts to Christianity in the early years generally consisted. The lowest of the vulgar will not easily be brought to think on subjects wholly new to them. As to the persons in the highest classes of life, they are chiefly swayed by their connections and very seldom have the courage to think and act for themselves.[21]

"The Race of Life": The Ideology of the Middle Class

Priestley envisioned a minimal and noninterfering state. This vision flowed quite easily from his commitment to religious freedom, for in the dissenting world view religious dogma was closely related to the political and economic concerns of the bourgeoisie. In addition to their often noted stress on worldly success and its relation to thrift, simplicity, frugality, and industry, the dissenting sects were all but unanimous in demanding the disestablishment of the Church of England

---

[20]Cited in Samuel Heywood, *High Church Politics: Being a Seasonable Appeal to the Friends of the British Constitution against the Practices and Principles of High Churchmen* (London, 1792), p. 102.

[21]Priestley, *Proper Objects of Education*, pp. 22, 39.

and the complete separation of church and state. Matters of religion and of conscience, they held, were totally beyond the competence of the magistrate. The state, they argued, ought not to interfere in religious matters; its concerns were purely civic. In a constant restatement of Locke's doctrine of toleration, dissenting clergy and political writers insisted that the power of government must be limited strictly to preserving the peace and protecting property. This constant invocation of the principle of religious laissez-faire, the withdrawal of the state from the realm of belief, became appropriated by secular arguments for economic laissez-faire. The centuries-old restrictions on economic activity inherited from medieval Christian dogma, guild-dominated feudalism, and Tudor paternalism came under attack by the entrepreneurs of industrializing England. Their arguments were reinforced by their religious brethren in the pulpit. Demands by generations of dissenting clergy and political writers for limits on governmental interference in the religious lives of Dissenters very easily became demands for limits on state interference in the economic lives of Dissenters. Such demands came easily, for example, to the Unitarian Josiah Wedgwood, who, as a founder of the General Chamber of Manufacturers, vigorously lobbied for a free-trade treaty with France in 1786, and they came easily to the Unitarian John Wilkinson, who remarked that "Manufacture and Commerce will always flourish most where Church and King interfere least."[22]

Here, too, Joseph Priestley spoke for his age, for his religious brethren, and for his class. In his religious and political tracts Priestley invoked the doctrinal notion of freedom of conscience, and in his economic writings he wrote of the need for the state to withdraw, to be "as little expensive and burdensome as possible." More important, Priestley articulated the new bourgeois demand that government give up its traditional involvement in and control over the economic process. Individualism was as crucial here as in the religious realm, he insisted. Man should be "left to himself." All the restrictions should be undone so that individuals could "revert to that natural condition of man from which we have departed." Priestley applied this doctrine most clearly in his attack on the poor laws, which for the taxpaying bourgeoisie were among the most onerous of the old order's interferences with economic liberty. In his criticism of the poor laws he captures beautifully the emerging bourgeois attitude toward the poor as well. "Some will become rich and others poor," he writes. The state has attempted too much in providing public funds for the poor. The poor became

[22]Quoted in Eric Robinson, "The English Philosophes and the French Revolution," *History Today*, February 1956, p. 121.

"improvident, spending everything they get in the most extravagant manner, knowing they have a certain resource in the provision which the law makes for them." They are not taught the necessity of prudence and foresight, they think only of the present moment, and are thus, he suggests, reduced to a condition lower than that of beasts. "Better," he recommends, "if government had not interfered in the case of the poor at all." All that such actions do is take taxes from the industrious and encourage the idle. His suggestion is that the deserving poor should, if need be, be taken care of by "the charity of the well disposed." The message was echoed by a chorus of middle-class ideologues that included Paine and Smith. The state should stop interfering in matters economic; it was only increasing the taxes and burdens on the middle class and interfering with economic individualism and self-reliance. The language flowed easily from one who spent so much of his time pleading for the state to get out of matters religious. Government was in general too much with us. It is quintessential bourgeois radicalism that Priestley articulates in a pamphlet addressed to Burke in 1791.

In this and many other things, government has taken a great deal too much upon it, and has by this means brought itself into great and needless embarrassments. In many things besides the article of religion, men have busied themselves in legislating too much, when it would have been better if individuals had been left to think and act for themselves.[23]

One obvious instance in which the state legislated too much was the passage of the dreaded Test and Corporation Acts, which interfered with both religious and civil liberty. They violated the natural religious rights of believers while intruding the state into the free competitive market of careers and rewards due by right to the talented and industrious. The ideological core of dissenting social thought is found here, in its opposition to the restrictive Test and Corporation Acts, for they violated the fundamental assumptions of the ethos of the self-made individual and of society disinterestedly rewarding people of merit and talent, people of hard and useful work. By excluding Dissenters from public office, the acts buttressed an aristocratic order of received and unearned status and rank. They rewarded idle and unproductive people of leisure and lineage. In an essay attacking the acts, Priestley

---

[23]Joseph Priestley, *An Account of a Society for Encouraging the Industrious Poor to Which Are Prefixed Some Considerations on the State of the Poor in General for the Use of J. Wilkinson's Iron Works at Bradley* (Birmingham, 1789), pp. 5, 7; Joseph Priestley, *Letters on History and General Policy*, 4th ed. (London, 1826), lecture 38, pp. 290–305 (in the American newspaper *Aurora*, February 27, 1798, he insists that the "fundamental maxim of political arithmetic" is the "state's not interfering in the economy"); Joseph Priestley, *Letters to the Right Honourable Edmund Burke* (Birmingham, 1791), p. 55.

ridiculed the values and the individuals they favored. They were designed to reward "gentlemen born," those "with family and connections respectable . . . of polished and engaging manners." It is the
bourgeois demand for the opening of careers to the talented and the
charge that aristocratic society blocks such advances that Priestley in-
tones in his mocking comment that "the door of preferment is so open
to him [the gentleman born] that he hardly needs to knock in order to
enter."[24] No matter how superior a Dissenter might be, it seemed to
some of them, the English would always have more respect and rewards for the old order's incompetents. Robert Bage, the Dissenter
novelist, wrote to a friend:

> In this country it is better to be a churchman, with just as much common
> sense as heaven has been pleased to give on average to Esquimaux, than a
> dissenter with the understanding of a Priestley or a Locke. I hope, Dear
> Will, experience will teach thee this great truth, and convey thee to peace
> and orthodoxy, pudding and stability.[25]

Priestley warned that if preferment would not come to the talented
and successful Dissenters, then as "citizens of the world" they would
get up and go where their virtuous achievements were recognized and
rewarded.[26] This was shorthand for America, and indeed, he went
there. The fiery Anna Barbauld did not leave, however, and in making
her case for the repeal of the Test and Corporation Acts she addressed
the social issue straight on. It was no favor for which she asked but "a
natural and inalienable right," which she claimed was hers and every
Dissenter's. It was not the religious issue that bothered the opponents
of repeal, nor, indeed, she added, was religion the main concern of the
Dissenters. The issue was "power, place and influence."

> To exclude us from jobs is no more reasonable than to exclude all those
> above five feet high or those whose birthdays are before the summer
> solstice. These are arbitrary and whimsical distinctions. . . . We want civil
> offices. And why should citizens not aspire to civil offices? Why should not
> the fair field of generous competition be freely opened to every one. . . ? We
> wish to buy every name of distinction in the common appellation of
> citizen.[27]

Barbauld articulated the very core of liberal-bourgeois social theory.
In the competitive scramble of the marketplace all citizens are equal in

---

[24]Joseph Priestley, "On the Repeal of the Test and Corporation Acts," in *Familiar
Letters*, letter 4, pp. 19–20.
[25]Quoted in "English Philosophes," p. 117.
[26]Priestley, "On the Repeal of the Test and Corporation Acts," p. 20.
[27]Barbauld, *Address to Opposers*, pp. 17–18.

their opportunity to win; no one has a built-in advantage of birth or status. Freedom involves unrestrained competition and equality, an absence of built-in handicaps. In the vulgar rhetoric of the bourgeoisie, life is competition, a race for goods and offices, and in this race all have an equal opportunity to win. It was, in fact, these Dissenters who popularized the metaphor of the race. John Aikin, for example, brother of Anna Barbauld, wrote in a letter published for his son: "For what is the purpose of equal laws, equal rights, equal opportunities of profiting by natural and acquired talents, but to annul artificial distinctions, and cause the race of life to be run fairly."[28] It is easy to forget the explosive radical thrust of this praise of talent, its progressive assault on the world of privilege and artificial distinction. For bourgeois radicalism only the natural distinctions of talent and industry and the success or failure they produce are just.

These early bourgeois ideologues were extremely sensitive lest their assault on hierarchy and aristocratic privilege be construed as a mere leveling to an absolute equality of conditions. They were also fearful that they were being read as enemies of private property. Burke, more than any other contemporary, seemed to them to have drawn these false conclusions. Nothing could be further from their intentions; property was sacred to them. The new order, they assumed, would still have inequalities. Thomas Walker, Manchester cotton manufacturer, lay Dissenter, and political activist, summed up the essence of this new radical creed in 1794.

We do not seek an equality of wealth and possessions, but an equality of rights. What we seek is that all may be equally entitled to the protection and benefit of society, may equally have a voice in elections . . . and may have a fair opportunity of exerting to advantage any talents [we] may possess. The rule is not "let all mankind be perpetually equal." God and nature have forbidden it. But "let all mankind start fair in the race of life." The inequality derived from labour and successful enterprise, the result of superior industry and good fortune, is an inequality essential to the very existence of society; and it naturally follows that the property so acquired should pass from a father to his children. To render the property insecure would destroy all motives to exertion, and tear up public happiness by the roots.[29]

Walker's plea that "all mankind start fair in the race of life" had already been endorsed by Adam Smith. The "race for wealth and

[28]John Aikin, *Letters from a Father to His Son on Various Topics Relative to Literature and the Conduct of Life* (Philadelphia, 1794), p. 205.
[29]Thomas Walker, *A Review of Some of the Political Events Which Have Occurred in Manchester during the Last Five Years* (London, 1794), pp. 46–47. See also Frida Knight, *The Strange Case of Thomas Walker: Ten Years in the Life of a Manchester Radical* (London, 1957).

honours and preferments," Smith wrote, should be fair and each run-
ner should have an equal opportunity to win. Each competitor will
"run as hard as he can, and strain every move and every muscle, in
order to outstrip all his competitors," but interfering with other runners or having special advantages is "a violation of fair play." Merit,
talent, virtue, and ability are, alas, not sure indications of success,
according to Smith, because in

> the courts of Princes, in the drawing rooms of the great, where success
> and preferment depend, not upon the esteem of intelligent and well-
> informed equals, but upon the fanciful and foolish favours of ignorant,
> presumptuous, and proud superiors, flattery and falsehood too often pre-
> vail over merit and abilities. In such societies, the abilities to please are
> more regarded than the abilities to serve.[30]

Government was too much involved in the race, according to Smith. By
reserving offices, power, and authority to the privileged, it tilted the
competition to an idle aristocracy devoid of all talent and virtue. Government was interfering in the natural freedom to "outstrip all competitors."

In his *Rights of Man,* Paine accused Burke of not having read Adam
Smith carefully enough. Paine sensed quite correctly that the sober
Scotsman Smith shared in a psychology basic to the radical bourgeois
vision. The runners in the race of life were urged on, he wrote, by the
"uniform, constant, and uninterrupted effort of every man to better his
condition." This restless ambition "comes with us from the womb and
never leaves us till we go to the grave." The winners of the race would
be those middle-class runners who learned the crucial principle of
frugality, the ability to postpone immediate gratification—"that self-
command, in the same manner, by which we restrain our present
appetites, in order to gratify them more fully upon another occasion."
The losers would be the profligate and idle aristocracy with "their
passion for present enjoyment," with no incentive to better their condition. The lower orders were also incapable of such postponement, but
at this stage of the ideology the primary enemy of the middle class was
the class above. The aristocracy would lose, that is, if governmental
authority stayed out of the race, and did not reserve all the rewards for
those privileged players incapable of postponing gratification. To fix
the race in this way was not only to violate fair play; for Smith it was to
reward "public enemies," to thwart the progress and improvement of

[30]Adam Smith, *The Theory of Moral Sentiments* (Edinburgh, 1813), 1:188, 136.

civilization, which requires the hegemony of the frugal and productive—the public benefactors.[31]

These frugal and productive men were, of course, men of property.
English bourgeois radicals, Burke notwithstanding, worshiped private
property. They may have had little respect for ancient baronial estates,
but they were bourgeois to the core. Along with their dissenting religion they learned respect for property, quite literally, in their infancy.
Priestley, for example, wrote in his *Memoirs* of an incident that happened when he was five. He was playing with a pin, and his mother
asked him where he had gotten it. From his uncle, the youngster
answered. "She made me carry it back again; no doubt to impress my
mind, as it could not fail to do, with a clear idea of the distinction of
property, and the importance of attending to it."[32] His mother died
when he was six. The adult Priestley remembered only two things
about her, the incident of the pin and that she had taught him the creed
of the Protestant Assembly.

Not only would bourgeois society have inequality; it would no longer look after the poor to the extent its predecessors had done, through
the mechanisms of a paternalist economy that ensured some government involvement and interference. As the bourgeois radicals called
for an end to the poor laws, they turned their sense of class virtue on
the people who benefited by those laws. In the wake of the Birmingham riots Priestley warned of a time

> when the labor of ages may be swept away in a day, and this whole
> country, at present the pride of the world, may become a scene of general
> desolation. It has within itself the ample seeds of such a calamity, in the
> prodigious number of the ignorant, the profligate, and the profane parts
> of the lower orders of the community, whom the impolicy of our poor laws
> chiefly, has rendered utterly averse to labor and economy, to a degree far
> below that of any of the brute creation.[33]

One wonders how sensitive the poor were to the aims of these new
antagonists. The rioters in Birmingham who burned down Priestley's
house and those in Manchester who burned Thomas Walker's were no
doubt whipped up by agitators for church and king. They saw both

[31] Adam Smith, *The Wealth of Nations*, ed. Andrew Skinner (Baltimore, 1970), pp. 441–
43. Adam Smith was, to be sure, no great champion of eighteenth-century industrialists.
His famous indictment of manufacturers can be found in chap 2, bk. 4, of *Wealth of
Nations* (pp. 438–39). What infuriated him was their action in *concert* to influence economic legislation and not their heroic functions as producers of wealth and social
benefactors.

[32] Joseph Priestley, *Memoirs of Dr. Joseph Priestley* (London, 1806), p. 3.

[33] Priestley, *Appeal to the Public*, p. 85.

Dissenters as supporters of the French Revolution, to be sure, but they may well have sensed that they were also representatives of a class that for all its indictment of the great and its defense of equality was exploitive and critical of them as well. This reading of the riots was not lost on Priestley.

> It is the opinion of many that envy of the property of the dissenters was one considerable stimulus to the mischief that was done to them at Birmingham. But the wanton destruction of wealth acquired by honest industry is not the way to make a nation flourish and enable it to bear its burdens.[34]

The adult writings of the bourgeois radicals represent a self-conscious glorification of the mission of the middle class in English society. Before James Mill and legions of Victorian apologists for the bourgeoisie, radicals in the 1770s, 1780s, and 1790s made the case for the superiority of men and women of the virtuous and industrious middle ranks. And who was more middle class than the Protestant Dissenters? John Aikin wrote of his radical associates: "Your natural connections are not with kings and nobles. You belong to the most virtuous, the most enlightened, the most independent part of the community, *the middle class.*" His sister, Anna Barbauld, was equally insistent that the Dissenters were fortunate to be "in that middle rank of life where industry and virtue most abound." Mary Wollstonecraft lamented that women were not more like middle-class men. "The middle rank," she wrote, "contains most virtue and abilities." It is there that "talents thrive best." Indeed, her *Vindication of the Rights of Woman* was written specifically, as she put it, for "those in the middle class, because they appear to be in the most natural state."[35]

Not only was the middle class most virtuous and most industrious, it was also the happiest. Interesting echoes of Jefferson's pursuit of happiness can be heard in Richard Price's observations on the good fortune of the Americans. America is lucky, he wrote in 1784, because the "happiest state of man is in the middle state between the savage and the refined, or between the wild and the luxurious state."[36] Priestley, too, was convinced that middle-class existence was the most felicitous. For several years in the late 1770s he lived in the great house of Lord

---

[34]Ibid., p. 104.

[35]John Aikin, *Address to the Dissenters of England on Their Late Defeat* (London, 1790), 18 (emphasis is Aikin's); Barbauld, *Address to Opposers*, p. 18; Mary Wollstonecraft, *Vindication of the Rights of Woman*, ed. Miriam Brody Kramnick (New York, 1975), pp. 147–48, 171, 181.

[36]Richard Price, *Observations on the Importance of the American Revolution and the Means of Making It a Benefit to the World* (London, 1784), p. 69.

Shelburne as librarian to this aristocratic patron of bourgeois radicalism. Price had held the job before Priestley, and later Shelburne would champion Jerry Bentham. Looking back in his *Memoirs* on his years as resident intellectual for the great, Priestley noted that he was above temptation.

> I was not at all fascinated with that mode of life. . . . These people are generally unhappy from the want of necessary employment; on which account chiefly there appears to be much more happiness in the middle classes of life, who are above the fear of want, and yet have a sufficient motive for constant exertion of the faculties, and who have always some other object besides amusement. I used to make no scruple of maintaining that there is not only the most virtue and most happiness, but even most true politeness in the middle classes of life.[37]

Asserting the superiority of the middle class involved not only putting down those above but also, as we have noted in Priestley, criticizing those below. The Aristotelian praise of the mean was sanctified by religion when the Cambridgeshire dissenting minister Robert Hall compared the Georgian middle class with the early converts to Christianity. Like them, "they were drawn from neither the very highest nor the very lowest classes. The former are too often the victims of luxury and pride, the latter, sunk in extreme stupidity. They were from the middle orders, where the largest portion of virtue and good sense has usually resided."[38] This parallel between the early Christians and the middle class produced by the Industrial Revolution was constantly evoked. They both had great historical missions as messianic agents of regeneration and rebirth. Joel Barlow, for example, the American entrepreneur who spent the 1790s in England and France pursuing profits and radical politics, expressed this theme in 1792:

> In mercy to them all, let the system be changed, let society be restored, and human nature retrieved. Those who compose the middle class of mankind, the class in which the semblance of nature most resides, are called upon to perform this task. . . . It will require some time to bring the men who now fill the two extremes in the wretched scale of rank to a proper view of their new stations of citizens. Minds that have long been crushed under the weight of privilege and pride or of misery and despair are equally distant from all rational ideas of the dignity of man. But even these classes may be brought back by degrees to be useful members of the state.[39]

[37]Priestley, *Memoirs*, p. 82.
[38]Robert Hall, *Miscellania* (Cambridge, Eng., n.d.), p. 205.
[39]Joel Barlow, *Advice to the Privileged Orders in the Several States of Europe* (London, 1792), pp. 97–98.

It was against this "weight of privilege and pride" that middle-class radicals, "the useful members of the state," waged war. The fundamental sin of the privileged order was their violation of what Thomas Cooper, the dissenting industrialist, called the "principle of talent." Government required "talents and abilities," which were not assigned at birth, but which manifested themselves in personal merit and achievement. While the privileged ruled the state, "the business of the nation is actually done by those who owe nothing to their ancestors, but have raised themselves into situations which the idleness and ignorance of the titled orders incapacitate them from filling." Moreover, Cooper argued, the privileged who acquire their control of politics and the social order by virtue of birth have no motive for industry or hard work. Everything they need or want is theirs through their station in life. "Take away these inducements by giving them in advance, and you stop the growth of abilities and knowledge and you nip wisdom and virtue in the bud." Public virtue flows not from the sated ranks of the privileged but from "insatiable ambition" and as a "reward for extraordinary talents or great exertions." The aristocracy by their monopoly of public offices blocked the virtuous citizen from the rightful fruits of his industry. Cooper's rhetoric is vintage bourgeois radicalism.

> The privileged orders are not required to earn their envied distinctions. . . . They have no concomitant duties to fulfill in consideration for the privileges they enjoy, their inutility is manifest . . . they are of no avail to any useful purpose in society. . . . It is well known that where business is to be done, it is best done with competition, and always comparatively ill done, by those who are careless of public approbation, because they are independent of public opinion. The privileged orders are unjust also to men of experience and abilities who are deprived in a great measure by the due reward of meritorious attainment.[40]

These men of "meritorious attainment" were the bearers of an ideology of equal opportunity. The bourgeois radical demanded political reform in order to destroy forever the aristocratic world of ascribed status. The demands of the reformers that the suffrage be extended to industrial and commercial wealth, that the new manufacturing centers such as Manchester and Birmingham be granted parliamentary representation, that expensive aristocratic institutions be streamlined or eliminated, that Dissenters be free to serve as municipal and governmental officials, all boil down to the bourgeois demand for the opening of careers to the talented. A public order managed by people of merit

---

[40]Thomas Cooper, *A Reply to Mr. Burke's Invective against Mr. Cooper and Mr. Watt* (London, 1792), pp. 16, 21, 32, 63, 65.

and achievement would in turn reward others for industry and effort. Poor laws would be abolished, taxes decreased, government withdrawn from the market and the pulpit, luxury discouraged, thrift and other middle-class values encouraged. Equality of opportunity was a social ideal that assumed that the have-nots were the truly skilled and industrious. Given a freely competitive environment, these talents would move them to the top, a victory for virtue as well as for merit.

Though equal opportunity may be an ideal of problematic application to a later age when the skilled have in fact become the haves, the bourgeois radicals of late eighteenth-century England faced no such problems. Equality of opportunity dominated their thought. One who pleaded for it was William Godwin, former dissenting minister and the philosopher of the English radicals during the French Revolution. In his immensely popular and influential *Enquiry Concerning Political Justice* he attacked the aristocrat as someone with "no motive to industry and exertion; no stimulus to rouse him from the lethargic, oblivious pool, out of which every human intellect originally rose." Privilege, Godwin wrote, enables a few to monopolize the rewards "which the system of the universe left at large to all her sons," and it "kills all liberal ambition in the rest of mankind." Godwin's treatise, justly remembered as the first important anarchist statement, is also a manifesto for the liberal individualistic world view that lashed out at the still powerful remnants of the corporate and hierarchical polity defended by Burke. Godwin proclaimed: "It is this structure of aristocracy, in all its sanctuaries and fragments, against which reason and morality have declared war. . . . Mankind will never be, in an eminent degree, virtuous and happy till each man shall possess that portion of distinction and no more, to which he is entitled by his personal merits." Godwin's plea for equality is that of the bourgeois radical. He demanded no leveling or arbitrary equalization, only equality of opportunity. He, too, invoked the metaphor of the race, the competitive symbol of self-reliant liberalism. "Remove from me and my fellows all arbitrary hindrances; let us start fair; render all the advantages and honors of social institution accessible to every man in proportion to his talents and exertions."[41] How fitting, then, that Thomas Holcroft, the radical dissenting novelist, Godwin's closest friend, and the acquitted conspirator in Pitt's treason trial of 1794, should have been the Englishman to translate Beaumarchias's *Marriage of Figaro* in 1784.

Along with Godwin, mention should be made of another bourgeois radical who in his day was considered the most influential and cer-

---

[41]William Godwin, *Enquiry Concerning Political Justice*, ed. Isaac Kramnick (Harmondsworth, 1976), pp. 470–75.

tainly the most widely quoted critic of the English political and social scene. Overshadowed now by Priestley, Price, and Paine, James Burgh, through his *Political Disquisitions* (1774), was literally the schoolmaster for a whole generation of bourgeois radicals in England and America. He wrote that the British government and all its profitable and prestigious jobs were parceled out to the nobility and gentry who dominated Parliament. Why has the nobleman any more claim to this respect than the artisan or manufacturer? he asked. "If the nobility and gentry decline to serve their country in the great offices of the state, without sordid hire, let the honest bourgeoisie be employed. They will themselves be sufficiently rewarded by the honour done them."[42]

Public jobs, he suggested, should go to men of merit rather than to "half our nobility . . . and over drenched court sponges." Burgh proposed, in fact, that public jobs, like public contracts, be filled by "sealed proposals." The offer of the individual most capable of serving his country would then be accepted. If men of the meritorious middle class took over the public service and the Parliament, public expenditures, he predicted, would decline dramatically, for these new men would not demand great salaries, they would not dance "at Mrs. Conneley's masquerades." They would "rise up early and sit up late and fill up the whole day with severe labor."[43]

Bourgeois Millenarianism

Those self-reliant middle-class men who got up early and worked hard all day were perceived, like the early Christians, as messianic agents of regeneration and rebirth. Idleness and sloth would give way to industry and virtue, and the millennium would be ushered in on the wings of science and technology. The bourgeois radicals, almost to a man, were scientists and engineers. Price was a renowned mathematician and developer of actuarial science; Paine was an engineer involved in the development of the iron bridge; and Cooper was a learned chemist. Priestley was all these things and more.

Their science was a bourgeois science. At the proliferating learned societies in provincial Britain, such as the Lunar Society in Birmingham, such industrialists as Boulton, Wedgwood, and Watt and such scientists as Priestley and Darwin exchanged papers on the latest chemical breakthroughs, on electricity, on theories of free trade and republican government. These societies bound science ever closer to

---

[42]James Burgh, *Political Disquisitions* (London, 1774), 1:98.
[43]Ibid., 3:169.

the new world of profit and power, the world that Burke would characterize as that of sophistry, economy, and calculation.[44]

Bourgeois science was closely linked to radical politics. These scientists were good bourgeois who in a closed aristocratic society of privilege and rank sought radical social changes, not the least of which were greater social and political rewards and power for themselves and their industrial friends. But science was also a powerful tool in the bourgeoisie's effort to demystify the universe. Here, too, its impact was radical. The aristocratic political world was defended by Burke and others because of its very mysterious and superstitious essence—the dark shadowy eminences of kings, queens, and lords with their cloaks of mysterious authority, crowns, scepters, and thrones. Government, it was held, was also a mysterious, complicated, and arcane realm. Only persons born to it could understand and manipulate it. Science expelled superstition from the heavens and could expel the mysteries that lay heavy on aristocratic society. With its new and corrosive ideals of truth, efficiency, and utility, science fueled the millennial social and political visions of the radical bourgeoisie. Science seemed to give reality to the radicals' unbounded faith in progress, the belief that human society could be perfected and suffering eliminated; in science as in politics, men of unrestrained pride soared high, seeking to rival even the gods. The radical millennial role of science is seen in a delightful aside in Wedgwood's correspondence with his partner:

> I am much pleased with your disquisition upon the capabilities of electricity, and should be glad to contribute in any way you can point out to me towards rendering Doctor Priestley's very ingenious experiments more extensively useful. . . . But what daring mortals you are! to rob the Thunderer of his bolts,—and for what?—no doubt to blast the oppressors of the poor and needy, or to execute some public piece of justice in the most tremendous and conspicuous manner, that shall make the great ones of the earth tremble![45]

Science for Josiah Wedgwood was the handmaiden of an anti-aristocratic radical politics. Men rivaled the gods. They, too, could terrify the great of this world.

[44]See Schofield, *Lunar Society of Birmingham;* S. H. Jeyes, *The Russells of Birmingham in the French Revolution and in America, 1791–1814* (London, 1911); L. S. Marshall, *The Development of Public Opinion in Manchester, 1780–1820* (Syracuse, N.Y., 1946); Eric Robinson, "The Derby Philosophical Society," *Annals of Science* 9 (1953); John Taylor, "The Sheffield Constitutional Society," *Transactions of the Hunter Archaeological Society* 5 (1943); W. H. Chaloner, "Dr. Joseph Priestley, John Wilkinson, and the French Revolution, 1789–1802," *Transactions of the Royal Historical Society,* 5th ser., 8 (1958); Robinson, "English Philosophes."

[45]Josiah Wedgwood, *Selected Letters of Josiah Wedgwood,* ed. Ann Finer and George Savage (London, 1965), p. 44.

Millennial fervor was basic to bourgeois radicalism. The vision of a social order purged of barbaric and feudal iniquity revived the millennial dreams of the Dissenters' seventeenth-century forebears. The Reverend Richard Price, for example, was convinced of the imminence of a new era. In an address to some wealthy backers of dissenting academies in 1787 he forcefully brought together the faith in progress of a philosophe and the messianic vision of English nonconformity. The English Enlightenment, the product not of freethinkers or antichristians but of deeply religious dissenting ministers, could produce in Price an enthusiasm so boundless that he could acknowledge and even glory in the anomaly that Carl Becker has pointed out: the kingdom of heaven that was fast approaching would be a heavenly city in this world. Price's prosperous bourgeois audience was witness to "a progressive improvement in human affairs which will terminate in greater degrees of light and virtue and happiness than have yet been known." No one could doubt, he noted, that the "present day world is unspeakably different from what it was." Superstition was giving ground, "the world out-growing its evils . . . Anti-Christ falling and the millennium hastening."[46]

But the sons of God must not sit still and merely await the coming of the new order. There was work to be done, Price urged, God's work, and the idle were His enemies. In his description of how his dissenting listeners could "facilitate this progress," Price reveals much about the theological roots of so much of radical bourgeois ideology. He speaks as a philosophe (indeed, he quotes Condorcet's life of Turgot), as Protestant minister, and as bourgeois idealogue.

> Providence works through the investigation and active exertions of enlightened and honest men. These are aimed directly at the melioration of the world, and without them it would soon degenerate. It is the blessings of God on the disquisitions of reasons and the labour of virtue, united to the invisible direction of his Providence, that must bring on the period I have in view. Inactivity and sleep are fatal to improvement. It is only (as the prophet Daniel speaks) by running to and fro, that is, by diligent inquiry, by free discussion, and by the collision of different sentiments, that knowledge can be increased and the dignity of our species promoted.

Progress is fueled by the anxious and industrious Protestant, "running to and fro" and avoiding "inactivity and sleep." The subscribers were urged to set up more dissenting academies where these values would

---

[46]Price, *Evidence for a Future Period of Improvement*, pp. 5, 22, 25; see Carl Becker, *The Heavenly City of the Eighteenth-Century Philosophers* (New Haven, Conn., 1959).

be practiced and taught. "Obey the care of Providence, and join our helping hands to those of the friends of science and virtue."[47]

It was Price's genius to anticipate even before the French Revolution that new day which would so dazzle Wordsworth and the others. Like the poets who sang of "joy" and "bliss" and like Jefferson and Bentham, who wrote of "happiness," Price saw the new era as felicitous liberation from misery and discontent. It was the theme of the age: "We live in happier times than our forefathers." The "shades of night are departing," Price noted characteristically, "the day dawns."[48]

In his radical millenarianism, as in so much else, Joseph Priestley surpassed even Richard Price, perhaps because he lived through the revolution and the fiery reaction to it which sent him to America. In 1791 Priestley wrote ecstatically of "the prospect of the general enlargement of liberty, civil and religious, opened by the Revolution in France." The language with which Priestley described the imminent regeneration of humanity is strikingly close to that later used by Marx to describe the impact of the proletarian revolution. The revolution in France, as well as the one that took place in America, were, Priestley wrote in reply to Burke,

> in many respects unparalleled in all history, they make a totally new, a most wonderful and important, era in the history of mankind. It is, to adopt your own rhetorical style, a change from darkness to light, from superstition to sound knowledge and from a most debasing servitude to a state of the most exalted freedom. It is a liberating of all the powers of man from that variety of fetters by which they have hitherto been held. So that, in comparison with what has been, now only can we expect to see what men really are, and what they can do.[49]

Priestley held out a wondrous and dazzling future, and America showed the way. Like the American colonies, first France, then England, and then the world would have governments "confining their attention to the civil concerns . . . and consulting their welfare in the present state only." As a result, all peoples would soon be "flourishing and happy." All animosity between the world's peoples would come to an end, and peace and goodwill would reign among nations. Priestley suggests, much like Kant, that "when the affairs of the various societies [should] be conducted by those who . . . truly represent them," colonial empires would be no more; no longer would one people be

---

[47]Price, *Evidence for a Future Period*, pp. 27, 51.

[48]Ibid., p. 53; see M. H. Abrams, *Natural Supernaturalism* (New York, 1971), for a good description of poetic millenarianism in England at the end of the eighteenth century.

[49]Priestley, *Letters to Burke*, letter 14, p. 251.

held in subjection by another. "The idle pageantry of a court" would be replaced by canals, bridges, roads, libraries, and laboratories. This "happy state of things," when wars would end and men would beat their swords into plowshares, was, Priestley noted, repeatedly foretold in the prophecies of 2,000 years earlier. But more than Providence stood behind this looked-for state of things, for it made "good sense, and the prevailing spirit of commerce" worked to bring it about. In "this new condition of the world," no men would be singled out by titles, "a profanation of epithets." The magistrates would be "appointed and paid for the conservation of order." Government would be of modest scope and "unspeakably less expensive than it is at present." The taxes now paid, "a most unreasonable sum . . . perhaps the amount of one half of our property," would "become superfluous" with the elimination of the state church and the aristocratic establishment.[50]

This new "glorious and happy" order described by Priestley and his contemporaries would be characterized by perfection and the elimination of all evil. Buoyed by their optimistic sense of progress and futurity, the bourgeois millenarians fully expected to see a world without anxiety, without suffering, and without sin. The enlightened men and women of the eighteenth century had finally and irrevocably set in train the events that would overcome original sin. In the new kingdom on earth, all people would be forever joyous and happy. Their lot would be ameliorated unto perfection. All that was imperfect, all that was inefficient, and all that was painful would be swept away by the fires of redemption with a little bit of help from practical bourgeois science. For bourgeois radicals, nothing seemed beyond their power. Their tools of science and reason could eliminate all life's pain and even life's mortality. Franklin wrote to Priestley:

> The rapid progress the sciences now make, occasions my regrets sometimes that I was born so soon. It is impossible to imagine the heights to which may be carried, in a thousand years the power of man over matter. . . . All diseases may by sure means be prevented or cured (not excepting even that of old age) and our lives lengthened at pleasure, even beyond the antediluvian standard.[51]

Godwin was caught up in the rapturous potential of this vision. If Franklin were right, he suggested, "if the power of intellect can be established over all other matter, are we not inevitably led to ask, why not over the matter of our own bodies?" It is surely possible, then, for

[50]Ibid., pp. 252–54.
[51]J. T. Rutt, ed., *The Life and Correspondence of Joseph Priestley* (London, 1831), 1:329.

us to correct the faults that tear down the heart and tire the limbs. We should be able to arrive at "a total extirpation of the infirmities of our nature." We shall live forever. Bourgeois optimism reaches its most prideful moment when Godwin concludes that "there will be neither disease, anguish, melancholy, nor resentment."[52]

For the bourgeois radicals the millenarian future lay in America. For Tom Paine America was the spark that set off the flame of bourgeois revolution in Europe. It was a new Athens, "the admiration and model for the present." America ushered in a new era in human history, the "birthday of a new world," a world dominated by republican principles and bourgeois ideals. This millenarian mission could be rendered in mechanical terms. Paine, the engineer, likened America's destiny to Archimedes' famous quest. "Had we, said he, a place to stand upon, we might raise the world. The Revolution in America presented in politics what was only theory in mechanics." What would move the world was the new system of government in America. The most impressive thing about it for Paine was that it was everything the British system was not. Taxation, as one might imagine, was front and center, followed closely by its consort—bloated and aristocratic retainers of no ability. The differences between America and England were, he wrote to Henry Dundas,

> in a great measure to be accounted for, not by the differences of proclamations, but by the difference of governments and the difference of taxes between that country and this. What the laboring people of that country earn they apply to their own use, and to the education of their children, and do not pay it away in taxes, as fast as they earn it, to support court extravagance, and a long enormous list of place-men and pensioners.[53]

America represented Utopia for the bourgeois radicals. America lived the very values that they preached against the age of chivalry. Had not Dr. Franklin, Thomas Cooper pointed out, claimed "that the people of America have a saying—that God Almighty is Himself a mechanic, the greatest in the universe; and He is respected and admired more for the variety, ingenuity and utility of His handiwork, than for the antiquity of His family"? Had not Jefferson written in 1788

---

[52]Godwin, *Enquiry Concerning Political Justice*, pp. 770–77. In contrast to this mood of optimism found in late eighteenth-century radicalism, it should be noted, is a strain of pessimism associated with criticism of and lamentation over the national debt. See, for example, Price's *Appeal to the Public on the Subject of the National Debt* (London, 1771) and *London Society for Constitutional Information* (London, 1782). Paine wrote critically of the national debt on some occasions, and on others he defended it.

[53]Tom Paine, *The Rights of Man*, ed. Henry Collins (Baltimore, 1969), p. 181, and *To Mr. Secretary Dundas* (London, 1792), in *The Writings of Thomas Paine*, ed. M. D. Conway (New York, 1895), 3:22.

that "there is not a crowned head in Europe whose talents or merits would entitle him to be elected a vestryman by the people of any parish in America"? America's cause "was the cause of all mankind," as Paine put it. Freedom would find an asylum here in a land where "no one by birth could have a right to set up his own family in perpetual preference to all others forever."[54]

[54]Franklin cited in Thomas Cooper, *Some Information Respecting America* (London, 1794), p. 230; Jefferson to Washington, May 2, 1788, in *The Political Writings of Thomas Jefferson*, ed. Edward Dumbauld (New York, 1955); Paine, *Common Sense*, p. 78.

CHAPTER 3

Joseph Priestley's Scientific Liberalism

I N 1794 Joseph Priestley fled England and the church-and-king sentiment that had set ablaze his Birmingham house and laboratory in 1791. His flight to America was noted by the United Irishmen with a public letter. This most radical group in the entire camp of British sympathizers with the French Revolution not only lamented English repression but also offered a marvelous hymn to the tripartite linkage of America, useful science, and radical change.

> The Emigration of Dr. Priestley will form a striking historical fact, by which alone future ages will learn to estimate truly the temper of the present times. . . . But be cheerful, dear Sir, you are going to a happier world, the world of Washington and Franklin. In idea we accompany you. . . . We also look to the new age when man shall become more precious than fine gold, and when his ambition shall be to subdue the elements, not to subjugate his fellow creatures, to make fire, water, earth, and air obey his bidding, but to leave the pure ethereal mind, as the sole thing in nature free and invincible. . . . The attention of a whole scientific people [here] is bent to multiplying the means and instruments of destruction . . . but you are going to a country where science is turned to better use.[1]

The relationship between science and progressive politics was by no means one-way. Just as science would ameliorate the human conditions, so a progressive politics would encourage scientific advances. In the very last scientific paper he wrote before his self-imposed exile, Priestley made a digression into politics, noting the extent to which

---

[1] J. T. Rutt, ed., *The Life and Correspondence of Joseph Priestley* (London, 1831), 2:218.

politics, ideology, and science were intertwined, and firmly identified himself and other radicals as the true virtuosos of science. His *Experiments on the Generation of Air from Water* (1793) notes that

> since . . . the friends of philosophy in this country *must* separate on the ground of *religion* and *politics* . . . may the separation have no farther consequences than that producing a generous emulation who shall most advance the cause of science; the friends of *Church* and *King,* as they affect exclusively to call themselves, or the friends of liberty, among whom, at all times, and in all circumstances, I shall be proud to rank myself. We are, it is true, but a small minority, but not deficient, I trust, in ability, activity, and energy, qualities which will always make men respected, though oppressed.[2]

Priestley cannot have been surprised to find that in his adopted America his champion was the founding father who similarly linked progress to the fortunes of science. Jefferson wrote Priestley in 1801:

> Our countrymen have recovered from the alarm into which art and industry had thrown them; science and honesty are replaced on their high ground, and you my dear Sir, as their great apostle, are on its pinnacle. It is with heartfelt satisfaction that, in the first moments of my public action, I can hail you with welcome to our land, tender to you the homage of its respect and esteem, cover you under the protection of those laws which were made for the wise and good like you. Yours is one of the few lives precious to mankind for the continuance of which every thinking man is solicitous.[3]

The Priestley-Jefferson connection is a close one. On numerous occasions Jefferson articulated the debt his own educational, theological, and political attitudes owed to Priestley's ideas and writings. He read Priestley's *History of the Corruptions of Christianity* "over and over again," and it became the basis of his own peculiar blend of anticlericalism and deism. Through Priestley Jefferson came to philosophical materialism, the associationist theories of David Hartley, and notions of the materiality of the soul. Jefferson's millenarian vision of science and scientists was derived at least in part from Priestley's works. Priestley's writings on education were influential in Jefferson's planning of the University of Virginia, and in 1786 Madison and Jefferson used Priestley's writings on the disestablishment of the Anglican

---

[2]Quoted in F. W. Gibbs, *Joseph Priestley: Revolutions of the Eighteenth Century* (New York, 1967), p. 243; emphasis is Priestley's.

[3]Thomas Jefferson to Joseph Priestley, March 21, 1801, in *The Works of Thomas Jefferson,* ed. P. L. Ford (New York, 1905), 9:216.

church and the separation of church and state in planning the statute to establish religious freedom in Virginia.

But it was more than just specifics that Priestley and Jefferson shared. It was an entire world view, an unabashed appreciation of modernity. Writing to Priestley in January 1800, Jefferson continued their running discussion on education. He agreed with Priestley that the study of Greek and Latin was not essential for a modern education. Jefferson then turned to broader concerns in a passionate defense of modernity against antiquity.

> The Gothic idea that we are to look backwards instead of forwards for the improvement of the human mind, and to recur to the annals of our ancestors for what is most perfect in government, in religion, and in learning, is worthy of those bigots in religion and government, by whom it is recommended, and whose purpose it would answer. But it is not an idea which this country will endure.[4]

These were Priestley's views, as well. He had written earlier: "Those times of revived antiquity have had their use and are now no more. . . . Their maxims of life will not suit the world as it is at present."[5]

"One of the Few Lives Precious to Mankind"

Priestley, known to later ages as the great scientist who discovered oxygen, or perhaps as the theologian who founded modern Unitarianism, was known to his contemporaries primarily as "Gunpowder Joe," the leading radical intellectual of his era. In the 1770s Priestley had been, along with Richard Price, one of the most ardent supporters of the American cause. This outspoken support for the Americans was, in fact, soundly rebuked by Samuel Johnson in his famous attack on the colonists in 1775. Priestley's marriage of science and radical politics was not to Johnson's taste, "Ah Priestley," Johnson is reported to have

---

[4]Ibid., p. 102.

[5]Joseph Priestley, *Lectures on History and General Policy* (London, 1782), lecture 45, p. 349. For documentation of Jefferson's debt to Priestley, see *Works of Jefferson*, 9:95, 102, 380, 404; 10:69. See also *The Writings of Thomas Jefferson*, ed. Albert E. Bergh (Washington, D.C., 1907), 10:228, 13:352, 14:200, 15:232; Adrienne Koch, *The Philosophy of Thomas Jefferson* (Chicago, 1964), pp. 24, 27, 34; Daniel J. Boorstin, *The Lost World of Thomas Jefferson* (Boston, 1960), pp. 17–19, 113–19, 159–62; Colin Bonwick, *English Radicals and the American Revolution* (Chapel Hill, N.C., 1977), p. 285; Nicholas Han, "Franklin, Jefferson, and the English Radicals at the End of the Eighteenth Century," in *Proceedings of the American Philosophical Society* 98 (1954): 406–26. For advice on commercial policy given Jefferson by Priestley and his disciple Thomas Cooper, see Drew McCoy, *The Elusive Republic* (Chapel Hill, N.C., 1980), pp. 176–77, 215–16, 246–47.

uttered, "an evil man, Sir. His work unsettles everything."[6] More significant for Priestley's "evil" reputation was his emergence in the 1780s as the leader of the English radicals who called for reform of Parliament, extension of the suffrage, and repeal of the onerous Test and Corporation Acts. To all this clamor Edmund Burke replied, "If I must, my choice is made. I will have rather George III or IV than Dr. Priestley."[7]

Priestley's pamphlets called not only for an end to the legal disabilities faced by Dissenters like himself and his fellow Unitarians but also for disestablishment of the Anglican church and total separation of church and state. His effort was of no avail, however, for in 1787, 1789, and 1790 Parliament refused to repeal the acts. In the last of these efforts, Burke led the forces for the status quo. To repeal these fundamental religious laws, Burke warned, would "proceed step by step" to a leveling of the "foundations" of first the church and then the state.[8]

Burke's argument reflected the pervasive popular linkage of the religious rebel Priestley with the cause of political radicalism. The assault on the Test and Corporation Acts did indeed come from the very same dissenting intellectuals and industrialists who were demanding reform of the archaic Parliament, in which such newly populated Midlands cities as Birmingham, Manchester, and Leeds were not represented but to which rural constituencies of fields and cows continued to send members. What frightened Burke and others, of course, was that the assault on the Test and Corporation Acts and the demands for political reform intensified with the news of the revolution in France; that fear provides the background for the mob's burning of Priestley's house in 1791.

Priestley was lyrical in his praise of the French Revolution, as were virtually all the Dissenters. For Priestley the revolution was, as we have seen, "unparalleled in all history," an event ushering in "a most wonderful and important era in the history of mankind."[9]

No surprise, then, that Burke's *Reflections on the Revolution in France,* published in November 1790, singled out Priestley (along with Price) as a leader of a plot to subvert the English social order as the French had subverted theirs. There was no mistaking Burke's intent to place Priestley at the head of this pack of seditious malcontents when he noted that "the wild gas, the fixed air is plainly broke loose." Priestley

[6]Quoted in Boswell Taylor, *Joseph Priestley: The Man of Science* (London, 1954), p. 11. See also Samuel Johnson, *Taxation No Tyranny* (London, 1775).

[7]Edmund Burke, "Speeches on Fox's Motion for Repeal of Certain Penal Statutes Respecting Religious Opinions," *Parliamentary History* 29 (1791–1792): 1389.

[8]Ibid., p. 1387.

[9]Joseph Priestley, *Letters to the Right Honourable Edmund Burke* (Birmingham, 1791), letter 14, pp. 143–44.

immediately replied in a pamphlet attacking Burke's *Reflections*. "Your whole book, Sir, is little else than a vehicle for the same poison, inculcating, but inconsistently enough, a respect for princes, independent of their being originally the choice of the people as if they had some natural and indefeasible right to reign over us, they being born to command, and we to obey."[10]

On July 14, 1791, many Dissenters in Birmingham gathered at the Hotel, Temple Row, to commemorate the French Revolution. The call to the meeting urged that "surely no free-born Englishman can refrain from exulting in this addition to the general mass of human happiness. It is the cause of Humanity! It is the cause of the People!" The people of Birmingham, alas, were not moved. Inflamed by Anglican preachers, as well as by free liquor, the mob that evening destroyed the Dissenter chapel and headed on to Priestley's house and laboratory. He was warned and fled, but he had no time to take anything with him. Priestley's house was burned to the ground and with it his manuscripts, library, and scientific equipment. For days the mob destroyed houses of other known Dissenters and radicals. Finally Henry Dundas, the home secretary, sent royal troops to restore order. Priestley had traveled through the night to London. George III took note of him in authorizing his secretary of state to send troops to Birmingham. The king wrote, "I cannot but feel better pleased that Priestley is the sufferer for the doctrines he and his party have instilled, and that the people see them in their true light."[11]

In 1794 Priestley sailed for America. Coleridge, still in his radical phase, wrote of this shame.

> Him, full of years, from his loved native land
> Statesmen blood-stained and priests idolatrous
> By dark lies maddening the blind multitude
> Drove with vain hate. Calm, pitying he retired,
> And mused expectant on these promised years.[12]

In America Priestley settled in rural Pennsylvania, at the fork of the Susquehanna River near Northumberland, where Coleridge and the poet Robert Southey had once dreamed of creating the utopian community they called Pantisocracy. Here Priestley lived until his death in

[10]Edmund Burke, *Reflections on the Revolution in France*, ed. Conor Cruise O'Brien (Baltimore, 1969), p. 90; Priestley, *Letters to Burke*, letter 3, p. 30.

[11]Gibbs, *Joseph Priestley*, p. 199; George III to Henry Dundas, July 14, 1791, in *The Letters of King George III*, ed. Bonamy Dobrée (London, 1935), p. 212.

[12]Samuel Taylor Coleridge, "Religious Musings" (December 1794), in *Selected Poetry and Prose of Coleridge*, ed. Donald A. Stauffer (New York, 1951), pp. 100–101, cited in part in Basil Willey, *The Eighteenth-Century Background* (Boston, 1961), p. 194.

1804, and here the American Chemical Society was founded in 1874, on the one hundredth anniversary of Priestley's discovery of oxygen. Nothing pleased Priestley more during his last ten years in America than Jefferson's election to the presidency in 1800. It marked a personal milestone for Priestley. He wrote, "I now for the first time in my life (and I shall soon enter my 70th year), find myself in any degree of favour with the government of the country in which I have lived, and I hope I shall die in the same pleasing situation."[13]

Science and the Liberal State

In Priestley and his circle the English had their eighteenth-century philosophes and their Enlightenment. They produced no *Encyclopedia*, but their influence was every bit as great as that of their French counterparts. As he sought to free religion from superstition so that it could be accepted by "philosophical and thinking persons," so Priestley's writings, politics, and science were permeated with an optimistic and progressive outlook. The advancement of science in the late eighteenth century was based on the nexus in England of rising industry, political reform, and liberal theology. At the center of this nexus stood Priestley.[14]

The quest for happiness on this earth preoccupied Priestley the philosophe. It informs his religion and it structures his science. In his *Catechism for Children and Young Persons*, he posed the question "What did God make you and all mankind for?" His answer: "He made us to be good and happy." Even more significant is the reply to the question "Will not an application to worldly business interfere with the duties of religion?" "No," Priestley replies, "we please God the most, by doing that which makes ourselves and others the most happy." He strikes the same theme in his *Sermons*. Our lives and work have one objective, "the glorious, animating prospect of the happy state of mankind."[15]

Priestley was convinced that the religious life was a life of temporal happiness, one most easily attainable by the hardworking bourgeois to whom he preached and for whom he wrote. When he looked back on his years near the great aristocrats in England—men such as Lord Shelburne, for whom he had once worked—it struck him that "These people are generally unhappy from the want of necessary employment."[16]

[13]Quoted in Anne D. Holt, *A Life of Priestley* (London, 1931), p. 205.
[14]Rutt, *Life and Correspondence of Priestley*, 1:75. See also J. D. Bernal, *Science in History* (London, 1965), p. 481.
[15]Joseph Priestley, *A Catechism for Children and Young Persons* (London, 1787), pp. x, 27; and *Sermons* (London, 1830), p. 190.
[16]Joseph Priestley, *Memoirs of Dr. Joseph Priestley* (London, 1806), p. 82.

What the great in the aristocratic houses were not doing was "carrying on improvements," which was, according to Priestley, along with "the remedy of abuses," the mission God had given human beings through his injunction that they be useful through "industry and zeal." Science was, of course, the "necessary employment" most central to increasing happiness, remedying abuses, and furthering progress. In the preface to *The History and Present State of Electricity* Priestley invokes Bacon. Knowledge becomes power as the scientist "is master of the powers of nature." This power is applied "to all the useful purposes of life." The scientist contributes to the "security and happiness of mankind." Less interested in unlocking secrets of the universe or in knowing God's ways, the scientist has the practical goal of making "human life . . . in its present state . . . more comfortable and happy . . . able to subsist with more ease." This is, indeed, a civic responsibility, for by his work the scientist serves the community. He is "a good citizen and a useful member of society."[17]

The practical and political aims of Priestley's science were most persuasively articulated by his most important disciple, Thomas Cooper. A fascinating man in his own right, Cooper, like Priestley, represents in one person all the strains—scientific, industrial, political, religious, and economic—that constitute the progressive-innovative nexus of bourgeois radicalism. A well-to-do Manchester cotton manufacturer as well as one of the leading chemical scientists in England, Cooper was an important figure in the Manchester Literary and Philosophical Society and the Manchester Constitutional Society, the groups to which he submitted most of his scientific, philosophical, and political tracts. His essays on materialism and Unitarianism were widely distributed, especially in America, where Cooper became Priestley's major publicist.

Cooper was also one of the period's leading political radicals. His political writings and his tireless efforts to repeal the Test and Corporation Acts had already placed him in the public imagination as a leading figure in English Jacobin circles when an incident in 1792 earned him widespread notice. He and James Watt, Jr. (the radical son of the inventor), traveled to revolutionary France to see the wondrous revolution at firsthand and to do some business for Cooper's textile firm and the iron firm of Watt and Boulton as well. Their visit to France infuriated Burke, who in a celebrated outburst in Parliament on April 30, 1792, singled them out as traitorous agents of subversion. The two would, he feared, return from Paris to fan discontent in Manchester and Birmingham. Upon his return Cooper wrote *A Reply to Mr. Burke's Invective against Mr. Cooper and Mr. Watt*, a landmark in the middle-class

[17]Joseph Priestley, *Proper Objects of Education in the Present State of the World* (London, 1791), pp. 2, 6; *Sermons*, p. 21; and *The History and Present State of Electricity* (London, 1769), pp. iv, 442.

political offensive of those revolutionary years. As for Mr. Burke's "privileged orders . . . hereditary monarchy, hereditary nobility, hereditary legislators and hereditary judges," Cooper wrote, "there is good reason to regard them as incumbrances, absurd and useless, dangerous and unjust."[18] Such sentiments had become suspect in Pitt's England, however, and Cooper soon left for America (a decision made easier, no doubt, by the failure of his Manchester mills). Like Priestley, he settled first in Pennsylvania.

In America the first thing Cooper did was write a pamphlet encouraging other dissenters, religious and political, to follow him across the Atlantic. "The first and principal feature of America," he argued, was "the total absence of anxiety, respecting the future success of a family." The pamphlet provides a fascinating insight into the nearly obsessive concern of the bourgeois with personal and business success and with the ability to pass their success on to future generations, as the aristocracy did. Priestley, too, worried about his children. One of his reasons for leaving England was that "the bigotry of the country in general made it impossible for me to place my sons in it to any advantage."[19]

In Great Britain, Cooper wrote, "the middle class of moderate fortune, must work incessantly, deprive themselves of comfort, and pay anxious attention to minute frugality, with little probability of ultimate success, especially those with a large family." In America, he contended, in language not uncharacteristically reminiscent of Bunyan's *Pilgrim's Progress*, this "whole weight is taken off the father of a family." In England "anxious industry deserves a better reward"; in America, he asserts, social mobility is a reality, success is easy, and hardworking families are rewarded with wealth and land.[20]

Cooper, like Paine, carved out a dramatic second career in America. Fierce partisan of Jefferson in the election of 1800, he was tried and convicted of sedition for libeling John Adams. After he was released from jail, the victorious Jeffersonians rewarded him with a judgeship on the Pennsylvania Supreme Court. Later he became a widely published professor of chemistry at Carlisle College in Pennsylvania. After teaching at the University of Pennsylvania and the University of Virginia, he became in 1821, at the age of sixty, professor of chemistry and president of the College of South Carolina at Columbia.

His social views developed in directions similar to those of other

[18]*Parliamentary History* 29 (1791–1792): 1303–39; Thomas Cooper, *A Reply to Mr. Burke's Invective against Mr. Cooper and Mr. Watt* (London, 1792), p. 16. On Cooper see Dumas Malone, *The Public Life of Thomas Cooper, 1783–1839* (New Haven, Conn., 1926).

[19]Thomas Cooper, *Some Information Respecting America* (London, 1794), p. 53; Priestley, *Memoirs*, 2:238.

[20]Cooper, *Some Information Respecting America*, pp. 55, 57.

Jeffersonians. He became a leading writer on laissez-faire economics and a leading southern opponent of the tariff. In the 1820s he was one of the most respected voices in defense of states' rights and one of the first to suggest nullification in South Carolina. He remained, however, an outspoken materialist and popularizer of Priestley's Unitarianism. Jefferson wrote in 1819, "Cooper is acknowledged by every enlightened man who knows him to be the greatest man in America, in the power of the mind, and in acquired information, and that without a single exception."

The Manchester radical is evident throughout Cooper's American career. American states, like individuals, he wrote, had to guard against "the despotic power of centralised government." If America was the answer to the dreams and aspirations of the anxious English bourgeoisie, then the least Cooper could do was lecture the Americans on the economic wisdom of bourgeois radicalism, and this he did. In England, he told his southern students, who were as strongly opposed to tariffs as he was, the public had

> arrived at the conclusion, that all legislative restrictions, prohibitions, encouragements, and directions applied to commerce or manufacture, have proceeded from ignorant and intermeddling men who know not that the motive of self interest is more effacious than all the laws that can be enacted; and that persons whose time and intellect are intensely devoted to the pursuit of their own good, by means of those occupations that furnish them with subsistence, are better judges how to conduct their own business, than legislators who have neither the same motives, the same knowledge, or the same exciting interest themselves. . . . In fact, a legislator might as well direct the analysis of the chemist, or the manipulations of the pin-maker, or the pursuits of the planter, the manufacturer, or the merchant. From the time of Colbert to the present time, every fact has tended to establish the reasonableness of the request, *laissez-nous faire;* let us manage our own business.[21]

In America Cooper also set out to develop Priestley's philosophy of science. The English as well as the French philosophes found inspiration in Bacon. Bacon's genius, according to Cooper, lay in his ability to turn men of scientific bent away from the games of the learned, "playing tricks with syllogisms, and the legerdemain of words." He turned them to experiments and facts, to practical ameliorative concerns. Chemistry was central in this practical turn. "Chemistry is of more immediate and useful application to the everyday concerns of life and

---

[21]Thomas Cooper, *Lectures on the Elements of Political Economy* (Columbia, S.C., 1826), p. 21.

it operates more upon our hourly comforts than any other branch of knowledge whatever." An equally crucial science, according to Cooper, was mechanics, the study of the laws of inorganic bodies, their size, shape, weight, forces, and properties. Mechanics had contributed to the riches of England and the comfort of all its inhabitants. "It is to this science in conjunction with chemistry that the great wealth and power of that nation is principally indebted."[22]

Science was, according to Cooper, the most praiseworthy pursuit of any would-be cultured man. Science was, in fact, the crowning glory of an advanced civilization, replacing literature, which was always suspect for the practical and ascetic Dissenter because it distracted attention from more productive things. Praise of science is also linked to middle-class disdain for the past, for history, and for custom. For the middle class, the mystery and awe of ancient institutions and ancient ideas were part of the barbaric feudal past, to be replaced by usefulness and efficiency. All that Burke found so comforting and so necessary for civilized existence Cooper swept away in his description of science's contribution to human progress.

> What should make the knowledge of those laws on which all useful manufacturers depend less interesting than a knowledge of the licentious poets and dramatists? It is in the infancy of society chiefly that works of mere fiction receive an inordinate share of public attention. It is in our boyish years that the poets and novelists, the writers who are disgracefully employed in furnishing stimulus to appetites that require to be bridled, engage our attention. When experience has taught us wisdom, we begin to estimate utility as the criterion for desert, and look back with some regret at the time misemployed in mere amusement. It is so with the progress of civilized society; in the infancy and the ignorance of all communities, the great objects of intellect in peace are poetry and oratory; as nations advance in knowledge, science gains a rightful ascendancy.[23]

Priestley's and Cooper's science is a science of material and physical domination; it is "a knowledge that multiples a thousandfold the physical force of a human being." It is a utilitarian and practical science, less concerned with ultimate theories and speculative systems than with "rendering every hour of existence more desirable." Few have better stated the Enlightenment's conception of science than Priestley's disciple Cooper, as he captures all the progressive and ameliorative overtones of the eighteenth-century worship of science. "Science compels

---

[22]Thomas Cooper, *Introductory Lecture of T. Cooper, Professor of Chemistry at Carlisle College* (Carlisle, Pa., 1812), p. 7.
[23]Ibid., pp. 13–14.

every object around us to contribute, in some way or other, to our pleasure, to our profit, to our comfort, or to our convenience . . . which multiplies not only human enjoyment, and alleviates human suffering, but multiplies also the human species; by providing more extensively the means of constant employment, and comfortable subsistence." All the while, of course, Cooper pays tribute to the more immediate materialistic benefits of science. "It is to science, chemical and mechanical, that England is indebted for having made her island the storehouse of the world, for having compelled the nations of the earth to pour into her lap their superfluous wealth, for having acquired the undisputed command of the sea. . . . Her merchants are as princes."[24] Through science, we compel objects, and nations compel other nations. Bacon has come a long way. In Priestley's circle, science is indeed power—the power of profits to transform merchants into would-be princes.

The model scientist for Priestley's circle was Benjamin Franklin. Here, in fact, one found the scientist as statesman-prince. And here was also the preacher of pleasure, profit, comfort, and convenience. Franklin and Priestley were close friends and corresponded often about politics and electricity, and Franklin, we know, was a religious freethinker as well. A veritable cult of Franklin emerged in Priestley's circle. Many a hero in the early children's books produced by writers in Priestley's circle was named Benjamin. Indeed, Anna Barbauld, whose poetry sang Priestley's praises and whose tracts defended his calls for the repeal of the Test and Corporation Acts, offered Franklin as the model of "true heroism" in the new age. In one of her stories for children she wrote, "Few wiser men have ever existed than the late Dr. Franklin. His favorite purpose was to turn everything to use, to extract some potential advantage from his speculations. He understood common life and all that conduces unto its comfort. He left treasures of domestic wisdom that were superior to any of the boasted maxims of antiquity."[25]

Priestley's science, like Franklin's, was a part of the newly organized and interlocking world of politics and economics at whose center he stood. Priestley got to the center of that world partly by good fortune. He had married Mary Wilkinson, the daughter of Isaac Wilkinson, an ironmaster. Though her father was poor, Priestley writes, "I had a little fortune with her. I unexpectedly found a great resource in her two brothers, who had become wealthy, especially the elder of them."[26] This brother-in-law, John Wilkinson, the founder of the Wilkinson steel

[24]Ibid., pp. 99, 96.
[25]John Aikin and Anna Barbauld, *Evenings at Home; or, the Juvenile Budget Opened,* 6 vols. (Philadelphia, 1792–96), 6:250.
[26]Rutt, *Life and Correspondence of Priestley,* p. 19.

fortune, introduced Priestley to his own wider circle of Dissenter industrialists in the Midlands. As a result, Priestley became a lifelong
friend of Thomas Bentley and Josiah Wedgwood. Bentley, Wedgwood,
and Wilkinson subsidized Priestley's scientific work throughout their
lives; he in turn investigated the practical problems of industrial physics and chemistry, and often turned his pen to the political, religious,
and social affairs that concerned them.

Priestley saw his science as the handmaiden of a radical politics. He
was so convinced that science undermined all "undue and usurped
authority" that he was certain the English hierarchy had "reason to
tremble even at an air pump or an electrical machine."[27]

Priestley often used apocalyptic scientific imagery to describe the
impending and irresistible reform of the antiquated religious-political
order in Britain. It was, in fact, just such a passage that earned him his
popular name, "Gunpowder Joe." "We are," he wrote,

> as it were, laying gunpowder, grain by grain, under the old building of
> error and superstition, which a single spark may hereafter inflame, so as
> to produce an instantaneous explosion; in consequence of which that edi-
> fice, the erection of which has been the work of ages, may be overturned
> in a moment and so effectually as that same foundation can never be built
> again.[28]

According to Priestley, science would "be the means, under God, of
extirpating all error and prejudice, and of putting an end to all undue
and usurped authority." Priestley assumed that science would create a
people "more easy and comfortable," who would "grow daily more
happy." Whatever was the beginning of this world, he wrote, "the end
will be glorious and paradisiacal, beyond what our imaginations can
now conceive."[29]

The institution critical for science and thus for the increasing ame-
lioration of human life was the dissenting academy, certainly not Oxford or Cambridge. Priestley was "sorry to see the ample revenues of
the two universities . . . applied in a manner so little favourable to the
real interests of science." The source of progress was, on the contrary,
the dissenting academy, such as Warrington, where Priestley put
"modern scientific subjects" at the center of the curriculum. He wrote
to Pitt in 1787, "While your universities resemble pools of stagnant

[27]Joseph Priestley, *Experiments and Observations on Different Kinds of Air* (London, 1774),
p. xiv.

[28]Joseph Priestley, "Reflections on the Present State of Free Inquiry in This Country"
(1785), in *Sermons*, p. 101.

[29]Quoted in Gibbs, *Joseph Priestley*, p. 62; see also Joseph Priestley, *Writings on Philosophy, Science and Politics*, ed. John Passmore (New York, 1965), p. 198.

water secured by dams and mounds, and offensive to the neigh-
borhood, ours are like rivers, which, while taking their natural course,
fertilize a whole country." The dissenting academies served and by no
means offended their other-minded neighbors. Located primarily in
the newer industrial communities and funded by dissenting industrialists, the academies taught subjects fit "for civil and active life," as
Priestley put it. The dissenting academy, he wrote, would break down
the traditional barrier between "the learned world and the common
world." Men trained for an active life would no longer receive a classical education. Science and mathematics would replace ancient languages and classical thought. "Those times of revived antiquity,"
Priestley wrote, "have had their use and are no more. . . . Their maxims of life will not suit the world as it is at present." What he did teach
his students was accounting, algebra, geometry, modern history, commerce, theories of manufacture, and politics. Even young men who
were preparing for the ministry, he insisted, should study mathematics
and science. The purpose of education was, after all, "to find expedi-
ents to remedy abuses and carry on improvements." The clergy was
shaped for that same endeavor. The graduates of these academies,
industriously working in "civil and active life," were modernizing
saints ushering in the social and political millennium. They would join
the pantheon of Priestley's heroes, would become "a Bacon or Newton,
a Locke or Hartley, a Hampden or Sidney, a William Penn, or Franklin,
a Washington."[30]

As we have noted, millenarian fervor was endemic among English
intellectuals in the last decades of the eighteenth century. Wordsworth's "dawn when it was such bliss to be alive" was but the metaphorical symbol of a widespread belief in progress and perfectibility.
Priestley, too, saw "the morning opening upon us, and we cannot
doubt but that, the light will increase, and extend itself more and more
unto the perfect day. . . . As all things (and particularly whatever de-
pends upon science) have of late years been in a quicker progress
towards perfection than ever; we may safely conclude the same with
respect to any political state now in being."[31]

Nearly two centuries later we remember the confident optimism of
the young Wordsworth and of the members of Priestley's circle as they
saw the progressive and ameliorative impact of science reflected in the
revolutionary ideals of the American and French revolutions. And we

---

[30]Joseph Priestley, *Letter to the Right Honourable William Pitt on the Subject of Toleration and Church Establishment* (London, 1787), p. 20; *Writings on Philosophy, Science and Politics*, p. 296; and *Proper Objects of Education*, pp. 6, 5.

[31]Joseph Priestley, "An History of the Corruptions of Christianity," in *The Theological and Miscellaneous Works of Joseph Priestley*, ed. T. J. Rutt (London, 1819–1832), 5:4.

remember the pathetic disillusion that soon descended on such as Wordsworth and Coleridge—though never, it should be noted, on Priestley. What we seldom remember, however, is the towering intellect that informed and shaped the optimism of Priestley and his circle, that of David Hartley. Physician and Christian philosopher, Hartley, in that characteristic eighteenth-century English way, combined scientific zeal with religious certainty. He was the author in 1749 of *Observations on Man*, the holy book of millenarian perfectionism. Praise was tendered Hartley in a variety of ways. Coleridge named his first son David Hartley; students in the 1790s at the dissenting academy of Hackney, such as William Hazlitt, read "Hartley for four and a half hours a week"; and Joseph Priestley reprinted Hartley's book, noting, "I think myself more indebted to this one treatise, than to all the books I ever read beside, the Scriptures excepted."[32]

Hartley's psychological theory of associationism provided the basis for his tremendous influence. "Dr. Hartley," Priestley wrote, "has thrown more useful light upon the theory of the mind than Newton did upon the theory of the natural world." Building on Hobbesian and Lockean sensationalism and its insistence that the source of knowledge is found in the sensations caused by external objects acting on the senses, Hartley argued that ideas, originating in this way and developing through physiological processes in the brain, became "associated" together in a certain necessary order in the mind. The mind was itself a natural mechanism, governed by scientific laws, and these laws were in turn discernible through observation and experimentation. Thus Hartley's associationism provided a materialist base for a theory of human learning. Its relevance for educational doctrine accounts for its impact on Priestley and explains the linkage of materialism with optimism. For Priestley and others, such as Jefferson and Benjamin Rush, "the most important application of Dr. Hartley's doctrine of the association of ideas is to the *conduct* of human life, and especially the business of education."[33] People's minds were formed by their circumstances. The actions of the environment and of teachers had a necessary effect on children that could not be otherwise, argued necessitarian deniers of free will such as Priestley. It was through education, then, that the millennium would be reached. John Stuart Mill understood this well as he reflected on his father's schooling in Edinburgh, a

[32]Quoted in J. W. Ashley Smith, *The Birth of Modern Education* (London, 1954), p. 177; Joseph Priestley, *An Examination of Dr. Reid's Inquiry into the Human Mind on the Principles of Common Sense* (London, 1774), p. xix.

[33]Priestley, *Examination of Dr. Reid's Inquiry*, pp. xv, xiii. See also Donald J. D'Elia, "Benjamin Rush, David Hartley and the Revolutionary Uses of Psychology," *Proceedings of the American Philosophical Society* 114 (April 1970).

center of Hartleyian medical/psychological materialism in the 1790s. Hartley's influence convinced his father and others, he wrote, of "the formation of all human character by circumstances, through the universal principle of Association, and the consequent unlimited possibility of improving the moral and intellectual condition of mankind by education."[34]

Hartley, without the evidence of the American or the French Revolution, read human history as one of inevitable progress. From its infancy, humankind, with its "mind a blank, void of ideas, as children now are born," had grown through the process of the association of ideas to an adulthood in which its knowledge and happiness would inevitably be paradisiacal. Presiding over the workings of the association principle was God and his "system of benevolence," which would lead individuals in society "to promote the welfare of others." This moral sense was not innate, as the Scottish philosophers argued, but "generated necessarily and mechanically."[35]

Inherent in Hartley's "optimistic materialism" and in that of his disciple Priestley is, of course, a paradox. As necessitarians they claimed humankind to be the passive product of circumstances; as reformers they preached active intervention in controlling and changing circumstances, in educating, in order to produce progress, perfection, and paradise. It is this latter perspective that most characterizes Priestley and his fellow Hartleyian reformers. Other close friends of Priestley who were also taken with Hartley's associationist theories were busy reforming all of England's institutions. Like Priestley, they were Protestant Dissenters fueled by a zeal to improve and reform. John Howard was developing the principles of the modern penitentiary, Thomas Percival of Manchester was developing the first modern hospital, and Josiah Wedgwood was developing in his factories the first modern principles of scientific management.[36] Priestley approached the polity, or Howard prisons, or Percival hospitals, or Wedgwood factories, as problems of mechanics in which active intervention through scientific manipulation of circumstances—in other words, education—could produce "improvements" by necessarily altering the causal chain of associations in the machine that was the human mind. Warrington, Hackney, and the other dissenting academies were thus the great agen-

---

[34]John Stuart Mill, *Autobiography* (Oxford, 1924), p. 91.

[35]David Hartley, *Observations on Man, His Frame, His Duty, and His Expectations* (London, 1749), 2:139; 1:473, 368, 510. For a good discussion of Hartley, see Willey, *Eighteenth-Century Background*.

[36]For John Howard, see Michael Ignatief, *A Just Measure of Pain* (New York, 1978); for Thomas Percival, see his *Medical Ethics* (1803), ed. Chauncy D. Leake (Baltimore, 1927); for Josiah Wedgwood, see Neil McKendrick, "Josiah Wedgwood and Factory Discipline," *Historical Journal* 4 (1961): 30–55.

cies of redemption. Their commitment to science and to the psychology of Hartley laid the basis for what they thought would be the perfecting of England through education.

Liberalism and the Scientific State

Priestley's scientific world view was at the core of his theory of the liberal state as well. To be sure, he began with conventional contractual convictions; he was thus a Lockean in more than merely his materialist psychology. He was, as his enemies never tired of noting, "the most eminent disciple" of the Lockean contractual natural rights school. Priestley's *Essay on the First Principles of Government* (1768) is a virtual gloss on Locke's *Second Treatise*. He begins by describing a state of nature in which people live "independent and unconnected"; they "voluntarily resign some part of their natural liberty" to magistrates, who then are the people's servants. These magistrates are accountable to the people, and if they abuse the trust given them, they can be deposed. Punishing their governors is a natural right of the people. Priestley dismissed out of hand all arguments for historical rights, specifically lost Saxon rights. England's Saxon era was a time of "idleness, treachery, cruelty, and insecurity of property," Priestley argued. It was no golden age or moment of pure principle to which one ought to return.[37]

Priestley described government in 1769 as set up to secure the rights of "my life, my liberty, my property, and my ease." In 1789, writing of Anglicans, Dissenters, Catholics, and Negroes, he insisted that there were "common rights of humanity." All the variety of Englishmen were "equally men . . . and therefore equally entitled to all the natural and just rights of man." To protect these rights civil government was established. But in good Lockean terms Priestley emphasized the contractual nature of civil power. Governors were mere servants, and "if such magistrates abuse their trust, in the people therefore lies the right of deposing and consequently of punishing them."[38]

Priestley's fundamental maxim of politics was the need to limit state interference in individual liberty. The spirit of the age, he wrote, "encourages us to relax the bonds of authority, rather than bind them

[37]Joseph Priestley, *An Essay on the First Principles of Government* (London, 1791), pp. 2–7, and *Lectures on History and General Policy* (London, 1788), p. 349.

[38]Joseph Priestley, *A View of the Principles and Conduct of the Protestant Dissenters with Respect to the Civil and Ecclesiastical Constitution of England* (London, 1769), p. 31; *Conduct to Be Observed by Dissenters in Order to Procure the Repeal of the Corporation and Test Acts* (Birmingham, 1789), p. 14; and *Writings on Philosophy, Science and Politics*, p. 206.

faster." That spirit required the magistrate to retreat from or resist entering three crucial areas—education, religion, and the economy. In all his political writings, these three concerns constantly intermingle, and the perspective is the same. "The advantage we derive from them will be more effectually secured when they are conducted by individuals, than by the state."[39] Priestley made specific the terms of the liberal revolution, under which much of human life that hitherto had been seen as part of the single public social realm presided over by church, paternalistic officials, or moral economic norms would be split off into separate social spheres, there to be the concern primarily of autonomous self-regarding individuals.

Priestley was an outspoken foe of public education. His insistence that the state play no role in such matters repudiated both past practice, in which education was the particular concern of the state church, and the contemporary arguments put forth by his reformer friends Paine and Wollstonecraft, who were calling for active state involvement in a system of public education. Priestley's opposition was grounded in his doctrinal individualism. State education would hinder the flourishing of truth, variety, and improvement. It would indoctrinate students with whatever authorities took to be truth or whatever served their interest. It would restrict individual inquiry and development. The pursuit of truth is carried on by individuals who "dread nothing so much as being confined and cramped by the unreasonable hand of power." To put education "into the hands of the civil magistrate" would be to stifle forever freedom of inquiry; it "would be like fixing the dress of a child, and forbidding its clothes ever to be made wider or larger." That was much more than liberals expected of the state, which was simply "the avenging of injuries, or redressing of private wrongs."[40]

Priestley develops the theory of the liberal state as neutral umpire even more self-consciously than Locke does. The state no longer has any positive role to educate, nurture, or provide moral standards. It is concerned with neither the classical ideal of illuminating the good life nor the republican ideal of providing an arena for fulfillment through public service and citizenship. The state, for liberal theory, has specific, limited, and negative functions that are implicit in its contractual origins. Its sole purpose is the protection of individuals and their rights. It is simply an agent performing the useful but limited service of keeping order and protecting individuals from harm. Nowhere is this liberal theory of the state better articulated than in Priestley's writings on the relationship between religion and the state. As in Locke before him,

---

[39]Priestley, *Writings on Philosophy, Science and Politics*, pp. 311, 305.
[40]Ibid., pp. 308, 305.

the most vivid articulation of the liberal theory of the state is found in an explanation of why it must be separated from the church.

The state, according to Priestley, deals with "things that relate to this life," while the church deals with "those that relate to the life to come." The liberal state, then, is restricted to a specific purpose. It does no more and no less than provide a "secure and comfortable enjoyment of this life, by preventing one man from injuring another in his person or property." The magistrate has no concern with opinions or beliefs. His sole duty "is to preserve the peace of society." The state punishes only "if I break the peace of society, if I injure my neighbor, in his person, property or good name," not if I believe in a different creed. "How," Priestley asks, "is any person injured by my holding religious opinions which he disapproves of?" If the answer is that such opinions endanger the salvation of others, it is still inappropriate for the state to interfere, for its "business is with the things of this life only." Like Jefferson denying the liberal state the right to regulate religion because another's belief "neither breaks my leg nor steals from my purse," Priestley excludes the state from religious life as a use of civil power beyond the limited terms of the state's contractual base. For early liberals such as Locke, Jefferson, and Priestley, the separation of church and state becomes the crucial defining feature of liberal politics. The realm of public power has been dramatically reduced. What right does the state or anyone else have to involve itself in my religion? Priestley asks Burke in 1791. "Does my conduct in this respect injure them? What, then, has the state, or my neighbors, to do in this business, any more than with my food or my medicine?"[41]

What Priestley the scientist and liberal theorist set out to do was to demystify the state. Much more dramatically than Locke, Priestley the scientist sought to free the state and political obligation from their conventional link to arcane religious sources, inscrutable and beyond human understanding. He severed deference to political power from the timeless realm of hereditary and religious mystery. He rendered the state a simple and useful artifact created by ordinary self-seeking people whose rational common sense prompted them voluntarily to consent to be governed. Priestley exulted in just the scientific demystification that Burke lamented. For Priestley the state was indeed,

---

[41]Ibid., p. 228; Joseph Priestley, *Considerations on Church Authority* (London, 1769), p. 4; *Conduct to be Observed by Dissenters*, p. 6; *Familiar Letters Addressed to the Inhabitants of the Town of Birmingham* (Birmingham, 1790–1792), letter 6, p. 18; and *Letters to Burke*, letter 2, p. 55. Like Locke, Priestley argues that the magistrate may interfere with religious practices if those practices threaten life or rights (*Writings on Philosophy, Science and Politics*, p. 230). Priestley goes beyond Locke, however, in his extension of toleration to Catholicism. Jefferson's *Notes on Virginia*, query 17, is cited in *Thomas Jefferson on Democracy*, ed. Saul Padover (New York, 1961), p. 109.

as Burke complained, "nothing better than a partnership agreement in a trade of pepper and coffee, calico or tobacco, or some other such low concern." It was indeed "taken up for a little temporary interest, and to be dissolved by the fancy of the parties." It was not to be looked on with "other reverence," as Burke insisted. Princes and magistrates, according to Priestley, are not shrouded in mysterious majesty. There is no rational grounds for "the superstitious respect for kings and the spirit of chivalry." Titles such as "most sacred or most excellent majesty" inaccurately describe mere "magistrates appointed and paid for the conservation of order." Political power is obeyed not, as Burke suggested, out of "generous loyalty," "proud submission," or "dignified obedience" but for the very mundane reason that "the good order of society requires it." Priestley would himself obey magistrates "only as the confidential servants of the nation, and the administrators of the laws."[42]

Like the principles of the natural universe, these laws and the institutions of civil society are simply and easily comprehended. They require no complex mysterious wisdom of specialized priests of statecraft schooled by ageless traditions in the impenetrable secrets of politics. Stripped of metaphysical and religious mystery, stripped of aristocratic complexity, the state for Priestley would be streamlined and simple. It would merely administer justice and preserve the peace. Such a government, "being thus simple in its objects, will be unspeakably less expensive than it is at present," and thus the industrious will no longer be taxed "the most unreasonable sum that we now pay for the single article of government."[43]

Priestley constantly answered the Burkean defense of baroque mystery with this theme of simplicity and austerity. "You are told that matters of the state and church are of great mystery, into which you shouldn't delve," Priestley informed the Dissenters of Birmingham in 1792. But such claims deceive, and Priestley replied with a vintage articulation of the cult of simplicity: "These things are not, in reality, of so difficult a nature as many things in your common trades and businesses. The most important questions [of state and church] are the plainest things in the world and require nothing but a common understanding, honestly applied to comprehend them." Like Burke, who saw the age of chivalry replaced by the age of economists and calculators, Priestley realized that European civilization was at a historic turning point. While this development enraged Burke, it thrilled Priestley. "The whole of the Gothic feudal system," Priestley wrote in

---

[42]Burke, *Reflections on the Revolution in France*, pp. 194, 169; Priestley, *Writings on Philosophy, Science and Politics*, pp. 247, 255, 248.
[43]Priestley, *Writings on Philosophy, Science and Politics*, p. 253.

1792, "embracing matters both of a civil and ecclesiastical nature, is beginning to shake to its foundation." "The system which had stood for ages," he told his congregation with great joy on another occasion, was vanishing "like an enchanted castle in a romance."[44]

Burke and Priestley bear witness to the emergence of the secular liberal state, the partnership agreement to protect the trade in calico or tobacco, or, as it has been caricatured, the state as joint-stock company. That this demystification of the state decisively separated it from the church was obvious to both of them. Burke, the secular man of affairs, repudiated the age of calculators and pleaded that "religion is the basis of civil society, and the source of all good and comfort."[45] Priestley, the scientist and Christian clergyman, replied with quintessential liberalism. The age of chivalry was indeed dead:

> Is there no good, or comfort in anything but religion, or what flows from it? Will religion feed or clothe us; or is there no comfort in food or clothing? It is not possible to make many wholesome laws to prevent men from injuring one another, and is it not possible to execute those laws, so as to preserve the peace of society, which I conceive to be the proper end of civil government, without calling in the aid of religion?[46]

Priestley's radical contemporaries shared his assumption that a new era was dawning in world history. The new order of scientific reasoning and self-interest would push aside mystery and superstition. The cults of science and simplicity come to the fore in Paine's pleas for cheap plain government and his constant evocation of the simplicity of American institutions. "The science of government is beginning to be better understood," Paine wrote in 1792. He was certain that "the age of faith and political superstition, and of craft, and mystery is passing away." In religion, as in politics, he wrote in his *Age of Reason*, "perfection consists in simplicity." Godwin, another apostle of simplicity, was persuaded by the revolutions in America and France of the "desireableness of a government in the utmost degree simple." There is, "no mystery in government which uninitiated mortals must not presume to penetrate." The masses of humankind had been duped, Godwin claimed, by talk of the "mysterious complicated nature of the social system." Joel Barlow joined the attack on defenders of "government as the most complicated system . . . without which it has been supposed impossible for men to be governed." He asked his readers to "conceive of the

---

[44]Priestley, *Familiar Letters*, 6:22; *An Appeal to the Public on the Subject of the Riots in Birmingham* (Birmingham, 1792), p. 14; and *Sermons*, p. 101.
[45]Burke, *Reflections on the Revolution in France*, pp. 186–87.
[46]Priestley, *Letters to Burke*, p. 86.

simplicity to which the business of government may be reduced, and to which it must be reduced, if we would have it answer the purposes of promoting happiness." Nature is simple and efficient; the old order is artificial, complicated, and ornate. "The essence of tyranny," wrote Barlow, "is to counteract the economy of nature, the essence of liberty is to promote it."[47]

This recurring tendency of Priestley's circle to link political arguments to conceptions of the natural world is central to an understanding of the radicalism of these English-speaking philosophers. Priestley's theory of the state is intimately connected to his scientific and theological materialism. He demystified the state just as he demystified the soul. In his essay, "The Materiality of the Soul" he noted "that there is not a simple idea of which the mind is possessed but what may be proved to have come to it from the bodily senses." The state, then, is what we touch, feel, and see. It is not any Burkean a priori ideal transcending time and generations. It is the actions of real people whose taxes impinge on and whose security protects physical beings. The state is a material entity, not a spiritual one. It acts on material beings through the careful distribution of rewards and punishments. "Governors," Priestley wrote, "will rule voluntary agents by means of rewards and punishments, and the governed, being voluntary agents, will be influenced by the apprehension of them." Government was for Priestley exactly what Burke denied it was—a thing of interest and calculation, not something spiritual and transcendental. The human being embodies nothing impenetrable and unknowable, according to Priestley, "no immaterial soul." Just as the whole "substance of man is material," there being no spiritual part "capable of subsisting before and after its union to the body," the whole substance of the state consists of calico and tobacco traders. There is no spiritual Burkean state; the state consists of nothing but material matter than attracts and repels according to the gravitational laws of interest.[48]

The despiritualization of the state renders it a mere machine whose operations are not only simple and knowable but mechanical, predictable, and manageable. The state as machine was a recurring metaphor in the rhetoric of Priestley's circle. For Paine the traditional British constitution was "like a complicated machine that never does right."

---

[47]Thomas Paine, "Letter Addressed to the Addressers on the Late Proclamation" (1792), in *The Writings of Thomas Paine*, ed. M. D. Conway (New York, 1895), 3:93, and *Age of Reason*, in ibid., 4:28; William Godwin, *Enquiry Concerning Political Justice*, ed. Isaac Kramnick (Harmondsworth, 1976), pp. 247, 552; Joel Barlow, *A Letter to the National Convention of France on Defects of the Constitution of 1791* (London, 1792), pp. 172, 220.

[48]Priestley, *Writings on Philosophy, Science and Politics*, pp. 145–66, 97, 115, and "History of the Corruptions of Christianity," pp. 480–81.

For Priestley, too, the old order was doomed by the laws of mechanics. Writing of England's "Gothic" constitution, he notes that "the more complex any machine is . . . the more liable it is to disorder." Robert Bage, the Birmingham Dissenter, manufacturer, friend of Priestley, and eminent novelist, was even blunter. In his novel *Barham Downs* he demanded that government become as straightforward, simple, and efficient as "a manufacture of buttons."[49]

If the state is but a machine and its inhabitants mere matter, then politics is a fit subject for experimentation by the likes of Priestley. Priestley, indeed, discusses politics in scientific terms. Since "we are so little capable of arguing a priori in matters of government," it is clear that "experiments can only determine how far this power of the legislature ought to expand." The magistrate should do little, in fact, "till a sufficient number of experiments have been made." Government is like everything else in this scientific world view. It stands "the fairest chance of being brought to perfection" if there "is opportunity of making the most experiments and trials." Priestley saw the world and history as a political laboratory in which "hypothesis built upon arguments a priori are least of all tolerable, where observation and experience are the only safe guides." The fruits of this scientific approach were facts of politics overwhelming in their consistency: "The old governments of Europe are arrived to a considerable degree of maturity; so that their several advantages and defects are become sufficiently conspicuous and the new government in North America and especially those of France and Poland are so many new experiments of which political philosophers cannot fail to make the greatest use."[50]

It is Hartley's influence, we must remember, that lurks behind the scientific optimism of Priestley's materialism. Priestley's popularization of Hartley, whom he ranked with Newton, made Hartley's ideas available after 1775 to dominate British social and psychological thought. As in the France of Holbach, Helvétius, and La Mettrie, advanced radical circles in Britain accepted the doctrine of human materiality and the parallel assumption that reform and improvement were a simple matter of changing the "associations" linked to external sensation. The materialist psychology, by eliminating the mind-body distinction, provided a scientific basis for the widespread belief that social and moral behavior could be changed by bodily discipline—by the application of pleasure and pain. The state literally becomes a laboratory in which its

[49]Thomas Paine, *Prospect Papers* (1804), in *Writings of Tom Paine*, ed. Conway, 4:333; Priestley, *Writings on Philosophy, Science and Politics*, p. 205; Robert Bage, *Barham Downs* (London, 1784), 2:9.

[50]Priestley, *Writings on Philosophy, Science and Politics*, pp. 219, 307, and *Lectures on History and General Policy*, p. 39.

citizens and institutions can be perfected, like machines, by trial and error. For some reformers this was the task of the statesman. James Burgh wrote, "An able statesman can change the manner of the people at pleasure." It was clear to him "that by management the human species may be moulded into any conceivable shape." For others this task was reserved for one special scientist, the medical doctor. La Mettrie had predicted in 1749, in his *L'Homme machine*, that statesmen and judges would be replaced "by the most skillful physicians."[51] Indeed, many of the radical reformers in Priestley's circle were medical doctors themselves, as Locke and Hartley had been. Five of Priestley's thirteen colleagues in the Lunar Society were medical doctors. James Watt's first partner, John Roebuck, was a doctor who, like James Kier and many others, turned to industry, especially chemical technology. The Manchester Literary and Philosophical Society, a hotbed of dissenting radicals, was founded by Thomas Percival, the great hospital reformer and close friend of Priestley. The great prison reformers—John Howard, John Aikin, and John Fothergill—were medical doctors, Dissenters, and friends of Priestley's. Two important political reformers, John Jebb and Thoms Beddoes, were doctors. And, of course, one of the closest American friends of this circle was Benjamin Rush, a former student at the medical school of Edinburgh, where Hartleyian materialism was at the heart of the curriculum. The medical doctor, then, plays a crucial role in eighteenth-century social attitudes. Scientific student of the human body, he becomes the empirical wizard of the body politic, revealed now in all its simplicity as similarly a mere material mechanism of action and reaction.

The contemporary of Priestley who spoke most directly to this vision of the medical doctor was his close friend Thomas Percival. "Strangers to superstition and enthusiasm," doctors were, for Percival, the symbol of "the present enlightened period" in its crusade against "Gothic ignorance" and "barbarism." The doctor was the apostle of science locked in combat with "the prejudices, the caprices, and the passions of the sick and their relatives." A crucial weapon in this struggle was the doctor's mastery of Hartleyian psychology, his "knowledge of the animal economy, and of the physical causes which regulate or disturb its movement and unites an intrinsic acquaintance with the laws of association."[52]

The doctor's role, for Percival, was not simply to cure the sick; he was also involved in social reform. His concern was the "moral improvement of the patients," which involved teaching them the princi-

[51]James Burgh, *Political Disquisitions* (London, 1775), 3:176–78; La Mettrie cited in Ignatief, *Just Measure of Pain*.
[52]Percival, *Medical Ethics*, pp. 73, 85, 87.

ple of private property and the necessity of wills. The hospital had as its purpose disciplining and regulating the poor, much like Howard's prison and Wedgwood's factory. It was the antidote to the "immoderate passion," the "vicious indulgences," the "sloth, intemperance and irregular desires" that were the sources of disease.

> It may be proved that a work hospital is an institution founded on the most benevolent principles, consonant to sound policy, and favourable to reformation and virtue. It provides relief for a painful and loathsome distemper, which contaminates in its progress the innocent as well as the guilty, and extends its baneful influence to future generations. It restores to virtue and to religion those votaries whom pleasure has seduced or villainy betrayed, and who now feel, by bad experience, that ruin, misery and disgrace are the wages of sin.[53]

Percival's hospital, locked and "removed from public inspection," was modeled on Howard's reformed prison. "The form best adapted (*mutatis mutandis*) to the essential paupers, appears to be that of the New Prison at Manchester, which is constructed on the well-known plan of Mr. Howard." Patients were kept in small separate rooms. They were isolated from society just as the new prison ended the easy access of friend and family to the prisoner. As Howard prescribed uniform clothes and washed walls for his prison, so Percival ordered the same for his hospital. Order and discipline in both institutions would conquer sloth and intemperance. Indeed, Percival's proposed board of health was to be a form of "hospital police." These state officials would inspect and approve the accommodations of the poor. They would require the houses of the poor to be washed twice a year. They would pay a bounty of one or two shillings to anyone who reported "the appearance of fever in any poor family." These "hospital police" or "inspectors" would then give over the feverish poor to the physicians in Percival's hospital. When the fever was cured and the reformed returned to his or her family, "a reward . . . shall be given to the head of the family, after the cessation of the fever, on condition that they have faithfully observed the rules prescribed for cleanliness, ventilation and the prevention of infection, amongst their neighbors."[54] Percival's hospital police would visit the poor, round up the sick, and send them to hospitals, there to be cured and reformed.

Priestley himself was not above social engineering. In 1787 he published *An Account of a Society for Encouraging the Industrious Poor*. The scheme was, significantly enough, intended primarily "for the use of

[53]Ibid., pp. 86, 74, 122–23, 85.
[54]Ibid., pp. 86, 173, 180, 69, 168, 179.

John Wilkinson's [his brother-in-law] iron works at Bradley." His society was Priestley's alternative to the poor laws, which he saw as merely encouraging idleness. How, he asked, "to remove the Temptations to idleness and profligacy?" How to hold out to a poor man "certain prospects of bettering his condition?" How to "enable him to do more for himself than he knows his parish will ever do for him?"

Priestley's answer was to give the manufacturer the means with which to fix firmly in the minds of the poor the association between present self-denial and future pleasure. Priestley proposed that Wilkinson set up a "club" and deduct 4.5 percent from the worker's pay each week as forced savings. The manufacturer must teach "the men to provide for themselves." Manufacturers would create middle-class attitudes in the poor through their intervention. The poor would thus learn to be ambitious and competitive, "be enabled to vie with their neighbors in the acquisition of everything which is comfortable."

Priestley was not unaware of the tension between the disciplinary tone of his proposed "society" and the emancipatory tone of his other writings. He acknowledged that his scheme involved "some restriction of liberty," that the worker was "not to be allowed to spend his money in whatever way he thought best." According to Priestley, such restrictions were, however, but invasions on brutes who were not yet self-directing individuals. Their intention was, in fact, quite the opposite, to render the poor truly autonomous individuals who internalized the values of a truly free and therefore human person. These restrictions on freedom were thus necessary and just, for they ensured that "the idle and thoughtless may be made, in some measure, to do for themselves what the industrious and thoughtful are now compelled to do for them." The poor laws were doing quite the opposite, "keep[ing] them in a state of greater submission and dependence." His suggestion would set the poor on the path of middle-class freedom, for "they would be much more within the influence of honourable ambition than they are in at present."[55]

Priestley's use and popularization of Hartley's associationism helped shape the world view of an entire generation of dissenting factory masters, scientists, and reformers. Human beings and social institutions were, like the human body, material contrivances whose operations were knowable and manageable. Another figure in this period who faithfully followed Priestley's lead in this realm was his friend and follower David Williams. Dissenting minister, schoolmaster, and friend of Franklin and Jefferson, Williams saw it as "the principal duty of man

[55]Joseph Priestley, *An Account of a Society for Encouraging the Industrious Poor to Which Are Prefixed Some Considerations on the State of the Poor in General* (Birmingham, 1787), pp. 3, 4, 7, 11, 13.

to transfer into social institutions, moral, civil, and political, the ideas he deduces from the natural world." Government should, then, be in the hands of "men of scientific minds." It was time, he wrote in 1782, "to discard the reveries of savages and apply the principles of science" to politics. Scientists in government would best understand the operations of the state, "the nature and construction of the machine" in which people live. Like the schemes of so many others in Priestley's circle, Williams's mechanistic politics was fundamentally optimistic. "As the development of a machine is owing to the prevalence of some constituent power or powers over others: so in a state, all inconveniences and injuries are to be ascribed to the want of sufficient counteraction and assistance in some of its parts, to balance the pressure of the others; and to assist in producing the ground effect."[56]

The men and women in Priestley's circle were the first generation to live with the machine and what they took to be its benign promise. The reality of the Industrial Revolution complemented the philosophical hegemony of Hartley. Mechanistic imagery is found everywhere. Wedgwood, pioneer in developing factory discipline with his bells and time clock, wrote that he would "make machines of men as cannot err." Bentham's Panopticon was conceived as "a machine for grinding rogues honest." Improving the human lot was for Bentham "a species of manufacture." Benjamin Rush, the American Hartleyian, wrote that "I consider it is Possible to convert men into republican machines. This must be done, if we expect them to perform their parts properly, in the great machine of the government of the state." Robert Owen, the industrialist reformer, who of all those schooled in psychological sensationalism would have the best opportunity to realize his utopian schemes in later years, once remarked that "the animate mechanisms" of New Lanark had been made as efficient as the "inanimate mechanisms" under his management. In a lighter but most revealing mood, Wedgwood reminds us how instinctive the use of mechanical imagery was among Priestley's friends. He wrote in 1782 to cheer up their fellow Lunatic James Watt, who was tired from overwork at his iron works. Hartley, thanks to Priestley, was everywhere.

> Your mind, my friend, is too active, too powerful for your body and harasses it beyond its bearing. If this was the case with any other machine under your direction . . . you would soon find a remedy. For the present permit me to advise a more ample use of the oil of delegation through your whole machinery. Seriously, I shall conclude in saying to you what Dr. Fothergill desired me to say to Brindley. "Spare your machine a little or like

[56]David Williams, *Preparatory Studies for Political Reformers* (London, 1810), pp. 19, 188, and *Lectures on Political Liberty* (London, 1782), pp. 4–5, 74–75.

others under your direction, it will wear out the sooner by hard and constant usage."[57]

Priestley's liberalism, then, had two dimensions, and his connection to this radical use of Hartleyian psychology makes them clear. He was committed to a natural rights liberalism on the one hand and to utilitarian liberalism on the other. Priestley was a bridge between the two variants of liberalism. They were not incompatible for him because they served his overriding concern, reform, which was a passion more pressing even than freedom. One part of Priestley's liberalism preached liberation, the freeing of all individuals and their rights from existing restraints—tyranny, the state, priests, and superstition. Another part of Priestley's liberalism wanted to subject individuals to new discipline and new forms of authority: factories, jails, schools, hospitals run by scientific minds, and scientific legislators who would teach, order, and manage people until they became industrious and hardworking. This latter aspect of Priestley's outlook explains why he and his circle— Howard, Percival, Wedgwood, and the rest—were such passionate reformers. They were not interested in simply sweeping away ancient and feudal barriers that hindered a free and good society. They were also convinced that one could then move to a positive stage of managing, engineering, and creating a good and happy life. Such a life would not emerge in and of itself by the mere elimination of priests, tyrants, and superstition. Science and materialism cut both ways. They undermined the old order, liberating and freeing men and women from timeless domination and mystery. They also promised a new day when scientific leadership would produce great happiness for great numbers of people by manipulating them and their motions, even if such happiness required an initial sacrifice of freedom.

For all its commitment to emancipation and liberation, its zeal to free human beings from political, spiritual, and economic restraint, the bourgeois radicalism of Priestley's circle casts an ominous shadow of discipline, regimen, and authority. Though these radicals preached independence, freedom, and autonomy in polity and market, they preached order, routine, and subordination in factory, school, poorhouse, and prison. In its liberating aspect, bourgeois radicalism was bent on toppling the aristocracy; in its repressive aspect, it was deter-

[57]Wedgwood to Bentley, October 1769, in *The Selected Letters of Josiah Wedgwood*, ed. Ann Finer and George Savage (London, 1965), p. 82; Bentham cited in Ignatief, *Just Measure of Pain*, p. 68; Benjamin Rush, "Of the Mode of Education Proper in a Republic," in *The Selected Writings of Benjamin Rush*, ed. Dagobert Runes (New York, 1947), p. 92; Robert Owen, *A New View of Society* (London, 1813), p. 95; Julia Wedgwood, *The Personal Life of Josiah Wedgwood* (London, 1915), p. 295.

mined to improve the poor. Members of the society who had not internalized self-reliance and self-discipline had to be bridled and tamed, taught to be methodical, clean, prompt, frugal, and industrious. One means to this end was to teach and preach middle-class values; another was to replicate the institutions over which these radicals presided—factories, schools, penitentiaries, and hospitals. Here the moral fiber required for running the race of life could be acquired from time clocks, bells, and whitewashed walls, since the ideology's psychology assumed a malleable human nature ultimately shaped by association and environmental influence. The need for discipline would be transitory. It was not permanent subordination but a temporary restriction of freedom that Priestley's circle sought through their new institutions. This temporary dictatorship of the middle class would end when these new or reformed institutions had rendered everyone self-reliant and industrious. There was no doubt in Priestley's mind that such a day would dawn. In both its liberating and its repressive aspects, scientific liberalism was indeed unabashedly optimistic.

Children's Literature
and Bourgeois Ideology

"I THINK I CAN, I think I can, I think I can," says the smiling little engine. I'm not very big, but I'll do my best, and "I think I can, I think I can, I think I can." Lo and behold, the little engine can. It pushes the broken-down train loaded with toys and good things to eat across the mountain to where the little boys and girls eagerly wait. Some big and important engines have said they can't, but by working hard and repeating over and over again "I think I can," the little engine does the job and everyone is very happy, not least Mabel C. Bragg, whose book *The Little Engine That Could* has sold over five million copies since its first appearance in 1926.

The success of that engine and of Mabel Bragg is itself a story. Written just before the Depression, the book caught fire during the thirties; it has succeeded in part because it has touched so deeply the well-spring of American ideology. Faced by a serious problem, the little engine met it head on and proved what could be accomplished by hard work and the simple will to achieve, the will to do. The American individualist ethos, its heritage of self-reliance and optimistic problem solving, is enshrined here. No collective solution is offered, no sharing of troubles. The engines don't cooperate to solve the problem, nor do they call on any outside solution, public or social. All that is needed is a resourceful and ingenious little engine that has faith and confidence in itself, an engine that knows that though it is little, it *can*.

Few English-speaking readers would dispute that much of contemporary children's literature has a high component of ideology. A good deal of work has been done in recent years to reveal the socioeconomic, racial, and sexist values in the stories we read to our children. Children's literature has always served political purposes. At its very beginnings in the late eighteenth century, children's literature in English was designed by bourgeois radicals to serve ideological objectives.

Industry, Machines, and the Family

Between 1760 and 1800 England was fundamentally transformed by the Industrial Revolution. All across England's "green and pleasant land" were rising "dark Satanic mills." These mills did more than mar the aesthetic landscape; they brought in their wake a new set of values and a new ideology—the values of the middle-class factory owners and managers, bourgeois values. This middle-class ideology was radical and progressive; it called for changes to liberate and unshackle the individual still bound by traditional restrictions.

The central tenet of the bourgeois ideology as it picked away at the old order was, as we have seen, that status and power should be achieved and not ascribed. What was important was what one had done and accomplished, rather than who one was by virtue of title or family connections. Merit, talent, and hard work should dictate social, economic, and political rewards, not privilege, rank, and birth. The individual stood alone. At the center of the new bourgeois ideology was the solitary individual responsible for his or her own fate—not the heir to a family title or the member of a guild but the self-reliant individual alone in the marketplace of merit and talent, who earned either success or failure. The three main battering rams used by the bourgeoisie in the late eighteenth century to destroy the aristocratic edifice that was still England were the machine, science, and the Protestant ethic. In all three the individualism basic to bourgeois ideology took on practical and concrete form.

A representative figure of the early Industrial Revolution was the great potter Josiah Wedgwood, whose factories were some of the largest in all England and whose china still is the pride of English workmanship. In 1783 Wedgwood assembled his workers and lectured them on the wondrous transformation wrought by factory masters such as himself. In his lecture the great potter captured vividly the world view of Priestley's circle as they effected their revolutions in the west of England. He suggested that the workers ask their parents to compare the countryside as it now stood with what they once knew. Had not poverty been replaced by affluence as wages rose to twice what they had been earlier? Had not miserable huts been replaced by new and comfortable homes? Had not the poorly cultivated land, nearly impassable roads, "and everything else" been replaced by "pleasing and rapid improvements"? Convinced that his young employees would agree with him that their lot was much better than that of their parents, a generation earlier, Wedgwood proceeded to note the source of this progress. It was industry, a word pregnant with meaning for the Unitarian Wedgwood.

> From where and from what cause did this happy change take place? The truth is clear to all. Industry has been the parent of this happy change—A well directed and long continued series of industrious exertions, both in masters and servants, has so changed, for the better, the face of our country and the manners and deportment of its inhabitants, too.[1]

The foundation of a new England was being laid by people who saw hard work as a command of God. Wedgwood, in fact, expanded the decalogue, heaping praise on workers "very good in keeping my eleventh commandment—*Thou shalt not be idle.*"

The rest of his lecture outlined what was necessary to ensure that this seemingly boundless improvement would continue. First, of course, the workers must respect the property that rightfully belonged to the masters; they must not, that is, destroy the machines. The industrialist Wedgwood articulated the liberal theory of the state as he digressed into political theory.

> If property is not secure there would be an end to all government, an end to the state. No man could be secure in the enjoyment of the fruits of his labor for a single day, no man, therefore, would labor . . . without the hopes of reaping for himself and being protected in his property.

Having finished with political theory, Wedgwood turned to liberal economic theory. If progress was to continue, he declared, government must withdraw from the marketplace. Tariffs should be abolished, followed by the "opening up of our seaports for the importation of foreign grain." These measures, he informed his workers, anticipating the argument of many a Manchester liberal in the 1840s, would drive down the price they paid for bread. They would drive down also the wages he would have to pay them, of course, but he failed to mention that detail. If the workers thought the landowners and farmers would keep up the price, they were mistaken, Wedgwood assured them. Sounding much like Adam Smith, he guaranteed his workers that "provisions will rise and fall in price, according to their quantity as naturally as water finds its level." Wedgwood was a firm believer in the principles of laissez-faire. As a founder of the General Chamber of Manufacturers

---

[1]This and the following quotations from Wedgwood's lecture may be found in his *Address to the Young Inhabitants of the Pottery* (New Castle, 1783), pp. 4–14.

of Great Britain in 1785, he vigorously championed Pitt's treaty of 1786, which provided for virtual free trade with France. It was no small payment for his efforts in the cause of free trade before the House of Commons that the treaty opened the markets of France to his china.

A final requirement for continued progress, Wedgwood told his workers, was the proper ordering of their own lives. While increased demand for manufactured goods would, he promised, "enable masters to give out over-work to their servants and therefore increase their wages," the workers, in turn, had their responsibility. And so Wedgwood turned to middle-class ethical theory.

> If a married man can maintain a wife and four or five children with no more than you do . . . who have only themselves to provide for, surely some small weekly saving may be made, which, I can promise you, you will afterwards find the comfort of, when you marry, and have a house to furnish, and other things to provide for a wife and growing family. Most of you visit public houses, wakes, and other places where TIME AND MONEY IS WASTED and where you acquire habits in your youth which entail poverty and distress on those who depend on you later.[2]

I will return to this statement later, for it provides revealing insight into the changes taking place in the family structure under the impact of the Industrial Revolution, but for now let me simply point out that Wedgwood practiced what he preached. He was a pioneer in factory discipline. He instilled bourgeois values in his workers. Time was a new idol, together with care and regularity. He trained his workers to notions of time by inventing the first punching-in clock. He also introduced a system of bells to summon them to work and to end the day. The bells stood in a central place on each floor, next to the clock. In addition to methodically organizing the day, he banned drinking in his potteries and insisted on cleanliness. He instituted penalties for wasting clay, and he posted detailed regulations for washing the floors and keeping the benches clean. He told his workers "to lay up the clay with as much cleanliness as if it were intended for food."[3]

Not far from Wedgwood's works in Staffordshire is Cromford, near Matlock, in Derbyshire. Here a more ambivalent response to the transformation of the west of England was articulated by the Honorable John Byng, fifth viscount of Torrington, when he happened on the town on his tour of the Midlands in 1790. What he saw there moved

---

[2]Josiah Wedgwood, *Selected Letters of Josiah Wedgwood*, ed. Ann Finer and George Savage (London, 1965), p. 247.

[3]Quoted in Neil McKendrick, "Josiah Wedgwood and Factory Discipline," *Historical Journal* 4 (1961).

him deeply. It disturbed him, but it also filled him with awe. His was a response common to the men who, unlike Wedgwood and Priestley, in fact governed England.

> These vales have lost all their beauties; the rural cot has given place to the lofty red mill, and the grand houses of overseers; the stream perverted from its course by sluices and aqueducts, will no longer ripple and cascade. Every rural sound is sunk in the clamour of cotton works, and the simple peasant (for to be simple we must be sequestered) is changed into the impudent mechanic. . . . The bold rock opposite this house [the Black Dog at Cromford] is now disfigured by a row of new houses built upon it; and the vales are everywhere blocked by mills. I saw the workers issue forth at 7. o'clock, a wonderful crowd of young people. . . . A new set then goes in for the night, for the mills never leave off working. . . . These cotton mills, seven stories high, and filled with inhabitants, remind me of a first rate man of war; and when they are lighted up, on a dark night, look most luminously beautiful.[4]

This giant man-of-war was Richard Arkwright's cotton works. For a much angrier William Blake it was one of the "dark Satanic mills" that forever doomed England's "green and pleasant land." For Priestley's artist friend, Joseph Wright of Derby, these mills were emblematic of a new world and as such fit objects to be put on canvas. He painted two versions of Arkwright's Cromford mill: a matter-of-fact depiction by day and a night scene of exquisite beauty in which the landscape is bathed in moonlight and in each of the hundreds of windows a candle burns. Wright was intoxicated by the new England. He painted memorable pictures of technological exhibits and scientific experiments. It is for his portraits, however, that Wright is renowned. In them he has frozen for eternity the faces of the men in Priestley's circle who were ushering in industrial civilization: the partners Thomas Bentley and Josiah Wedgwood; the textile magnates Arkwright, Jedediah Strutt, Samuel Crompton, and Samuel Oldknow; the philosopher-poet-scientist Erasmus Darwin; the political radical Thomas Day; the dissenting minister, mathematician, and reformer Richard Price.[5]

Wright's portraits are free of mystery and awe. They suggest no majesty, no theatrical grandeur or charisma. No aristocratic adornments or symbols clutter the canvas and we see none of the classical themes or modes that so intrigued his French contemporary Jacques-Louis David. Instead a penetrating steady light reveals plain men in

---

[4]*Torrington Diaries, Containing the Tours through England and Wales of the Hon. John Byng (Late Fifth Viscount of Torrington) between the Years 1781–1794*, ed. C. Bruyn Andrews (London, 1935), 2:194–95.

[5]See Benedict Nicolson, *Joseph Wright of Derby, Painter of Light* (London, 1968).

sober and simple settings. Their milieu was the countinghouse, not the manor house; the mill, not the drawing room. They meant business. Wright's subjects were entrepreneurs and men of business, or intellectual spokesmen for that class. They were not cosmopolitan public men from London or Bath. They were provincials from Derby, Manchester, and Birmingham. They were industrious men hard at work changing the face of English society.

The machine seemed to provide a concrete basis for these men's belief in unlimited progress and improvement. Others might react with fury to the pain and hurt inflicted by the machine, but the people in Priestley's circle had few regrets. Tradition, custom, all of the status quo must give way to felicitous progress. There is an ominous foretaste of social Darwinism in the vision of endless innovation and improvement conjured up in 1780 by a pamphleteer who sought to enlighten the machine breakers of Lancashire.

> Every new invention, every useful improvement must unavoidably interfere with what went before it and what is inferior and less perfect must give way and ought to give way, to what is better and more perfect. The transition indeed cannot always be made without inconvenience to some individuals, but this proceeds from the progressive nature of things, and the general order of Providence; and cannot be prevented without destroying the main springs and first elements of the moral world.[6]

The machine was the new standard of value. In terms that speak strikingly to later themes of reification and alienation, Wedgwood calmly informed a correspondent that he had "been turning models, and preparing to make such *Machines* of the *Men* as cannot err."[7]

This was, of course, the great age of "inventions" and "useful improvements." The mechanical innovations of James Hargreaves, Richard Arkwright, Samuel Crompton, Edmund Cartwright, Henry Cort, James Brindley, John Kay, and James Watt underwrote the phenomenal expansion of the great new industries—cotton, steel, and pottery—in the last half of the eighteenth century. The great industrial masters—Oldknow, Strutt, and Arkwright in textiles; Wilkinson, Boulton, and Watt in steel; and Wedgwood in pottery—were, if not themselves inventors, certainly the entrepreneurial backers of men who were. The tremendous economic power of these masters was based in great measure on their use of these technical improvements as well as their

---

[6]*Letters of the Utility and Policy of Employing Machines to Shorten Labor* (London, 1780), p. 16.

[7]Wedgwood to Thomas Bentley, October 7, 1769, in *Selected Letters of Wedgwood*, p. 83; the emphasis is Wedgwood's.

ability to exploit them privately, free from public control. In the past the guilds, town and municipal governments, the church, and Parliament had exercised a great deal of social control over industry. By the late eighteenth century, however, sentiments of economic individualism had extensively replaced the earlier notions of group and public control with a conviction that unrestrained use of the instruments of production and invention by their owners was natural, just, and in the national interest. One very important way in which capitalist owners hastened this shift from external restraints to their own unchallenged hegemony was to locate their factories in unincorporated towns, where guild and corporate restrictions on employment practices, on prices and wages, and on work conditions would not interfere. This lack of interference, in addition to the presence of water to run Watt's new steam engines, was the major reason, in fact, that industry developed in the Midlands, northern and western counties, outside the corporate grasp of the southern and home counties. Another strategy was frequent and increasingly successful petitioning of Parliament for the repeal or suspension of traditional, often centuries-old legislation providing for minimum wages, restricting apprenticeship practices, and guaranteeing that workers would not be replaced by machines.

The decline of public and corporate power as a counterweight to the private power of the factory owner was further hastened by a general discrediting of public authority during much of this early period of industrialization. From the Wilkes crisis in the 1760s through the American crisis in the 1760s and 1770s and the rise of radical agitation in the 1780s, George III and his ministers seldom dealt decisively and successfully with domestic agitation or colonial wars. There was one exception, however, to the government's inability or lack of desire to preserve traditional public restraints on merchants, landlords, and manufacturers: at no time did public authority retreat from its traditional controls on workers. Workers still, for example, were restrained by the force of public authority from combining in associations. No such restraint, of course, was applied to Wedgwood's General Chamber of Manufacturers.

The greatest impact of these developments was felt in the cotton and steel industries. These two industries came to symbolize the Industrial Revolution, and with them emerged two new social heroes—the entrepreneur and the engineer. Shortly behind them stood another new hero, the scientist. Science was seen as the source of endless improvement; it was a practical, ameliorative enterprise. Science was applied physics, mechanics, electricity, and chemistry, all with useful and material applications. Not theoretical astronomy but the empirical chemistry of Priestley was the ideal. It was a science that would serve industry and manufacture well. In Manchester, Birmingham, and Sheffield, philosophical societies sprang up at whose meetings manufacturers and scientists read papers on the chemical properties of dyes or on the principles of steam or electricity.

In these societies and in the dissenting academies all the diverse strains of the bourgeois innovative nexus played their parts. Dissenting manufacturers such as Wilkinson and Wedgwood subsidized dissenting scientists such as Priestley. Richard Price, dissenting schoolmaster, radical, and mathematician, was the principal developer of actuarial science and a member of the board of Equitable Life Insurance. Erasmus Darwin, one of the great biological scientists of the day, was a friend of the great Birmingham circle of industrialists, a political radical, the father-in-law of one of Wedgwood's daughters, and a poet whose verses eulogized steam and the industrialization of England. William Shipley, the founder of the Royal Society of Arts, had been a member of the Northampton Philosophical Society, which was an offshoot of the academy run by the distinguished dissenting theologian Philip Doddridge. At his academy "the study of divinity was blended with scientific experiments." It was Shipley, along with Doddridge, who hit upon the idea of annual prizes to stimulate scientific skills. The Royal Society of Arts, the product of this idea, symbolized the marriage of science and industry. Competitions would be held "to embolden enterprise, to enlarge science, to refine art, to improve our manufactures, and extend our commerce."[8] All the while, of course, Priestley's curriculum reforms and his own example spread the study of practical and experimental science throughout the dissenting academies that educated the nonconformist middle class.

Alongside the leadership role they played in science, industrialism, and political radicalism, the Dissenters inserted into the emerging cultural ideals linked to industrialism a heavy dose of the Protestant ethic so critical for the development of capitalism. Their writings praised thrift and self denial. They attacked idleness and luxury while praising simplicity, productivity, and usefulness. The juxtaposition of these good and bad qualities became at the same time a symbolic contrast between the middle class and the aristocracy. The middle class was resourceful, hardworking, frugal, productive, and useful. The aristocracy was lazy, idle, luxurious, thoroughly unproductive, and useless.

Like most marginal minorities, the Protestant Dissenters were convinced of the importance of transmitting their values to their children. They were, indeed, preoccupied, as we have seen, with education. Through their academies they could pass on their virtuous special

[8]D. G. C. Allen, *W. Shipley—Founder of the Royal Society of Arts* (London, 1968).

traits to the next generation. Another means to socialize young people to the Dissenters' values was to produce a literature specifically intended for them. It was from the ranks of those Dissenters that most writers of the first English children's books came, and, as one might expect, they came with their ideological baggage intact.

One of the reasons that little or no specific literature for children was written before this period is that until the industrial era people had little or no notion of childhood as a special time of life that needed special things such as literature. Philippe Ariès revised traditional notions of the family and of children with his claim that at a definite period in time (the seventeenth and eighteenth centuries) the middle class withdrew from contact with the collective community and sought privacy and solitude far from the "pressure of the multitude or the contact of the lower classes." In doing so, these people organized themselves around the private and nuclear family. In parallel with this development, Ariès suggested, evolved a new notion of childhood. Children no longer went from dependent infancy into the immediate fellowship of old and young alike, mixing freely with adults in work and play. Childhood for the bourgeoisie, Ariès argued, came to be a special time of learning and play, of transition from dependency to responsibility.[9] It was this new notion of childhood that Rousseau codified in his *Emile*.

In the preindustrial era more children died than lived. It was hard to invest emotional energy in an infant who probably would not live long. There was no separate world for children. They shared the games, toys, and fairy tales of the adult world. They lived together with older generations, not apart from them. Children were not considered precious things requiring special clothes, entertainment, living areas, or protection from the crudeness and exigencies of adult life.[10]

Ariès's thesis, to be sure, has been severely questioned in some quarters, but it has received an important restatement concerning England.[11] In their *Children in English Society*, Ivy Pinchbeck and Margaret Hewitt confirm Ariès's argument for eighteenth-century bourgeois England. In pre-Restoration England, they claim, families tended to extend to older relatives, cousins, in-laws, servants, apprentices, and the like. The increasing wealth of the middle class in the eighteenth century encouraged a new, more comfortable mode of living. Separate

---

[9]Philippe Ariès, *Centuries of Childhood* (New York, 1962), pp. 411, 415.

[10]See Peter Laslett, *The World We Have Lost* (London, 1965); J. H. Plumb, "The Great Change in Children," *Horizon* 8 (1971); J. H. Plumb, "The First Flourishing of Children's Books," in *Early Children's Books and Their Illustrations* (New York, 1975); Lloyd Demause, ed., *The History of Childhood* (New York, 1975).

[11]For criticism, see David Hunt, *Parents and Children in History* (New York, 1970).

living quarters for servants and apprentices, apart from the family's, encouraged

> more intimate family relationships and a degree of family self-con-
> sciousness in a way hitherto impossible. Just as the institutional develop-
> ment and acceptance of formal education in schools, with the consequent
> isolation of the child from adult society, was a prerequisite of the emer-
> gence of modern sociological and psychological concepts of childhood, so
> also the gradual isolation and individualization of the family as a social
> and psychological entity ultimately contributed to the same end. The ties
> between parent and child were necessarily strengthened in a family re-
> duced to parents and children, a family from which servants, clients and
> friends were excluded. . . . In the main these influences were far more
> observable among the middle classes of eighteenth-century England than
> among any other section of contemporary society.[12]

It is not possible or necessary to settle here the question whether or
not childhood was an invention or major contribution of the bourgeoisie to modern life. At least in England, however, the bourgeoisie
did indeed invent a specific genre of literature for children. Harvey
Darton, the definitive historian of children's books in England, has
written that "children's books did not stand out by themselves as a
clear but subordinate branch of English literature until the middle of
the eighteenth century." Pinchbeck and Hewitt are even more specific.
"Not until 1780," they write, "did professional authors turn their attention to writing juvenile literature." Darton links the growth of this
literature to the rise in the eighteenth century of the "large domesti-
cated middle-class," literate and leisured, and freed from the passions
of religious and civil strife. Like others—Ian Watt, for example—he
sees the rise of children's literature as related to the birth of the novel in
general in England and thus as reflective of increased literacy and the
"spread of the reading habit into middling social life."[13] Neither Darton nor Pinchbeck and Hewitt go beyond this vague identification of
children's literature with an increase in the literate middle-class readership. When one reads these books, however, it becomes apparent
that they self-consciously expressed the values of that middle class and
served as an important vehicle for the socialization of children to those
values. The writers of these children's books were very much a part of
the bourgeois radical nexus. Their connections overlapped extensively

[12]Ivy Pinchbeck and Margaret Hewitt, *Children of English Society*, 2 vols. (London,
1969), 1:206–7.
[13]Harvey Darton, *Children's Books in England* (Cambridge, Eng., 1958), pp. 1, 5;
Pinchbeck and Hewitt, *Children in English Society*, 1:299. See also Ian Watt, *The Rise of the
Novel* (Berkeley and Los Angeles, 1959).

with dissenting political, scientific, industrial, and religious circles; the writers' values were the Dissenters' values.

Though we cannot doubt the importance of Ariès's thesis that the notion of childhood is a relatively modern development, he fails to relate this idea in great detail to the equally important transformation of the family unit itself under industrialization, most particularly the changes in the life and role of the mother. Ariès and others have made the evolution of the private, nuclear, middle-class family, the family Wedgwood idealized in his talk to his workers, appear to be a self-conscious choice, whereas in fact it was a major structural consequence of industrial capitalism and to a great extent beyond people's control.

In preindustrial England there was little differentiation between domestic life and productive work, between home and workplace.[14] Before industrialization women played a central economic role. They controlled the dairy and the spinning wheel. They were the bakers and the brewers. Large numbers of women were millers, butchers, and fishmongers, and they dominated shopkeeping. Occasional women were even smiths and ironmongers. Most of these economic enterprises were carried on at home. A woman thus functioned as a producer, not simply as a provider of child care. The preindustrial home had few walls dividing the interior space into rooms with particular functions; it had no separate cooking, eating, and sitting rooms. When the preindustrial mother worked in the dairy or at the wheel, her relationship with her children was quite different from that of the postindustrial middle-class mother. In addition, the high rate of infant mortality discouraged parents from forming a sentimental attachment to any individual child.

Childhood was short. Children were little adults, themselves important economic units. Many children who survived infancy left home at seven or eight to become servants or apprentices. The preindustrial mother did not see child care as her major role because she was busy doing economically productive work, and children were not yet the focus of a cult of innocence, precious objects to be protected. More important, perhaps, less concern was focused on child rearing when a woman had little time for it and when it did not exclusively define her usefulness. One might also note that the preindustrial father was around the home or farm a good part of the time, to lend a hand with the children.

The unity of work and home collapsed. Men and some women were separated from the intimate daily routine of the household. Many

[14]See Eli Zaretsky, *Capitalism, the Family, and Personal Life* (New York, 1976); Sheila Rowbotham, *Woman's Consciousness, Man's World* (London, 1974); *Hidden from History* (New York, 1975); Ann Oakley, *The Sociology of Housework* (New York, 1975).

women were increasingly separated from productive enterprise as more and more of their former work was mechanized or centralized in factories. Single women often worked in factories, to be sure, but these developments had their most dramatic impact on the lives of married women. Formerly they were financially independent, or at least partners; they now became increasingly dependent economically on men. Housework and child rearing in the increasingly more private home and nuclear family became their major concerns, and with these activities developed the role that has stereotyped most married middle-class women throughout the modern period. This transformation is already abundantly clear in the passage quoted from Wedgwood's speech to his male employees in 1783. He envisioned wives at home tending to their children, totally dependent economically on their husbands.

This new role created for women is also a critical variable in the evolution of a literature intended for children. It is to industrialism that we owe the form of family life widely thought to embody "traditional values"—the man at work and the wife at home. And it is in this familial context that children's literature could develop. Books that the mother could read to her children became important adjuncts to her new role as child rearer.

Books for Children

To claim that this literature for children was new is by no means to suggest that it sprang out of nowhere, with no antecedents. Behind the emergence of children's literature in this period lay the literary traditions of the fable, the folktale, and the fairy tale. In the late seventeenth century, Aesop's fables and the story of Reynard the Fox were translated into English. Perrault's fairy tales (1628–1703) were translated from the French in the eighteenth century, and several of them—"Cinderella," "Sleeping Beauty," "Little Red Riding Hood"—later became staple fare in the nursery. By and large, however, the fable and the fairy tale were not intended exclusively for children, and throughout the eighteenth century they were not regarded as suitable reading for children.[15] Only in a later age would these stories be seen as children's literature. Much the same can be said of three books that eventually became giants in the children's book trade. Though *Pilgrim's Progress*, *Robinson Crusoe*, and *Gulliver's Travels* have become classics in the liter-

[15]See Plumb, *Early Children's Books*, passim; M. E. Thwaite, *From Primer to Pleasure* (London, 1963), p. 35.

ature for children—and indeed they had already begun to emerge as children's books by the end of the century—they were not, of course, written for children. The fact that *Robinson Crusoe* and *The Pilgrim's Progress*, at least, became children's books is explained in part by their ideological affinity to the kind of literature that was specifically written for children, a literature concerned with and expressive of the values emerging in the new bourgeois civilization of England.

Another thread of influence on the development of a self-conscious children's literature was the didactic Puritan tract designed for children which flourished after the Act of Uniformity of 1662. These "good Godly books" preached of sin, hell, gloom, and doom. The Puritans were preeminently concerned with children and their stern moral training, and echoes of this concern can be heard in the books Dissenters wrote for children in the late eighteenth century. Perhaps the most important link between the Puritan children's tract and the dissenting children's novel was the work of Dr. Isaac Watts (1674–1748), the great hymn writer and nonconformist divine. He wrote many volumes of hymns "for use of children" in easy-to-memorize rhymed verses, verses learned by heart to this day. His rhymes contain less fear than moral humility. They were, he wrote, "intended to deliver children from the temptation of learning idle, wanton, or profane songs."[16]

The commercial outlet for much of this early children's literature, the fables and fairy tales adapted for children and the Puritan moral and religious tracts, was the chapbook. Quite literally cheap books—they could be bought for a halfpenny or a penny—these small and flimsy publications were printed and sold by "running stationers" (itinerant peddlers or "chapmen") at fairs or from house to house. Many of these abbreviated and vulgar stories taken from popular folk or religious tales were illustrated by woodcuts specifically designed for children. By the middle of the eighteenth century, however, the gaudy fifteen- to twenty-page chapbook had ceased to be the major venue for children's literature.[17] In its place developed a fictional literature written specifically for children by respectable and well-known public figures and published by respectable men and women in the London publishing trade, a literature that reflected the values arising in the new bourgeois society that was England.

John Locke himself played a minor but not insignificant role in the evolution of this bourgeois children's literature. In *Some Thoughts Concerning Education* (1693) Locke applied the principles of his *Essay Concerning Human Understanding* to the education of children. Instead of

[16]Thwaite, *From Primer to Pleasure*, p. 53.

[17]See Victor E. Neuberg, *The Penny Histories: A Study of Chapbooks for Young Readers over Two Centuries* (Oxford, 1968).

losing themselves in abstract speculation and imaginative flight, children, he wrote, should use their powers of observation and experience in examining the world close at hand. They should be taught to read books that dealt with their world, not with imaginative other worlds. The child should not be given books, he wrote, "such as should fill his head with perfectly useless trumpery." In this category he placed fairy lore, superstition, stories of "goblins and spirits." Avoiding useless trumpery meant eschewing enthusiasm and imagination for the sober world of common sense. Locke was moved to comment on the scarcity of such books for children and to advise that such be written.[18] How well his advice was taken! If nothing else, children's literature as it evolved after 1750 was eminently practical and commonsensical. The fairies had fled, and what replaced them as themes was by no means useless trumpery. Goblins and spirits gave way to subjects that Locke, the theorists of liberal capitalism, would have found much more congenial.

Particularly instrumental in bringing together children and the world of bourgeois capitalism was the entrepreneurial wizardry of John Newberry. His *Little Pretty Pocket-Book* of 1741 was tremendously successful, as was his *Tom Telescope* in 1761 and his *Goody Two-Shoes* in 1765. Newberry was a commercial innovator who virtually invented the children's publishing trade. With his *Little Pretty Pocket-Book*, for example, he provided a ball or a pincushion for an extra twopence. In each of his stories he carried advertisements and a preview of another he was publishing. He published his books cheaply and quickly, and he provided them with delightful illustrations. The books often sold for a halfpenny, like the chapbooks, easily in the range of even a working-class family.[19]

Newberry brilliantly sensed the potential for exploiting childhood in the capitalist market. The later years of the eighteenth century, indeed, saw a veritable explosion in consumer products directed at children, an interesting but seldom explored addendum to the Ariès thesis. Games— board games, card games—mechanical toys, scientific toys, doll houses, rocking horses all flourished. In the early part of the century there was no such thing as a shop specializing in toys for children; by 1780 such shops were found everywhere. Perhaps the most spectacular success story in this area was that of the jigsaw puzzle, invented in 1762 by a young Englishman, John Spillsbury, who produced cut-up maps for teaching geography. His creation became an

[18]John Locke, *Some Thoughts Concerning Education* (1693), ed. R. H. Quick (London, 1899), pp. 149, 156.
[19]William Noblet, "John Newberry, Publisher Extraordinary," *History Today* 22 (1972): 265–71.

instant sensation. Children were a new and large market, ripe for a capitalist economy geared to home demand. Parents spent money on them. Mothers, of course, were also spending on other elements of the bourgeois household. We know now that it was, in fact, the purchase of crockery, buckles, textiles, pins, and buttons that fueled the Industrial Revolution.[20] We also know that coincidentally women's journals developed and flourished in the 1760s. But there is an important difference between children's books and these other consumer goods: the books were bought for motives more complex than utility, comfort, entertainment, adornment, or amusement. They were bought to instruct.

Robins, Engineers, and Heroism: Themes for Children

The first truly important novel written in English for children was *The History of Little Goody Two-Shoes,* published in 1765 by John Newberry. Its author is to this day unknown (one of the leading candidates is Newberry the publisher). *Goody Two-Shoes* is as fine an introduction to the genre as one could hope for. Its basic theme was to be repeated again and again in subsequent books—success comes to the self-reliant, hardworking, independent individual.

The story is about a young girl, Margery Meanwell, who is orphaned at the beginning of the book. Many of the characters in these early children's stories are orphans (as they are in modern works, too). Several explanations can be offered for the popularity of this device, not the least important of which is that it deals with an obvious area of anxiety for young readers, the death or absence of parents. At least in these early children's books orphanhood also permits an important ideological statement. An orphan allows a personalization of the basic bourgeois assumption that the individual is on his or her own, free from the weight of the past, from tradition, from family. It intensifies and dramatizes individuals' responsibility for their fate by dint of their own hard work, self-reliance, merit, and talent.

In this story Margery and her brother Tommy are wretched, like most orphans. Tommy has only one pair of shoes and Margery is even worse off, for she has only one shoe when the reader first meets her.

[20]See J. H. Plumb, *The Commercialization of Leisure in Eighteenth-Century England* (Reading, Pa., 1973); Alison Adburgham, *Women in Print* (London, 1972); Linda Hannas, *The English Jig Saw Puzzle, 1760–1890* (London, 1972); Neil McKendrick, "Home Demand and Economic Growth: A New View of the Role of Women and Children in the Industrial Revolution," in *Historical Perspectives: Studies in English Thought and Society,* ed. McKendrick (London, 1974).

The children are so ragged and poor that their relatives will have nothing to do with them. A worthy clergyman, Mr. Smith, takes charge, however. He sends Tommy off to sea as a sailor and takes Margery into his family. The first thing he does for her is to buy her a pair of shoes. Margery is so thrilled at the novelty of having two shoes that she shows them to everyone she meets. The neighbors call her Goody Two-Shoes as a result, and the name sticks.

We thus settle the mystery of her name. "Goody two-shoes" survives in our own time as a familiar sobriquet for a woman or girl of affected propriety, but originally the name had nothing to do with Margery's manner. It was merely a shortened locution of "Good Dame Two-Shoes." One can only speculate that the popularity of this first real children's book in English spread the name of its heroine—who in the course of the book does become an almost sickening do-gooder—and thus it developed that her name seemed apt for such an exemplary child.

As the story unfolds, Goody Two-Shoes overcomes adversity, teaches herself to read, and becomes an itinerant teacher. She turns out to be a very popular and successful teacher, partly because she gives her pupils little rhymes and homilies with which to learn spelling and reading. The book is filled with these lessons, and they are of an interesting ideological nature.

> He that will thrive
> must rise by five.

> Where pride goes . . . shame will follow.

> Where vice enters the room . . . vengeance is near the door.

> Industry is fortune's right hand, and frugality her left.

> Make much of three pence, or you ne'er will be worth a groat.

> Abundance, like want, ruins many; contentment is the best fortune.[21]

Goody Two-Shoes's success as a teacher leads to a promotion; she becomes the principal of the school. From this point on, she is called Margery Two-Shoes. At her school she continues to give moral instructions to her pupils. Many of these hortative tales are virtual prototypes of the themes developed in all these early children's books. In one such

[21]*The History of Little Goody Two-Shoes* (London, 1965), pp. 36, 41, 67.

tale she tells her students of one Mr. Lovewell, an apprentice in London who became a servant to a city merchant. He spent his leisure not as servants usually do, "in drinking and in schemes of pleasure, but in improving the mind." One of the things he did was to make himself a complete master of accounts. Needless to say, these achievements and his sobriety and honesty recommended him to his master. He was given an office of trust in the countinghouse. He became in time so useful to the merchant that he was given a share of the business. In addition, as one might suspect, Mr. Lovewell married the niece of his former master. Margery Two-Shoes makes the moral clear to her students: "See what honesty and industry will do for us. Half the great men in London, I have been told, have made themselves by this means; and who would not be honest and industrious, when it is so much our interest and our duty."[22]

As principal, Margery Two-Shoes continues her good deeds. At night she teaches poor servants to read and write. The only payment she asks is that they say their prayers and sing psalms. Even this philanthropy has a double payoff, spiritual and material. She comments: "By this means the people grew extremely regular. The servants were always at home, instead of being at the alehouse, and more work was done than ever."[23]

A well-to-do man, Mr. Jones, asks Margery to be his wife. With her marriage, Goody Two-Shoes becomes a lady. Moreover, who should appear on her wedding day but her long-lost brother. Tommy arrives rich and successful from beyond the sea, where he has made a large fortune. He is thus able to provide a large marriage settlement for her. Six years later Mr. Jones dies and Margery, now Lady Jones, is left with a large fortune. Unchanged by it, she continues to live a life of simplicity and noble philanthropy. One of her many achievements is to offer a free loaf of bread to every poor person who attends church. At the end of the story, however, Lady Jones does confess to her young readers that after she married she had in fact been tempted to live a life of idle luxury with all her riches. She had resisted that life, though. The book ends with a beautiful rendering of the peculiar tension at the heart of the bourgeois and Protestant ethic. Bourgeois and ascetic Protestants must accumulate and acquire wealth, but they must also deny themselves. They cannot consume all; they must disdain show and luxury. They must plow some capital back; they must save. Self-denial is the cornerstone of capitalism, and this is in fact the final message of

[22]Ibid., pp. 67–68.
[23]Ibid., p. 96.

the book. Meanwhile, presiding over the whole process is the ever-watchful Calvinist God. The book ends:

> Ah said I, why did I long for riches. Having enough already why did I covet more? This is a lesson, a load of riches bring instead of felicity, a load of troubles; and the only source of happiness is contentment. Go therefore you that have too much and give it to those who are in want. . . . This is a precept from The Almighty, a precept which must be regarded, for the Lord is about your path and about your bed, and spieth out all our ways.[24]

God was not the only patient one in these early tales for children; animals, too, were about the path and by the bed. The greatest teller of animal tales in this formative period of children's literature was Sarah Trimmer (1741–1810). Though ubiquitous in folktales and fables, animals had not appeared before in literature specifically written for children. Mrs. Trimmer is usually given credit for teaching the English to be kind to animals, a trait that some people regard as peculiar to the middle class and opposed to the attitudes of both the lower and upper classes. It might be noted that in their infinite wisdom the librarians at Cornell University have put Trimmer's books in the library of the College of Veterinary Medicine.

Trimmer's animal tales were in fact thinly disguised vehicles for the transmission of bourgeois values. The message of her very successful *Fabulous Histories Designed for the Amusement and Instruction of Young People*, written in 1786, is simple: we can learn a lot from animals. Consider "the exact regularity with which they discharge the offices of cleanliness and economy. Idle persons, for instance, may be admonished by the bee, a thoughtless mother by a hen, an unfaithful servant by a dog and so on."[25]

When Sarah Trimmer tells a story about a bird family, it turns out to be a good bourgeois bird family. The little birds love and respect their parents; the parents dote on their offspring. The bird father is industrious, spending most of his day away from the nest gathering food while the mother sits home keeping the nest clean and tending to her loved ones. The father bird lectures his children about not associating with birds that do not respect the property of others. It is most important to choose carefully the birds with whom you keep company, he tells them.

Mrs. Trimmer's message is that being kind to animals not only is good in itself but also pays off in the end. In the last chapter of her

---

[24]Ibid., p. 127.

[25]Sarah Trimmer, *Fabulous Histories Designed for the Amusement and Instruction of Young People* (Philadelphia, 1794), p. 69.

Fabulous Histories she gives a reckoning of what happened to all the humans who appeared in the story. The boys and girls who were good to animals did well in the world. They were respected by all. The young boy who beat his animals and cared only for himself was despised by all who knew him, and even worse, was finally killed by a horse he was beating. The good farmer Wilson, a neighbor to the bird family, always took good care of his cattle; "his prosperity increased with every succeeding year and he acquired a plentiful fortune, from which he gave portions to each of his children, as opportunities offered for settling them in the world."[26]

This theme is not unlike those stressed by another woman who wrote children's stories in the 1790s and early 1800s, Maria Edgeworth (1767–1849). Edgeworth grew up among her father's friends in that hotbed of scientific and political excitement, the Lunar Society of Birmingham. She later became an important Anglo-Irish novelist, author of *Castle Rackrent* (1800) and *Belinda* (1801). Edgeworth's stories for children are fine examples of the various motifs and themes of this early literature. One of her stories, "The Purple Jar," teaches the lesson of self-control and self-denial, or, in more modern jargon, the need to postpone immediate gratification.

Passing shops on a trip to buy a pair of shoes, seven-year-old Rosamund wants to buy everything she sees. What particularly strikes her fancy is a pretty purple jar. Her mother reminds her that she desperately needs shoes, that hers are falling apart, but headstrong Rosamund chooses the jar instead. No sooner does she get the jar home, however, than she realizes it is useless and not even purple. It seems to have been filled with a purple liquid. She soon despises the jar, but her parents drive home the lesson by requiring her to wear her old broken-down shoes for a month.[27]

In another story, "The Little Merchants," Edgeworth offered the classic format that much of children's literature took in those years and has indeed kept to this day. It is a tale of two boys and their differing paths to success and failure. The genre is full of contrasting sons, daughters, brothers, sisters, cousins, horses, dogs, what have you. One member of every pair is energetic and hard-working, the other lazy, idle, and profligate. The ideological message is clear. Each pair contrasts virtuous middle-class values with despised aristocratic values or occasionally lower-class values, which the middle class, of course, often saw as the same. After all, both the upper and the lower classes drank,

---

[26]Ibid., p. 209.
[27]Maria Edgeworth, *The Most Unfortunate Day of My Life and Other Stories* (London, 1931), pp. 40–45. For details of Edgeworth's life, see Marilyn Butler, *Maria Edgeworth* (Oxford, 1972).

gambled, and were lazy, according to the sober, hard-working bourgeoisie. "The Little Merchants" contrasts two twelve-year-old street entrepreneurs in Naples, Piedro and Francisco. Piedro is the son of a less than honest fishmonger, who teaches the boy to be sharp and cunning, to deceive customers on value and price, to take advantage of the customer's ignorance. Piedro is lazy and sleeps most of the day, habits he also learns from his father. Francisco, on the contrary, is the son of an honest gardener, who has taught him to be scrupulous and truthful when he sells fruit. He is taught that lying never pays and that cheats and thieves come to no good. "His industry was constant, his gains small but certain. . . . He realized his father's maxim that honesty is the best policy."[28]

Some English tourists in Naples, apparently cheated wherever they go, are very impressed by Francisco's honesty. They tender him the ultimate compliment an Englishman can bestow: "Bless you my good boy, I should have taken you for an Englishman by your ways of dealing."[29] Honest Francisco, it seems, had shown them the bruised half of a melon when they picked it out. Piedro, on the contrary, had tried to sell them old fish as fresh. All this honesty pays off in the end for hard-working Francisco. One of the English gentlemen with whom he has been so honest takes him back to England and makes him a famous artist. Piedro, however, lives a life of crime in Naples and suffers the disdain of all his peers. One may note that nothing is said about Francisco's dear old father and how he takes to having his son carted off. In the scheme of values of the readers, that is irrelevant in comparison with the wondrous luck of being lifted from Naples and planted in the natural home of honest tradesmen, England.

By far the most important and enduring of Maria Edgeworth's children's books was her *Harry and Lucy,* a tale of brother and sister in which many of the ideological themes sketched earlier are emphasized. It is a hymn to science and industry and the godlike figures who have made England what it was in the 1790s—the factory of the world. The family setting described in the book is also interesting. The father is a teacher, the mother a housewife superintending the development of her children, a bright inquiring son and, of course, a scatterbrained and ineffectual daughter.

As in many of these early stories, the family is constantly performing scientific experiments, with thermometers, barometers, hygrometers, water pumps, and air pumps. Occasionally they experiment in the fields, with flowers and plants. The most exciting parts of the book,

[28]Maria Edgeworth, *The Parents' Assistant; or, Stories for Children* (New York, 1877), p. 325.
[29]Ibid., p. 327.

however, describe the trips the family takes to various industrial sites around England. When holidays arrive, no trips to castles, cathedrals, battlegrounds, or great homes for them; such places enshrine the past. In the new bourgeois age the family visits industrial factories. The young reader is treated, for example, to a fifty-page description of the workings of cotton mills, with the father lecturing on the spinning jenny. The particular factory was one of Arkwright's. His fortune is well deserved, lectures the father, unlike most fortunes in England. Arkwright is being paid for his inventiveness, his industry, and his perseverance. The father waxes rhapsodic about the romance of cotton. He informs Harry and Lucy that the machinery in these mills earns nearly £1,000 in a working hour and that in only three minutes 40,000 pounds of cotton is spun into thread—more than enough to circumscribe the whole earth.[30]

From the cotton mills the family moves on to Staffordshire for a visit to Wedgwood's potteries. Here the father teaches the children the various chemical processes involved and then delivers his social message:

> 'It was by this attention to little as well as to great objects and by steadily adhering to one course of pursuits, that Wedgwood succeeded in accomplishing all that he began . . . the consequences of his success we all know, and we all rejoice in them. He made a large fortune for himself and his children, with a character, and reputation above all fortune. He increased amazingly the industry, wealth, and comforts of the poor in the neighbourhood; raised at home and abroad the fame of the arts and manufactures of his own country, extended her commerce, and spread her own name with his productions to the most remote regions of the civilised world.'[31]

Some of these holiday outings elicit veritable poetic flights from Edgeworth. After the potteries, for example, the family visits a steel mill, where they see

> half smoldering heaps of coal, clouds of smoke of all colors, from the chimneys and foundries and forges. The hands and faces of everyone were covered with soot. Lucy said it was the most frightful country she had ever beheld. Harry acknowledged that there was nothing beautiful here to be seen; but it was wonderful, it was a sort of sublime. He could not help feeling a great respect for the place, where steam engines seemed to abound, and in truth, to have the world almost to themselves.[32]

[30]Maria Edgeworth, *Harry and Lucy: Being the Last Part of Early Lessons*, 2 vols. (London, 1825), 1:229–30.
[31]Ibid., 2:19–20.
[32]Ibid., p. 162.

Even more typical is the praise of Watt and his steam engine. He is given godlike qualities. The father lectures:

'Watt is the man whose genius discovered the means of multiplying our national resources, to a degree, perhaps even beyond his own stupendous powers of calculation and combination in bringing the treasures of the abyss to the summit of the earth. He has commanded manufactures to arise, as the rod of the prophet produced water in the desert, and thus afforded the means of dispensing with that time and tide which wait for no man, and of sailing without that wind, which defied the commands and threats of Xerxes himself. This potent commander of the elements, this abridger of time and space, this magician whose cloudy machinery has produced a change in the world, the effects of which, extraordinary as they are, perhaps are only now beginning to be felt, was not only the most refined man of science, the most successful combiner of powers, and calculator of numbers as adapted to practical purposes; but one of the best and kindest of human beings.'[33]

Children's literature has always had as one of its functions the provision of heroes and models for young children, and here at its beginning children's literature in English makes quite clear that statesmen, clerics, chivalric knights, and warriors have been replaced as fit heroes for children by new bourgeois models—engineers, scientists, and industrial entrepreneurs.

These books are never subtle about their ideological message, the superiority of the bourgeois world to the aristocratic. A friend of Harry and Lucy's father tells the children of some foreigners who have recently visited England. They are used to make the obvious point. If the middle class is the superior class, then surely the nation where the middle class looms so significant is the superior nation. Bourgeois ideology is joined to nationalism for the young readers. These foreigners were accustomed to wealth, but Edgeworth notes:

They were surprised by the comfortableness of persons in the middle ranks of life, here. They were struck by the liberty enjoyed and the equal justice done to all, as far as they could see in England. They found that many of our most distinguished men have made their own fortunes, many risen by their own talents and exertions, from the lower ranks of life. They found that in this country though birth has great advantages, education does more, and industry and genius have the road to fame, and wealth, and honours open to them.[34]

---

[33]Ibid., p. 335.
[34]Ibid., p. 77.

At the end of this passage Maria Edgeworth adds, "Harry understood all this, though it might seem a little above his years." That any eight- or ten-year-old would relate easily to this kind of language indeed seems strange to the modern reader; but this observation speaks to the point made earlier. We live now in an age that assumes a specific language and conceptual ability distinctly appropriate for a stage of life called childhood. These books, though produced in an age when childhood was emerging as a separate time of life, are still written as if this time of life does not come complete with its own level of language facility. The language is still for children as small adults. It is also worthwhile to note that Edgeworth singles out Harry as understanding; she makes no such claim for Lucy. Harry, moreover, is awed by the sight of the steel mill and is moved to compare it with the sublime; Lucy is merely frightened by it.

Harry and Lucy was an important vehicle in transmitting the sexual stereotypes emergent in the new notion of the family—the superiority and usefulness of men. It is the new family we see in the book. It is always the father who lectures, who knows about and deals with the world out there, outside the household, while the mother tends to the home. In a revealing incident, the factory master takes Harry and Lucy by the home of one of his workers. They happen to arrive as the husband is beating his wife. Immediately thereafter they see the children and the wife waiting on the husband hand and foot. Harry and Lucy asks the master why he does not intervene in this family scene. He replies that he has "no right to do this. Every man has the liberty to do as he pleases in his own home and in his own affairs."[35] This is liberal freedom. The new bourgeois home and family structure are sanctified by laissez-faire ideology.

This factory master, Mr. Watson, is indeed a most significant symbolic figure in *Harry and Lucy*. He is the model bourgeois master, the new heroic model. He sets rigorous limits on his own pleasures and devotes his principal concern to business. Edgeworth describes a visit to his house:

The dinner was plentiful though plain and there were creams and sweet things in abundance, for the master loved them . . . and his wife and sisters were skilled in confectionary arts. . . . As soon as the cloth was removed, Mr. Watson swallowed a glass of wine and pushing the bottle to his guests, rose, saying . . . 'I must leave you now to take care of yourselves. . . . I must go to my business.'[36]

[35]Ibid., p. 185.
[36]Ibid., p. 173.

He takes Harry on his rounds to the factory and to the workmen's homes. He teaches him about "balance of accounts" and about the fascinating and mysterious world of debts, credit, and so forth. Several of the workmen, Harry is told, leave Mr. Watson part of their money to be put into the savings bank. "By so doing the men obtained a provision for the time when they might be sick, or must grow old." On their walk, Mr. Watson and Harry come upon a worker dressed in rags. The master lectures the poor man:

> 'You earn a great deal . . . if you would put less of your money into your cup you would have more on your back.' . . . The ragged man walked away ashamed, while his companions laughed at him. . . . Mr. Watson was steady as well as good-natured to the people. . . . The industrious and the frugal he encouraged, the idle and the drunken he reproved, and he took pains to see that justice was done to them all.[37]

Mr. Watson has taken over the varied social, political, and cultural roles of the traditional landed aristocrat. His visits to the workers' cottages, dispensing justice and bourgeois homilies as he goes, have replaced the paternal care of the gentry on their rounds of the cottages. Like the landed justice of the peace, the factory master is responsible for justice in his domain, for the well-being of his charges. Edgeworth makes clear this new and significant role of the factory master in bourgeois England through young Harry's report to his father about the trip with Mr. Watson to the factory and to the workers' homes.

> 'Father,' said Harry, after a long silence and looking very serious. 'I thought that a great mechanic was only a person who invented machines and kept them going to earn money and to make things cheaply. . . . But now I perceive that there is a great deal more to be done. . . . And if I ever grow up to be a man, and have to manage any great works, I hope I shall be as good to my workmen as Mr. Watson is. . . . I think I will be as just and as steady, too, if I can. . . . I see it is not so very easy to be just, as I should have thought it was. . . . There is a great deal to be considered. . . . I feel that I have much more than I knew of before to learn.'[38]

Meanwhile, as Harry resolves on the noble mission of his glorious future, Lucy is told that she should have no such great expectations. She should simply listen to father and Harry as they teach her what is important for her to know. "By acquiring knowledge, women not only increase their power of being agreeable companions to their fathers, brothers, husbands or friends, if they are so happy as to be connected

[37]Ibid., pp. 177, 179.
[38]Ibid., p. 200.

with sensible men, but they increase their own pleasure in reading and learning of scientific experiments and discoveries." If there can be any doubt about the sex roles ascribed by the bourgeois ideal, Maria Edgeworth dispels them in her preface to the book. She apologizes to readers if Harry appears "too knowledgeable for his age" and Lucy "too childish and volatile," with "no respect for accuracy." But, she adds, Lucy's character provides the "nonsense and the action necessary to relieve the reader's attention."[39]

The fundamental messages of *Harry and Lucy* were not lost on posterity. Decades later Louisa May Alcott invoked them in her *Little Men*. Father Baer criticizes his young boys for their lack of industry and self-denial, their fondness for cakes, candy, and fairy tales. They read too much useless literature, such as the *Arabian Nights*, he charges. Better, he notes, that they read such books as *Harry and Lucy*, which are "not fairy books and are all full of barometers and bricks and shoeing horses and useful things."[40]

In the eighteenth century, children's literature was part of the political assault on aristocratic England. Some of the most important radicals wrote children's literature. In *Dramas for Children* (1808), for example, the former dissenting minister and anarchist philosopher William Godwin gives a moving speech to a middle-class character who has just been ridiculed by an idle and supercilious aristocrat. It is a fitting sentiment from Godwin, a friend of Thomas Holcroft, the English translator of Beaumarchais's *Marriage of Figaro*.

'My ancestors were respectable heads of families, who filled each his station in the world with credit and with honour. They bequeathed to me, it is true, a condition in which I am called upon to labour; but I inherit also from them a love of independence, and an abhorrence of every mean or dishonest action. . . . The man who toils to gain an honourable subsistence is infinitely more entitled to the esteem of the virtuous than he whose greatest merit consists in a gaudy equipage and a costly expenditure."[41]

Mary Wollstonecraft also wrote children's stories. In her *Vindication* she announced that she wrote for middle-class women against the "pestiferous purple" of aristocratic society, for the middle class where "talents thrive best." Her *Original Stories from Real Life*, written in 1791,

---

[39]Ibid., 1:10, xiii.

[40]Louisa May Alcott, *Little Men* (1871; rpt. New York, 1963), pp. 38–39.

[41]William Godwin, *Dramas for Children* (London, 1808), p. 129. See also Thomas Percival, *A Father's Instructions: Consisting of Moral Tales, Fables, and Reflections, Designed to Promote the Love of Virtue, a Taste for Knowledge and an Early Acquaintance with the Work of Nature* (Manchester, 1775).

emphasizes one particular bourgeois theme for young readers—time. Mrs. Mason, the governess-tutor whose towering, all-knowing presence dominates the book, continuously lectures Mary and Caroline, the little heroines of fourteen and twelve, on the importance of time. Mrs. Mason, Wollstonecraft tells the reader, "always regulated her own time and never loitered her hours resolutely away." She instructed her girls to read every day at a precise time, and she became angry when "whole hours were lost in thoughtless idleness." To make her point, she relates to the girls the sad tale of the young man who lost his fortune because he never planned and organized his time. The moral is clear. One "must never loiter away in laborious idleness the precise moments." Mrs. Mason insists that the girls be kept constantly busy, the better to resist the assaults of Vice. She is also preoccupied with neatness and has contempt for luxurious ornaments. She notes that "economy and self-denial are necessary in every station." She cautions the girls not to give in to their caprices and appetites, or to squander their money. "If you wish to be useful, govern your desires," she tells them; "do not spend money in indulging the vain wishes of idleness and a childish fondness for pretty things."[42]

Next to Wollstonecraft, perhaps the most important woman radical in the 1790s was Anna Barbauld (1743–1825). A close friend of Priestley and Price, she also was a writer of children's stories—indeed, one of the most important figures in these early years of the genre. This outspoken opponent of the Test and Corporation Acts was a leading member of the Stoke Newington Dissenter community. She wrote radical tracts and poetry; and with her brother, the physician John Aikin, she wrote one of the most famous early pieces of children's literature, *Evenings at Home; or, The Juvenile Budget Opened.*[43] Like most early works in this genre, this one consists of a lengthy series of short moralistic tales for young readers. The content of Barbauld's stories is also typical of the genre. They are full of science and antislavery arguments, natural rights and anticolonialism. And, of course, they sing the praises of the new industrial order and the heroic industrialist.

One such story depicts Richard Arkwright's rise to fame and fortune. His powers know no limits. The father in the story notes that "this is what manufacturers can do; here man is a kind of creator, and like the great Creator, he may please himself with his work and say it is

---

[42]Mary Wollstonecraft, *Vindication of the Rights of Woman,* ed. Miriam Brody Kramnick (New York, 1975), pp. 81, 150, and *Original Stories from Real Life with Considerations Calculated to Regulate the Affections and Form the Mind to Truth and Goodness* (London, 1791), pp. 78–97, 116.

[43]Most of the book is Barbauld's. For details of Barbauld's fascinating career, see Betsy Rodgers, *Georgian Chronicle: Mrs. Barbauld and Her Family* (London, 1958).

good." When the father tells the children that he will take them to a real factory, he emphasizes the good middle-class fun of it all. There is, he notes, "more entertainment to a cultivated mind in seeing a pin made, than in many a fashionable diversion which young people half ruin themselves to attend."[44]

In another story, "The Female Choice," Barbauld repeats Wollstone-craft's new middle-class ideal of working women in contrast to useless and idle aristocratic women. Two visions appear to a sleeping girl; one, a beautifully dressed woman, offers the sleeping girl endless amusement and excitement; the other, plainly dressed, tells her:

'I am the genie who has ever been the friend and companion of your mother. I have no allurements to tempt you with like those of my gay rival. Instead of spending all your time in amusements, if you enter yourself of my train, you must rise early, and pass the long day in a variety of employments, some of them difficult, some laborious, and all requiring some exaction of body or mind. You must dress plainly and aim at being useful rather than shining.'[45]

Barbauld calls one vision "dissipation," the other "housewifery."

Things are much more exciting for Barbauld's boy readers. Like Edgeworth, Barbauld is concerned to provide new heroes for the young male reader. She makes this point rather dramatically in two of the stories in *Evenings at Home,* "True Heroism" and "Great Men." Great men, she informs her youthful readers, are no longer "kings, lords, generals, prime ministers," and other traditional figures of status. The new heroes that children should look up to are

those that invent useful arts, or discover important truths which may promote the comfort and happiness of unborn generations in the distant parts of the world. They act still a more important part, and their claim to merit is generally more undoubted than that of the former, because what they do is more certainly their own.[46]

Most of these ingenious true heroes are engineers. In this particular story Barbauld has the young son taken by his father to see the "Great Man" James Brindley, the engineer responsible for the new canal system. The father speaks of Brindley just as Burke spoke of nobility or royalty: "I wish you to look upon him as one of those sublime and uncommon objects of nature which fill the mind with a certain awe and

---

[44]John Aikin and Anna Barbauld, *Evenings at Home; or, The Juvenile Budget Opened,* 6 vols. (Philadelphia, 1792–1796), 2:191.
[45]Ibid., 3:329.
[46]Ibid., 6:223; see also 5:203.

astonishment." Another true hero and great man held up to the readers of *Evenings at Home* was Benjamin Franklin, a figure who persistently turns up in the classics of early children's literature. "Few
wiser men have ever existed," Barbauld wrote, "than the late Dr.
Franklin."[47]

We know, of course, that not everyone shared Mrs. Barbauld's conception of true heroism. All this moral and technical instruction was
wasted on the purity and innocence of childhood, Lamb wrote in a
famous exchange with Coleridge:

> Mrs. Barbauld's stuff has banished all the old classics of the nursery. . . .
> Science has succeeded to poetry no less in the little walks of children than
> with men. Is there no possibility of averting this sore evil? Think what you
> would have been now, if instead of being fed with tales and old wives'
> fables in childhood, you had been crammed with geography and natural
> history!
>   Damn them! I mean the cursed Barbauld crew, those blights and blasts
> of all that is human in man and child.[48]

Wordsworth agreed. These stories filled children with useless knowledge, far beyond their capacity to understand. He satirized these children's books in the well-known lines of his *Prelude*.

> A miracle of scientific lore,
> Ships he can guide across the pathless sea,
> And tell you all their cunning; he can read
> The inside of the earth, and spell the stars;
> He knows the policies of foreign lands;
> Can string you names of districts, cities, towns,
> The whole world over, tight as beads of dew
> Upon a gossamer thread; he sifts, he weighs;
> All things are put to question. . . .[49]

Tommy, Harry, and Little Jack: Thomas Day and the New Genre

Thomas Day's *Sandford and Merton* is a book unknown to most people
today. Its characters have not lived on in the English vocabulary as
Goody Two-Shoes has done, yet *Sandford and Merton* was one of the
most widely read English books for many decades, deep into the Vic-

---

[47]Ibid., 6:227, 250.
[48]Quoted in Rodgers, *Georgian Chronicle*, p. 123.
[49]William Wordsworth, *The Prelude; or, Growth of a Poet's Mind*, bk. 5, ll. 315–23.

torian era. Published in the 1780s, it went through some forty-five editions in England, Ireland, and the United States. It was translated into French and German, and many an English literary figure—Dickens was one—wrote about its importance in his youth.

Day (1748–1789) was a fascinating figure. A political radical, he championed America in the War of Independence, opposed slavery, and called for suffrage extension and reform of Parliament. He was also a leading English disciple of Jean-Jacques Rousseau and, through Rousseau, an early pioneer in the development of what later came to be called progressive education. Day was at the same time a close friend of Wedgwood, Wilkinson, Watt, Priestley, and Edgeworth through his membership in the Lunar Society of Birmingham.[50] One might expect that a Rousseauean primitivist would have little to do with these apostles of industrialism and science, but the two tendencies could exist side by side, and indeed in the same person. Primitivism and industrialism could come together because they had a common enemy, the idle and unproductive aristocracy.

Sandford and Merton is a story of two boys, Tommy Merton, a rich boy of good family, and Harry Sandford, a son of an honest farmer. As in Rousseau's *Emile*, however, the central character of this novel is a tutor, the Reverend Mr. Barlow. It is he who seeks to shape and mold Harry and Tommy into good and virtuous citizens. The vague plot is concerned with poor Harry's education to life, his sojourn with the rich and elegant family of Tommy, and his repudiation of that family and its values. The importance and popularity of the book can be attributed not to the plot, however, but to the stories and fables—hundreds of pages of them—told by Mr. Barlow to educate the boys. It is in these tales that the morals are made and the ideological values proclaimed.

All of the stories and fables contain the familiar antithetical pairs: two men, dogs, horses, or what have you. One is invariably rich and lazy; the other is humble and hardworking. One rejects riches and luxury; the other wallows in them. Needless to say the humble hardworking boy, dog, or horse always triumphs. In one recurrent variation, the pair is deserted—on an island, on the desert, in a cave. The place varies but the contrasting duo always must resort to primitive and basic means to survive. This device involves Day in a reworking of *Robinson Crusoe*, and the ideological lesson is the same as in Defoe's book. The humble child, dog, or horse is always ingenious, resource-

[50]Michael Sadler, *Thomas Day—An English Disciple of Rousseau* (Cambridge, Eng., 1928); G. W. Gignilliat, Jr., *The Author of "Sandford and Merton": A Life of Thomas Day, Esq.* (New York, 1932); Robert Schofield, *The Lunar Society of Birmingham* (Oxford, 1963). For details on the impact and influence of *Sandford and Merton*, see William Stewart and William MacCaun, *The Educational Innovators*, 2 vols. (London, 1967), 1:23–26.

ful, inventive, and self-reliant. He responds creatively to adversity by making tools, food, and shelter. The overly sophisticated and gentler of the pair, never having worked for himself and used to servants, is ineffectual. The humbler can cope and survive. He is usually rescued and returned to his home, where he soon, of course, makes his fortune.

Like *Robinson Crusoe*, the tales told by Barlow in *Sandford and Merton* repeat the myth that informs liberal capitalist ideology. They depict a man on his own (the contrasting character is no help), independent of family, independent of the corporate ties of guild, church, and locality. He is free of history, free of tradition, free of association and society. He forges his own life through his merit and hard work. These tales also bear the imprint of Day's radical politics in the 1780s. On one hand they proclaim that if the aristocracy continues to govern, England will not cope and will decline. If, on the other hand, the inventive, ingenious, and clever middle class were to govern, the island would prosper and thrive. Rousseau, one might also note, is by no means inappropriate here. Mr. Barlow, after all, reminds Harry and Tommy that when Emile's tutor tells him not to read books because all books are worthless, he does make one exception, *Robinson Crusoe*. So did Priestley. In his *Memoirs* he tells of his early "aversion to plays and romances, so that I never read any works of that kind except *Robinson Crusoe*."[51]

Sandford and Merton is a veritable catalog and summary of the values and concerns of bourgeois radicalism. Opposite the title page appears an epigraph: "I don't know that there is upon the face of the earth a more useless, more contemptible, and more miserable animal than a wealthy, luxurious man without business or profession, arts, sciences, or exercises." Harry Sandford describes Tommy Merton's family as totally lacking in worthwhile traits:

> As to all the common virtues of life, such as industry, economy and punctuality in discharging our obligations, or keeping our words, these were qualities which were treated there as fit for nothing but the vulgar. . . . Instead of their being brought up to produce anything useful, the great object of all their knowledge and education is only to waste, to consume, to destroy, to dissipate what was produced by others.[52]

The aristocracy are never on time; they don't keep promises, they waste, and they consume. They disgust the bourgeoisie.

Sandford and Merton even contains a lesson on property rights. In a

[51]Joseph Priestley, *Memoirs of Dr. Joseph Priestley* (London, 1806), p. 15.
[52]Thomas Day, *Sandford and Merton* (New York, n.d.), pp. 256–57.

moving scene the boys give their clothes and some of Mr. Barlow's bread to a poor urchin. Proud of themselves, they appear before the good reverend for what they expect will be his praise. Instead, Mr. Barlow coldly answers, "You have done very well in giving the boy clothes, because they are your own; but what right have you to give away my loaf of bread without asking my consent?" The boys answer that the beggar was hungry and poor. Mr. Barlow replies, "This is a very good reason why you should give away what belongs to yourself, but not why you should give away what is another's . . . here is a story you may read on that subject."[53]

In his attitude toward women, Thomas Day strikes a careful compromise between the feminism of Wollstonecraft and the sexism of Rousseau's *Emile*. Like Rousseau, Day sees women as by nature dependent on and in the service of men, but he also accords them an important role in the enterprise of the home as opposed to the useless role of the aristocratic lady. Day, like Wollstonecraft and Rousseau, has assimilated the new postindustrial notion of the family. His ideal woman, like theirs, is the home-centered, republican mother working hard within the home and raising good republican children. In *Sandford and Merton* Day has an old farmer reminisce about changes in the family. A great deal of the upheaval, confusion, and transformation of the role of women in the eighteenth century can be glimpsed in the farmer's comments:

> 'When I was young we all did our duty and worked hard . . . this brought down a blessing upon our heads and made us thrive in all the worldly concerns. We were all at work by four, women then knew something about work. . . . The girls today all they want is finery, but scarcely one of them can milk a cow, or churn, or bake, or do anything that is necessary in a family. . . . Bring us a cargo of plain honest housewives, who have never been at boarding schools. They go to boarding schools and learn French, and music, and wriggling about the room. And when they come back who must boil the pot, or make the pudding, or sweep the house, or serve the pigs.'[54]

In addition to *Stanford and Merton*, Day wrote one other children's book, *Little Jack*, published in 1786. This book is almost a perfect summing up of all that I have said about such books. It could be the mold for the Horatio Alger stories that socialized the children of the next century to bourgeois values. It has the additional noteworthy feature of a plot that is developed throughout the book—the majestic rise and triumph of Little Jack.

[53]Ibid., pp. 55–56.
[54]Ibid., pp. 414–15.

Little Jack is an orphan (of course) raised by a poor and elderly soldier in the north of England. When the old man first finds Jack deserted on the moor, a note of predestination is struck. The old man exclaims, "Who knows but Providence which has preserved this child in so wonderful a manner may have destined it to something equally wonderful in his future life."[55] Right he is.

When Little Jack is twelve, the old man dies, and the youth sets out to find work. His first job is in a small iron factory, where he turns into "the most honest, sober, and industrious lad in the place." One unfortunate day, however, he gets into a fight with another worker and is fired. As luck would have it (and luck is very important in all stories of this genre, including Horatio Alger's), this is the day a group of elegant ladies and gentlemen are visiting the factory. They have come, as Day puts it,

> to view with astonishment the different methods by which that useful and necessary ore of iron is rendered fit for human use, to examine the furnaces where it is melted down, to disengage it from the dross, with which it is mixed in the bowels of the earth, and whence it runs down in liquid torrents like fire. They beheld with equal pleasure the prodigious hammers which, moved by the force of the water, mould it into massy bars, for the service of man.[56]

One of these visiting ladies is impressed by Little Jack's independence, and when he is dismissed for fighting, she offers him a job as her stable boy.

In the lady's service Little Jack has a good deal of extra time, which he uses to study mechanics and science. He is, we are told, "sober, temperate, hardy, active, and ingenious." This program of self-improvement continues for several years, until trouble appears in the person of a relative of the gracious lady, "a young gentleman who, having been educated in France and among genteel people in London, had a very great taste for finery, and a supreme distaste for the common. He constantly strutted, pranced, and dressed himself."[57] Harry and Tommy are recreated. As we have learned to expect, Little Jack and the precious relative clash. After a nasty fight, Jack loses his job and is picked up by a recruiting sergeant, who immediately presses him into the navy.

Little Jack's ship stops at an island. Little Jack (unlike Goody Two-Shoes, he never seems to acquire a more adult name as he grows up)

[55]Thomas Day, *The History of Little Jack* (London, 1797), p. 5.
[56]Ibid., pp. 20–21.
[57]Ibid., p. 27.

becomes separated from the others and is left behind. There ensues the liberal myth à la *Robinson Crusoe*. "Little Jack found himself now abandoned upon a strange country, without a single friend, acquaintance or even anyone who spoke the same language."[58] But Jack copes. He builds a house, eats fish and berries, and is generally as self-reliant and ingenious as one could be. Finally, a boat bound for India picks him up. In India he is put into the service of His Majesty's army, but unfortunately his regiment is captured by what Day calls the "Tartars." As a prisoner Jack has the good fortune to save the life of the chief's favorite horse. This act so endears him to the chief that he is put in charge of all the horses of the tribe.

Procuring some iron, Jack makes horseshoes, much to the astonishment of the Tartars (and to the reader, who never is told where the iron came from). Jack "could not help observing that it was a great pity that they had not learned to make a horseshoe instead of dancing and dressing hair." Jack and the whole regiment are finally freed by the Tartars through the intervention of the English ambassador. The chief loves Jack and hates to see him go. As a parting gesture, he gives him horses and skins as presents. Rather than cart them about, unsentimental Jack sells the chief's gifts and finds himself in "possession of a moderate sum of money."[59]

Good Jack is above temptation. He does not squander his money on useless trinkets in India, as most of the other soldiers do. He saves his windfall and takes it back to England with him. In England, of course, he is too virtuous to sit and merely live off his new wealth. He is, as Day tells us, "too active and too prudent to give himself up to idleness." Instead, he goes into the iron and steel business. He returns north to his old master. In a few years he is a partner, and eventually he takes over the whole business. "He improved the business so much as to gain a considerable fortune, and became one of the most respectable manufacturers in the country."[60]

But even with this great wealth, Little Jack has no taste for prideful and luxurious show. He remains simple and frugal. Most of his money goes to improving the business. He builds himself "a small but convenient house on the spot of his daddy's hut. Hither he would sometimes retire from business and cultivate his garden with his own hands, for he hated idleness." And so with this final note of middle-class sentimentalism, the house on the site of daddy's hut, the story of Little Jack ends—except, that is, for Jack's final words. He has told his life story to children everywhere "in order to prove that it is of very little conse-

---

[58]Ibid., p. 39.
[59]Ibid., p. 50.
[60]Ibid., p. 51.

quence how a man comes into the world, provided he behaves well and discharges his duty when he is in it."[61] The ideological message is clear. Little Jack is a bourgeois and Protestant model for all would-be successful young people—preferably, of course, boys.

How wonderfully that message of children's literature has persisted over time! One can almost hear prideful, self-assured Little Jack repeating at various crises in his life on the way to the top, "I think I can, I think I can, I think I can."

[61]Ibid., pp. 53, 54.

CHAPTER 5

Tom Paine:
Radical Liberal

I N THE seventh issue of his periodical *Crisis,* addressed in 1778 "to the People of England," Thomas Paine described his feelings on arriving in America four years earlier. An unknown Englishman of thirty-seven undistinguished years, he was plunged into tumultuous Philadelphia: "I happened to come to America a few months before the breaking out of hostilities. . . . The world could not then have persuaded me that I should be either a soldier or an author. . . . But when the country, into which I had just set my foot, was set on fire about my ears, it was time to stir. It was time for every man to stir."[1] Few men have "stirred" as much as Paine did in the last quarter of the eighteenth century.

Paine the Revolutionary

Paine's life reads like one of the stories written for children by Edgeworth, Barbauld, or Day. Not bred to privilege, Paine was forever forced to use his wits. He personified the clever, hardworking, forever planning and scheming man of talent and ability. Restless, rootless, and versatile, Paine in his constant remaking of himself symbolized the new age.

He was born in the country town of Thetford, Norfolk, on January 29, 1737. His father, Joseph Paine, was a respected Quaker staymaker, his mother the daughter of an attorney. Tom was raised a Quaker and

---

[1]Thomas Paine, "To the People of England," *Crisis,* no. 7 (Philadelphia, November 21, 1778).

schooled in the village from his sixth to his thirteenth year. In 1750 he was apprenticed to his father, in whose shop he learned to make women's corsets and insert their steel or whalebone ribs. He ran away from home at the age of sixteen and went to sea on a merchant ship, only to be brought back by his father. Three years later he left Thetford for good.

Staymaking was his trade. In 1757 he was a journeyman staymaker in London and a year later in Dover. He then moved on to the small village of Sandwich, on the coast, where he opened a shop of his own. There he met and married, in 1759, Mary Lambert, a maid in service to the local woolen draper's wife. It was a short-lived marriage, for she died the next year. Two years later Paine abandoned staymaking and started a new career as exciseman, a customs official assigned to collect the internal duties levied on beverages, tobacco, and other household items. For the next few years he was assigned to Lincolnshire. In 1765 he lost his job because he had stamped goods that he had not in fact examined. A one-year return to staymaking in the village of Diss, in Norfolk, was followed by some months of teaching English in London and several more as tutor and itinerant preacher. Paine was reinstated in the excise service in 1768 and assigned to Lewes, in Sussex, where he remained for the next six years.

Throughout these itinerant years Paine pursued a disciplined regimen of self-education. He bought books and scientific equipment with his meager earnings and attended lectures whenever possible. After settling down in Lewes at the age of thirty-one, he turned to politics, business, and family. He became a regular at the White Hart social club, where national and parish politics were constant topics of conversation. Contemporaries later noted what a joy it was to hear young Tom Paine take on the town officers in debate after a few beers. It was a reputation that would haunt Paine all his life. In addition to politics and drink, Paine devoted a good deal of the time left over from his official excise duties to a snuff, tobacco, and grocery business. He had little head for business and the shop fared poorly. He also remarried in Lewes. His second wife was the daughter, ten years his junior, of the former owner of his shop. In April 1774 the business failed. The marriage did no better; he and his second wife separated permanently.

Paine managed one important and enduring achievement in those six years in Lewes, however. He found his first cause and he threw himself into it with the same zeal that he would later bring to the American and French revolutions. Excise officers throughout Britain were seeking higher salaries in the 1770s, and in 1772 Paine drafted a pamphlet, *The Case of the Officers of Excise*, to make their case. He went so far as to spend a winter in London distributing copies to members of

Parliament. The cause failed, too, but Paine was in print, and his appetite for social reform had been whetted. The six months in London cost him his job in the excise service, however; he was dismissed in 1774 for having left his post.

Bankrupt, separated, and jobless, Paine left Lewes in 1774 and headed for London. He had not done much with his life in his thirty-seven years. He had failed in business, in marriage, and in vocation. America tempted him. It offered a fresh start far from the drudgery of collecting taxes and making ladies' stays. Through connections made in the unsuccessful excise campaign Paine was introduced in London to Benjamin Franklin, then acting as agent for Pennsylvania. Franklin agreed to give Paine some letters of introduction to take to America. Franklin's note indicates how little he or anyone else expected of Paine. He wrote to his son-in-law, a Philadelphia merchant:

> The bearer Mr Thomas Paine is very well recommended to me, as an ingenious, worthy young man. He goes to Pennsylvania with a view of settling there. I request you give to him your best advice and countenance, as he is quite a stranger there. If you can put him in a way of obtaining employment as a clerk, or assistant tutor in a school, or assistant surveyor (of all which I think him very capable) so that he may procure a subsistence at least, till he can make acquaintance and obtain a knowledge of the country, you will do well, and much oblige your affectionate father.[2]

Paine was, according to Franklin, an "ingenious, worthy young man." "Ingenious" was a favorite word of Franklin's. In using it to describe Paine, Franklin brings us to the heart of Paine's significance for the ideology of revolution in the late eighteenth century. Ingenious Paine was self-made Paine; he had created himself, generated himself, given birth to himself. Ingenious men were authors of themselves, in contrast to men bred to privilege, in contrast to those to the manner born. The eighteenth-century revolutionary spirit was the spirit of ingenious, self-made men such as Franklin and Paine, men who assaulted the vestiges of feudalism and the hierarchical and hereditary principles by which the old order, the ancien régime, ascribed place, power, and privilege: in accordance not with talent and achievement but with birth.

Paine recognized that in this simple replacement of the privileged by the ingenious lay the revolutionary spirit of the age. He was one of the first, in fact, to see that the radical social and political transformations sought by the Franklins and the Figaros constituted what we now call a revolution. It was in the late eighteenth century that the modern sense of the word *revolution* replaced its old meaning of the rotation of a

---

[2]Quoted in D. F. Hawke, *Paine* (New York, 1974), p. 20.

heavenly body about its axis or its movement around its orbit, and by extension a change of regime in the ordinary course of events.

> What were formerly called Revolutions, were little more than a change of persons, or an alteration of local circumstances. *They* rose and fell like things of course, and had nothing in their existence or their fate that could influence beyond the spirit that produced them. But what we now see in the world, from the Revolutions of America and France, are a renovation of the natural order of things, a system of principles as universal as truth and the existence of man, and combining moral and political happiness and national prosperity.[3]

A revolution, Paine insisted, did not return a government to an earlier starting point, nor did it have anything to do with the inevitable rise and fall of dynastic fortune; it initiated a totally new system. For Paine a revolution was a sharp break from the past, as it has been for the rest of us since the late eighteenth century. "Our style and manner of thinking," he wrote, "have undergone a revolution . . . we see with other eyes; we hear with other ears, and we think with other thoughts, than those we formerly used."[4]

Returning to Paine's life, we find him in Philadelphia trying his hand at teaching. But the printer of the *Pennsylvania Magazine,* a recently arrived Scotsman, soon persuaded him to write. Throughout 1775 Paine wrote short miscellaneous pieces for Philadelphia newspapers and magazines. One was an outspoken attack on slavery. In the *Pennsylvania Magazine,* of which Paine became the editor, he wrote scientific articles as well as political ones. His interests were wide-ranging and instinctively progressive.

In November 1775 Paine began to write an essay on what seemed to him to be the logical outcome of the increasing tension between Britain and the American colonies. Ever since 1763 the colonies had been aboil with outrage over the British government's levies of taxes and customs duties, which were intended to make the colonists pay some of the huge expenses of the recently concluded French and Indian Wars (the Seven Years' War, in its European phase). Only in 1773 and 1774, however, with the Boston Tea Party and Britain's harsh reprisals, did tensions rise to the point where armed clashes developed and talk of independence could be heard. It was by no means certain even as late as 1775 that reconciliation was not possible—that is, until Paine published *Common Sense,* with its simple and dramatic call for America to declare its independence.

[3]Thomas Paine, *The Rights of Man,* ed. Henry Collins (Harmondsworth, 1975), p. 166.
[4]Thomas Paine, "Letter to Abbé Raynal on the Affairs of North America," in *Writings,* 2:105.

Other Englishmen had spoken for the Americans. The elder Pitt and Edmund Burke had urged conciliation in 1774 and 1775. But as impressive and useful as the support of such statesmen was to the Americans, it was to English radical circles that patriots in the colonies really looked for support. English radicals such as the Reverends Price and Priestley and politicians such as John Wilkes sought reform of Parliament and the English constitution in the name of the same natural and historical rights as those to which the Americans appealed. They, too, demanded representation in Parliament for subjects taxed by the crown. In 1775 John Wilkes, by then lord mayor of London, strongly defended the colonists in Parliament and was soon involved with the French playwright Beaumarchais in a clandestine arrangement by which the French sent aid to the colonies.

Radicals in England stressed the similarity of American and English grievances and predicted that should a revolution break out in America, another would follow shortly in the mother country. Efforts seemed to be afoot to set up provincial associations of English radicals to send aid to the Americans as well as to bring down the wicked tyranny that oppressed the Americans and the English alike. In October 1775 some colonists in Middletown, Connecticut, were speaking of "committees of association . . . forming throughout the Kingdom of Ireland and England," committees that would bring down George III. The king, meanwhile, was well aware of the existence of what he called "traitorous correspondence, counsels and comfort of divers wicked and desperate persons within this realm." He called upon his subjects "to use their utmost endeavours to withstand and suppress . . . rebellion, and to disclose . . . all treasons and traitorous conspiracies which they shall know to be against us, our crown and dignity."[5] The citizens of Middletown notwithstanding, no supportive insurrections materialized in England. The Americans had to proceed on their own, aided, to be sure, by the ingenious newcomer, Mr. Paine.

Paine's bold but anonymous plea for independence in *Common Sense* caught the public imagination. The pamphlet "struck a string which required but a touch to make it vibrate," a contemporary noted. "The country was ripe for independence, and only needed somebody to tell the people so, with decision, boldness and plausibility." Edmund Randolph of Virginia later noted that "the public sentiment which a few weeks before [the publication of *Common Sense*] had shuddered at the tremendous obstacles, with which independence was environed, overleaped every barrier." General Washington commented that increased hostilities, "added to the sound doctrine and unanswerable reasoning contained in the pamphlet *Common Sense*, will not leave numbers at a

[5]Quoted in Pauline Maier, *From Resistance to Revolution* (New York, 1974), pp. 257–58.

loss to decide upon the propriety of a separation." In Massachusetts a citizen noted that he believed "no pages was ever more eagerly read, nor more generally approved. People speak of it in rapturous praise." In Philadelphia the book made numerous converts. In sending the pamphlet to a friend in London a contemporary of Paine's noted that "*Common Sense* which I herewith send you is read to all ranks; and as many as read, so many became converted; though perhaps the hour before were most violent against the least idea of independence."[6]

George Trevelyan has summarized the impact of this pamphlet, which by February everyone knew was from the pen of Tom Paine: "It would be difficult to name any human composition which has had an effect at once so instant, so extended and so lasting. . . . It was pirated, parodied and imitated, and translated into the language of every country where the new republic had well-wishers. It worked nothing short of miracles and turned Tories into Whigs." It is estimated that almost 100,000 copies of *Common Sense* were sold in 1776. Translated immediately into French, with the antimonarchical passages deleted, it became an instant success in Paris. Silas Deane, the American emissary in France, noted that *Common Sense* "has a greater run, if possible, here than in America."[7]

Paine's pamphlet had influential opponents as well. John Adams, who shared Paine's views on independence, feared the radicalism of the pamphlet and the effect "so popular a pamphlet might have among the people." He replied to Paine in his *Thoughts on Government*, a draft of which he circulated among influential patriots in the spring of 1776. Adams, a much more conservative thinker than Paine, agreed with his call for separation, but he trembled at the pamphlet's popular tone and its prescription of a simple political system for independent America, with none of the complex balancing and separation of powers inherent in the British model. The system that Paine sketched in *Common Sense*, Adams wrote, was "so democratical, without any restraint or even an attempt at any equilibrium or counter poise, that it must produce confusion and every evil work."[8]

John Adams notwithstanding, far fewer Americans criticized Paine's pamphlet than praised it. Paine found himself famous when it became known that he was the author of *Common Sense*. But he was not a man to sit idly in his newly acquired literary and political glory. He enlisted in the American army in July 1776 and soon became aide-de-camp to

[6]Quoted in Hawke, *Paine*, pp. 47–48.

[7]George Trevelyan, *The American Revolution* (New York, 1903), 1:150; *The Deane Papers, 1774–1790*, New York Historical Society Collections (New York, 1887–1890), 1:214.

[8]John Adams, *The Diary and Autobiography of John Adams*, ed. Charles Francis Adams (Boston, 1850–1856), 2:330.

General Greene. For the next seven years, while the war with Britain dragged on, Paine combined his military role with journalism and produced a series of remarkable pamphlets designed to maintain American morale as well as to make the case for America in England and Europe. The first of these papers, later to be published together as *The American Crisis*, appeared on December 23, 1776, addressed to all Americans as much as to Washington and his troops huddled in the New Jersey cold. Its opening lines have remained to this day the most frequently quoted of all that Paine wrote. All America must persevere, must suffer, he wrote, for all history awaited the battle's outcome:

> These are the times that try men's souls: The summer soldier and the sunshine patriot will, in this crisis, shrink from the service of his country; but he that stands it now, deserves the love and thanks of man and woman. Tyranny, like hell, is not easily conquered; yet we have this consolation with us, that the harder the conflict, the more glorious the triumph. What we obtain too cheap, we esteem too lightly.

In addition to serving in the army and writing inspirational journalism, Paine played an active role in the politics of the war period. In 1777 he was appointed secretary to the Committee of Foreign Affairs by the Congress, and in this capacity he worked tirelessly to obtain supplies, loans, and military assistance from France. In the course of arranging this aid Paine found himself embroiled in a bitter controversy with Silas Deane. Paine contended that the supplies America received from France through the offices of the ever-present adventurer and playwright Beaumarchais were a gift and not a loan. Deane claimed they were a loan and demanded a commission. Never one to hide his anger, Paine rushed into print with a public attack on Deane, which led ultimately to Paine's dismissal from his congressional position by a coalition of Deane's supporters and others who had felt all along that the appointment of such a radical was a mistake. Gouverneur Morris, one of the latter, insisted that it was inappropriate for such a delicate position to be held by "a mere adventurer from England, without fortune, without family or connections, ignorant even of grammar."[9]

Paine was also active during these years in the local politics of Pennsylvania. He was an ardent supporter of its constitution of 1776, the most radically democratic of all the thirteen state constitutions. By 1780 Paine had, in fact, been appointed clerk of the Pennsylvania Assembly. One of his acts as clerk was to draft the legislation that provided for the gradual emancipation of slaves in that state, the first such legislation

---

[9]Quoted in Introduction to *The Complete Writings of Thomas Paine,* ed. S. Philip Foner (New York, 1945), p. xviii.

passed in the United States. During this period Paine also helped several well-to-do merchants and bankers to found the Bank of Pennsylvania. For Paine this seemed the only way to allow Pennsylvania to answer Washington's call for money to pay and provision his troops. Some people took Paine's defense of this bank against attacks by farmers and radicals in 1786 as a sign that he had moved to a more conservative position. Paine argued, however, that the bank was essential for commercial growth and would ultimately contribute to the well-being of all. He contended that the people had no right to revoke economic contracts entered into by the legislature of Pennsylvania.

Throughout this period when America was governed by the states-focused Articles of Confederation, Paine was a self-proclaimed advocate of a stronger central government, the cause that was to triumph in the Constitution of 1787. He opposed Virginia's claim to land in the West, for example, insisting that such land belonged to the nation and not to any individual state. He also urged the individual states to approve amendments to the Articles which would have granted Congress the power to levy national tariffs to support the war.

Paine's writings on the Bank of Pennsylvania as well as his opposition to unlimited state sovereignty may well have fueled speculation that he had been bought off by the merchants of Philadelphia or by the elites who called for constitutional reform. But this was not the case. His views were shaped by his vision of America as a powerful and flourishing nation, the better to represent the democratic ideal; and he was virtually penniless throughout this period of his life. Over the years most of his earnings from *Common Sense* and from his political appointments had gone to support the revolutionary army and to facilitate the printing and distribution of his writings. In 1783 Paine was forced to ask Congress for financial assistance. He received nothing from the central government. Pennsylvania, however, gave him $500 in cash, and New York gave him a farm in New Rochelle, confiscated from a loyalist.

Like many of his contemporaries in England and America— Priestley, Price, Jefferson, and Franklin, among others—Paine combined political liberalism with a dream of technological and scientific progress. The ease with which scientific and technical principles could be applied to political arguments is illustrated beautifully by the discussions of weights and forces in *Common Sense*. A project to which Paine devoted considerable energy in the 1780s was the construction of an iron bridge over the Schuylkill River in Philadelphia. His efforts to develop and finance his bridge led him in April 1787 to leave America and return to Europe. France was the place where engineering was best understood, Paine felt, and he went there hoping to find backers for the single-arch bridge he contemplated. This innocent quest brought about the third development of Paine's meteoric career. First a failure, then an American revolutionary, Paine was destined next to emerge not as a great engineer but as an English revolutionary.

English radicalism had persisted from its first explosion in the 1760s, gathering momentum with the American Revolution in the 1770s and the growth of the County Association movement in the 1780s. The French Revolution brought to a head middle-class discontent with the archaic and unreformed constitution. A new and progressive order had come with such apparent ease to the French that English reformers assumed that change in English institutions would follow quickly and painlessly. A heady faith in progress and the dawning of a new era swept through English intellectual and radical circles. Paine was in France furthering his bridge-building interests in the winter of 1789. The hero of America, he was toasted by the circles of Lafayette and Jefferson, who was then serving as American ambassador to France. From Lafayette Paine received the key to the Bastille to take back to Washington. He was present during the early stages of the French Revolution and was pleased by what he saw.

One Englishman much less pleased than Paine was Edmund Burke, whose *Reflections on the Revolution in France* appeared in 1790, while Paine was in England ostensibly still en route to America. Burke's attack on the French Jacobins and their English sympathizers was vicious. They had no reverence for the past, no respect for the church and the aristocracy, he fumed. They tore down the entire political and social edifice and built completely anew, making no effort to repair damaged parts. Government and society, Burke wrote, were fragile and complex entities, the products of generations of slow and imperceptible growth. No reformer's plans or blueprints could substitute for the experience of the ages. Burke's message was clear: English radicals should not copy their French counterparts; the aristocratic and hierarchical English past and present must be defended against its enemies. Legions of intellectuals among those enemies replied to Burke. Godwin rose to the occasion with his *Inquiry Concerning Political Justice*, Wollstonecraft with her *Vindication of the Rights of Woman;* but no other response was so powerful or so popular as Paine's *Rights of Man*, which appeared in 1791.

Once again Paine's uncomplicated, unscholarly, and unsophisticated rhetoric brought him unprecedented popular success. He was an instant hero in England, not only to the intellectual radicals among whom he moved, such as Blake, Holcroft, Horne Tooke, Godwin, and Wollstonecraft, but to hundreds of thousands of artisans and journeymen who bought *The Rights of Man* for sixpense or read it reprinted by their provincial radical association. Paine's book was more than a simple defense of the French against the obloquy heaped upon them by Burke; it was also a call to the British to replace the aristocratic institutions that Burke praised with new liberal institutions, to replace the principle of privilege and heredity with the new ideals of talent and merit. The monarchy and the aristocracy were relics of a feudal past. Republican government rested with the people and was designed to serve their interests alone. Paine's message was that every age and every generation acted for itself, set up its own political and social order to meet its own needs. "The vanity and presumption of governing beyond the grave," he wrote, "is the most ridiculous and insolent of all tyrannies. Man has no property in man; neither has any generation a property in the generations which are to follow."[10] Paine championed the rights of the living, not the hoary rights of classes privileged from time immemorial.

Paine was no hero to George III's prime minister, William Pitt the younger. Burke wrote to dissuade people from entering the radical camp; Thomas Reeves and his mob in the Church and King Society literally burned down the insurgents' camps; the role of Pitt and his agents in the repressive atmosphere of the early and middle 1790s was to arrest radicals, try them, and throw them in jail. In 1792 charges of seditious writings were lodged against Paine, and a trial was scheduled. Pitt would not allow a writer, especially one so widely read, to state freely as Paine had done in the introduction to part II of *The Rights of Man:* "If universal peace, civilization and commerce are ever to be the happy lot of man, it cannot be accomplished but by a revolution in the system of governments."[11]

The mood of England had shifted dramatically in the two years since that dawn when Wordsworth felt it was such bliss to be alive in the reflected glory of the French Revolution. On the night of November 22, 1792, a patriotic mob burned Paine's effigy at Chelmsford, Essex. A newspaper reported:

> On Wednesday last, the Effigy of that Infamous Incendiary, Tom Paine, was exhibited in this town, seated in a chair, and borne on four men's shoulders;—in one hand he held the 'Rights of Man' and under the other arm he bore a pair of stays; upon his head a mock resemblance of the Cap of Liberty, and a halter round his neck.
> On a banner carried before him, was written,
> 'Behold a Traitor!
> Who, for the base purposes of Envy, Interest and Ambition,
> Would have deluged this Happy Country in BLOOD!'[12]

[10]Paine, *Rights of Man,* pp. 63–64.
[11]Ibid., p. 183.
[12]Quoted in Audrey Williamson, *Thomas Paine* (New York, 1973), pp. 160–61.

All they had was Paine's effigy, for, sensing the justice he would receive in an England inflamed by Pitt, Burke, and Reeves, Paine had fled to France two months earlier. The trial nevertheless took place in December. Paine was found guilty in absentia of seditious libel, and outlawed from ever returning to Britain.

Paine now entered the historical stage as a French revolutionary. He was chosen delegate to the National Convention by a constituency that included Calais and Oise, and threw himself into the chaotic politics of the revolution in the critical year of internecine fighting between Girondin and Jacobin. Once again Paine was no mere bystander. In October 1792 he was appointed to the Committee of Nine to frame the new French constitution. But all was not easy for Paine in the suspicious atmosphere of Paris. He became entangled in the labyrinth of revolutionary personalities and politics. His associations with the moderate Girondins was to anger the more radical Jacobins when they came to power. Most particularly he alienated Robespierre and Marat by pleading in the Convention that Louis XVI's life be spared. No one was so criminal, he argued, as to deserve the barbarity of the death penalty. In addition, he pleaded, whatever Louis Capet's manifest faults, he had after all "aided my much-loved America to break its chains." The English-speaking Paine became further suspect when war broke out in 1793 between France and England. In October his allies the Girondins were tried and condemned. In December foreigners in the Convention were denounced. Paine was arrested and imprisoned.

For ten months of his imprisonment Paine busied himself working on *The Age of Reason*, a penetrating attack on theistic Christianity and defense of a natural deistic religion free from supernatural trappings. In it he examined the Bible and regaled his readers with its contradictions, its false chronology, and its tales of barbarism, slaughter, and inhumanity. This was not, he argued, the work of a God who presided over the natural universe. In an age of reason, he predicted, men and women would replace such superstition with science and nature. In place of a mysterious and brutal God, they would have God the first cause, the Supreme Being. While he wrote on religion, Paine also worked on his release from prison through the good offices of the new American minister, James Monroe. After some confusion about his status as American or British, Paine was released in the autumn of 1794.

One of Paine's first works after his release from prison was a stinging attack on George Washington, whom he held responsible for the length of his imprisonment. In fact, the much more likely culprit was Paine's old conservative nemesis Gouverneur Morris, who was the American minister to France before Monroe. It was he, not Washington, who apparently saw no reason to speed Paine's release. Nevertheless, Paine lashed out at Washington in rage-filled pages that denounced the president's military skills as well as his Federalist politics. Once again Paine was voicing his deepest feelings in print.

The Jacobins had fallen in the meantime, and Robespierre himself had been guillotined. Paine was reelected to the Assembly in December 1794 and sat through the following year, but he had contracted a malignant fever in prison and for the most part could summon energy enough only to write. His last years in Paris, therefore, were less political than polemical. He produced a second part of *The Age of Reason;* a political essay, *Dissertation on First Principles of Government;* and a major piece of social and economic criticism, *Agrarian Justice.*

In 1802, after ten years in France, Paine returned to America for the final and tragic chapter in his career. The America he found was very different from the Philadelphia he had known in 1774 or even in 1783. The social ferment of those years had been stilled by a federal constitution and a Federalist ideology that seemed to throw the balance of political and social power into the hands of the powerful and well-to-do. *Common Sense* was a thing of the distant past. Paine was no longer the celebrated author of the pamphlet so influential in its day. He was now the notorious author of the godless *Age of Reason,* with its assault on Christianity. Jefferson was man enough to renew his old ties with Paine, but to most Americans Paine was evil personified. The Federalist press wrote of him as a "lilly-livered sinical [sic] rogue," a "loathsome reptile," a "demi-human archbeast," an "object of disgust, of abhorrence, of absolute loathing to every decent man except the President of the United States." A Boston newspaper summed up the feelings of polite and privileged America: Paine was a "lying, drunken, brutal infidel."[13]

The aging Paine, with no family and few close friends, became cantankerous and argumentative. He turned more and more to the solace of drink and to bitter reflections on the fickleness of the public that had once acclaimed him. He had come full circle. An unknown self-educated parvenu in 1774, he had climbed the heights of world fame. Now he was once again ignored or mocked. It was a difficult fate for a man whose arrogance and conceit knew no bounds. Paine's ego was colossal. Had he not claimed that the success of *Common Sense* "was beyond anything since the invention of printing"? Had he not told a friend that his "*Rights of Man* could take the place of all the books in the world," and that "if it were in his power to demolish all the libraries in existence he would do it, so as to destroy all the errors of which they are the depository—and with the *Rights of Man* begin a new chain of

[13]Quoted in Foner, Introduction to *Complete Writings,* p. xliii.

ideas and principles"? Paine seemed to Morris "to become every hour more drunk with self-conceit."[14]

The aristocratic Morris had always held Paine in contempt as an outsider, an arriviste. In this age of gentlemen Paine stood out for more reasons than the ignorance of grammar of which Morris accused him; "he was coarse and uncouth in his manners, loathsome in his appearance, and a disgusting egoist, rejoicing mostly in talking of himself and reading the effusions of his own mind."[15]

Parvenus often seem uncouth to the established; at the same time, it is not unusual for angry newcomers to cultivate vulgarity. Paine was convinced that his was a superior talent and he lashed out at the aristocratic belief that rewards were due only to people born to privilege, to the nobility, whom he called men of "no-ability." Paine's writings are filled with defiance of and disrespect toward kings, ambassadors, titled persons, presidents, and pious priests. How better to subvert these untalented superiors in a world of polished privilege than by repudiating the pattern of civility they dictated?

Paine's last years were spent in New York City, in what is now Greenwich Village, or on his farm in New Rochelle, northeast of the city. He died on June 8, 1809. Few people saw the coffin carted from the city to the farm. Even fewer were present at the burial site, merely a handful of New Rochelle neighbors and friends. There were no dignitaries, no eulogies, no official notices of his death. The staymaker from Thetford who had shaped the world as few people have ever done, who had known and been known by many great men of America, France, and England, was laid to rest in a quiet pasture with no ceremony, no fanfare, no appreciation. The irony of such a funeral for such a man was too much for Madame de Bonneville, who had acted for several years as Paine's housekeeper, and who was one of the few mourners present. She later wrote:

> This interment was a scene to affect and to wound any sensible heart. Contemplating who it was, what man it was, that we were committing to an obscure grave on an open and disregarded bit of land, I could not help feeling most acutely. Before the earth was thrown down upon the coffin, I, placing myself at the east end of the grave, said to my son Benjamin, "stand you there, at the other end, as a witness for grateful America." Looking round me, and beholding the small group of spectators, I exclaimed, as the earth was tumbled into the grave, "Oh! Mr Paine! My son stands here as testimony of the gratitude of America, and I, for France!" This was the funeral ceremony of this great politician and philosopher![16]

[14]Quoted in David Powell, *Tom Paine: The Greatest Exile* (London, 1985), pp. 197, 206.
[15]Ibid., p. 123.
[16]Quoted in Williamson, *Thomas Paine*, p. 275.

Self-made men, not bred to families with age-old vaults entombing generations of privilege, must suffer the uncertainty of the marketplace of fame. So it was, indeed, that the irony of Paine's eclipse had not yet run its full course. Ten years after his unnoticed interment, William Cobbett, an enthusiastic convert to Paine's radicalism, decided on a whim to dig up Paine's bones and return them to England, intending to erect over this new resting place some memorial to Paine's achievement. Paine's body reached Liverpool, and it may have reached London. No one knows for sure, however, for the final indignity to Tom Paine was that Cobbett lost the bones. Such was the gratitude of America and England.

Tom Paine's *Common Sense*

The United States of America may owe its birth in part to *Common Sense*, but with the exception of a brief line in the introduction, neither America nor independence is mentioned until well along in the pamphlet. Why should it be otherwise? Paine had been in the colonies for only fourteen months when he published *Common Sense*. He was English, after all, and his Englishness breathes through every page of his remarkable work. He brings to the burning issues of Philadelphia in 1776 the theoretical mind and raging anger of English radicalism.

The pamphlet begins with an exposition of general liberal theory and gathers momentum with an attack on the English constitution in particular and on aristocratic institutions in general. Only then does it make sense to talk of the messianic mission of America, when it can be seen in its broadest theoretical context. An independent America beheld by a chastened England represents the triumph of radical principles and comes as close to the theoretical ideal sketched at the beginning of the pamphlet as any English radical could envision.

The intellectual roots of Paine's first section are the ideas of John Locke and the radical critique of English society found in the writings of English Dissenters. Their principal assumption was, as Paine put it, that human beings originally lived as isolated, free, and solitary individuals in a "state of natural liberty." A thousand reasons draw them together; in society they provide each other with essential mutual assistance. But society and government are entirely different: "The one encourages intercourse, the other creates distinctions." How, then, does government come about? What is "the design and end of government"? People voluntarily set up government, according to Paine, because it "will unavoidably happen" that these free and autonomous individuals have divergent interests that endanger one another's natural rights to life, liberty, and property. Like James Madison, Paine insists that it is because men are not angels that they submit themselves to government. Government, then, is a product of human wickedness and its sole end is to ensure "freedom and security." It should do no more than this minimal chore: protect natural rights. It has no positive function, as classical and Christian theorists had argued, no mandate to promote virtue, the good life, or the true faith. It is a necessary evil and should be involved in nothing more than what it is unfortunately required to do.[17]

Government's role, then, should be strictly limited. It should be simple and cheap. "Securing freedom and property to all men, and, above all things, the free exercise of religion," he writes, requires neither great expense nor complicated bureaucratic apparatus.[18] That liberal government is simple was a persistent theme in eighteenth-century literature. Monarchic and aristocratic government was pictured as interfering government, an overblown taxing machine that intruded too much into the private world of free individuals, preventing the realization of rights and achievements.

Paine's ideal was shared, as we have seen, by Adam Smith, whose *Wealth of Nations* that same year drew the economic conclusion implicit in their common notions. Government, Smith wrote, was to refrain from interfering "with that natural liberty, which it is the proper business of law not to infringe." Smith's and Paine's is the basic liberal vision. The social order and the economy are spontaneous and self-regulating mechanisms, peopled by rational, self-seeking individuals. It is a harmonious society, as Smith put it, where without "any intervention of law, the private interests and passions of men naturally lead them to divide and distribute the stock of every society among all the different employments carried on in it, as nearly as possible in proportion which is most agreeable to the interest of the whole society." Government, according to both Paine and Smith, merely presides passively over this self-regulating economy and spontaneously harmonious polity. At most, it is the umpire that enforces the rules, the most important of which is the right of the individual to the "secure enjoyment of the fruits of his own labour." It is "only under the shelter of the civil magistrate," Smith wrote, "that the owner of that valuable property which is acquired by the labour of many years or perhaps of many

---

[17]Thomas Paine, *Common Sense*, ed. Isaac Kramnick (Harmondsworth, 1976), pp. 65–68.

[18]Ibid., p. 68.

successive generations can sleep a single night in security."[19] Both Paine and Smith had read their Locke.

But Paine brought more than Lockean liberalism to *Common Sense;* he also brought the rage of English bourgeois radicalism. He attacked British government with all the savagery that one finds in the London defenders of John Wilkes and all the fiery passion that one finds among the Unitarian and Calvinist opponents of the Test and Corporation Acts. Nowhere in the pamphlet did Paine itemize the grievances of the colonies. He simply took it for granted that their treatment by the English government violated universal reason and natural rights. That government was an "exceedingly complex" and exceptionally corrupt engine of oppression that pressed as a weight on the energetic Americans, as it did on the virtuous English.

Armed with a vision of "mankind being originally equal in the order of creation," Paine attacked the dominance of idle monarchs and useless aristocrats in society and politics and demanded an end to all elements of traditional privileges that froze individuals into permanent inequality.[20] What mattered was not lineage but talent and merit. Here, too, the British were sinful violators of God's natural equality, as they set up luxurious and foolish men of no skills to rule over the industrious, hardworking, and unenfranchised middle class.

One is reminded how critical a component of bourgeois ideology dissenting Protestantism was by Paine's stress on scriptural, primarily Old Testament, injunctions against monarchy and aristocratic distinctions in general. The Dissenters link the leveling radicals of the seventeenth-century civil war sects, many of whose descendants had emigrated to the more egalitarian shores of America, with the many religious entrepreneurs of the late eighteenth century who threatened to leave for America if the religious exclusiveness of the Anglican establishment were not modified. The Quaker Tom Paine knew his audience well and knew that biblical arguments against the British and even an occasional anti-Catholic note would move them. He also knew that hardworking, self-reliant Americans had no love for the hereditary principle by which a man has "a right to set up his own family in perpetual preference to all others forever." Not only can few titles bear close inspection without being revealed as founded in plunder and conquest, but more critically the whole system of frozen ranks and ascribed status was "unwise," "unjust," and "unnatural."[21]

---

[19]Adam Smith, *The Wealth of Nations,* ed. Andrew Skinner (Baltimore, 1970), pp. 340, 594–95, 508, 610.
[20]Paine, *Common Sense,* p. 71.
[21]Ibid., p. 74.

After his assault on aristocratic and hereditary principles Paine turns finally to "the present state of American affairs." His interest is that of an English radical convinced that America's destiny transcends the mere livelihood of the people of the thirteen colonies in January 1776. America stands as the living repudiation of the old aristocratic and monarchic order. Her independence will strike the first blow in the battle to overthrow the ancien régime. It will help undermine the dominant position of the crown in public life. It will subvert the corrupt system of George III and the burdensome taxes of his ministers. But Paine's vision is more grandiose still. America's independence has metahistorical significance—it will usher in a new era in world history.

Paine's rhetoric in *Common Sense* reminds his readers, indeed flatters his fundamentalist readers, that the independence of the thirteen colonies is an event of momentous importance, not unlike the dramatic events told of in the Scriptures. Like the Hebrews, the Americans are invested with a messianic mission. "The cause of America is in a great measure the cause of all mankind," Paine points out. The scriptural tone is repeated when he notes that "posterity are virtually involved in the contest, and will be more or less affected, even to the end of time, by the proceedings now." American independence is a flood that will wipe clean the slate of history. America has it in her power, Paine writes, "to begin the world over again. A situation, similar to the present, hath not happened since the days of Noah until now. The birthday of a new world is at hand." Paine's flight of fancy, his sense of the American mission, reads on occasion like pure poetry. There is no more stirring passage in *Common Sense* than the evocation of America's destiny which to this day expresses an aspect of American idealism:

> O ye that love mankind! Ye that dare oppose, not only the tyranny, but the tyrant, stand forth! Every spot of the old world is over-run with oppression. Freedom hath been hunted round the globe. Asia, and Africa, have long expelled her.—Europe regards her like a stranger, and England hath given her warning to depart. O! receive the fugitive, and prepare in time an asylum for mankind.[22]

Paine is seldom concerned with the petty details of colonial grievances. He had little time to learn them in his fourteen months in Philadelphia. No recital here of confiscations or unjust taxation, massacres or ignored charter rights. What is important, he tells his readers, is that America dissociate itself from England. It is a matter not of grievances but of a world-historical mission. America's destiny is to usher in a new

[22]Ibid., pp. 63, 120, 100; Paine, *Rights of Man*, p. 181.

age, in which master staymakers will no longer chafe under stifling and oppressive aristocratic institutions.

Paine's pamphlet was no mere recital of ministerial blunders, no learned disquisition on constitutional or imperial theory. His readers were summoned to greatness, recruited for a crusade against the Old World and the values from which so many Americans had fled. America was crucial to Paine's vision of the New World order, and, not surprisingly, the fervor of the pamphlet is to be found in the first part of the work and in the passages describing America's mission. When Paine begins to argue in detail the case for separation and independence, his tone changes and he starts to talk the language of common sense.

The practical case for independence is impressive. America has no need for commercial ties with England, Paine insists. American corn will have markets enough "while eating is the custom of Europe." Reconciliation with England will, on the other hand, involve America in all the quarrels and wars of Europe. An independent and thus peaceful America will provide security for property. Under the English, property is precarious. The mother country cares for the good of America only if it serves her own interests. When these interests conflict with colonial interests, "her own interest leads her to suppress the growth of ours." Prospective emigrants will think twice about coming to America if it offers no security for property, if property is always to be at the mercy of England's interest. "The property of no man is secure in the present unbraced system of things." Nor can English rule ever really be effective, according to Paine. The thousands of miles, the months of delay make it impossible for England properly to manage the colonies.[23]

This is the common-sense case for independence. Occasionally, however, Paine lifts his pen from the commercial ledger and points to reasons for separation which transcend the mundane. Independence is, for example, historically decreed, "an event which sooner or later must arrive." Elsewhere he notes that America's continued dependence on England is "repugnant to reason, to the universal order of things."[24] This is more than the effrontery of an island ruling a continent; it is also a violation of the rights of humanity derived from God and nature.

Should some of his readers be reluctant to separate from England for lack of any alternative system of government, Paine offers his own constitutional plan. A popular convention consisting of provincial del-

[23]Paine, *Common Sense*, pp. 83, 94.
[24]Ibid., p. 89.

egates will produce a charter guaranteeing the freedom and free exercise of religion for all. The new government will be cheap, operating "with the least national expence." Property will be secure. No kings or ministerial taxes will interfere with property rights, nor will "the desperate and the discontented" sweep away the liberties of the continent. In America "the law is King."[25]

The argument turns next to America's ability to exist free of English influence and to resist English rule. Paine is convinced that America can raise a fleet and equip an impressive army. He betrays some confusion about a national debt: on one page he delights that America is free of this burden, on another he boasts that to fight a long war America will incur a huge debt and that "no nation ought to be without a debt."[26] In the realm of common sense, in fact, the pamphlet bogs down. Paine moves few readers with his excursions into finance and commerce.

Only in its final pages, when Paine again leaves common sense for rhetorical exhortation, does the pamphlet come to life once more. The attack launched by the Quaker Paine against the passivity and non-resistance of the Quaker is a warning to the American not to be "the quiet and inoffensive subject of any and every government which is set over him." He proclaims that "setting up and putting down Kings and governments" is the natural right of citizens. In a land without given ranks of authority and subordination we need not fear appearing "to be busy bodies about our station."[27] This is the angry Paine that Americans took to heart when they devoured his pamphlet. It was not Tom Paine's common sense but his rage that turned hundreds of thousands of Americans to thoughts of independence in the winter of 1776.

Paine and Bourgeois Radicalism

No one rejected the aristocratic world more enthusiastically than Thomas Paine. Burke wrote that Paine sought "to destroy in six or seven days" the feudal and chivalric past that "all the boasted wisdom of our ancestors has laboured to bring to perfection for six or seven centuries." Paine's every reflex was egalitarian. The "quixotic age of chivalric nonsense" must come to an end, and kings must be the first nonsense to go. Doing nothing more than make war and give away positions, they were paid "eight hundred thousand sterling a year and worshipped into the bargain." They were useless and unproductive:

[25]Ibid., pp. 96–98.
[26]Ibid., pp. 101–2.
[27]Ibid., pp. 127, 126.

"of more worth is one honest man to society . . . than all the crowned ruffians that ever lived."[28]

After kings, the nonsense of aristocracy must go. Is there anything more absurd than the hereditary principle, Paine asked in *The Rights of Man*, "as absurd as an hereditary mathematician, or an hereditary wiseman, and as ridiculous as an hereditary poet laureate"? What mattered was not pedigree but productivity. Society should be led by men of "talents and abilities," yet its offices of privilege and power were filled by men of "no-ability." Paine, like Wat Tyler, could scan "all the vocabulary of Adam" and find there "not such an animal as a duke or a count." The great of the world could shout Leveller at such Jacobin sentiments, and proud citizen Tom Paine would reply, "France has not levelled, it has exalted. It has put down the dwarf, to set up the man." Monarchs and aristocrats were unproductive idlers, "drones . . . who neither collect the honey, nor form the hive, but exist only for lazy enjoyment."[29]

Behind the power of these drones lay the deception that government and society were mysterious and arcane realms whose secrets were known to only a few, and that knowledge enabled the few to lead, to govern, to oppress. For Paine, "the age of fiction and political superstition, and of craft, and mystery is passing away." The "craft of courts" would be banished from popular government. "There is no place for mystery, no where for it to begin" when the people govern themselves.[30] Such a government would be simple and uncomplicated. Defenders of balanced or separated powers, such as John Adams, were criticized for their glorification of complexity, which Paine insisted was merely a return to the fiction, craft, and mystery of the predemocratic age.

In the age of mystery and "chivalric nonsense" the poor fared worst of all. To their defense, in moving and bitter language, sprang Paine, the former staymaker, in terms no less meaningful two centuries later. "The present state of civilization," he wrote in *Agrarian Justice*, "is as odious as it is unjust. It is absolutely the opposite of what it should be, and it is necessary that a revolution should be made in it. The contrast of affluence and wretchedness continually meeting and offending the eye is like dead and living bodies chained together." There is nothing wrong with riches, he adds, "provided that none be miserable in con-

---

[28]Edmund Burke, "Letters on a Regicide Peace," in *The Works of the Right Honourable Edmund Burke*, ed. Henry Bohn (London, 1877–1884), 5:395; Paine, *Rights of Man*, p. 72, and *Common Sense*, p. 83.

[29]Paine, *Rights of Man*, pp. 105, 128, 249.

[30]Thomas Paine, "Letter Addressed to the Addressers on the Late Proclamation," in *Writings*, 3:93; *Rights of Man*, p. 206.

sequence of it."[31] In *The Rights of Man* he laments that nations are "governed like animals, for the pleasure of their riders." "When . . . we see age going to the workhouse and youth to the gallows" in a civilized country, he adds, "something must be wrong in the system of government." Why is it "that scarcely any are executed but the poor"? The young should be instructed and the aged supported; instead, Paine fumes, "the resources of a country are lavished upon kings, upon courts, upon hirelings." What pathetic irony that the poor themselves "are compelled to support the fraud that oppresses them"! Paine calculates that

> the millions that are superfluously wasted upon government are more than sufficient to reform those evils. . . . Were an estimation to be made of the charge of aristocracy to a nation, it will be found nearly equal to that of supporting the poor. The Duke of Richmond alone (and there are cases similar to this) takes away as much for himself as would maintain two thousand poor and aged persons.[32]

Paine's solution is for the authorities to grant the poor £4 a year for children under fourteen, and to require that the children be schooled. For the elderly there would be, at age fifty, £6 a year, and £10 after sixty. "It is painful," Paine writes, "to see old age working itself to death, in what are called civilised countries, for daily bread." He calculates how much a poor person pays in taxes over a lifetime, and notes, in anticipation of modern social security, that "the money he shall receive after fifty years, is but little more than the legal interest of the net money he has paid." Is it more civilized, he asks, to render comfortable the old age of 140,000 people, "or that a million a year of public money be expended on any one individual, and him often of the most worthless or insignificant character"?[33]

Public education could be provided for all, according to Paine, at a cost of 10 shillings a year for 400,000 children. Women would receive 20 shillings immediately after the birth of a child, and couples 20 shillings upon marriage. Paine insisted that this was not the Christian philanthropy of traditional paternalist attitudes toward the poor. In striking anticipation of a doctrine that even two hundred years later is unacceptable to many Americans, he is certain that "this support, as already remarked, is not of the nature of a charity, but of a right." No one else in that age of revolution, none of the "sober and cautious"

---

[31]Thomas Paine, "Agrarian Justice," in *The Thomas Paine Reader*, ed. Michael Foot and Isaac Kramnick (Wandsworth, 1987), p. 486.

[32]Paine, *Rights of Man*, pp. 248–50.

[33]Ibid., pp. 264–66.

democrats who were America's founders, proclaimed as Paine did: "When it shall be said in any country in the world, my poor are happy, neither ignorance nor distress is to be found among them; my jails are empty of prisoners, my streets of beggars; the aged are not in want, the taxes are not oppressive . . . when these things can be said, then may that country boast its constitution and its government."[34]

Such sentiments endeared Paine to democratic working people. He was applauded by the artisans of Philadelphia and by the members of the London Corresponding Society in the 1790s. His writings were quoted by the Chartists and the early trade unionists in the nineteenth century. But it is a mistake to read Paine's radicalism as protosocialism, as some people have done. His merciless indictment of an aristocratic polity and society did serve the interests of the workers and touched their souls, but Paine's radical egalitarianism also served, and was bound up with, the interests of bourgeois liberals, the principal architects and beneficiaries of the destruction of "chivalric nonsense."

It detracts in no way from Paine's radicalism and his egalitarianism to note their liberal sources. Such, indeed, were the terms in which a progressive and humanitarian assault on the old order had to be couched in his age. The limitations liberalism placed on his radicalism become clearer in a later age. In his day no incompatibility was seen between his democratic ideals and his defense of individualism, property, and business enterprise. In his mind bourgeois ideals were intimately linked to an egalitarian vision of society. The stratified society of privilege and rank would be leveled in a bourgeois world of competitive individualism—a world in which political and social place would be determined by talent, merit, and hard work.

His political theory was vintage liberalism. Like Adam Smith and James Madison, Paine assumed that cooperation and fellowship were strangers to the political arena, which he saw as a place of conflict and competition. A nation, he wrote, "is composed of distinct, unconnected individuals, following various trades, employments and pursuits; continually meeting, crossing, uniting, opposing and separating from each other, as accident, interest, and circumstances shall direct."[35]

Government had no positive agency to promote justice or virtue among these clashing individuals and interests. It was merely to preside as umpire over a world where individualism was the central value. Its sole justification was its provision of a stable and secure setting for the operation of a commercial society: "Every man wishes to pursue his occupation and to enjoy the fruits of his labour and the produce of

[34]Ibid., pp. 265, 286.
[35]Thomas Paine, "Dissertations on Government: The Affairs of the Bank and Paper Money," in *Writings*, 3:137.

his property in peace and safety and with it the least possible expence. When these things are accomplished, all the objects for which government ought to be established are answered."[36]

Paine was read by artisans and the poor, but among his natural friends were also the manufacturers, who were fast destroying traditional society. Paine the entrepreneur, the salesman forever hawking his iron bridge, had great respect for the Wedgwoods, the Arkwrights, the Watts, and their counterparts in America who chartered the Bank of Pennsylvania. These enterprising individuals stood outside government; indeed, their achievements occurred in spite of government:

> It is from the enterprise and industry of the individuals and their numerous associations, in which, tritely speaking, government is neither pillow nor bolster, that these improvements have proceeded. No man thought about the government, or who was in, or who was out, when he was planning or executing those things; and all he had to hope with respect to government, was that it would let him alone.[37]

Paine's entrepreneurial friends were engaged in the same egalitarian crusade as he was. Like him, they sought a redistribution of wealth and power which would be based on equality of opportunity and which would enable individuals of real ability to replace those of "no-ability." Paine's most progressive writings, his *Agrarian Justice* and the justly celebrated Part II of *The Rights of Man*, while advocating the redistribution of much wealth to the poor, still served the greater interest of individuals of "enterprise and industry," for Paine sought to relieve them of that most burdensome of weights, the poor rates. Relief would come to both the middle and lower classes; indeed, in greater measure to the former. Equal conditions, equal results, were not his goal or theirs. The end of "chivalric nonsense" would bring not leveling but equal opportunity in a competitive individualistic society. "That property will ever be unequal is certain," he wrote in 1795. This outcome was neither unjust nor unfair, but "simply a result of industry, superiority of talents, dexterity of management, extreme frugality and fortunate opportunities." His political creed was a simple one—pure liberalism at its most radical and progressive historical moment: "Establish the Rights of Man; enthrone equality . . . let there be no privileges, no distinctions of birth, no monopolies; make safe the liberty of industry and trade, the equal distribution of family inheritances."[38]

---

[36]Paine, *Rights of Man*, p. 220.
[37]Ibid., p. 219.
[38]"Dissertations on First Principles of Government," in *Writings*, 3:268, 270.

"Society in every state is a blessing, but government even in its best state is but a necessary evil," wrote Paine in *Common Sense*.[39] With this formula Paine distills the essence of liberal social theory. From Locke through Paine and even unto Milton Friedman, the liberal sees civil society as peopled by self-reliant individuals. Such a society is benignly innocent, self-regulating, and harmonious. Government is pernicious, a threat to individual freedom; it, along with its ally the established church, is in essence tyrannical. Coercion and abuse are the fruits only of government, never of the social and economic institutions of civil society.

Poverty, for example, according to Paine, is a direct result of governmental interference with "the great laws of society," the "laws of nature and reciprocal interest." "How often is the natural propensity to society disturbed or destroyed by the operations of government?" he asks. Instead of "consolidating society, it divided it; it deprived it of its natural cohesion, and engendered discontents and disorders, which otherwise would not have existed." The "excess and inequality of taxation" have but one effect: "A great mass of the community are thrown thereby into poverty and discontent." Governments thus create the poor; the economic institutions of civil society do not. In America there is little or no government, according to Paine. Society performs there quite naturally, with "order and decorum." It follows, according to Paine, that poverty is unknown in America.[40]

Paine's preoccupation with government as the source of all coercion, his conviction that civil society is the realm of true freedom, is nowhere better revealed than in his obsession with taxation. The real threat to individual freedom, for Paine, was taxation. Taxation was the symbol of tyranny and corruption. His self-appointed mission was to defend "the cause of the poor, of the manufacturers, of the tradesmen, of the farmer, and of all those on whom the real burden of taxes fall." Monarchy, aristocracy, and taxes were all of a piece in Paine's mind. In his "Anti-Monarchical Essay" of 1792 he insisted that "whoever demands a king, demands an aristocracy, and thirty millions of taxes." Royalty "has been invented only to obtain from man excessive taxes." The turmoil of his revolutionary age was produced, he said, by taxpayers who had had enough. He wrote in 1792: "There are two distinct classes of men in the nation [England]. Those who pay taxes and those who receive and live upon the taxes. . . . When taxation is carried to excess, it cannot fail to disunite these two, and something of this is now beginning to appear."[41]

[39]Paine, *Common Sense*, p. 65.
[40]Paine, *Rights of Man*, pp. 187–88.
[41]Thomas Paine, "Prospects on the Rubicon" (1787), in *Writings*, 3:204; "Anti-Monarchical Essay," in ibid., p. 107; "Letter Addressed to the Addressers," in ibid., p. 55.

America represented for Paine "a revolution in the principles and practice of governments." He meant its repudiation of monarchy and the hereditary principle and its commitment to representative government. In addition, America represented liberal utopia, the triumph of civil society over government. Like Locke, who had claimed that "in the beginning all the world was America," Paine contended that "the case and circumstances of America present themselves as in the beginning of a world." Paine was struck by how well revolutionary America performed with little central direction: "A little more than what society naturally performed was all the government that was necessary." American government was also cheap. Paine calculated the costs of this country, ten times as large as England, as "a fortieth part of the expense which government costs in England." No vast patronage network here; no costly system of jobs. The civil list for the support of one man, the king of England, Paine noted, was "eight times greater than the whole expense of the federal government in America." What little government the Americans had was simple, local, and understandable. They put into practice Paine's maxim that the "sum of necessary government is much less than is generally thought." In America "the poor are not oppressed, the rich are not privileged. Industry is not mortified by the splendid extravagance of a court rioting at its expense. There taxes are few." The English were envious of Americans, and calls for change were coming fast, Paine wrote in 1792, because "the enormous expense of government has provoked men to think."[42]

Paine's vision of the triumph of civil society over government, of cheap and simple self-regulation over expensive and tyrannical taxation, is seen in his acknowledged preference for local over centralized government. England, he suggests, really governs itself, with constables, assizes, magistrates, and juries. It does so at virtually no expense, at no great intrusion of taxation on individual freedom. Central government, on the contrary, or "court government," while useless, is a leviathan, an overblown monster spewing forth jobs and wars. It is the "most productive machine of taxation that was ever invented."[43] Centralized monarchical government is unnecessary and a constant threat to individual liberty. Self-regulation by local society is natural, cheap, and really not government at all. It is thus no threat to individual rights or to the self-realization of talented individuals.

For the liberal Paine there is but one villain: government. Merchants, manufacturers, and bankers, even magistrates and justices of the peace are parts of benign and wholesome civil society. Traditional republican

---

[42]Paine, *Rights of Man*, pp. 147, 183–84, 189, 206; "Answer to Four Questions on the Legislative and Executive Powers," in *Writings*, 3:245; "Letter Addressed to the Addressers," p. 81.

[43]Paine, *Rights of Man*, pp. 148, 216, 234.

doctrine is turned on its head: self-serving individuals further the common good, and public government serves its own selfish and corrupt interest. "The greedy hand of government" is thrust "into every corner and crevice of industry" to grasp "the spoil of the multitude." Governments are evil incarnate. They engage in wars abroad and practice "oppression and usurpation" at home. They "exhaust the property of the world." Reversing the conventional identification of courts and the great with civility, and provincial manufacturers and artisans with vulgarity, Paine holds that governments work for the forces of barbarism, society for the forces of civilization. "Governments . . . pervert the abundance which civilised life produces to carry on the uncivilised part." Paine pushes aside what most people take to be the political issues that divide them and finds not class war but a heroic and quintessentially liberal struggle between individuals and governments: "It is not whether this or that party shall be in or not, or Whig or Tory, or high or low shall prevail; but whether man shall inherit his rights, and universal civilisation take place? Whether the fruits of his labours shall be enjoyed by himself, or consumed by the profligacy of government? Whether robbery shall be banished from courts, and wretchedness from countries?"[44]

It was inconceivable to Paine and other liberals that civil society and its institutions, economic, familial, or cultural, could be a source of coercion, of "oppression" and "usurpation." That concentrations of power and wealth in nongovernmental institutions could be the source of inequality and poverty was incompatible with the liberal urge to indict political institutions and to seek progressive change through political reform. Threats to freedom come only from the state, from churches and tyrants in the liberal world, not from factory owners, corporations, or financial manipulators.

Nowhere is this assumption more apparent than in Paine's strident defense of the Bank of Pennsylvania, a defense that alienated him from many of his Jeffersonian friends in 1786. Paine rejected the fears of the bank's radical critics, who charged that its directors would wield so much economic power that they could control the state and the government. On the contrary, Paine answered, the bank illustrated the superiority of civil institutions over state institutions. Society had little need for government; citizens could supply their internal wants and needs by private cooperative activity. Nongovernmental institutions such as the bank by definition could not be oppressive; the ability to oppress came only with the power to tax. The bank came into being, he wrote, because government was inadequately financing the war: "A

---

[44]Ibid., pp. 233–34, 239–40.

public spirit awakened itself with energy out of doors." The bank "facilitates the commerce of the country." More significant,

> if merchants by this means or farmers by similar means among themselves can mutually aid and support each other, what has the government to do with it? What right has it to expect emolument from associated industry, more than from individual industry? It would be a strange sort of government that should make it illegal for people to assist each other, or pay a tribute for doing so.[45]

The real threat to individual freedom here was not from any potential or real economic power of the bank and its directors, according to Paine. The enemy was government. Such corporate groups as the bank must be free of government. They must not be dependent on government each year for renewal of their charters: "The citizens who compose those corporations are not free; the government holds an authority and influence over them in a manner different from what it does over other citizens, and by this means destroys that equality of freedom which is the bulwark of the republic."[46]

When he wanted to, Tom Paine could summon citizens to collective action with stirring phrases: "These are the times that try men's souls; the summer soldier and the sunshine patriot will, in this crisis, shrink from the service of his country."[47] But common action and fraternity, for Paine, were found only in the angry response of a basically individualistic society to public oppression and injustice. When the stimulus of rebellion and war against tyrants and aristocrats was removed, equal individuals would pursue their own livelihoods, and seldom would they be moved to cooperate for common purposes. Equal citizens had little or no sense of community; a self-regulating society, yes, but no consciousness of solidarity, no real emotional sense of unity. Society had little need for popular power; there were, after all, no collective goals.

Democratic egalitarian citizens for Paine were free, not powerful. Power was something governments had, and with it they taxed, coerced worship, and gave jobs to incompetent second sons of elderly peers. Its abusive association with government permanently tainted power for the individualist Paine and for liberals like him. America was a beacon in an otherwise dark world because its equal citizens were free, not because its people had power. Americans did not tax, establish churches, or give away public jobs. The possibility that power

[45]Paine, "Dissertations on Government," in *Writings*, 3:166–67.
[46]Ibid., p. 172.
[47]Thomas Paine, "The American Crisis," in Foot and Kramnick, *Paine Reader*, p. 116.

might serve less abusive ends could not occur to individualistic liberals such as Paine, for free people were not united in pursuing communal ends, nor were they even interested in community. Such a linkage of power, community, and freedom could come only with democratic theorists such as Rousseau, less wedded to an individualistic vision of society. For such democrats, it was not power that corrupted but the wielders who corrupted power.

Blinded as he was by liberal social theory to extragovernmental threats to freedom, equality, and democracy, Paine still assaulted privilege more passionately than all but a precious few in the liberal camp. Few liberals were so fervently committed to democracy and egalitarianism. Should we forget the radical Paine, we need remember only how he was hated by the conservatives of his day. For John Adams he was the symbol of mischievous radicalism. Adams wrote in 1805:

> I know not whether any man in the world has had more influence on its inhabitants or affairs for the last thirty years than Tom Paine. There can be no severer satyr on the age. For such a mongrel between pig and puppy, begotten by a wild boar on a bitch wolf, never before in any age of the world was suffered by the poltroonery of mankind, to run through such a career of mischief. Call it the Age of Paine.[48]

[48]Quoted in Hawke, *Paine*, p. 7.

PART TWO

REPUBLICAN REVISIONISM AND ANGLO-AMERICAN IDEOLOGY

CHAPTER 6

Republican Revisionism Revisited

F OR OVER a hundred years the world of scholarship agreed that Locke was the patron saint of Anglo-American ideology in the eighteenth century and that liberalism, with its stress on individuality and private rights, was the dominant ideal in that enlightened and revolutionary era. To the Victorian Leslie Stephen it was self-evident that "Locke expounded the Principles of the Revolution of 1688 and his writings became the political bible of the following century." To the more recent Harold Laski it was equally clear that Lockean liberalism dominated English political thought in the eighteenth century. Colonial Americans, it was assumed, were also schooled on Locke and became, in fact, his most self-conscious disciples. Thus for Carl Becker "the lineage is direct, Jefferson copied Locke," and for Merle Curti the "Great Mr. Locke" was "America's philosopher." Louis Hartz has summarized this scholarly consensus. "Locke," he wrote in 1955, "dominates American political thought as no thinker anywhere dominates the political thought of a nation."[1]

Dethroning Locke

Revisionism comes to all orthodoxies, and this received wisdom has been assaulted with a vengeance. Over the last few decades eigh-

[1] Leslie Stephen, *A History of English Thought in the Eighteenth Century,* Harbinger ed. (New York, 1962), 2:114; Harold Laski, *The Rise of European Liberalism* (New York, 1936) and *Political Thought in England from Locke to Bentham* (New York, 1920); Carl Becker, *The Declaration of Independence: A Study in the History of Political Ideas* (New York, 1922), p. 79; Merle Curti, "The Great Mr. Locke, America's Philosopher, 1783–1861," *Huntington Library Bulletin,* no. 11 (1939), pp. 107–51; and Louis Hartz, *The Liberal Tradition in America* (New York, 1955), p. 140.

teenth-century Anglo-American social and political thought has undergone a fundamental reinterpretation. To a great extent, the liberal individualist heritage preoccupied with private rights has been replaced by a republican tradition emphasizing citizenship and public participation, a tradition with roots deep in the classical and Renaissance worlds. Fundamental to this republican revisionism has been a rethinking of the hegemony of Locke. As Stanley N. Katz has noted, "*Locke et praetera nihil*, it now appears, will no longer do as a motto for the study of eighteenth century Anglo-American political thought. The state of nature, doctrine of consent, and theory of natural rights were not as important before 1776 as the ideas of mixed government, separation of powers and a balanced constitution. We are only in the opening phases of a major reassessment of our constitutional heritage."[2] Replacing Locke as the vital center of political discourse in the century is the "country," opposition ideology of the Walpole years. These ideas are themselves read as part of a larger tradition—the civic humanist, or republican, tradition.

The revisionist school makes two distinct claims. The first deemphasizes the role of Lockean ideas in the early eighteenth century. The second questions Locke's influence on the entire century, including the radicalism of post-Wilkes England and the ideology of the American founding. In its first claim, revisionism is on solid ground. Locke's influence early in the century deserves the deemphasis it has received. In its second claim, however, the revisionist position is much more dubious; here it has gone too far.

The republican revisionist reading has replaced Lockean liberalism with civic humanism. Part Aristotle, part Cicero, part Machiavelli, civic humanism conceives of human beings as political animals who realize themselves only through participation in public life, through active citizenship in a republic. The virtuous person is concerned primarily with the public good, *res publica*, or commonweal, not with private or selfish ends. Seventeenth-century writers such as James Harrington and Algernon Sidney adapted this tradition, especially under the influence of Machiavelli (according to J. G. A. Pocock),[3] to a specifically

[2]Stanley N. Katz, "The Origins of American Constitutional Thought," *Perspectives in American History* 3 (1969): 474. Also see Robert E. Shalhope, "Toward a Republican Synthesis: The Emergence of an Understanding of Republicanism in American Historiography," *William and Mary Quarterly* 29 (1972): 49–80.

[3]For J. G. A. Pocock's arguments, see his *Machiavellian Moment: Florentine Political Thought and the Atlantic Republican Tradition* (Princeton, 1975); "Virtue and Commerce in the Eighteenth Century," *Journal of Interdisciplinary History* 3 (1972): 119–34; *Politics, Language, and Time: Essays on Political Thought and History* (New York, 1971); and "Early Modern Capitalism—The Augustan Perception," in *Feudalism, Capitalism, and Beyond*, ed. Eugene Kamenka and R. S. Neale (Canberra, 1975).

English context. This significantly English variant of civic humanism, "neo-Machiavellianism" or "neo-Harringtonianism," became, through the writings of such early eighteenth-century English Augustans as Charles Davenant, John Trenchard, Thomas Gordon, and especially Henry St. John, Viscount Bolingbroke, the ideological core of the "country" ideology that confronted Walpole and his "court" faction. Bolingbroke provided a crucial link in this intellectual chain by associating corruption with social and political themes, a critical concept in the language of eighteenth-century politics.[4] Much richer than simple venality or fraud, the concept is enveloped by the Machiavellian image of historical change: corruption is the absence of civic virtue. The corrupt are preoccupied with themselves and oblivious of the public good. Such failure of moral personality and such degeneration from the fundamental commitment to public life fuel the decline of states and can be remedied only through periodic revitalization. Calls for a return to the original and pristine commitment to civic virtue, for *ridurre ai principii* (Machiavelli's phrase), form the response to corruption.

Bolingbroke's achievement was to appropriate this republican and Machiavellian language and apply it to the social and economic tensions developing in Augustan England over the rise of government credit, public debt, and central banking as well as to political issues, such as Walpole's control of Parliament through patronage and the concern over standing armies. Bolingbroke deployed the themes of independence and dependence, so critical to the republican tradition (the former essential to any commitment to the public good), over a social map of independent country proprietors opposed to placemen and stock jobbers and a political map of a free Parliament opposed to a despotic court. In the process Bolingbroke's rejection of egalitarianism as well as of commercialism gave this eighteenth-century republican-country tradition its socially conservative and nostalgic quality. But this court-country reading eschews class analysis, at least in terms of the conventional dichotomy of progressive bourgeoisie and reactionary aristocracy. Its categories and frames of reference are older and more complicated.

To a great extent, the innovative scholarship of J. G. A. Pocock has shaped this new way of looking at English political thought. His writings on Harrington and his magisterial *Machiavellian Moment* (1975) have made the concept of civic humanism a strikingly useful tool with which to explore the political mind of late seventeenth- and early eighteenth-century England. The more ambitious extension of the reign of

---

[4]See my *Bolingbroke and His Circle: The Politics of Nostalgia in the Age of Walpole* (Cambridge, Mass., 1968).

civic humanism, however, is questionable. In the hands of Pocock and others, such as John Murrin and Lance Banning, this insightful reading of early eighteenth-century politics through Bolingbroke's dichotomy of virtuous country and corrupt court does not stop with Augustan England.[5] It becomes the organizing paradigm for the language of political thought in England as well as America throughout the century. As a result, the revisionists also insist on the irrelevance of class in political discourse, which in conventional progressive or liberal scholarship has been linked to the emergence of the Industrial Revolution in the later decades of the century. Analyses of the late eighteenth century which refer to class consciousness or conflicting class ideologies or which use such concepts as aristocracy, capitalism, feudalism, and bourgeoisie are thus dismissed by republican scholarship as simplistic and proleptic. Challenges to the "primacy" or "omnipresence" of "civic ideology," of "Aristotelian and civic humanist values," sprang throughout the century not from "simple bourgeois ideology" or from visions of "economic" or "capitalist man" but from a court ideology, part commercial and part elite, that was not representative of a class in any conventional sense. There is no dialectical tension between middle and upper classes. To claim that such tension existed is to engage in "much distortion of history." There is for Pocock only one proper dialectical reading, which sees everywhere "the dialectic of virtue and commerce." All of Anglo-American political thought in the eighteenth century involves, then, "a continuation, larger and more irreconcilable, of that Augustan debate."[6]

Locke and possessive individualism in this scheme have obviously had to go.[7] And a chorus of distinguished scholars has joined John Dunn in deemphasizing the importance of Locke throughout eighteenth-century Anglo-American thought. "Eighteenth-century English political thought," according to Gordon Wood, "perhaps owed more to Machiavelli and Montesquieu than it did to Locke." Indeed, Bernard Bailyn has persuasively argued that "the effective triggering convictions that lay behind the [American] Revolution were derived not from common Lockean generalities but from the specific fears and formula-

---

[5]See John Murrin, "The Great Inversion, or Court versus Country: A Comparison of the Revolution Settlements in England (1688–1721) and America (1776–1816)," in *Three British Revolutions: 1641, 1688, 1776*, ed. J. G. A. Pocock (Princeton, 1980), pp. 368–455; and Lance Banning, *The Jeffersonian Persuasion: Evolution of a Party Ideology* (Ithaca, N.Y., 1978).

[6]Pocock, "Virtue and Commerce," pp. 130–34.

[7]The term "possessive individualism" is, of course, C. B. Macpherson's in *The Political Theory of Possessive Individualism: From Hobbes to Locke* (Oxford, 1962).

tions of the radical publicists and opposition politicians of early eighteenth-century England."[8]

J. G. A. Pocock has been the most insistent in repudiating Locke's influence on the entire century. He has seen the history of political thought as "dominated by a fiction of Locke," whose importance "has been wildly distorted." He and others are engaged in what he has called "a shattering demolition of [Locke's] myth." Their concern is to prove that the predominant language of politics for the eighteenth century, even for its radicals, "is one of virtue, corruption and reform, which is Machiavellian, classical and Aristotelian, and in which Locke himself did not figure." We have come, Pocock has insisted, to the end of "the image of a monolithically Lockean eighteenth century," the end of "a convention of writing as if Locke dominated the thought of the eighteenth century, and imposed on it a pattern of liberal individualism." Indeed, he concludes, to understand the debates of eighteenth-century politics does "not necessitate reference to Locke at all."[9]

Pocock has applied this revisionist verdict on Locke to an alternative reading of America and its founding. American political culture has been haunted by myths, the most mistaken of which is the role of Locke as "the patron saint of American values." The proper interpretation "stresses Machiavelli at the expense of Locke." The Revolution was, Pocock writes, "the last great act of the Renaissance . . . emerging from a line of thought which staked everything on a positive and civic concept of the individual's virtue." The Revolution was a Machiavellian *rinnovazionne* in a new world, "a republican commitment to the renovation of virtue." America was born in a "dread of modernity," according to Pocock. In its early years "the country ideology ran riot." The debate over Hamilton's economic policies in the 1790s "was a replay of court-country debates seventy and a hundred years earlier." In Jefferson's polemics, however, "the spirit of Bolingbroke stalked on every page." John Murrin concurs. The Jeffersonians, he writes, "like an English country opposition . . . idealized the past more than the future and feared significant change, especially major economic change, as corruption and degeneration."[10] From this perspective, Garry Wills's book on

---

[8]John Dunn, "The Politics of Locke in England and America in the Eighteenth Century," in *John Locke: Problems and Perspectives,* ed. John W. Yolton (Cambridge, Eng., 1969), pp. 45–80; Gordon Wood, *The Creation of the American Republic* (New York, 1972), p. 29; and Bernard Bailyn, *The Origins of American Politics* (New York, 1972), pp. ix–x, 56–58. Also see Bailyn's *Ideological Origins of the American Revolution* (Cambridge, Mass., 1976).

[9]Pocock, *Machiavellian Moment,* p. 424; "Virtue and Commerce," pp. 124, 127, 129; and *Politics, Language, and Time,* p. 144.

[10]Pocock, *Machiavellian Moment,* pp. 469, 529, 548, and "Virtue and Commerce," pp. 130–31, 134; and Murrin, "Great Inversion," p. 406.

Jefferson's Declaration of Independence is welcome.[11] Wills, too, gets rid of Locke; behind Jefferson he sees not Locke but Francis Hutcheson and the Scottish Enlightenment.

Perhaps the best summary of this more ambitious school of revisionist scholarship in making the claim for both the early and late eighteenth century can be found in Donald Winch's work on Adam Smith. Winch sets out to rescue Smith from the scholars who have misread him as a theorist of individualism and liberal capitalism, from those whose scholarship Winch has labeled Marxist and Whig—"those who come to bury capitalism as well as those who come to praise it." To read Smith in this way is to disregard "the remarkable body of revisionist literature" that depicts the entire eighteenth century as free of Locke and free of the bourgeoisie:

> Those political theorists and historians who are committed, for one pre-sent-minded reason or another, to the enterprise of constructing a genealogy of liberal or bourgeois individualism which is continuous from Locke to the nineteenth century and beyond have suffered a major casualty as a result of recent research on eighteenth century political thought and ideology. That casualty is no less a figure than Locke himself, the "founder" of liberal constitutionalism.

Winch then describes "the remarkable historiographic upheaval . . . which converges on the conclusion that Locke's *Two Treatises*[sic] was of strictly limited significance to many of the most lively as well as profound developments which took place in Anglo-American political thought during the eighteenth century." Nor were the traditional issues of liberalism important. Political thought in the period, Winch concludes, "owed far less to Locke's concern with questions of obligation, original contract, and natural rights than was originally thought to be the case."[12]

The "historiographic upheaval" has indeed been "remarkable." Republican revisionism has sharpened our perceptions of the ideological currents operating in the eighteenth century, but its two claims must remain distinct. The revisionists have informed us of the continuity and hold of older political and cultural ideals, competing with a Lockean emphasis on natural rights and individualism, on the early eighteenth-century mind. But in its efforts to free the entire eighteenth century of Locke, of socioeconomic radicalism, and of bourgeois liberalism, this new broom has also swept away much that is truth.

[11]Garry Wills, *Inventing America: Jefferson's Declaration of Independence* (New York, 1978).
[12]Donald Winch, *Adam Smith's Politics: An Essay in Historiographic Revision* (Cambridge, Eng., 1978), pp. 28, 36, 41, 54, 180.

There are serious difficulties in applying the model of court and country or the dialectic of virtue and commerce to Anglo-American politics after 1760. These difficulties derive from the basic revisionist assumption that such concepts as corruption and virtue had a continuous meaning throughout the century. The nostalgia, hierarchism, and anticommercialism of the earlier part of the century cannot be so easily read into the later years of the century. The writings and politics of British reformers from 1760 to 1800 illustrate the problematic nature of such a reading. Is Locke irrelevant to the reformers' radicalism? Are their ideological paradigms republicanism and civic humanism? Is theirs the politics of nostalgia untainted by bourgeois liberal or individualist ideals?

"Celebrated Assertions of Mr. Locke"

The verdict of recent republican scholarship is that Locke and progressive liberal ideals were in fact unimportant in the agitation for parliamentary reform in Britain from the 1760s through the French Revolution. Relying heavily on the work of such British historians as Herbert Butterfield and Ian Christie, the revisionists emphasize the nostalgic and even reactionary quality of the reform movement.[13] What the reformers were seeking was lost historical rights, Anglo-Saxon rights. Alternatively, the reformers were country ideologues concerned only with mixed government and an independent House of Commons. Republican scholarship denies that any social or economic motives or grievances were at work among the reformers, either democratic or bourgeois. Continuity and nostalgia are the key, not radical appeals to abstractions such as human or natural rights. In such a configuration of ideas Locke is seldom to be found.

For Pocock, the reform movement was simply civic humanism and country rage. "Georgian radicals in the era of the Revolutionary War and its aftermath used a language indistinguishable from that of their American peers." That same language of corruption and virtue was being used "against the ministries of George III" by the foes of Bute "and the friends of Wilkes." This was no casual flirtation with the language of civic humanism by the radicals. Pocock has noted that the country ideology of republican virtue which the Americans adopted "had originated in England and was still very much in use there. In the

---

[13]See Herbert Butterfield, *George III, Lord North, and the People, 1779–80* (London, 1949), esp. pp. 229–56, 337–52; Ian Christie, *Myth and Reality in Late Eighteenth-Century British Politics and Other Papers* (London, 1970); Introduction to G. S. Vetch, *The Genesis of Parliamentary Reform* (London, 1964); and *Wilkes, Wyvill, and Reform* (London, 1962).

mind of James Burgh, John Cartwright, or Richard Price, it was as obsessive and terrifying as in any American mind." It was the "conceptual framework" behind "radical demands for parliamentary and franchise reform." In *The Machiavellian Moment*, Pocock describes Christopher Wyvill, Price, and Cartwright as using "a vocabulary of corruption and renovation little different from that of their American contemporaries." In an earlier article Pocock placed Burgh, Wilkes, the Yorkshire movement, the Society for Constitutional Information, and, *miracula mirabilis*, John Thelwall in the tradition of country and civic humanism. They are "key points in the long continuous history of a political language and its concepts." The terminology and ideas of country ideology, Pocock has concluded, "were extensively borrowed by the radical left when one began to appear in George III's reign."[14]

This backward-looking reading of British reform is shared by Gordon Wood, who has also described Price, Burgh, and even Paine as members of this camp of virtue-obsessed republicans.[15] Bernard Bailyn has agreed, as we have seen. "The leaders of the [American] Revolutionary movement were radicals—but they were eighteenth-century radicals concerned, like the eighteenth-century English radicals, not with the need to recast the social order nor with the problems of economic inequality and the injustice of stratified societies but with the need to purify a corrupt constitution and fight off the apparent growth of prerogative power."[16] But this is not my reading of these radicals and of the British reformers in general between 1760 and the French Revolution. Locke was very much alive and well in their arguments.

The radicals of the later eighteenth century, both English and American, were much more likely to base their arguments on natural rights than on historical rights; they were preoccupied less with nostalgic country concerns than with very modern socioeconomic grievances. They shared a deeply felt sense that the unreformed British constitution failed to serve the interests of the talented and hardworking middle class.[17] Locke was, indeed, unimportant to the earlier Augustan country ideology. Its basic hierarchical commitment, in fact, led Bolingbroke to repudiate all notions of the state of nature, with its

---

[14]Pocock, "Virtue and Commerce," pp. 133, 122; *Machiavellian Moment*, pp. 507, 547; and *Politics, Language, and Time*, pp. 133, 145–46. Also see Iain Hampshire-Monk, "Civic Humanism and Parliamentary Reform: The Case of the Society of the Friends of the People," *Journal of British Studies* 18 (1978–79): 70–89.

[15]Wood, *Creation of the American Republic*, pp. 21, 23, 36, 47, 56–57, 92, 100.

[16]Bailyn, *Ideological Origins of the American Revolution*, p. 283.

[17]This is by no means to take the case as far as Staughton Lynd did in his *Intellectual Origins of American Radicalism* (New York, 1969). He was quite correct in stressing the social content of the English radicals read by Americans during the revolutionary era but quite mistaken in reading this content as critical of private property.

egalitarian overtones.[18] But two great historical developments operated to change the context of ideological discourse, especially among the radicals. The 1760s represent the crucial turning point. The concerns of the earlier part of the century—the mixed constitution, annual Parliaments, the independent Commons, anti-place legislation, and the standing army controversy—were shunted aside. America and the crisis over taxation introduced new noncountry issues into politics. The taxation controversy raised to the center of debate the issue of representation, which brought to the fore basic concerns about the origins of government and of authority in general. Taxation was the curse of all, yet few were enfranchised. An emphasis on taxation flew in the face of ideas of virtual representation and expanded the notion of property beyond landed wealth or freehold. This emphasis on movable property, as John Brewer has noted, enabled radicals such as Burgh and Cartwright to extend "the debate about parliamentary reform far beyond its previous confines."[19] It transcended the paradigms of country ideology to more class-based categories.

[18]Kramnick, *Bolingbroke and His Circle*, pp. 95–106. Also see my "An Augustan Reply to Locke: Bolingbroke on Natural Law and the Origin of Government," *Political Science Quarterly* 82 (1967): 571–94.

[19]As should be clear, I share this point of view with John Brewer, who has argued it brilliantly in his *Party Ideology and Popular Politics at the Accession of George III* (Cambridge, Eng., 1977), p. 255. This chapter does not address, except in passing, the question of Locke in America during these years. Other scholars, such as Joyce Appleby and Ronald Hamowy, have been questioning republican revisionism on that score. It might be noted here, however, that if Locke was indeed alive and well in the circles of British reform during these later eighteenth-century years, there must be a high presumption that he thrived in America too, if only because such writers as Burgh, Price, and Priestley were the staple reading of Americans in the revolutionary era. See Joyce Appleby, "The Social Origins of American Revolutionary Ideology," *Journal of American History* 64 (1977–78): 935–58, and "What Is Still American in the Political Philosophy of Thomas Jefferson?" *William and Mary Quarterly* 39 (1982): 287–309; and Ronald Hamowy, "Jefferson and Scottish Enlightenment: A Critique of Garry Wills' *Inventing America*," *William and Mary Quarterly* 36 (1979): 503–23. Also see earlier investigations of the relation between English and American radical thought: Thad W. Tate, "The Social Contract in America, 1774–1787: Revolutionary Theory as a Conservative Instrument," *William and Mary Quarterly* 22 (1965): 375–91; and Curti, "Great Mr. Locke," pp. 107–51. For the vogue of English radicals in America, see the writings of Bailyn and Wood. Also see Lynd, *Intellectual Origins of American Radicalism;* Jack P. Greene, "Political Mimesis: A Consideration of the Historical and Cultural Roots of Legislative Behavior in the British Colonies in the Eighteenth Century," *American Historical Review* 75 (1969–70): 337–60; Pauline Maier, *From Resistance to Revolution: Colonial Radicals and the Development of American Opposition to Britain, 1765–1776* (New York, 1972); Oscar Handlin and Mary Handlin, "James Burgh and American Revolutionary Theory," *Proceedings of the Massachusetts Historical Society* 73 (1963): 38–57; Edmund S. Morgan, "Slavery and Freedom: The American Paradox," *Journal of American History* 59 (1972–73): 5–29; Nicholas Hans, "Franklin, Jefferson, and the English Radicals at the End of the Eighteenth Century," *Proceedings of the American Philosophical Society* 98 (1954): 406–22; H. Trevor Colburn, *The Lamp of Experience: Whig History and the Intellectual Origins of the American Revolution* (Chapel Hill, N.C., 1965); and Colin Bonwick, *English Radicals and the American Revolution* (Chapel Hill, N.C., 1977).

The American crisis coincided with a second crucial development, the early years of the Industrial Revolution and the emergence of a new middle-class radicalism. The first decades of industrialization in England saw, as D. E. C. Eversley has calculated, a greatly expanding middling level of English society, families with an income between £50 and £400. This "free, mobile, prudent section of the population" was turning to politics.[20] These owners of small and movable property, as well as the new entrepreneurs like Wedgwood and Wilkinson, felt excluded from a political process that affected them daily in their credit transactions, in their tax burden, and in the proliferation of intrusive statute law.[21]

This is not to dismiss out of hand the existence of lingering country content in the radical ideology of Wilkes, Burgh, Cartwright, or John Sawbridge. It had been, after all, the ideological reflex of the excluded for a century. Calls for frequent elections and a reformed suffrage along with attacks on placemen were often still uttered in the Machiavellian language of corruption, restoration of first principles, and historical analogies with Rome. But beneath the familiar surface of the new radicalism that began to emerge during the 1760s were different themes. The new radicalism went beyond praise of wise and virtuous landed MPs independent of both the crown and constituent pressure. It went beyond the Rockingham Whigs' sense that all was well with the political system and that only a change of leadership in which men of virtue replaced wicked men was needed to end "the present discontents." The new radicalism had a new dimension, the conviction that the people now excluded—the urban and commercial interests—wanted in, wanted to be represented in Parliament and wanted their MPs to be their spokesmen, serving their interests, not serving as wise men independent of both court and the people who elected them. Thus, in their anger, the new radicals turned on *both* the landed classes and the court government.

Precisely in this context of a critical shift in the nature and aims of the opposition, Lockean ideas made a dramatic and decisive comeback in the 1760s and 1770s. In Locke far more than in Bolingbroke and his ilk, the unenfranchised middle class and especially the Protestant Dissenters found intellectual authority and legitimacy for their radical demands. Locke's ideas, reflecting the revolutionary upheavals of the previous century, spoke more directly to a Burgh, a Paine, or a Priestley than did the nostalgia of a St. John, a Pope, or a Swift.

---

[20] D. E. C. Eversley, "The Home Market and Economic Growth in England, 1750–1780," in *Land, Labour, and Population in the Industrial Revolution: Essays Presented to J. D. Chambers*, ed. E. C. Jones and G. E. Mingay (London, 1967), pp. 206–59.

[21] See John Brewer, "English Radicalism in the Age of George III," in Pocock, *Three British Revolutions*, pp. 334–36.

The revival of Lockean influence is apparent in the pamphlet that contained the first important call for the reform of Parliament. The anonymous *Reflexions on Representation in Parliament* was published in 1766. Although the pamphlet ostensibly provides a sympathetic reading of James Otis's arguments on taxation and representation, over its defense of the colonies and its plea for reform of the suffrage hovers the spirit of John Locke. The author expounds the principles of the British constitution, offering an idea "of what it was in its original purity." This discourse could well have represented the civic humanist quest for first principles or the search for lost Anglo-Saxon rights, but it represented instead a search for "principles of truth and reason." At the heart of these principles is the "cession which every man, on entering into civil government makes of some of his natural rights, to enjoy the rest in greater security." On the principles of "equity," the author demands an "equal representation in Commons." (The Saxon past is cited, but the justification for "equal" representation is the ahistorical "principle of equity.") Representation is a "a question of right." The pamphlet ends with a direct invocation of "the celebrated assertions of Mr. Locke's . . . that there remains still inherent in the people a supreme power to remove or alter the legislature, when they find the legislative act contrary to the trust reposed in them; for when such trust is abused it is thereby forfeited and devolves to those who gave it."[22]

Locke, whose principles "so favour the natural rights of mankind," is central to this opening salvo in the campaign to reform Parliament, and his use here set the pattern for the next thirty years. His notion of contract, of governors as trustees, subject to dismissal if they forfeited this trust, was the intellectual weaponry used in the assault on the unreformed Commons. This is abundantly clear in Wilkes's agitation and its offshoot, the Society of the Suporters of the Bill of Rights. By 1771 the society, led by Horne Tooke, had moved from merely defending Wilkes's right to a seat in Commons to offering a comprehensive program for parliamentary reform. Central to that program was an oath to be required of all parliamentary candidates that they "endeavour to obtain a more fair and equal representation of the people." Echoes of the 1766 pamplet are clear. "Equitable and equal" became "fair and equal." John Wilkes moved in the House of Commons on March 21, 1776, "that leave be given to bring in a bill, for a just and equal representation of the people of England in Parliament." In his speech he cited "the present unfair and inadequate state of the representation of the people in Parliament. It has now become so partial and unequal from the lapse of

---

[22]*Reflextions on Representation in Parliament* (London, 1766), pp. 4, 6–7.
[23]Quoted in Society for Constitutional Information, *Minutes of a Meeting on Friday 29th of March 1782* (London, 1782), pp. 11–12. For Wilkes, see Christie, *Wilkes, Wyvill, and Reform;* and Brewer, *Party Ideology and Popular Politics,* chap. 9.

time."[23] The language used in Wilkes's bill is important. For the next thirty years the reform movement used the phrases "fair and equal representation" and "just and equal representation." This abstract language of reason and nature does not derive from specific calculations from the Saxon past, and the principal author of these abstract phrases is none other than John Locke.

In a most striking case of historical oversight, few who have written on this period have noted that this formulation, so central to reform politics and writing for the remainder of the eighteenth century, is lifted directly from Locke, who in paragraphs 157 and 158 of *"The Second Treatise of Government* wrote:

> It often comes to pass that in government where part of the legislative consists of representatives chosen by the people that by tract of time this representation becomes very unequal and disproportionate to the reasons it was at first established. . . . For it being the interest as well as intention of the people to have a fair and equal representative, whoever brings it nearest to that is an undoubted friend to and establisher of the government and cannot miss the consent and approbation of the community.[24]

The key phrase of the reform movement was Locke's of nearly one hundred years earlier. Scholars' failure to note the textual derivation from Locke is all the more striking since most eighteenth-century users of the "fair and equal" demand cited Locke as their authority. So it was that Wilkes in his speech of March 21, 1776, noted that "this evil has been complained of by some of the wisest patriots our country has produced. I shall beg leave to give that close reasoner, Mr. Locke's ideas in his own words. . . . [He then read paragraphs 157 and 158.] After so great an authority as that of Mr. Locke, I shall not be treated on this occasion as a mere visionary."[25]

Even more important than this textual linkage between Locke and the reformers, however, is the far deeper theoretical bond the reformers constructed between themselves and such Lockean themes as contract, state of nature, natural rights, and government as a trust in all of their writing on taxation and representation. This bond becomes evident when the focus is shifted from Wilkes to more respectable and learned reformers. But Wilkes and his supporters both in London and in the provinces—by and large merchants, manufacturers, and entrepreneurs—forged the link for the enduring character of reform agi-

---

[24]John Locke, *The Second Treatise of Government* (New York, 1952), paras. 157–58. This link between Locke and the reformers in the late eighteenth century is not developed by either J. R. Pole or John Cannon; see Pole's *Political Representation in England and the Origins of the American Republic* (London, 1966) and Cannon's *Parliamentary Reform, 1640–1832* (Cambridge, Eng., 1973).

[25]Society for Constitutional Information, *Minutes*, pp. 14–15.

tation: its antiaristocratic, middle-class bias. Wilkes the fool, Wilkes the court jester, was a living repudiation of hierarchical piety and the due subordination of rank and degree.[26]

John Cartwright, the grand old man of British reform, illustrates how Lockean ideas, not the more hierarchical views of country ideology, were at the heart of the reform movement. In 1776 he noted that "the all wise Creator hath likewise made men by nature equal as well as free. . . . None are set above others prior to mutual agreement." Freedom implies choice and equality excludes degrees of freedom. "All the commons have a right to vote in the elections of those who are to be the guardians of their lives and liberties . . . , and no man shall be taxed but with his own consent, given either by himself or his representative in Parliament." The antiaristocratic flavor of the reform movement is apparent in Cartwright, too: "What right has 1/7 of the people who wear laced coats and eat white bread to tell 6/7 who have plain coats and eat brown bread that they have no right to interfere in the election . . . because their want of riches deprived them of many other indulgences, enjoyed by the wearers of laced coats and eaters of white bread?" The source of his arguments is nature, not history. Cartwright insisted that "mankind universally have in all ages had the same unalienable rights to liberty. . . . No charters, exclusions, prescriptions can add to or diminish this right."[27]

The middle years of the 1770s saw an outpouring of radical texts in England. The crisis with the colonies did indeed raise fundamental questions of authority and obligation, which the civic humanist reading of the period sees as secondary to themes of corruption and virtue. In 1774, for example, James Burgh's three-volume *Political Disquisitions* appeared. From 1747 to 1771 Burgh ran the influential Dissenter academy at Newington Green, where he taught legions of Dissenter youth. His huge tome schooled more generations of British radicals and their American cousins. Republican scholars have made much of Burgh's writings in constructing a case for nostalgic, civic humanist, country ideology at the heart of the reform movement.[28] They have good reason for this claim. In his three volumes Burgh often cited Bolingbroke, *Cato's Letters,* and even Machiavelli. He also wrote at great length about an independent Commons, placemen, corruption, standing armies, annual Parliaments, and lost Saxon rights. But there is much more to Burgh than this simple dependence on mid-eighteenth-century argu-

[26]For this picture of Wilkes, see Brewer, *Party Ideology and Popular Politics,* pp. 197–99.

[27]John Cartwright, *The Legislative Rights of the Communality Vindicated; or, Take Your Choice* (London, 1776), pp. 1–2, 31, 27, 116–17.

[28]See, in addition to the literature cited in n. 19 above, Carla H. Hay, "The Making of a Radical: The Case of James Burgh," *Journal of British Studies* 18 (1978–79): 90–118.

ments and formulas, and it has generally been overlooked. He is very much in the Lockean individualist tradition, and he injected into the reform movement not only a strong dose of Locke but also a good deal of the bitter middle-class resentment of the aristocratic quality of the British constitution, as we shall see in the next chapter.

Burgh began and ended his massive work with Locke. At the outset he provided a declaration of his political beliefs which is pure Locke. Authority originates from the people, who, he suggested, receive that power back when their governors betray their trust. When Burgh turned to the inadequate state of representation in Britain early in volume 1, the first authority cited on "the monstrous inequality of parliamentary representation" is Locke. Three volumes later, in concluding his huge tome, Burgh called for a popular association movement to push Parliament to reform. Here he again quoted Locke. Those who accept the trust of governing are answerable to the people, who can refuse obedience and take back power into their own hands. Locke is made the theorist of a popular movement against a corrupt legislature.[29]

Richard Price's *Observations on the Nature of Civil Liberty,* another critical text in the reform tradition, appeared in 1776. Price left no room for doubt about his source, for in his preface he noted that "the principles on which I have argued form the foundation of every state as far as it is free; and are the same with those taught by Mr. Locke." Government for Price is a trust; the people set up governors to serve particular ends. When the trust is betrayed, government is dissolved. Price insisted that the rights of the Americans were the natural rights of all free people, not the products of history, tradition, statute, charter, or precedent. Enemies of the colonists, such as Josiah Tucker, denigrated the American colonists as "Mr. Locke's disciples." "What a glorious title," Price replied.[30]

Price's praise of America provides an interesting insight into the Lockean world view that aroused such excitement in British reformers when they looked to America. America was, as Locke himself had noted, as it was "in the beginning." Price and others saw America as a land of individual freedom and equality, where hierarchy and subordination were unknown. The colonies had no rich or poor, he wrote, no beggars and no "haughty grandees." The Americans were strangers to luxury, and they worked hard. They had no large government and few taxes. Most important of all, Price claimed, in America merit was

[29]James Burgh, *Political Disquisitions: An Enquiry into Public Errors, Defects, and Abuses,* 3 vols. (London, 1774), 1:3–4, 72–73; 2:279; 3:449.

[30]Richard Price, *Observations on the Nature of Civil Liberty, the Principles of Government, and the Justice and Policy of the War with America* (London, 1776), pp. ix, 16, 32, 93.

the only path to distinction. To his dying day Price repeated these themes: in his speech in 1789 and in his *Discourse on the Love of Our Country,* which so infuriated Burke that he answered with his *Reflections on the Revolution in France.* In a sermon at Old Jewry in 1789, Price alleged that the greatest defect of the British constitution was representational inequality and that its remedy lay in a representational structure that was "fair and equal"—Locke again.[31]

To be sure, other strains are found in Richard Price's work. We note, for example, a deeply pessimistic tone in much of his writings, especially in his repeated fears over the national debt—fears that are also found in the writings of Horne Tooke and James Burgh and, indeed, in the works of most of the radicals.[32] Given as well Price's fascination with the independent farmer in his writings on America, republican scholars do seem to have a point when they insist that such as Price were not individualist liberals and optimistic modernizers who spoke for an insurgent middle class but antimarket nostalgics steeped in civic humanism's "Renaissance pessimism" over the direction of social change and the inevitability of degeneration and decline. In short, the English radicals and their American counterpart Jefferson seem to be direct descendants of Bolingbroke.

There are, however, serious problems with this republican reading. By the end of the century criticisms of the debt, of paper money, and of banks and praise of independent farmers could not automatically be translated into a politics of nostalgia or a repudiation of capitalism or even of urbanism. Fear of national ruin from an ever-growing national debt was as widespread in the entrepreneurial and manufacturing circles as it was among the middle-class intellectuals in the Dissenters' chapels and academies. People who made money in the funds or through the manipulations of the credit system were seen as idle and unproductive. They were part of the immoral, nonindustrious camp that included the nobility, most of the landed gentry, and the nonworking poor. The talented members of the middle class were unknowingly revising the classical, Thomistic dichotomy between natural and artificial economies. No longer was a subsistence economy "natural" and

---

[31]Richard Price, *Observations on the Importance of the American Revolution and the Means of Making It a Benefit to the World* (London, 1784), pp. 68–70; and *A Discourse on the Love of Our Country Delivered November 4, 1789* (London, 1789), p. 39.

[32]See Price, *Observations on the Importance of the American Revolution,* pp. 60–83; *An Appeal to the Public on the Subject of the National Debt* (London, 1771); *Observations on the Nature of Civil Liberty,* pp. 70–85, 109–30; and *Additional Observations on the Nature and Value of Civil Liberty and the War with America* (London, 1777), pp. 44–46; Horne Tooke, *Causes and Effects of the National Debt and Paper Money on Real and Natural Property in the Present State of Civil Society* (London, 1795); and Burgh, *Political Disquisitions,* e.g., 1:408, 2:298.

a market economy for profit "artificial." A natural economy was now characterized by productive hard work and industry, profit notwithstanding; an artificial economy was characterized by idleness and nonproductivity, and its practitioners were the useless aristocrats by birth and the equally useless parasites by profession, the money men who lived off the national debt. Protestant Dissenters looked with little favor on the ill-gotten gains of gaming, whether at the table or in the funds.

More important still in accounting for middle-class and modernist sentiment against the debt was its symbolic role as the endless fountain of corruption, the source of jobs and patronage that not only corrupted Parliament but gave society's rewards to people without talent or merit. Critical here was the popular identification (well founded in fact) of the growing national debt and war. A vast military establishment generated the debt and left the impression in the virtuous, hardworking middle class of an immoral and unholy alliance. To wage useless wars, to pay for a useless court establishment, to provide jobs and pensions for useless men of no merit, the government incurred a vast debt, which saddled the useful and productive manufacturers and artisans with burdensome taxes and high prices. The national debt, moreover, drained capital from industry and raised interest rates and thus was the very symbol of unproductivity and uselessness. The apparent gloom and pessimism of Price and the other reformers has thus been misread. Although Price and Burgh shared a deep Calvinist appreciation of human depravity, they also shared a hatred of the idle. For them, the idle "monied interest" along with idle aristocrats posed a grave threat to the creation of a truly just and moral society, in which hard work and productive enterprise were the central values.

It may well be that Price and Burgh were wrong and that those whom they considered immoral and idle funders and bankers would be essential in the creation of the very world they sought.[33] It is a mistake, however, to read their views in the light of later economic knowledge. Their opposition to the national debt, the funding system, and the system of paper credit was not reactionary; it went hand in hand with their vision of a moral, middle-class society. Indeed, the

[33]For an important discussion of the relationship between the entrepreneurial manufacturer and the banking and credit system, see the essays in François Crouzet's *Capital Formation in the Industrial Revolution* (London, 1972). Most manufacturers could decry the national debt and the banking system at this stage in the development of British capitalism because they in fact made little use of that system for their capital. Much more characteristic was the self-generation of capital. A good sense of industrial anger over the national debt can be found in Thomas Walker's *A Review of Some of the Political Events Which Have Occurred in Manchester during the Last Five Years* (London, 1794). Walker, a wealthy cotton manufacturer and leading Dissenter, concluded his book with an attack on the growth of the national debt and "the tremendous burden it makes of additional taxes on the manufacturers."

national debt enshrined for them much that their new order sought to replace.

It is also true that Price praised America as the home of the independent farmer, and in his writings he warned lest this noble species be overrun by cities, debts, and taxes. But, as is the case with Jefferson, this agrarian bias must again not be automatically translated into nostalgia, antimodernism, and anticommercialism, for it is by no means clear that the city was perceived in the late eighteenth century as standing for modernity and capitalism and the countryside for reaction and agrarianism. Yeoman farmers operated very much in the capitalist marketplace and had highly developed commercial networks. The yeoman ideal of both Price and Jefferson was not, as Richard Hofstadter depicted it, "non-commercial, non-pecuniary, self-sufficient." In defending American agriculture against the Hamiltonian system, Thomas Cooper recognized that encomia for farming did not necessitate a nostalgic repudiation of a commercial society. Although agriculture was a morally superior pursuit, its superiority did not lie in any more virtuous, precapitalist ideal. Commerce had less value only insofar as it drained away resources: "To foster every, or any other employment of capital at the expense of agriculture—by diminishing the savings of the farmer and forcing him to maintain the manufacturer—or by tempting the capitalist from agriculture into manufacture, is plainly contrary to our most undoubted policy."[34]

Price, Cooper, Paine, and Jefferson were no less committed to a commercial society than others in this period. What distinguishes their economic vision is its individualistic, decentralized, and non-hierarchical flavor. Thus when Jefferson preached the virtues of unrestrained free trade, he had in mind an idealized, individualistic marketplace. "Our interest will be to throw open the doors of commerce, and to knock off all its shackles," he wrote, "giving perfect freedom to all persons for the vent of whatever they may choose to bring into our ports, and asking the same in theirs." As Joyce Appleby has noted, "what was distinctive about [Jefferson's] economic policy was not an anticommercial bias, but a commitment to growth through the unimpeded exertions of individuals" with "access to economic opportunity."[35]

[34]Price, *Observations on the Importance of the American Revolution*, pp. 69–77; Richard Hofstadter, *The Age of Reform* (New York, 1955), pp. 23–24; Thomas Cooper, ed., *Emporium of the Arts and Sciences*, new ser., 1, no. 1 (1813): 8.

[35]Thomas Jefferson, *Notes on the State of Virginia*, ed. W. Peden (Chapel Hill, N.C., 1955), p. 174; Appleby, "What Is Still American?" p. 297. Price, as we know, was intimately connected with the Dissenter industrialist community, and as a mathematician his work in actuarial science became the basis of that most commercial of enterprises, the life insurance industry. Jefferson was not above having labor-saving machines and man-

The rural-urban dichotomy and the preference for the rural is compatible with the emerging middle-class vision. The countryside (where, after all, the early English manufacturers established their operations) represented hard work, simplicity, frugality, industry, and productivity. The city represented courts, officehholders, pensioners, luxury, waste, money, and funds. In the city congregated the idle, both the very rich and the very poor. In the city were gaming, opera, theater, and other useless, time-wasting activities. To label the city corrupt and the countryside virtuous need not, then, immediately connote a dread of modernity. The ideological thrust of such activities is never simply read. Who is virtuous and who is corrupt is not reducible to who is engaged in agriculture and who in commerce, who lives on the land and who on city streets. Hard work, talent, and productivity are what are really critical in the distribution of moral worth, and the secondary distinctions based on geography have to be read in the light of these much more crucial, more primary issues.

Joseph Priestley is a case in point. He did, to be sure, become involved with Coleridge in the Pantisocracy, a scheme for a rural utopia in America, and he finally settled in the Pennsylvania backcountry, near Northumberland. Yet no more zealous a modernizer and liberal apologist for the middle class can be found in the ranks of British reform in these years. Even more than Price, Priestley leaned on Locke in the 1770s, as we have seen. *An Essay on First Principles of Government* (1771) describes a natural society of "independent" and "unconnected" people who voluntarily give up their "natural liberty" to magistrates, and may replace any who abuse the trust reposed in them. Thus revolution was a natural right of the people. Priestley was so keen on arguments from nature that he totally rejected the relevance of historical rights.[36]

In his economic thought Priestley offered a vigorous defense of laissez-faire and individualistic attacks on the poor laws. He also attacked the national debt. But, again, this was the politics not of nostalgia but of a modernizing middle class. He complained that, among

---

ufacturing mills at Monticello. Indeed, as Merrill Peterson has noted, "Here was no pastoral Eden but belching smoke and clanging hammers": *Thomas Jefferson and the New Nation: A Biography* (New York, 1970), pp. 535–36. Industry and manufacture on a small scale were clearly compatible with a virtuous life of hard work and productivity. For a late eighteenth-century argument that factories and manufacturing contribute "to paths of virtue, by restoring frugality and industry" while counteracting aristocratic corruption and luxury, see Trench Coxe, "An Address to an Assembly of the Friends of American Manufacturers," *American Museum* 2 (1787): 251, 253–55.

[36]Joseph Priestley, *An Essay on the First Principles of Government and on the Nature of Political, Civil, and Religious Liberty, Including Remarks on Dr. Brown's Code of Education* (London, 1771), pp. 2–7, and *Lectures on History and General Policy* (London, 1788), p. 349.

other things, the growing debt raised prices. Particularly distressing was the rising price of bread, for when the price of bread is kept at a reasonable level, "workmen's wages are kept lower, and more fixed, a thing of the greatest consequence in manufactures."[37]

The spirit of John Locke hovers as well over Priestley's writings on religious individualism, which so influenced Jefferson and which derive directly from Locke's *Letters on Toleration* and from Locke's views of government in the *Second Treatise*. Government, Priestley wrote, should not be involved in the religious beliefs of citizens, because "the magistrate's concern is not with opinions and beliefs. His proper duty is to preserve the peace of society, or to see that no member of it injures another man in his person or his property."[38]

Once again Locke lives, for it was clear in the late eighteenth century that behind such ideas as these stood, among others, Locke. In America a well-known cartoon of 1769, labeled "An Attempt to Land a Bishop in America," shows the bishop hastily sailing back to England. The angry crowd is hurling at him epithets labeled "Calvin's Works," "liberty and freedom of conscience," and "Locke."[39]

Locke also flourished in the two major organizational expressions of British reform in these years, the Society for Constitutional Information (SCI) of the 1780s and the London Corresponding Society (LCS) of the 1790s. Founded in the early 1780s, the SCI circulated to its members excerpts from books, speeches, and pamphlets that the society's leaders—Horne Tooke, Capel Lofft, Christopher Wyvill, John Jebb, and John Cartwright—felt argued for reform of Parliament or more generally praised freedom. Here, as in Burgh's *Political Disquisitions*, much use was indeed made of Bolingbroke, *Cato's Letters*, and the whole arsenal of country opposition to Walpole. There is even occasional talk of Machiavellian *ritorno ai principii*, signifying a return to the lost rights and purer principles of Saxon times. The SCI leader most likely to use this older country language was Christopher Wyvill. His letters and political papers are full of pleas to the other reformers to back Pitt's more moderate reform bills, to avoid plans of "theoretical perfection" or schemes "to form a government on a perfect theory." He spoke less of natural than of Saxon rights, and he spent a good deal of energy in

---

[37]Priestley, *Lectures on History and General Policy,* p. 394. For his critical views of the poor and the poor laws, see ibid., pp. 295–305, and *An Account of a Society for Encouraging the Industrious Poor to Which Are Prefixed Some Considerations on the State of the Poor in General* (Birmingham, 1787).

[38]Joseph Priestley, *Conduct to Be Observed by Dissenters in Order to Procure the Repeal of the Corporation and Test Acts* (Birmingham, 1789), pp. 6–7.

[39]This cartoon is fully described in Herbert D. Foster, "International Calvinism through Locke and the Revolution of 1688," *American Historical Review* 32 (1926–27): 476.

the 1790s criticizing the abstractions and ahistorical arguments of Thomas Paine.[40]

But alongside Wyvill's country ideology and civic humanism spoke another and more dominant voice in the SCI, the voice of Locke, of natural rights, of compact, of government as trust, of natural equality, and of the people's power to change governments. John Jebb, the Peterhouse Anglican who converted to Priestley's Unitarianism, rejected Wyvill's expectation that Parliament would reform itself. It was too subject to the will of the prime minister. Better for the people themselves in public association and assembly to reassert their natural right to change governments. This was their residual right from the original compact. Only by popular pressure outside Parliament, Jebb insisted, could the fair and equal representation that Wilkes sought be realized.[41]

Capel Lofft, another major figure in the SCI leadership, offered a gloss on Locke in 1779, applying the principles of natural law and the social compact to the reform of Parliament. All men were equal "by the law of nature," and the power of governors derives "only from consent and contract." Neither Saxon nor seventeenth-century commonwealth history are the sources of Lofft's radicalism: "As to our liberty, we derived it not, if we mean the right from our forefathers or from the Revolution; we had it from God, from the nature of man, and the nature and ends of society. We respect human authority so far as it is founded in public consent and directed by that principle to public utility." In the 1790s Lofft repeated the superior claim of natural rights over historical rights. The former "is of date far higher, and of origin transcendentally more venerable. It is an inheritance coeval with the commencement of humanity." In general, Lofft defended the Dissenters against Burke's wrath, and he invoked the familiar cry that no longer should "those of useful industry" be barred from "public counsel." It was time, he urged, to break down the barrier "separating the useful from the honored classes in the Community." The "temples of honour" were open only to the "mere presumptions of merit." Reformers meant, he wrote, to "expand the gates and enlarge the avenues" to these temples.[42]

---

[40]Christopher Wyvill, *Political Papers*, 4 vols. (London, 1794), 2:605; 3: Appendix, 154; and 4:75–90.

[41]John Jebb, *The Works of John Jebb* (London, 1787), 3:180, 455–84. Also see Jebb to Wyvill, August 7, 1781, in Wyvill's *Political Papers*, 4:497–521.

[42]Capel Lofft, *Elements of Universal Law and Particularly of the Laws of England* (London, 1779), pp. 10–15; *Observations on Mr. Wesley's Second Calm Address* (London, 1777), p. 55; and *Remarks on the Letter of the Right Honourable Edmund Burke Concerning the Revolution in France* (London, 1790), pp. 3, 31, 35.

The Butterfield-Christie reading of English reform in the late eighteenth century, so crucial for republican scholarship, needs rethinking. Far from being principally backward-looking seekers of lost Saxon rights, uninterested in socioeconomic themes, those who called for the reform of Parliament in the late eighteenth century were, in fact, very much preoccupied with the social question. Moreover, in the SCI documents, lost Saxon rights were read as natural rights. The purpose of the Saxon constitution, according to the SCI leadership, was to preserve natural rights. To reestablish the Saxon constitution, then, was to recapture inalienable natural rights. This is a very different emphasis from that of Bolingbroke and his circle. Most of the pamphlets circulated by the SCI affirm that reason and nature, not custom and history, are the points of reference. All men are free and possess absolute rights, by the dictates of reason and the "immutable laws of nature." Among these rights are the right to be taxed only with consent and the right to "fair and equal representation." Here, too, the SCI held up America as the beacon for a corrupt Britain, and not because it represented a repudiation of modernity but because it stood behind the rights of nature, of equity, and of reason.[43]

Locke is quoted extensively in SCI documents on the people's responsibility when their natural rights are violated. The SCI's pamphlets never tire of describing governors as trustees who may be turned out when they have violated the people's trust. Locke was the source of the judgment that the people could remove legislators who violated that trust. The people have a recourse for a corrupt, despotic House of Commons. They have "a just and natural control" and a right "to a just resistance . . . to an invasion of their natural and inalienable rights." An SCI pamphlet of 1780 calls this Lockean theory down to the world of practice: "Mr. Locke is of the opinion, that "there remains inherent in the people a power to remove or alter the legislative, when they find the legislative act contrary to the trust reposed in them; for when such a trust is abused, it is thereby forfeited, and dissolves to those who gave it." If this conclusion is just in theory, it must be just in practice, and . . . may be adopted and argued from under the present dispensation of government."[44]

This translation of Locke from theory to practice was even more apparent in the London Corresponding Society. This artisan-based,

---

[43]Society for Constitutional Information, *Minutes of the Meetings . . . Held at No. 2 in New-Inn* (London, 1782), pp. 1–30.

[44]Ibid., p. 37 (also see Society for Constitutional Information, *An Address to the Public . . .* [London, 1780], pp. 1–8, and *A Second Address to the Public . . .* [London, 1780], pp. 1–15); *A Letter from the Right Honourable Lord Carysfort to the Huntingdonshire Committee* (London, 1780), pp. 4–5.

more radical group of the 1790s also shows the unmistakable stamp of John Locke. The call to establish the LCS in 1792 describes how men voluntarily give up some of their rights the better to secure the possession of others. Among the rights an individual retains is "the right to share in the government of that society of which he is a member." To ensure that right, Thomas Hardy, the secretary of the society, advocated "a fair, equal and impartial representation." Like the SCI, the LCS cited as the source of these rights both "our Saxon inheritance" and "our inheritance from nature and the immutable principles of justice." But much more typical of these friends of liberty and ideological kinsmen of Tom Paine was the invocation of nature.[45]

It is important to note the imprint of Locke on the LCS, for E. P. Thompson has made much of the LCS as an example of early working-class ideology in action.[46] Radical the members of the society were, granted, but radical petty bourgeois. Their *Declaration of Principles* is a fascinating document, very much influenced by the spirit of Locke. Principle 1 proclaims "that all men are by nature free, equal and independent of each other." No reference is made to Locke, but this passage is, of course, taken verbatim from the opening of paragraph 95 of the *Second Treatise*. Principle 2 states that, "to enjoy all the advantages of civil society, individuals ought not to relinquish any more of their natural independence than is necessary to preserve the weak against the strong, and to enable the whole body to act with union." The LCS *Declaration of Principles* also includes a list of the civil rights of every individual. At the top is "equality of protection for his liberty, life and property." Farther down another important civic right is claimed, one that is by now familiar as a critical issue for these reformers. It is "equality of encouragement for the exercise of his talents, and consequently the free enjoyment of the advantages thereby obtained."[47]

The LCS pamphlets and manifestos abound in references to the membership as "taxpaying, industrious and useful inhabitants" or "industrious and worthy citizenry." The society's world view, like that of the reform movement in general, saw two classes in British society, the useful and the useless: "We take pride in acknowledging ourselves a part of that useful class of citizens which placemen (pensioned with the extorted produce of our daily labour) and proud nobility wallowing in riches (acquired somehow) affect to treat with a contempt too degrad-

---

[45]London Corresponding Society, *The . . . Society to the Nation at Large* (London, 1792), pp. 1–2, 6, and *An Account of the Proceedings of the British Convention Held in Edinburgh, the 19th of November 1793* (London, n.d.), pp. 10–12.

[46]E. P. Thompson, *The Making of the English Working Class* (New York, 1963), esp. pp. 152–57.

[47]London Corresponding Society, *Report of the Committee Appointed to Revise and Abridge a Former Report of the Constitution of the . . . Society* (London, n.d.), pp. 1, 2.

ing for human nature to bear, unless reconciled to it by the reflection that though their inferiors in rank and fortune, we equal them in talents and excel them in Honesty." Nor was the LCS an enemy of private property. It acknowledged "that differences of strength, of talents, and of industry, ought to afford proportional distinctions of property which when acquired and confirmed by the laws, is sacred and inviolable."[48]

When these talented and industrious citizens convened in a huge open-air meeting at Chalk Farm on April 14, 1794, they knew full well the mood of Pitt's government and the growing evidence of repression. Their unanimous resolution, critical of the government, was a paraphrase of Locke. It was sound constitutional doctrine, to be sure, but in the context of the mid-1790s even the spirit of Locke was suspect. The LCS resolved "that any attempt to violate those yet remaining laws, which were intended for the Security of Englishmen against the Corruption of dependent judges ought to be considered as dissolving entirely the social compact between the English nation and their Governors, and driving them to that incontrovertible maxim of eternal Justice, that the safety of the people is the supreme, and in cases of necessity, the only law."[49]

Locke and the "Ranks in Society"

What better proof could there be of Locke's importance in the late eighteenth century than a crusade to root out his ideas? So common was the reformers' use of Locke's "close reasoning" that their Tory and clerical opponents often singled out Locke as the sinister influence behind radical agitation. Richard Hey and Bishop William Paley ridiculed the reformers'—that is, Lockean—notions of contract, the state of nature, and natural rights. The *Anti-Jacobin* lamented that "Price, Priestley, Rousseau, Paine could justify on the principles of Locke, their own visionary doctrines, pregnant with consequences so mischievous to society and so different from what Locke himself intended."[50]

---

[48]London Corresponding Society, *Addresses and Resolutions* (London, n.d.), p. 1; *Address of the . . . Society to Other Societies of Great Britain United for Obtaining a Reform in Parliament* (London, 1793), p. 8; and *Address from the . . . Society to the Inhabitants of Great Britain on the Subject of a Parliamentary Reform* (London, 1792), pp. 2–3.

[49]*Annual Register* (London, 1794), p. 264.

[50]See Richard Hey, *Happiness and Rights: A Dissertation upon Several Subjects Relative to the Rights of Man and His Happiness* (York, 1792); and William Paley, "Elements of Political Knowledge," in *The Collected Works of William Paley,* vol. 3 (London, 1838), bk. 6. The *Anti-Jacobin* is quoted in Anthony Lincoln, *Some Political and Social Ideas of English Dissent, 1763–1800* (Cambridge, Eng., 1938), p. 114.

George Horne, bishop of Norwich and chaplain to George III, criticized Locke's notion of natural equality and independence in the state of nature, "since from the beginning, some were born subject to others." Samuel Horsley, bishop successively of St. David, Rochester, and St. Asaph, chimed in that Locke's descriptions of an original compact and an independent state of nature were "absurd and unphilosophical creations of something out of nothing." In his annual sermon marking the anniversary of the execution of Charles I, Horsley linked together in unholy alliance Lockean doctrine, Protestant Dissenters, and French Jacobins. "Contractual ideas of popular sovereignty inflamed the phrensy of that fanatical banditti," and the "dissemination of those infernal maxims that kings are the servants of the people, punishable by their masters," had led now to the murder of Louis XVI. Behind it all, Horsley lamented, was English seventeenth-century doctrine.[51]

The most vocal denouncers of Locke in this period, however, were Josiah Tucker, the dean of Gloucester, and Edward Tatham, an Anglican divine from Oxford. Tucker's *Treatise Concerning Civil Government* (1781) is one long diatribe against Locke and those whom Tucker called his "eminent disciples"—Priestley and Price. What particularly upset Tucker about Locke, Price, and Priestley was their conviction "that government is a work of art, and that nature has no share in forming it, in predisposing or inclining mankind to it." He repudiated their notion that men were ever "independent and unconnected beings" who voluntarily chose to set up governments. He also rejected what he described as their conviction that "civil government is a necessary evil, rather than a positive good." What folly, he wrote, to describe men as "all equal, all free, and independent, all masters of self." Against Locke and his late eighteenth-century radical disciples Tucker invoked Aristotle, who, Tucker insisted, had correctly described the inherent sociability of human beings and the naturalness of the political community. Tucker was particularly angered by the Americans' use of Locke, for they had taken to heart his pernicious doctrines and would create a "Lockean Republic, where all taxes are to be free gifts! and every man is to obey no further, and no otherwise, than he himself chooses to obey."[52]

Edward Tatham in 1791 continued the assault on Locke and those he called "the two captains" of his teachings in England, Price and Priestley. And Tatham had the same alternative to Locke. Priestley

---

[51]George Horne, *Discourses on the Origins of Civil Government* (London, 1800), p. 271; Samuel Horsley, *A Sermon Preached before the Lords Spiritual and Temporal . . . , January 30, 1793* (London, 1793), pp. 4, 22–23.

[52]Josiah Tucker, *Selections from His Economic and Political Writings*, ed. R. L. Schuyler (New York, 1931), pp. 407–553 *passim*, esp. 464.

should have read more Aristotle and less Locke, Tatham suggested. The Aristotle Tatham invoked is not, however, Aristotle the theorist of citizenship and the *zöon politikon* so dear to twentieth-century republican scholarship but Aristotle the theorist of hierarchy and privilege. Aristotle, Tatham wrote, "took men as he found them and as history informed him they have been always found, connected in society, subordinate and dependent on each other." Against Locke, Price, and Priestley, Tatham preferred an Aristotle who taught "that men are made by their Creator different and unequal, some formed for authority, and others for subjection." Locke and his eighteenth-century captains, Tatham insisted, would "throw down all ranks and distinctions of man."[53]

Late eighteenth-century observers thus made a clear link from Locke to British reform and socioeconomic change, a link that has been denied by the republican school. The real threat of Locke and his "eminent disciples" was their leveling tendencies, their assault on traditional aristocratic society. In *The True Basis of Civil Government in Opposition to the System of Mr. Locke and His Followers,* Tucker criticized the reformers for denying what he saw as basic in human nature: "a certain ascendancy in some, a kind of submissive acquiescence in others." There are, Tucker insisted, certain natural "ranks in society" and "stations in life," which contract theory undermines in its subversive preoccupation with natural freedom and equality. These critics perceptively understood the intentions of the "eminent disciples" of Locke. The praise of achievement and talent, the ideology of equal opportunity, and the cult of industry and productivity, all wrapped in doctrines of natural equality and independence, were in fact self-consciously directed at "the age of chivalry." The true nostalgics were the likes of Burke, Tucker, and Tatham. Theirs was the defense of a world with "Kings, princes, nobles and gentlemen. . . . For in the whole scale of beings, and in the nature of things, there must be regular gradations and regular distinctions."[54]

Less concerned with nostalgia than with repression, Pitt's government brought numerous leaders of the reform movement to trial for treason. Even above the trials hovered the spirit of John Locke. So subversive were his ideas considered that to say anything consonant with them in the 1790s was itself grounds for suspicion. According to Priestley, "any sentiment in favour of liberty that is at all bold and manly, such as till of late, was deemed becoming Englishmen and the

[53]Edward Tatham, *Letters to Edmund Burke on Politics* (Oxford, 1791), pp. 7, 12, 22, 26.
[54]Tucker, *Economic and Political Writings,* p. 477; and Matthew Goodenough, *Plain Thoughts by a Plain Citizen of London* (London, 1792), p. 11.

disciples of Mr. Locke, is now reprobated as seditious." No surprise, then, that sympathy with Locke's ideas was raised as an issue in the trials of Hardy, Joseph Gerrald, and Paine.[55]

Despite these attacks, Locke had his proud defenders. Thomas Erskine, the eloquent defense attorney for so many of Pitt's victims, still invoked Locke as a warning to the government. "It is justly observed by Locke," he declared, that "after much neglect and provocation the people will be roused to a reasonable and justifiable resistance." Robert Hall, the dissenting minister, was unafraid to praise Locke in his published reply to Bishop Horsley's anniversary sermon. Hall proudly proclaimed that the doctrine of Locke and his followers "is founded on the natural equality of mankind; for as no man can have any natural or inherent right to rule any more than another, it necessarily follows, that a claim to dominion, wherever it is lodged, must be ultimately referred back to the explicit or implied consent of the people." The "immortal Locke" is, indeed, the patron of English reform.[56]

In *A Vindication of the Political Principles of Mr. Locke* Joseph Towers, the dissenting minister in Highgate and a friend of Price and Priestley, praised the reformers' use of Locke, describing him as "an ornament and an honour to the country which gave him birth." Towers met the historical objections to Locke head on, insisting that the "great excellence of his maxims" is that they are based not "upon the iniquities of a dark and intricate and disputable nature" but upon the more indisputable "principles of reason and justice . . . apparent at all times." As for objections to Locke's doctrine of changing governors who act "contrary to the trust given them," Towers responded, "You might as well say, honest men may not oppose robbers or pirates, because it may occasion disorder or bloodshed." Towers even wrapped himself in Locke when he demanded the suffrage for Birmingham, Manchester, and Leeds. Had Locke not begun it all, Towers asked, with the passage on "bringing Parliament to a fair and equal representation"? Far from denying Locke's role, the Presbyterian Towers praised it: "It may be readily admitted, that Mr. Locke and his followers wish to extend the present partial representation of the people, and to make it more

[55]Joseph Priestley, *An Appeal to the Public on the Subject of the Riots in Birmingham* (Birmingham, 1792), pp. 113–14. See Thompson, *Making of the English Working Class*, pp. 88–89, 128–29; F. D. Cartwright, ed., *The Life and Correspondence of Major Cartwright* (London, 1826), 1:214–17; and Lloyd Paul Stryker, *For the Defense—Thomas Erskine* (Garden City, N.Y., 1947), p. 224.

[56]Thomas Erskine, *A View of the Causes and Consequences of the Present War with France* (London, 1797), p. 22; Robert Hall, *An Apology for the Freedom of the Press and for General Liberty, to Which Are Prefixed Remarks on Bishop Horsley's Sermon* (London, 1793), pp. 40, 72, 62.

agreeable to reason and to justice . . . , but this is not one of the defects of Mr. Locke's system, but one of its principal excellencies."[57]

Even more telling than Towers's *Vindication* was a pamphlet of 1794,
The Spirit of John Locke, written by Henry Yorke of Sheffield, who in that
same year was tried for treason. The pamphlet widely distributed to all
radical associations by the Constitutional Society of Sheffield, was a
popular abridgment of Locke's *Second Treatise of Government*, designed
to bring Locke's ideas more readily to "that part of the community who
have not leisure to employ themselves in perusing the whole of the
work." The abridged Locke, Yorke wrote, was

> applicable to the present times.—It may serve to open the eyes of our
> deluded Countrymen, who are persecuting and hating us, because we are
> vindicating the ancient Liberties of our Country. It will expose the fall-
> acious reasoning of those who would persuade the People that they have
> no other rights but what their rulers please to give them. It will prove
> passive obedience to be folly, and RESISTANCE AGAINST OPPRESSION to be
> the duty of the people.

Locke's credentials were good, Yorke informed the reader, and his
ideas had served well in the recent American "cause," so sacred to the
Dissenters and the reformers:

> While America was gloriously struggling to throw off the yoke of British
> oppression, the name of John Locke resounded even in the British Senate,
> and was echoed in Congress. The principles, which he had so admirably
> digested from amidst the crude volumes of remoter times, were, to op-
> pressed Humanity, the alarum of Liberty. They taught the criteria of good
> and bad Government, and instructed the injured how, and when, to tram-
> ple Despotism under foot.

Locke's writings might be dull, Yorke conceded, but Locke was relevant and his spirit alive. Speaking for his reforming colleagues in
Sheffield, he commended Locke to readers who were less familiar with
the "close reasoner" than they: "We commit to your wisdom and pru-
dential reflection, the following Abstract from a book, difficult to be
purchased, and, throughout the greatest part, uninteresting even
when purchased. We have declined making any notes to the body of
the work. But he who runs may read, and the Man who cannot take a
broad hint from the *last* century, must not expect one from the *present*."
In trying to make the strongest case he could for knowledge of Locke,

---

[57]Joseph Towers, *A Vindication of the Political Principles of Mr. Locke* (London, 1782), pp.
13, 16, 40, 65.

Yorke noted that Edmund Burke, "Knight Errant of Feudality," had claimed on the floor of the House of Commons that "Locke's Treatise on Civil Government, was the worst book ever written." Yorke was therefore "certain it needs no farther recommendation."[58]

Locke and the Radicalism of Protestant Dissent

To paraphrase Mark Twain, the scholarly consensus on Locke's death in the late eighteenth century is greatly exaggerated. Late eighteenth-century English reformers dramatically worked Lockean themes into the heart of their critique of traditional England, turning to Locke because his *Second Treatise of Government* was uniquely appropriate to their peculiar problem. Parliament, the representative body, was itself the barrier to reform. Locke's belief in the residual power of the people against their governors legitimized the reformers' campaign against the unreformed House of Commons. Locke's political theory legitimated their demands, both substantive and procedural, for a reform of the suffrage and of parliamentary representation. His concept of a limited secular magistrate legitimated their demand for the separation of church and state.

The reformers also turned to Locke because their ideological concerns were similar. These spokesmen for an insurgent middle-class radicalism were drawn to this liberal theorist of possessive individualism. No one had better expressed their economic and social convictions than Locke had done. His socioeconomic vision was perfectly compatible with—indeed, had helped shape—their image of a world peopled by hardworking, industrious property owners. Locke had often written on the themes of industry and talent and was perceived as a crucial part of the Protestant tradition that so informed much of this reform movement. In the libraries of the dissenting academies, Locke's works were standard references, not only for psychology and education but also for politics and commerce. Had not, in fact, the *Second Treatise* contended that God had set some men to be more industrious than others and thus to acquire more property? Locke's conviction that God "gave the world to the use of the industrious and Rational . . . , not to the Fancy or the Covetousness of the Quarrelsome

---

[58]Henry Yorke, *The Spirit of John Locke on Civil Government* (Sheffield, 1794), pp. iii–iv, viii. For Yorke's fascinating career, see J. Taylor, "The Sheffield Constitutional Society," *Transactions of the Hunter Archaeological Society* (Sheffield) 5 (1943): 133–46; and G. P. Jones, "The Political Reform Movement in Sheffield," *Transactions of the Hunter Archaeological Society* 4 (1937): 57–68. Later in his career (after a long prison term), Yorke moved to the right and published an attack on his former radical colleagues.

and Contentious," was critical to his thought; it symbolized a central tension in his work: the struggle between the industrious and the idle—a struggle at the core of the world view of those late eighteenth-century dissenting reformers who read Locke in the libraries of their academies.[59]

The praise of industry, of what the seventeenth and eighteenth centuries commended as "skill, assiduity, perseverance and diligence," and the denunciation of idleness were, of course, by no means unique to Locke.[60] Protestant writers, especially Puritans such as Richard Baxter, had long made them a crucial part of their notions of work, of the obligation to labor, and of the importance of one's calling. What Locke did was wed these earlier views to a political theory of private rights and individualism with his argument that property was an extension of self, the injection of personality into nature through work.[61] Less apparent, however, is the extent to which other Lockean texts read in these dissenting academy libraries spoke to the themes of industry, idleness, and the glory of work. Indeed, so great was Locke's concern with these themes that it is little exaggeration to suggest that he saw industriousness as the central characteristic of the human personality, of personal behavior, and of social and personal activity.

In his *Essay Concerning Human Understanding*, Locke linked activity to anxiety, a connection not unfamiliar to later readers of Weber and Tawney. "The chief, if not the only spur to human industry and action," he wrote, "is uneasiness." This feeling of uneasiness drove men to enterprise and unrelenting activity. Once motivated, they were permanently active, for they had a never-ending "itch after honour, power and riches."[62]

Activity and industry, according to Locke, also characterized childhood. His widely read *Thoughts Concerning Education* is a veritable diatribe against idleness. Children are the model for the species. They "generally hate to be idle. All they care then is, that their busy humour should be constantly employ'd in something of use to them." All life is industrious activity, Locke wrote; even in recreation human beings are never idle. "For *Recreation* is not being idle (as every one may observe)

---

[59]Lincoln, *Some Political and Social Ideas of English Dissent*, p. 87; Locke, *Second Treatise*, chap. 5, secs. 48, 35.

[60]For a discussion of the word "industry," see Raymond Williams, *Culture and Society, 1780–1950* (London, 1958), p. 13.

[61]The following argument owes a good deal to the interesting work of E. J. Hundert. See his "The Making of *Homo Faber*: John Locke—Between Ideology and History," *Journal of the History of Ideas* 33 (1972): 3–22, and "Market Society and Meaning in Locke's Political Philosophy," *Journal of the History of Philosophy* 15 (1977): 33–44.

[62]John Locke, *An Essay Concerning Human Understanding*, ed. A. C. Fraser (Oxford, 1894), vol. 2, bk. 20, sec. 6.

but easing the wearied Part by Change of Business: and he that thinks *Diversion* may not lie in hard and painful Labour, forgets the early Rising, hard Riding, Heat, Cold and Hunger of Huntsmen, which is yet known to be the constant Recreation of Men of the greatest Condition." Recreation should not just delight and provide ease, it should refresh one for "regular business" and "produce what will afterwards be profitable." Uneasiness again preoccupied Locke, as he prescribed that parents keep their children busy and fight "the dead weight of unemployed Time lying upon their hands," since "the uneasiness is to do nothing at all."[63]

Children should be taught to keep account books, according to Locke, for this activity not only would keep them busy but also would teach them frugality. Such practices would contribute to the habitual and orderly management of their lives. Industriousness required that children also learn to postpone immediate gratification: "He that has not a mastery over his Inclinations, he that knows not how to *resist* the Importunity of *present Pleasure* or *Pain*, for the sake of what Reason tells him is fit to be done, wants the true Principle of Virtue and Industry."[64]

Two groups in the community—some aristocrats and all of the poor—were not, however, active and industrious. According to Locke, they provided the "fancy or the covetousness of the Quarrelsome and contentious." As Burgh, Price, Priestley, and all dissenting middle-class reformers eventually did, Locke divided society into an industrious, enterprising middle beset by two idle extremes. In his essay of 1691 on lowering the interest rate, Locke criticized the profligate aristocrat, whose plight was produced by "debauchery and luxury beyond means." He was not criticizing the "industrious and rational" among the aristocracy, only the "covetous" and "contentious," who "will have and by his example make it fashionable to have more claret, spice and silk." Such men would soon lose their power and authority to "men of lower condition who surpass them in knowledge."[65]

While only some of the aristocracy were lazy and "debauched," Locke presumed that most of the poor were idle and inactive, and his harshness toward them knew no bounds. He urged that the provisions of the poor law be made stricter so that the poor could be taught industry, hard work, and frugality. One way to break them of their wasteful idleness was through the establishment of what Locke called "working schools." A full century before Bentham and his "industry

[63]John Locke, *Some Thoughts Concerning Education* (Cambridge, Eng., 1892), pp. 110–11, 180–81.

[64]Ibid., pp. 183, 29.

[65]John Locke, *Some Considerations on the Consequences of Lowering the Interest and Raising the Value of Money* (1691), in *The Works of John Locke*, ed. J. Law (London, 1801), 5:53, 60.

houses," Locke proposed that all children of the poor "shall be obliged to come" at the age of three to live in "schools" where the only subjects taught would be spinning and knitting. This regimen would cure them of idleness, for they would then "from infancy be inured to work, which is of no small consequence to the making of them sober and industrious all their lives after." Rounding up the children of the poor and incarcerating them in order to teach them industry and hard work would, Locke conceded, cost the parishes dearly; but it would ultimately prove profitable in the account books of the spinning and knitting managers, for "the earnings of the children [would] abat[e] the charge of their maintenance, and as much work [would] be required of each of them as they are reasonably able to perform," so that "it [would] quickly pay its own charges with an overplus."[66]

Such Lockean schemes and the values they embody are directly linked not only to Bentham but to the middle-class Protestant reformers of the late eighteenth century. Priestley's proposal for a "Society for Encouraging the Industrious Poor," submitted to Wilkinson the ironmaster in 1787, contains similar sentiments. But the clearest link is in the equally repressive plan offered by James Burgh to eliminate idleness and encourage industry. He proposed in his *Political Disquisitions*, as we shall see, that the police and press gangs "seize all idle and disorderly persons, who have been three times complained of before a magistrate, and to set them to work during a certain time, for the benefit of great trading or manufacturing companies."[67] These are expressions neither of nostalgic country ideology nor of republicanism but of an ideology of hard work and industry. Middle-class reformers in the late eighteenth century were more likely to read the world and assess its institutions—economic, social, and political—in terms of the dialectic of industry and idleness than in those of "virtue and commerce." Here, too, they bore the indelible imprint of "that close reasoner, Mr. Locke."

Chapter 5 of the *Second Treatise*, "On Property," became the received wisdom in advanced radical circles in the late eighteenth century. Priestley described "a difference in industry" as introducing and legit-

---

[66]Locke, *Some Thoughts Concerning Education*, pp. 189–90. Bentham's industry houses are discussed below and in Gertrude Himmelfarb, "Bentham's Utopia: The National Charity Company," *Journal of British Studies* 10 (1970): 80–125.

[67]Burgh, *Political Disquisitions*, 3:220–21. It should be noted that Francis Hutcheson, so favored by Gary Wills as the intellectual gray eminence behind Thomas Jefferson, went even further. Although Hutcheson opposed the slavery of Africans, he insisted that slavery should be "the ordinary punishment of such idle vagrants, as, after proper admonitions and tryals of temporary servitude, cannot be engaged to support themselves and their families by any useful means": *A System of Moral Philosophy* (London, 1755), 2:202.

imating inequalities of property, "so that in time some will become rich and others poor." In turn, those with property are led to create civil society by "the desire of securing the undisturbed enjoyment of their possessions." The philologist and radical Horne Tooke is a less likely spokesman for these views, but he, too, felt the impact of Locke's economic ideas. His essay on the nature of property and wealth, published in 1795, begins by proclaiming that "industry, the bodily labour of the human being is the foundation of all property." The idle, however, "according to the original and natural constitution of things have no right or property in anything." But, by his reckoning, this was by no means the case in Tooke's England. With the exaggerated flair of the middle-class apologist, he asked, "Though it may be easily conceived that this was the case originally when men lived in a state of nature . . . , how is it that [today] the most industrious and laborious are scarcely able to procure even the common necessities of life" at the same time that "the idle, those who never work at all are rolling in luxury, and possess all the property in the kingdom, an inversion of the laws of nature"?[68]

Middle-class reformers in the late eighteenth century used the older language of civic humanism and corruption, to be sure. They and their American friends, such as Jefferson and Franklin, complained often of the corruption that hung heavy over Britain.[69] But corruption was a very different notion for these reformers from what it had been for Bolingbroke and his country ideology. A corrupt man for Burgh, Price, and Priestley was idle, profligate, unproductive, and lacking in talent and merit. A corrupt system was one in which such drones held important public offices, one in which privilege, not merit, distributed the prizes in the race of life, and one in which patronage ensured the rule of unproductive—that is, corrupt—men of no ability instead of that of deserving men of talent. When Francis Place complained that "the whole system of our Government is essentially corrupt," he was not invoking a court-country equation with commerce and modernity, he was using a new public language that saw government as a reserve for privileged parasites. It was the same language used by the Sheffield reformer Henry Yorke in linking corruption to the aristocratic system:

> From the privileged orders where birth supplies the lack of ability, virtue, knowledge and experience the executive officers of the nation are selected. . . . They preclude the industrious citizen from all honourable en-

---

[68]Priestley, *Lectures on History and General Policy*, pp. 303, 297; Tooke, *Causes and Effects*, pp. 2–4.

[69]See Drew R. McCoy, "Benjamin Franklin's Vision of a Republican Political Economy for America," *William and Mary Quarterly* 25 (1978): 605–28.

terprise and patriotic exertion. . . . Intrigue and corruption are the only
trades of the aristocracy. In these they excell. By these they enrich themselves. By such criminal means they monopolise all the offices of the
church, the law and the army . . . ; they first corrupt you, and then they
intrigue against you; they purchase you, in order to sell themselves. . . .
The aristocracy desire to be distinguished from you, not to be distinguished by you. In a government where such a system is prevalent
what is to be expected, but the extension of that corrupt influence by
which it is upheld.[70]

These useless idlers presided over a system that denied careers to
the talented. The real nation was, as earlier in the century, seen as
outside that corrupt government, but that nation was not a warmed-
over Augustan country. Now it consisted of the virtuous, hardworking, and frugal middle class and artisanry, who were as uninterested in
a republican order of civic virtue as they were in an aristocratic order of
deference and privilege. What they wanted was a meritocracy of talent.
Had not Locke written, after all, that God "gave the world to the use of
the Industrious and the Rational"?

Pocock and other revisionists have been quite right to see the court-
commerce connection earlier in the century. But by the late eighteenth
century the country reform tradition came to terms with the market
and, indeed, middle-class industrial Dissenters turned that reform tradition into a wholehearted ideology of the market. The court, while
bound to the market and commerce from Walpole and Defoe on, was
enmeshed in the principle of patronage, which ultimately flew in the
face of market notions of careers neutrally open to talent and hard
work. It is here that the conflict emerges. Patronage and privilege are
principles that pitted the court against the bourgeois reformers. Middle-class radicals inveighed against the corruption of patronage, but it
was a new sense of corruption, the corruption of jobs and places going
to undeserving, untalented men of high birth. It was the privileged
court that in this period responded with a nostalgic defense of the
ancient constitution, hierarchy, and paternalism. Its defenders ridiculed the leveling ideas of moneyed men and provincial bumpkins.

A court-country reading of the later eighteenth century becomes too
confusing to be useful, because, with the emergence and eventual
supremacy within the country "outs" of a class-conscious bourgeoisie,
the court-commerce linkage becomes obsolete. In the eyes of the middle-class radical "outs," the earlier equation was reversed. The "ins,"

[70]Henry Yorke, *Thoughts on Civil Government Addressed to the Disenfranchised Citizens of
Sheffield* (London, 1794), pp. 55–59. Place is quoted in Graham Wallas, *The Life of Francis
Place, 1771–1854* (New York, 1919), p. 256.

the court and all it stood for, were identified not with the market and commerce but with idle, unproductive privilege. The commercial and financial revolution stood behind the court-country split of the Augustan era. Its relevance receded, however, in the early years of the Industrial Revolution, when new dichotomous distinctions, not the least of which was virtuous commerce versus corrupt privilege, captured the fancy of reformers. The marriage of industrial England with Dissenter reform doomed court-country politics and introduced class politics.

What emerged in the course of the late eighteenth century—and most vividly in the writings of the middle-class radicals—was a new notion of virtue, one that dramatically rejected the assumptions of civic humanism. Citizenship and the public quest for the common good were replaced by economic productivity and hard work as the criteria of virtue. It is a mistake, however, to see this change simply as a withdrawal from public activity to a private, self-centered realm. The transformation also involved a shift in emphasis on the nature of public behavior. Now the moral and virtuous man was defined not by his civic activity but by his economic activity. One's duty was still to contribute to the public good, but such contributions could best be made through economic activity, which actually aimed at private gain. Self-centered economic productivity, not public citizenship, became the badge of the virtuous man.

A new cultural ideal was taking shape in the work and writings of these radicals. *Homo civicus* was being replaced by *homo oeconomicus*. In his letters, Josiah Wedgwood, Priestley's patron, described how he had "fallen in love" with and "made a mistress" of his pottery business. To be productive was merely to abide by the will of God. Wedgwood obeyed what he called the "eleventh commandment—Thou shalt not be idle." His friend the dissenting cotton manufacturer Jedediah Strutt was convinced, "whatever some Divines would teach to the contrary," that the "main business of the life of man was the getting of money." As we have noted, the early classics of children's literature produced in England from 1760 to 1800 by these very same middle-class radicals in Priestley's circle contain few lectures or parables extolling civic responsibility (unlike *Emile*), but they continually praise productive hard work. Anna Barbauld, we remember, wrote that great men were no longer those who devoted themselves to public life—"Kings, lords, generals, and prime ministers." There were new heroes, men who instead "invent useful arts, or discover important truths which may promote the comfort and happiness of unborn generations in the distant parts of the world." A pamphleteer of 1780 spelled out even more clearly who these new heroes were: "Consider the gradual steps of civilization from barbarism to refinement and you will not fail to discover that the progress of society from its lowest and worst to its highest and most perfect state, has been uniformly accompanied and chiefly promoted by the happy exertions of man in the character of a mechanic or engineer!"[71]

The middle-class radical praise of economic man no longer shared what Pocock described as the republican dread of Aristotle's banausic men, who were "less than citizens because they specialised in the development of one's capacity."[72] Specialization for the radicals, far from a sign of corruption, was a characteristic of the virtuous. It did not render economic man dependent on government or make him the servant of others, such as priests, lawyers, rentiers, or soldiers. The specialist, like the entrepreneur, the scientist, the engineer, the inventor, or any man of talent, was the true social hero, who through his ingenious productivity and private pursuits shaped the public good. The older praise of the public citizen as a nonspecialized amateur smacked too much of the aristocratic rule of idle and untalented privilege. A self-conscious glorification of specialization against Aristotle's "ethos of *zöon politikon*" is implicit in an ideology that extols talent, merit, and skill. Hence not just Adam Smith but a chorus of writers in the last decades of the eighteenth century sang the praises of specialization and the division of labor. The very heart of civic humanism was repudiated and its values reversed by the radical crusade to professionalize and specialize, to replace what the middle class saw as corrupt political man with virtuous and productive economic man.

Josiah Wedgwood approached civic life as a specialist in industry and commerce. "Sunk again I find into politicks" was how he described himself, reluctantly having to leave his business for citizenship. Not "fame" but "money getting" was his concern. When his friend the great engineer James Brindley died, Wedgwood noted that it was talents like his that truly benefited mankind. The public good done by such men of genius, the contribution to the commonweal by such men of "ingenuity and industry," far surpassed the contribution of political men, of "many noble lords." The economic benefactors "will be remembered with gratitude and respect" when the others "are totally forgotten." For Thomas Cooper, virtue and privilege were incompati-

---

[71]Josiah Wedgwood, *The Selected Letters of Josiah Wedgwood*, ed. Ann Finer and George Savage (London, 1965), pp. 46, 247; Strutt quoted in R. S. Fitton and A. P. Wadsworth, *The Strutts and the Arkwrights: A Study of the Early Factory System* (Manchester, 1972), pp. 109–10; John Aiken and Anna Barbauld, *Evenings at Home; or, The Juvenile Budget Opened*, 6 vols. (Philadelphia, 1792–1796), 6:223; *Letters on the Utility and Policy of Employing Machines to Shorten Labour* (London, 1780), p. 3.

[72]Pocock, *Politics, Language, and Time*, p. 92, and *Machiavellian Moment*, p. 499.

ble. Only those with "insatiable ambition" could be able, wise, or virtuous.[73]

The middle class wrapped itself in this new notion of virtue. They were "not adorn'd, it's true with coats of arms and a long Parchment Pedigree of useless members of society, but deck'd with virtue and frugality." When Jedediah Strutt in composing his own epitaph wrote that "he had led a life of honesty and virtue," thoughts of country purity and citizenship could not have been farther from his mind. His life was virtuous in comparison with the corruption of the idle nobility and the wretched poor, for he had worked harder than they and contributed more with his talent, ingenuity, and industry to the increased productivity and wealth of his nation. He was typical of a new species of self-centered virtuous men—men like those seen in Birmingham by an eighteenth-century chronicler of the middle class: "I was surprised at the place, but more so at the people: they were a species I had never seen: they possessed a vivacity I had never beheld: I had been among dreamers, but now I saw men awake: their very step along the street showed alacrity: Everyman seemed to know and prosecute his own affairs: the town was large, and full of inhabitants and those inhabitants full of industry." When such self-centered, virtuous men addressed themselves to public issues, they did so in accordance less and less with the paradigms and language of civic humanism or classical republicanism and more and more with the conceptual framework they knew best, the market. Joel Barlow—financial speculator, international entrepreneur, radical friend of Jefferson, Paine, Price, Wollstonecraft, Godwin, and Priestley—wrote of the French Revolution in the language and the paradigms he knew best: "It must be of vast importance to all classes of society . . . to calculate before hand what they are to gain or to lose by the approaching change; that like prudent stock jobbers, they may buy in or sell out, according as this great event shall effect them."[74]

Barlow and his friends, British and American, knew their Aristotle, their Machiavelli, and their Montesquieu. But they also knew their Locke. The world view of liberal individualism was fast pushing aside older paradigms during the last four decades of the century in the wake of the American crisis and the inventions of Watt and Arkwright.

---

[73]Wedgwood, *Selected Letters*, pp. 233, 81, 136, 182; and Thomas Cooper, *A Reply to Mr. Burke's Invective against Mr. Cooper and Mr. Watt* (London, 1792), p. 16.

[74]Joseph Stit, *A Sequel to the Friendly Advice to the Poor* (Manchester, 1756), p. 17; Strutt quoted in Fitton and Wadsworth, *The Strutts and the Arkwrights*, p. 108; William Hutton, *An History of Birmingham to the End of the Year 1780* (Birmingham, 1781), p. 63; Joel Barlow, *Advice to the Privileged Orders in the Several States of Europe* (London, 1792), p. 3.

Two hundred years later, republican revisionism depicts these late eighteenth-century figures as preoccupied with public virtue and civic humanism and as uninterested in Lockean liberal ideals. When allowed to speak for themselves, however, these radicals seem to tell a different story.

CHAPTER 7

James Burgh and "Opposition" Ideology in England and America

THE IDEA OF an "opposition ideology" in eighteenth-century England had preoccupied such contemporaries as Burke and Bute. More recently its very mention infuriated the great Sir Lewis Namier and his students; but only in the 1960s did it become reality—a post hoc academic reality, to be sure. The work of Caroline Robbins, J. G. A. Pocock, Bernard Bailyn, Gordon Wood, Gerald Stourzh, Forrest McDonald, H. Trevor Colbourn, Lance Banning, John Murrin, and Colin Bonwick has convinced many readers that there did indeed exist what Wood calls "an opposition view of English politics," or what Bailyn describes as "opposition theorists, country politicians and publicists." Equally convincing has been the claim by this group of scholars that this country opposition "more than any other single group of writers . . . shaped the mind of the American Revolutionary generation." A final truth seemingly established by the recent discoverers of opposition ideology is its nostalgic, backward-looking orientation; its proponents "urg[ed] a return to an ancient, balanced constitution that had been steadily undermined since the Glorious Revolution by the rise of ministerial influence and government by money."[1]

---

[1]Gordon Wood, *The Creation of the American Republic, 1776–1787* (New York, 1972), p. 14; Bernard Bailyn, *Ideological Origins of the American Revolution* (Cambridge, Mass., 1967), pp. 34, 35; Lance Banning, *The Jeffersonian Persuasion* (Ithaca, N.Y., 1978), p. 130. See also Caroline Robbins, *The Eighteenth-Century Commonwealthman* (Cambridge, Mass., 1959); J. G. A. Pocock, *The Machiavellian Moment: Florentine Political Thought and the Atlantic Republican Tradition* (Princeton, N.J., 1975) and "Virtue and Commerce in the Eighteenth Century," *Journal of Interdisciplinary History* 3 (1971): 119–34; Gerald Stourzh, *Alexander Hamilton and the Idea of Republican Government* (Palo Alto, Calif., 1970); Forrest McDonald, "A Founding Father's Library," *Literature of Liberty* 1 (January–March 1978), and *Novus Ordo Seclorum: The Intellectual Origins of the Constitution* (Lawrence, Kans., 1985); H. Trevor Colbourn, *The Lamp of Experience: Whig History and the Intellectual Origins of the*

Few writers assigned to this tradition of eighteenth-century English opposition loom as significant as James Burgh. His three-volume *Political Disquisitions* collected and reproduced in 1774 the writings of the earlier opposition theorists in the age of Walpole: Davenant, *Cato's Letters*, and Bolingbroke, as well as selections from the intellectual giants behind the country tradition, Machiavelli, James Harrington, and Algernon Sidney. For Caroline Robbins, Burgh's *Political Disquisitions* was "the most important political treatise which appeared in England in the first half of the reign of George III." For Bernard Bailyn it was "the key book of this generation." In its own day *Political Disquisitions* achieved virtual canonical status. "Have I read my Bible, sir?" Samuel Parr is alleged to have replied when asked if he had read Burgh's three volumes. Reprinted immediately in Philadelphia, they listed as their "encouragers" George Washington, Samuel Chase, John Dickinson, Silas Deane, John Hancock, Thomas Jefferson, Roger Sherman, and James Wilson.[2]

Burgh's importance for scholars consists for the most part in his role as transmitter of English republicanism and opposition ideology to Americans. In 1790, when Jefferson advised Thomas Mann Randolph on the proper reading for a young man going into law, he listed Adam Smith, Montesquieu, Locke's "little book on government," *The Federalist*, and Burgh's *Political Disquisitions*. John Adams "set himself to make the *Disquisitions* more known and attended to in several parts of America," and it was "held in as high estimation by all."[3]

Eighteenth-Century Opposition: Alternative Readings and Social Context

In addition to the consensus on Burgh's transatlantic preeminence, the secondary literature on Burgh is in agreement on two other themes. His writing is depicted as part of a single continuous country or opposition discourse, which at various times might include Whigs and Tories, but which, even in its reformist incarnation from the 1770s

American Revolution (Chapel Hill, N.C., 1965); John Murrin, "The Great Inversion; or, Court versus Country: A Comparison of the Revolution Settlements in England (1688–1721) and America (1776–1816)," in *Three British Revolutions: 1614, 1688, 1766*, ed. J. G. A. Pocock (Princeton, N.J., 1980); Colin Bonwick, *English Radicals and the American Revolution* (Chapel Hill, N.C., 1977).

[2]Robbins, *Eighteenth-Century Commonwealthman*, p. 365; Bailyn, *Ideological Origins*, p. 41; for the Parr anecdote, see *Dictionary of National Biography*, s.v. "Burgh, James"; for the "encouragers," see Oscar Handlin and Mary Handlin, "James Burgh and American Revolutionary Theory," *Proceedings of the Massachusetts Historical Society* 73 (1963): 51.

[3]Handlin and Handlin, "James Burgh," pp. 38, 52.

to and 1790s, has the corrupt court and king's ministers as its enemies, just as it did in the era of Walpole. A second assumption of writers on Burgh is that this continuous opposition tradition was always more interested in political than in economic questions, or at most was defensive of the social status quo against the inroads of commercial society. This social and economic defensiveness is accompanied by a reformist political preoccupation with the independence of Parliament and the restoration of the balanced constitution. Both opposition crusades, social nostalgia and political reform, have as their enemy corruption, be it the role of luxury and money in society in general or the ministerial purchase of parliamentary majorities in particular.

Caroline Robbins played an important role in the rediscovery of Burgh, as of so many other eighteenth-century reformers, and in doing so set forth what would become the conventional interpretation of his work. "Burgh attributed all the trouble of the period to the absence of an independent Parliament," she wrote. His concern was an end to parliamentary corruption through frequent elections, secret ballot, public debates, and the abolition of pensions and places. Robbins also noted Burgh's concern with the standing army. Still, his work was "chiefly occupied by his consideration of parliamentary abuses." For Oscar and Mary Handlin, Burgh was a reformer whose main concern was restoring the House of Commons as a check on royal and ministerial tyranny. "His writings aimed to strengthen rather than to overturn the existing order. . . . The perspective was entirely negative . . . there are, therefore, frequent though vague appeals to an earlier England."[4]

Bernard Bailyn reads Burgh as part of a great reformist triumverate in the 1770s. Along with Price and Priestley, he "renewed the earlier ideas" of *Cato's Letters* and Bolingbroke. Their reformist zeal in the 1770s, according to Bailyn, sought "to purify a corrupt constitution and fight off the apparent growth of prerogative power." Neither Burgh nor his colleagues were interested, Bailyn notes, in changing "the social order nor with the problems of economic inequality and the injustices of stratified societies." Similarly, Gordon Wood puts Burgh at the end of a tradition of radical intellectuals on the left of the ruling Whig establishment, who were unwilling "to accept the developments of the eighteenth century." Like John Trenchard and Thomas Gordon, Thomas Hollis and Richard Price, Wood has Burgh preserving the earlier republican ideals of Harrington, Milton, and Sidney.[5]

[4]Robbins, *Eighteenth-Century Commonwealthman,* pp. 365, 366; Handlin and Handlin, "James Burgh," pp. 49–50.

[5]Bailyn, *Ideological Origins,* pp. 41, 132, 283; Wood, *Creation of the American Republic,* pp. 15–16.

Colin Bonwick's *English Radicals and the American Revolution* also offers a traditionalist reading of Burgh and his fellow reformers. "They
were at one with the society in which they lived. They respected property rights and accepted the normality of a stratified society." Bonwick
describes Burgh and other English radicals as unwilling "to examine
the problems flowing from social inequality. . . . In this respect they
were incurably conservative."[6] It is Forrest McDonald, however, who
makes the classic case for the continuity of eighteenth-century opposition ideology. "Without exception," he writes, opposition writers
throughout the century were "writing in fierce opposition to the new
financial order."

> Davenant . . . warned of the evils to come. . . . *Cato's Letters* . . . the most
> quoted book in all the American's pre-revolutionary writings was pub-
> lished in 1721, in the wake of the financial corruption of the South Sea
> Bubble, and prophesied that doom was at hand. Bolingbroke's works . . .
> codified the thinking of the opposition. . . . Burgh, in a series of works of
> which the most influential was his *Political Disquisitions,* penned and pub-
> lished a popularized version of the *Cato* cum Bolingbroke gospel.[7]

Lance Banning, like Forrest McDonald, links Burgh to Cato and
Bolingbroke:

> Cato, Bolingbroke and Burgh were the most eloquent proponents of an
> ideology that occupied a central place in eighteenth-century British
> thought, headmasters of a school in which five generations of less able
> advocates were trained. From the Restoration to the French Revolution,
> English arguments were bound by a constitutional consensus. Through all
> those years, all loyal oppositions justified their presence by starting with
> the charge that men in power were conspiring to subvert the balanced
> constitution.[8]

J. G. A. Pocock reads Burgh the same way. Along with Wyvill, Price,
and Cartwright, Burgh represents a latter-day expression of a long
tradition of country rage at modernity, focusing by turns on corruption
and renovation. "Their radical demands for parliamentary and franchise reform" were simply the latest manifestation of the century-old
quest for republican virtue. In *Virtue, Commerce, and History,* Pocock
insists on an unbroken continuity in opposition ideology through the
later years of the century. Those in opposition, he writes, whoever
they might be, "were all employing much the same ideology," based

---

[6]Bonwick, *English Radicals*, pp. 18, 260.
[7]McDonald, "Founding Father's Library," p. 13.
[8]Banning, *Jeffersonian Persuasion*, p. 61.

"on an ideal of the ancient citizen." The ideology of opposition, be it "country," "commonwealth," Tory, dissenter, or radical, was "moral and neo-classisist in its arguments and assumptions." Radicalism in the entire century, Pocock writes, was "conducted largely in the name of classical-republican and agrarian-military values." Pocock singles out Burgh for special mention. Burgh's world view is "unmistakeably republican" because, in large part, his scenario for reform envisioned creation of associations for popular renewal of "moral and political virtue."[9] This, finally, is also the reading of Burgh found in the first full-length monograph devoted to him. In her *James Burgh, Spokesman for Reform in Hanoverian England*, Carla Hay concludes by describing

> the fundamentally conservative aspiration of English radicals, like Burgh, to restore some mythic yesteryear when virtue flourished and an harmo-nious equilibrium governed men's social and political rela-tionships. . . . Burgh aspired not to destroy the existing order and create anew. Instead he advocated radical reforms to achieve a conservative goal—the restoration of the ancient constitution.[10]

This conventional reading of Burgh and opposition ideology in the eighteenth century, emphasizing its continuity and its politics of nos-talgia from the age of Walpole to the French Revolution, is compatible with a second reading of the eighteenth-century opposition found in some of the same writers. In this reading a break in opposition con-tinuity occurs in the 1790s with the emergence of a working-class radi-calism that does seek to "recast the social order" in order to meet the "problems of economic inequality" and "the injustices of stratified so-cieties," to use Bailyn's distinctions. Burgh, Price, and Priestley are still depicted as "reformist radicals" preoccupied by threats to constitu-tional liberties and still committed to the social and economic past. However, John Thelwall, Thomas Spence, Thomas Evans, and Joseph Gerrald, writing in the 1790s, are considered to be urban radicals; their vision of a new future severs the opposition's link to the nostalgic country ideology of both real Whigs and corruption-hating Tories. This is the view of Ian Christie and Colin Bonwick as well as of Bailyn. Bonwick distinguishes between "old" and "new" radicalism and sees the corresponding societies of the 1790s as the artisan-based source of the "new" radicalism. Arthur Sheps also writes of "an increasing con-sciousness of the social dimensions of reform" in the 1790s. No longer

[9]Pocock, "Virtue and Commerce," p. 122; J. G. A. Pocock, *Virtue, Commerce, and History* (Cambridge, Mass., 1985), pp. 257, 260–61.

[10]Carla H. Hay, *James Burgh, Spokesman for Reform in Hanoverian England* (Washington, D.C., 1979), pp. 104–5.

were liberty and public virtue seen as the benefits of political reform. They were replaced, he writes, by "social justice or economic benefits." This is, of course, also the position of E. P. Thompson, who locates the entrance of plebeian radicalism into English politics in 1792.[11]

This second interpretation of opposition ideology in the eighteenth century, with its assumption of a transformation from a nostalgic seeking of lost liberties and virtue to a more radical and more progressive quest for economic and social justice, seems to describe accurately the shift in social composition which occurs with the entrance of artisan-based associations and their redistributive demands into the opposition in the 1790s. At the same time, it preserves intact the principal claim of the first reading, that the radical friends of the American Revolution were in the camp of Cato and Bolingbroke and that their American readers were, too.

Another reading of opposition history in the eighteenth century, however, sees nostalgic resistance to change as being abandoned earlier than the 1790s, and in a different social milieu. This perspective suggests, as we have seen, that the English reformers of the American revolutionary era were, in fact, committed partisans of modernity, of liberal individualism, and of market society. The break in opposition history, in this reading, occurred in the 1750s and 1760s, with Cato and Bolingbroke falling on one side of the divide and Price and Priestley on the other. Burgh is, in fact, the crucial figure in this third reading. His writings from the 1740s through 1774 span the all-important transition from the nostalgic opposition to the progressive opposition. In his writings opposition ideology moved from its republican, country concerns with lost civic virtue, encroaching luxury and commercialism, independent Commons, and fear of placemen, stock jobbers, and standing armies to a self-consciously more urban, more middle-class, more definitively individualist Protestant orientation. In the process of this shift Lockean influence revived, and from the 1760s the opposition more enthusiastically embraced commercial values and commercial society. The nostalgic politics of the Bolingbroke opposition, in other words, were replaced by the bourgeois radicalism of Price's and Priestley's opposition.

This reading of opposition ideology need not negate the claim that a shift did occur in the 1790s. It simply suggests that the entrance of

[11]Bailyn, *Ideological Origins*, p. 283; Ian Christie, *Wilkes, Wyvill, and Reform* (London, 1962), p. 222; Bonwick, *English Radicals*, p. 217; Arthur Sheps, "The American Revolution and the Transformation of English Republicanism," *Historical Reflections* 3 (1975): 26; E. P. Thompson, *The Making of the English Working Class* (New York, 1963). See also Iain Hampsher-Monk, "John Thelwall and the Eighteenth-Century Radical Response to Political Economy," forthcoming.

artisan groups and their demands introduced a third stage that pushed beyond middle-class radicalism. It assumes that such reformers as Price and Priestley were already concerned with recasting the social order and abolishing the injustices of stratified society, albeit from the perspective of an aggrieved, talented, and hardworking middle class. The Bolingbroke opposition, based on country and city against court, was transformed to an opposition based on city against court and country. It is in Burgh, as we shall see, that this transition from a country to a middle-class opposition can best be seen, as befits a career that straddles the two periods.

To be sure, Burgh often reads like Bolingbroke. He is, after all, a transitional figure, still steeped in country and civic humanist perspectives. My reading of Burgh reveals, however, that even when he articulates the very concerns Bolingbroke did, such as fear of paper credit and the national debt or parliamentary corruption via placemen, the grounds of Burgh's argument were often very different from those of Bolingbroke's. Burgh's principal objection to the role of the national debt and "money men" in politics, for example, was informed less by country revulsion at the replacement of traditional elites by new men in public life than by middle-class and Protestant arguments in support of the triumph of work and talent over idleness. Burgh may sound like Bolingbroke in his quest for legislation against placemen in Parliament, but his concern was not that placemen were pushing out leisured country gentlemen but rather that they were useless parasitic drones who excluded the more deserving and talented middle class.

Behind this dramatic shift in the language opposition writers used "to present their society and cosmos to themselves and to each other" lay profound social forces at work in eighteenth-century England.[12] The Protestant ethic was being politicized as the struggle between sinful idleness and virtuous hard work was translated into the political dichotomy of useless grandees and the useful middle class. As we have seen, Dissenters' repeated efforts to repeal the Test and Corporation Acts drove home this formulaic Protestant distinction.

The American crisis of the 1760s and 1770s introduced into English politics new noncountry issues of taxation and representation, which inevitably raised questions of class. These same years also saw the first impact of industrialization, with its creation of a greatly expanding middling level of English society. Around the new credit networks of borrowing and lending in regional and provincial exchange markets large numbers of men of movable property, professionals, indus-

---

[12]The phrase is Pocock's in *Virtue, Commerce, and History*, p. 290. One scholar who does see discontinuity in opposition ranks between Bolingbroke and Cato on the one hand and Burgh on the other is C. B. Cone in *The English Jacobins* (New York, 1968), pp. 45–50.

trialists, tradesmen, and shopkeepers (perhaps as many as one million of the seven million English) emerged between the few patrician elites and the many laboring poor. These men read the burgeoning political press, which not only spoke to their sense of the liberty of the subject but also provided reliable business news to calm the anxiety rampant in the new, uncertain world of credit. These were also the years of John Wilkes, whose movement for parliamentary reform and a broadened franchise was based on what John Brewer has characterized as a "commercially freer, politically self-reliant body politic."[13]

The middle years of the century saw a mobilization and politicization of the middle class. Implementation of capitalist principles of market society and laissez-faire required constant attention to Parliament and the quest for repeal of one after another of age-old pieces of paternalistic legislation. The middle class was slowly freeing itself from cliental relationships with the great. Professional men, intellectuals, and manufacturers sought to cut themselves loose from the aristocratic world of dependence and connection.

Brewer has depicted this process in the setting of that quintessential Lockean voluntary association, the private club.[14] The world of the "middling sort" organized itself in societies, lodges, fraternities, and trade and professional clubs. Perhaps the most dramatic example was the burgeoning number of Masonic lodges and pseudo-Masonic societies. Brewer argues most convincingly that the proliferating clubs provided a social network where trustworthiness and mutual aid flourished among the vulnerable actors in the new credit economy. Many provided insurance and protection for members against economic calamity; Masonic lodges especially helped cushion their members against indebtedness and social misfortune. The clubs and societies also gave members access to a substantial number of potential customers, creditors, and partners in an atmosphere of brotherhood and conviviality. Subscriptions to the clubs became a vital source of pooled investment, which freed many of the middle class from economic dependence on local aristocrats or magnates. Large numbers of entrepreneurial and philanthropic projects were funded by the subscriptions to the club box, which more often than not were invested with the publican or innkeeper where the members met to eat and drink.

---

[13]John Brewer, "Commercialization and Politics," in *The Birth of a Consumer Society: The Commercialization of Eighteenth-Century England*, ed. Neil McKendrick, John Brewer, and J. H. Plumb (Bloomington, Ind., 1982), p. 233. See also H. T. Dickinson, "The Precursors of Political Radicalism in Augustan Britain," in *Britain in the First Age of Party, 1680–1750* (London, 1987), and H. T. Dickinson, *Liberty and Property: Political Ideology in Eighteenth-Century England* (New York, 1977).

[14]Brewer, "Commercialization and Politics," p. 233.

Of crucial significance were the implications of club membership for the political culture of an emerging bourgeois society. In clubs and societies men were "free," independent of the deferential authority relationships assumed by the external political and social world. The societies determined their own activities. Members held regular elections, and offices tended to rotate within the group. Within the club or the society members were equal. The club became a major force, then, in the emancipation of the bourgeoisie from both the cliental economy and the political control of social superiors. Sir William Jones wrote in 1783 that "a free state is only a more numerous and more powerful club."[15]

Of immense importance to this new political culture of independent middle-class professionals were the provincial learned societies that sprang up in the second half of the eighteenth century. The scientists, inventors, poets, industrialists, politicians, and dissenting ministers who met monthly at the Lunar Society of Birmingham circulated and discussed literary, political, and scientific papers. The phenomenon was repeated often as many a similar middle-class assemblage met for talk and learning in the societies of Derby, Durham, Manchester, New-castle, Norwich, and Sheffield.[16] The role of the clubs and the learned societies as schools for a new politics was not lost on the young American John Vardill, who wrote a friend in New York about English life in 1774:

> The numerous societies for disputation, for the cultivation of the arts and sciences, and for political and religious purposes, furnish an unending variety of amusement, and constant source of instruction. The free association of persons of all orders at clubs, and the numerous coffee-houses, and the openness and familiarity which prevail, give a contemplative mind every hour some new matter for its advantage. Personages of the greatest importance affect not that distance and magisterial reserve, which is so common among those who can only preserve their dignity by the mysterious appendage of greatness.[17]

[15]Ibid., p. 231.
[16]See Robert E. Schofield, *The Lunar Society of Birmingham* (Oxford, 1963); L. S. Marshall, *The Development of Public Opinion in Manchester (1780–1820)* (Syracuse, N.Y., 1946); Eric Robinson, "The Derby Philosophical Society," *Annals of Science* 9 (1953); John Taylor, "The Sheffield Constitutional Society," *Transactions of the Hunter Archaeological Society* 5 (1943); W. H. Chaloner, "Dr. Joseph Priestley, John Wilkinson, and the French Revolution, 1789–1802," *Transactions of the Royal Historical Society*, 5th ser., 8 (1958); Thomas Fawcett, "Eighteenth-Century Debating Societies," *British Journal for Eighteenth-Century Studies* 3 (1980).
[17]John Vardill to Peter Van Schaack, April 5, 1774, in H. C. Van Schaack, *The Life of Peter Van Schaack* (New York, 1842), p. 22.

This, then, is the context in which Burgh must be read. In his works these changing historical forces are reflected in new themes of opposition ideology appearing alongside older and more venerable ones. What concerns us is the existence in his writings of Protestant and individualist liberal themes quite different from Bolingbroke's republicanism and its nostalgic repudiation of modernity.

Corruption and the Calvinist Nightmare in Burgh's Early Writings

Like so many others who made their mark in the political, scientific, and intellectual life of eighteenth-century England, Burgh was not English. He was born in rural Scotland in 1714. His father was a Presbyterian minister and his mother the aunt of the Scottish historian William Robertson. Burgh enrolled at St. Andrew's with the intention of studying for the ministry. An illness prevented him from completing his degree and he entered the linen trade. Failure at that endeavor sent him to seek his fortune in England in the early 1740s. A short period as a printer's helper was followed by a job as assistant in the free grammar school at Great Marlow, Buckinghamshire. In 1746 Burgh became assistant master of the Dissenter academy in Enfield, north of London. He became master of his own academy in Stoke Newington in 1747. In 1750 he moved the school to Newington Green, and there he remained for the rest of his life, educating hundreds of middle-class Dissenter youth for professional careers in the ministry, business, and public life.

Most of Burgh's creative years were characterized, then, by involvement in two vital communities. The first was the world of the Dissenter academy. As we have seen, the Dissenters of the eighteenth century perfected an alternative and innovative educational system at such centers as Burgh's in Newington, Priestley's in Warrington, and Price's in Hackney. Stoke Newington and Newington Green made up the other community central to Burgh's life.[18] Located in what is now the Islington section of London, Newington had been throughout the century a center of dissenting intellectual culture. Daniel Defoe and Isaac Watts had lived there. Thomas Day and John Howard spent part of their youth there. The latter half of the century saw Price as preacher in the chapel at Newington Green, and central figures in Priestley's cir-

---

[18]The best study of the intellectual ambiance of Stoke Newington is Betsy Rodgers, *Georgian Chronicle: Mrs. Barbauld and Her Family* (London, 1958); see also Nicholas Hans, "Franklin, Jefferson, and the English Radicals at the End of the Eighteenth Century," *Proceedings of the American Philosophical Society* 98 (1954): 406–22.

cle—John Aikin, Anna Barbauld, Thomas Rogers, and Mary Wollstone-craft—lived nearby. Priestley often visited, as did Benjamin Franklin. The Dissenter community gathered at Newington was self-conscious of its critical mission. Like their seventeenth-century forebears, they had a God-given mission to change England, to reform it, albeit with ideas rather than swords. It was from this Dissenter setting and inspired by its critical commitment that Burgh offered the English in 1746 his first work, *Britain's Remembrancer; or, The Danger Not Over.*

In this essay Burgh interpreted the Jacobite invasion of 1745 and that year's dearth of corn as divine retribution for Britain's abandonment of its virtuous ways. All about him Burgh saw corruption and the need for "the moral improvement of mankind."[19] But corruption was a very different thing for Burgh than for Bolingbroke. Nowhere in this essay does he refer to constitutional imbalance, an independent Commons, placemen, standing armies, the national debt, or any of the other themes traditional in Bolingbroke's circle. What Burgh attacks instead is his fellow Englishmen's concern with self-indulgence, pleasure, and appearance.

Bolingbroke and the civic humanist tradition did, to be sure, often attack luxury as a sign of public duty overcome by private interest. Burgh, however, nowhere suggests that Britain's moral regeneration requires a return to civic virtue, a transcendence of self through renewed moral commitment to the *res publica*. His analysis is utterly apolitical. What is required is a return to personal virtue—that is, Protestant virtue, understood as frugality, sobriety, and asceticism. Britain's salvation lies in a reformed private life, not in political or constitutional reform. Nowhere in the essay does Burgh call on the gentry to take back political power from court-sponsored money men; nowhere does he complain about the role of commerce, trade, or credit in society. Burgh's and Britain's enemies are "idleness, gluttony, drunkenness, lewdness, gaming." Indeed, in selecting an example of corruption Burgh overlooks the decline of civic participation in the wake of commercial, self-centered life to focus on the sad vision of formerly hardworking tradesmen turned into idle fops. "Their clothes bespatched with lace, their hands unfitted for business by being muffled up in cambrick to their finger ends . . . these french fopperies thus fill the heads and disguise the persons of our citizens." These tradesmen have "abandoned the sober and regular manners of our fathers." No longer do they "rise early, spend the morning examining their accounts, adjusting warehouses and shops and preparing for the busy hours of the day." Nor do they now "spend their evenings at

---

[19]James Burgh, *Britain's Remembrancer; or, The Danger Not Over* (London, 1746), p. 1.

home instructing their children, apprentices and servants in the principles of virtue and religion." In corrupt England "they are up at ten, dressed by two," and spend the rest of the day at "bottle, jockey club, playhouse, music garden."[20]

Burgh's sense of corrupt England in 1746 is quite unlike Bolingbroke's. Burgh is worried not by a decline of classical virtue but by the Protestant nightmare. Indolence, sloth, gluttony, and extravagance have triumphed over self-fulfillment through work, industry, and frugality. Burgh injects into opposition discourse a heavy dose of Protestant social theory, moving it from its secular and deistic base in the early eighteenth century to the dissenting Protestant focus of the end of the century. He condemns luxury and extravagance not because they divert citizens from public life but because they "lead only to dreaded bankruptcy, which makes a shipwreck of life, fortune and soul at once." He attacks the "races, cock matches, plays, music-gardens, balls, assemblies, operas, concerts, masquerades, breakfasting houses, ridottos and fireworks" not because they take precious time and energy from civic pursuits but because they bring shame to London, "once the seat of frugality, trade, industry, sobriety and religion."[21]

Burgh introduced into eighteenth-century opposition rhetoric the Protestant vision of life as a cosmic struggle between the virtuous forces of industry and the corrupt camp of indolence. Opposition texts after Burgh resonated less with the dialectic of virtue and commerce than with the more personal, less public dialectic of productive hard work on the one hand and unproductive sloth on the other. With this Protestant vocabulary the opposition could indict the useless aristocrat as well as the idle speculator in public credit, both of whom became targets in radical Dissenter texts of the last third of the century. Burgh wrote in 1746:

> No son or daughter of Adam has any indulgence from heaven to live a life of absolute indolence and pleasure, without filling up a certain station and doing the duties of a certain sphere. . . . We censure our time in a manner altogether useless to ourselves or our fellow creatures . . . we pass away the time of our trial for an everlasting state in pleasure.[22]

In his *Virtue, Commerce, and History* Pocock depicts a republican, civic humanist Burgh, in large part because he finds in Burgh's writings repeated calls for the creation of "associations" for renewal of "moral and political virtue."[23] *Britain's Remembrancer* does indeed contain such

[20]Ibid., pp. 6, 13.
[21]Ibid., pp. 14, 16.
[22]Ibid., p. 17.
[23]Pocock, *Virtue, Commerce, and History,* p. 261.

a call. Burgh asks "men of the first rank" to lead the general reformation. But what Burgh has in mind is not a Machiavellian *ricorso*. His is no call for a return to a *vivere civile*, only a plea for a reform of individual private lives. Burgh's reading of virtue is personal and apolitical.

> Let but the quality and Gentry enter into an association to live mostly in the country upon their estates, and within their incomes, to countenance the public worship of God, and to support a due decorum in their own families, and observe how long extravagance and impiety will continue in Britain. . . . [Let them] enter into associations for the restoration of the frugal, the industrious, the virtuous, and religious manners of your fathers, against a flood of deism, of French foppery, and of bewitching pleasure, which overruns the land.[24]

Nor should Burgh's assault on luxury and extravagance be read as a nostalgic indictment of the exchange relationships of a commercial society. In *Britain's Remembrancer* he pleads with London, whose "superior virtue and piety" as well as its "enormous wealth, trade, and magnificence" have made it "the chief of the cities of the earth," to recognize the danger that threatens it. London's merchants are princes and its commerce is "extended from sea to sea and from the rising to the setting of the sun." All this magnificence will be lost, however, if London's citizens abandon what made it possible, "a pattern of industry, sobriety and economy."[25]

Burgh's achievement was to develop the city side of Bolingbroke's country-city opposition to the court. He also appropriated Defoe's ideological defense of the new political economy, which he turned against both the court and Bolingbroke's country gentry. In this undertaking he revived the radical Protestant lexicon of Richard Baxter and John Bunyan. Opposition ideology would never be quite the same again. Moral transcendence of the self through a *vita activa* in pursuit of the public good was being replaced by the realization of the self in a *vita activa* of work. The self was on its own in a lonely, solitary pilgrimage that was the true test of virtue. An ancient and Renaissance ideology of leisured men expressing their personal virtue through participation in civic life was being replaced by one that envisioned individuals as practicing virtue through actualization of their God-given talents by hard work and achievement. How this radical Protestantism could become expressed in opposition political discourse becomes clearer in Burgh's second work, his *Thoughts on Education*, published in 1747.

---

[24]Burgh, *Britain's Remembrancer*, pp. 40–41.
[25]Ibid., p. 41.

Thoughts on Education was never as popular as *Britain's Remembrancer*, which by 1754 had sold more than 10,000 copies in numerous editions in England, Scotland, and Ireland. Even in America it went through four editions, the first printed by Benjamin Franklin in 1747.[26] In his *Thoughts on Education* Burgh, like so many of the dissenting radicals, is preoccupied with the preparation of young Dissenters for a virtuous and useful life in practical affairs. He recommends studies heavily weighted to an active life. Grammar, spelling, writing, history, "political principles," drawing, "keeping accounts" are important studies. French is necessary, as is some knowledge of Latin and Greek, "not for their own sake" but because they are "the foundation of most modern languages." Typical Dissenter that he was, Burgh also placed great emphasis on science, insisting on "astronomy, anatomy and microscopic observations." He repeats the theme of his earlier tract as he warns the young "to eschew luxury, sensual pleasure," and "to respect simplicity."[27]

What makes *Thoughts on Education* worthy of attention, however, is its anticipation of the important future political application of the radical Protestant impulse. The struggle located within the individual between virtuous hard work and the temptations of indolence is projected onto a social landscape of hardworking and idle collectivities. Burgh introduces a theme that was to become, as we have seen, the dominant element in the Dissenters' attacks on the Test and Corporation Acts later in the century, the notion of equal opportunity and careers open to the talented. This move was essential for the politicization of the Protestant ethic. Burgh laments that "we see the most laborious, industrious and useful part of mankind generally treated with neglect and contempt, and at the same time the idle, the inactive, and most restless part of the species, I mean, the rich who feed and riot and fatten on the labours of their fellow creatures, adored as Gods upon earth."[28]

Burgh is transforming the Neoclassical assumptions about virtuous and corrupt societies. As he praises hardworking farmers and tradesmen who have useful productive callings, he condemns "those wild beast warriors who butcher their fellow men and are called heroes."[29] A virtuous society is one where useful and industrious men of merit are heroes adored as gods; that is, receive the rewards of office and status. Corrupt society, however, sees idle men of little talent (the

[26]See Hay, *James Burgh*, p. 15.
[27]James Burgh, *Thoughts on Education* (London, 1747), pp. 11, 25.
[28]Ibid., p. 14.
[29]Ibid., p. 15.

privileged) as preordained winners in the competition for the prizes of life.

Middle-Class Maxims for Middle-Class Children: Burgh's Writings in the 1750s

The conventional reading of Burgh has him firmly planted in a continuous opposition tradition that is republican and Neoclassical in its politics, nostalgic and critical of commercial society in its economics. To the extent that Burgh is seen as the crucial link between the metropolitan and colonial oppositions, this reading is basic to a republican interpretation of the American founding fathers as well. This ideological portrait of Burgh, however, is deeply flawed. Not only is it based on a much too selective reading of the *Political Disquisitions* of 1774, but it is also drawn with little attention paid to Burgh's earlier writings, many of which brought him a wide reputation long before the *Political Disquisitions* appeared, the year before his death.

The book that in fact earned Burgh a permanent reputation in the Dissenter community appeared in 1754. *The Dignity of Human Nature* is a central work for properly understanding both Burgh's social theory and the transformation that opposition ideology underwent in the latter half of the century. Written after he had become master of his own academy in Newington, the book appears to be utterly at odds with the discourse of civic humanism or country ideology. We find in it no trace of either Gothic nostalgia or the ancient constitution. *The Dignity of Human Nature* is written in a different language, a language of Protestantism wedded to a clearly articulated middle-class consciousness. Burgh offers an elaborate psychological and cultural world view basic to emerging bourgeois radicalism in England. Its sources are less overtly Lockean than generalized Protestant ideals, but its flavor is equally individualistic and noncivic. It not only is at ease with market society but in fact unabashedly endorses modernity. Had Max Weber not found Franklin's *Poor Richard's Almanack*, he could have used Franklin's friend's *Dignity of Human Nature*, for it is essentially the Protestant ethic rendered in maxims for the English middle class. Burgh's essay preceded Franklin's by two years and the similarities are striking.

The book's theme is trumpeted in its subtitle: *A Brief Account of the Certain and Established Means for Attaining the True End of Our Existence.* That true end is neither citizenship nor civic commitment; it is "success and credit in life."[30] The text, some 430 pages long, provides "a series

---

[30]James Burgh, *The Dignity of Human Nature* (London, 1754), p. 94.

of directions" for young readers structured on numerous maxims or homilies, so that it reads like an English *Poor Richard*. The focus is completely apolitical. The successful man is not enjoined to commit himself to public service. Far from offering a life of civic virtue, Burgh prescribes a thoroughly Protestant regimen of individual improvement and achievement through rigorous management of the self. The keys to "success and credit" are self-control, economy, frugality, method, regularity, trusting no one, knowing how to deal with superiors and inferiors, and the proper management of time.

To make a figure in the world, according to Burgh, one must first internalize self-restraint. "If ever you was in a passion, did you not find reason afterwards to be sorry for it?" Such a "weakness" will be followed by "repentance" and "pain." Should one go to a "party of mirth," it is best to be mindful "of the hazard you run of misbehaving." Do not "forget yourself." And when you leave, "reflect how you have behaved." Silence, not public speech, is a good rule, for "men repent speaking ten times for once that they repent keeping silent." The successful man is always restrained and under control.

> It is by giving a loose to folly, in conversation and action that people expose themselves to contempt and ridicule. The modest man may deprive himself of some part of the applause of some sort of people in conversation, by not shining altogether so much as he might have done. Or he may deprive himself of some lesser advantages in life by his reluctancy in putting himself forward. But it is only the rash and impetuous talker, or actor, that effectually exposes himself in company, or ruins himself in life. It is therefore easy to determine which is the safest side to err on.[31]

The crucible where self-control is forged, where discipline is internalized, is childhood. Much of *The Dignity of Human Nature* is therefore devoted to maxims on proper child rearing. Totally absent are the liberating exhortations for the development of a social and moral sense soon to be found in *Emile*. Childhood for Burgh is a time for bridling the passions and developing a disciplined and autonomous individual firmly in control of self. Parents must be taught neither to indulge nor to be partial to their child. Instead, they must "break and form his temper." Children must be given no expectations of wealth or status, but must be raised to make their own way in the world, "by their own industry." Important for this internalization of self-reliance is a switch from corporal to psychological punishment; Burgh advises parents "to punish rather with shame and the loss of your favor," "to mortify him

[31]Ibid., pp. 22, 24, 25.

from time to time," to treat him "above all [with] disgrace." In many cases internalizing self-discipline will require solitary confinement, "shutting him up and keeping him from his diversions, and play fellows." Such confinement will give the child "an opportunity for what he most wants . . . consideration and attention to his weakness."[32] As we have noted earlier, other Dissenter reformers—Percival with his hospitals for the poor and Howard with his new-style prison—shared Burgh's conviction that solitary confrontation with an errant self would lead to a disciplined and reformed character.

Dissenter parents, according to Burgh, should not train their sons for careers in public service or benevolent philanthropy. Their concern ought to be to raise up children who are "diligent in . . . studies and active in Business." To this end they will give their sons "books, not sweetmeats, play things, and fine clothes as the most valuable presents, and the richest rewards." They will constantly encourage self-improvement. "Lying a-bed in a morning, or passing, at any time, a whole day without doing somewhat, toward his improvement, if he is in health, ought by no means to be allowed in a child."[33]

Idleness is, indeed, the grand temptation to be overcome by the virtuous self, that self which "employs his peculiar talent or advantage for the most extensive usefulness." The virtuous man for Burgh is not a political man but one who fulfills God's intention that he be useful in the improvement of this life. "Idle people make no improvements"; they "are dead before their time." Governments, therefore, "should see to it, that there be no encouragement given to idleness." They should give "encouragement to anyone who enriches or adorns his country by any valuable discovery, or noble production in arts and science." Burgh describes with great precision the corrupt man who lacks virtue. "The character of a sluggard must, I think, be owned to be one of the most contemptible. . . . And if all idle people in a nation were to die in one year, the loss would be inconsiderable, in comparison of what the community must suffer by being deprived of a very few of the active and industrious."[34]

To improve oneself is the only way "to have credit among mankind." (Burgh consistently uses "credit" in this ambiguous way.) Pursuit of knowledge, usefulness, and self-improvement "raise us above vice, and confirm us in a steady course of virtue." This Protestant transformation of virtue from its civic humanist sense is best exemplified in Burgh's insistence that the useful man who "expects to raise himself in the world," who seeks to arrive at "the safety and success of business,"

[32]Ibid., pp. 55, 57, 63, 58.
[33]Ibid., pp. 64, 58.
[34]Ibid., pp. 276, 23, 77, 270, 34.

must live a life of "method and regularity." No classical *telos* here, no transcendence of self as "civic being." This is the world of Poor Richard, where the self is transcended as "working being." All must live lives "of constant and unwearied application to the main pursuit." It is only "by dint of indefatigable diligence that a fortune is to be got in business." Methodical and regular persons are moral, for they are useful. Burgh offers a striking picture of the new cultural ideal—a day in the life of a moral man.

> Let a man set down in his memorandum-book every morning, the several articles of business he has to do through the day; and beginning with the first person he is to call upon, or the first place he is to go to, finish that affair (if he is to be done at all) before he begins another; and so on to the rest. A man of business who observes this method, will hardly ever find himself hurried or disconcerted by forgetfulness. And, he who sets down all his transactions in writing, and keeps his accounts and the whole state of his affairs in a distinct and accurate order, so that he can at any time, by looking into his books presently see in what condition his business is, and whether he is in a thriving or declining way; such a one, I say, deserves properly the character of a man of business, and has a fair prospect of carrying his schemes to an happy issue. But such exactness as this will by no means suit the man of pleasure, who has other things in his head than industry, or frugality, or affecting a useful part in society.[35]

Such methodical bookkeeping will instantly provide anxious Protestant Dissenters with a sign of whether they are "thriving or declining." Burgh is well aware, then, of the darker dimensions of Protestant anxiety. To be in debt "is one of the most substantial and real evils of life." To be "so plunged" (an evocation of Luciferian descent) and "to have no prospect of ever getting clear" is to "be in a state of despair." In some countries, Burgh suggests, not at all disapprovingly, insolvency "is punished with death." Success and failure are the only two outcomes in the challenge the Protestant God has set for each individual. He has given people talents, which "are parts of their respective trials; and they will be judged according to the use they have made of them."[36]

The verdict is likely to be favorable, the condition thriving, if the young learn to practice economy and frugality. "Next to diligence and assiduity in business," they are "the most necessary for anyone who would raise himself in the world by his own industry." Generalized themes of Protestant self-restraint join the capitalist need for saving and limited consumption in Burgh's maxims.

[35]Ibid., pp. 96, 101, 33, 32.
[36]Ibid., pp. 87, 287.

> If you can express yourself to be perfectly understood in ten words, never use a dozen. . . . He who will in his youth lavish away half-pence, when he comes to manhood, will be apt to squander away guineas. . . . He has a good income, who has but few occasions of spending, not he who has great rents, and great vents.[37]

Returning to themes of his *Britain's Remembrancer,* Burgh attacks "those pleasures of life which cost the most," such as balls, plays, elaborate coaches and powdered footmen. Such spending is "a waste of money." Better "improving barren land, raising buildings, encouraging manufacturing" than "keeping an open house and blood sucking servants." There will come a time when everyone is "called to give an account of the use he has made of his time." Better, in fact, Burgh suggests, to be a miser, "to save and hoard," than to be "a spendthrift." He is quite specific on how much one should save. Saving three or four shilling a day, he reckons, will amount to 60 or 80 pounds a year, "which sum saved up yearly over 30 years, the ordinary time a man carries on business, would amount to nearly 2000 pounds, reckoning interest, and still more if you supposed it laid out in an advantageous trade." Parents, in fact, should encourage their children

> to save a piece of money some little time, on the promise of doubling it, and, which is to the same purpose, lessening his allowance in case of misconduct, obliging him to give an exact account of his manner of laying out his money, by memory at first, and afterwards in a written account, regularly kept; putting in a purse by itself a penny or six pence for every penny or six pence given him, and showing him from time to time the sum and so forth. . . . Keeping the account he will thereby acquire a habit of frugality, attention and prudence.[38]

Burgh would not deny the "man of business" all pleasures and amusements, only expensive and wasteful ones. He offers "reading, viz. history, lives, geography and natural philosophy, with a very little choice poetry." He also recommends "riding on horseback once or twice a week," nothing to excess. Music is doubtful, especially if "there is too great a desire to excell in it." Such ambition will invariably lead to "an expense of time and money, above what the accomplishments carried to the greatest length is worth." We see that Burgh, so frugal with money, is also concerned about time. Here Burgh most perfectly plays the English Franklin. Time should not be squandered, for "it is to

[37]Ibid., pp. 35, 28, 59, 86.
[38]Ibid., pp. 38, 9, 37, 59.

you of inestimable worth." Burgh has his priorities straight about the proper uses of time. Conspicuous by its absence is time devoted to civic duties.

> Every moment of time ought to be put to its proper use, either in business, improving the mind, in the innocent and necessary relaxations and entertainments of life, or in the care of souls . . . and as we ought to be much more frugal of our time than of our money, the one being infinitely more valuable than the other; so ought we to be particularly watchful of opportunity . . . the thorough knowledge of the probable rise and fall of merchandise, the favorable seasons for importing and exporting, a quick eye to see, and a nimble hand to seize advantages as they turn up. These are talents which raise a man from low to affluent circumstances.[39]

Burgh's concern with the efficient use of time and energy, his preoccupation with keeping written accounts by which one could know at a glance whether one was "thriving" or "declining," and his general tendency to mix together commercial practices and Christian virtues were by no means unique. Such themes were traditionally found in Protestant pietist writings. Richard Baxter, for example, had written in 1673:

> Think how much work is behind, how slow thou hast wrought in the time which is past and what a reckoning thou shouldst make, if thy Master should call thee this day to thine accounts. Be therefore careful henceforth to make the most advantage of thy short time that remains, as a man would of an old lease, that were near expiring; and when thou disposest to recreate thy self remember how small a time is alloted for thy life.[40]

The proper use of time turns up in some surprising places in *The Dignity of Human Nature*. In his plea for the centrality of science in children's education and in his insistence that all men of affairs furnish themselves with "a few of the principal instruments used in experimental philosophy" (air pumps, condensing engines, microscopes, telescopes, artificial magnates, and electrical machines are mentioned), Burgh offers two arguments. First, experimental science is the best example of activity committed to "usefulness for life or futurity." But for the dissenting Protestant science has more to offer: it occupies a person's time. It renders busy the idle hands that might be doing the devil's work.

[39]Ibid., pp. 38, 26, 34.
[40]Richard Baxter, *A Christian Directory; or, A Summ of Practical Theology, and Cases of Conscience* (London, 1673), p. 4.

> A regular series of experiments and observations . . . likewise, might by supplying an inexhaustable fund of entertainment, supply the continual want of taverns, plays, music or other less innocent amusements to fill up the vacant hours. For it is only the want of something within themselves, to entertain them, that drives people to routs, rackets, or masquerades, to the fatal waste of time and money.[41]

If experimental science is a virtuous use of time, studying the classical-humanist curriculum is a wasteful one. The "scholastic rubbish of Latin and logic," Burgh writes, has been cleared away, though universities still "dispute endlessly subtle variations of words." Burgh ridicules the learned who consider themselves superior to "ordinary people." There is "more knowledge today in shops and counting houses than an age or two ago could be found in the universities." People in trade are, he contends, as "knowledgeable as any one else." What, then, should such knowledgeable people spend their time reading? Certainly not classical writers. Young people should learn modern languages, geometry, geography, history, "the theory of government, law, commerce, economics and ethics." Burgh recommends "Bacon, Locke and Sidney on government," and secondarily, Harrington, Thomas More, Hugo Grotius, Samuel von Pufendorf, John Milton, William Temple, and Montesquieu. If one wants "to have any place in politics," Burgh suggests, "one needs to know the theory of commerce."[42]

In *The Dignity of Human Nature* Burgh offers only occasional and practical glimpses of what such a theory of commerce might look like. Among his maxims are many on how to carry on and succeed in business; some, to be sure, are deeply reflective of a "theory of commerce." One should, for example, never trust anything of consequence to another. "Self love will ever be the ruling principle." Beware the crafty, Burgh advises; write detailed and exact agreements and contracts. "Try a friend before you trust him. Trust him no more than is necessary." People seldom act in pursuit of right, "but more according to present interest." Burgh perceives the marketplace as a competitive scramble; to succeed in a business deal is "to get the better of" the other party, "to secure your advantage." One must be shrewd to win in business; one must know the rules of self-serving human nature.

> Wait on a courtier, when he, or any friend, whose interest he espouses is a candidate for some place or preferment. He will not then venture to give you a flat denial (however he may gull you with promises) for fear you

[41]Burgh, *Dignity of Human Nature*, pp. 127, 122.
[42]Ibid., pp. 19, 23, 96, 125, 133.

should have it in your power to traverse his design. Or when he has just had success in some of his schemes, for being then in good humour, he may give you a more favourable negotiation. Do business with a phlegmatic slow man, after he has drank his bottle, for his heart is open. Treat with a gay man in the morning, for then, if ever, his head is clear.[43]

The Burgh of *The Dignity of Human Nature* is not the Burgh described by recent republican scholarship. This primer for youth nowhere commends the classical conception of a virtuous polity, its active, public-spirited, leisured citizens seeking the common good. By no means disdainful of modernity and commercial life, Burgh champions in this text business and middle-class values. One might still ask, however, to what extent he can be read as a spokesman for the middle class. In other words, to what extent are his recognizably Protestant concerns linked to class consciousness or class interests? Are not Pocock and Donald Winch still quite right to suggest that such claims are proleptic attributions of nineteenth-century categories to eighteenth-century ideology?[44]

Throughout *The Dignity of Human Nature* Burgh does, in fact, specify his audience as a Dissenter business class set in the middle between social superiors and social inferiors. His maxims repeatedly indicate, for example, the behavior proper to those above and to those below. On this score he is indebted to Aristotle—not, however, in championing the civic humanism of participatory citizenship but in positioning the middle class as the virtuous mean between extremes. The development of middle-class consciousness required (perhaps too obviously to be often noted) a real sense of being in the middle. Efforts to single out a stratum above and a stratum below the virtuous people in the middle are important indications, therefore, of a middle class aware of itself. This is exactly what one sees again and again in Burgh's writings. *The Dignity of Human Nature* instructs the young who aspire to success in business how to act with both their betters and their subordinates.

Young people who seek worldly success are told that if "they fall into the greatest company," they must not be humbled. "Do not sneak, nor suffer any one to treat you unworthily." Should the great "be rude, over-bearing, or purse proud," it is "less troublesome to retire than to wrangle with them." This cautious reluctance to confront the great is reinforced by Burgh's advice that "if a great person" forgets to reward service, "do not talk of it." He may not have an opportunity; he has, after all, many people to pay, "and the clamorous are too generally

---

[43]Ibid., pp. 34, 43, 83, 90, 44.
[44]For such claims, see Pocock, *Virtue, Commerce, and History,* and Donald Winch, *Adam Smith's Politics: An Essay in Historiographic Revision* (Cambridge, Eng., 1978), p. 181.

gratified before the deserving." More to the point, "it is a way to draw his displeasure upon you, which can do you no good, but will make bad worse."[45]

Burgh shares the ambivalence toward the socially superior which was to characterize the ambitious middle class in the second half of the eighteenth century. Wedgwood cultivated the aristocracy while detesting its ways. Adam Smith saw such behavior as the curse of the restless arrivé, "who serves those whom he hates, and is obsequious to those whom he despises." Thus Burgh, on the one hand, advises the study of "proper phrases" and "civilities to superiors," the acquisition of "a graceful and easy manner" by "attention and imitation of well bred people," and on the other hand, sometimes depicts the aristocracy as unworthy of emulation. Best, in fact, "to keep quite clear of the great." If one "must be thrust into their company," be dignified, for "if you sneak and cringe they will trample upon you." Burgh cautions his Dissenter students against being "meanly betrayed into an admiration of a person of high rank" whom "if he were your equal in station you would despise." Only fools and children, he writes, "are struck with tinsel."[46]

Alongside Burgh's advice on dealing with people above is a concern for his students' behavior toward those below. Let the "illiterate" stay "in their own way," he writes. If you demand from them "logical rules, you will quite confound them." At the same time, there is no greater rudeness than entertaining one's company "with scolding your servants." Indeed, an ambitious man should treat people above and below similarly. "Never contend," Burgh writes, "with superiors nor with inferiors. If you get the better of the first you provoke them. If you engage with the latter you debase yourself." Contend not, but the middle class must still deal with people beneath them. Burgh is therefore very clear on how inferiors are to be treated. One should neither scold nor swear at them lest

> they . . . despise you for a passionate, clamorous fool. Do not make them too familiar with you; they will make a wrong use of it and grow saucy. Do not let them know the value you have for them, they will presume upon your goodness and conclude that you cannot do without them. Do not give them too much wages; it will put them above their business. Do not allow them too much liberty, they will want still more and more.[47]

[45]Burgh, *Dignity of Human Nature*, pp. 19–20.
[46]Ibid., pp. 27, 77, 87. For Wedgwood, see *Selected Letters of Josiah Wedgwood*, ed. Ann Finer and George Savage (London, 1965), and Neil McKendrick, "Josiah Wedgwood and the Commercialization of the Potteries," in McKendrick et al., *Birth of a Consumer Society.*
[47]Burgh, *Dignity of Human Nature*, pp. 20, 28, 30, 84.

Not only is the middle class set apart from people above and those below by temperament and by interests, it is also morally superior to both. Frugal, ambitious, and industrious, it is free of the vices that the great and the poor equally display. Gaming, drinking, idleness, debauchery, and the constant quest for the pleasure of the moment are their only concerns. Only people in the middle lead virtuous lives.

> Great people think their inferiors do only their duty in serving them and that they do theirs in rewarding their services with a nod or a smile. The lower part of mankind have minds too sordid to be capable of gratitude. It is, therefore, chiefly from the middle rank that you may look for a sense and return of kindness.[48]

Burgh writes for people aware of themselves as a virtuous mean. He turns on the presumptuous lower orders as easily as on the people he would have taxed for "their luxury and superfluity." He ridicules the "lowest of the mob" who think themselves able "to take to task the governors of the state." Burgh's radicalism requires him to champion people who, like his students at Newington Green, "hope for success and credit in life." He is no apologist for the poor. Indeed, the existence of a virtuous mean requires the existence of persons "in an inferior station," "knowing their duty" to be faithful, diligent, and obedient.[49]

Behind this middle-class sense of moral superiority lay the need for objective evidence of one's own virtuous triumph over temptation and self-indulgence. A corrupt class of grandees above and of idle poor beneath, both incapable of resisting ease and indolence, ratified the achievements of the middle-class Protestant Dissenters. They had succeeded in God's trial and realized their calling. To condemn the way of life of both extremes was to lash out and subdue a potential wayward part of the self, and the resultant moral arrogance was the just fruit of this effort. Successful resistance in the face of temptation provided, then, no small part of the moral basis of middle-class consciousness.

The Utopian Impulse: Burgh's Writings in the 1760s

Burgh published next an essay on, as he put it, "rather what a good man would wish a nation to be, than the true account of a state of one really existing."[50] Burgh's *Account of the First Settlement, Laws, Forms of*

---

[48]Ibid., p. 93.

[49]Ibid., pp. 270, 94, 276.

[50]James Burgh, *An Account of the First Settlement, Laws, Forms of Government and Police of the Cessares, a People of South America* (London, 1764), p. iii.

Government and Police of the Cessares, a People of South America, published in 1764, borrows extensively from Harrington, but it by no means offers a Neoclassical utopian vision or a gentry-based republic in which independent, arms-bearing citizens realize their moral selves in public life. On the contrary, Burgh's utopia is a disciplined and regimented Calvinist world of publicly enforced industry and sobriety.

Cessares was ostensibly settled in 1606 by 150 families fleeing religious persecution in Europe. This was not their only motive in fleeing, however. These "honest, sober and industrious families" also sought to find in South America "a comfortable subsistence" for "them and their posterity." Burgh articulates here a theme we have met often in the Dissenters' literature, anxiety over the prospects for their children's future. In Cessares the original settlers divided land equally among themselves but each family was allotted only enough, thirty-five English acres, "to answer every necessary and useful purpose." All coal and iron mines—indeed, "whatever else is of public use and benefit"—was publicly owned, with "full satisfaction given to the one on whose estates they are found." The settlers of Cessares planned their environment with meticulous regularity. They divided the land into square parishes of four miles a side; twenty-five parishes (a hundred miles square) made up a county. Each road in the colony was thirty yards wide and met others at right angles.[51]

Cessares's civil government was the product of a social contract drafted by two of its original leaders and signed by all male settlers over the age of twenty-one. The contract produced a constitution of "mixed form," preserving "due balance" among executive, legislative, and judicial branches. The settlers rejected total popular government because such regimes, according to Burgh, were "giddy and inconstant, rash and tumultuous, full of discord and confusion." Executive power was vested in the office of governor, held initially by one of the two drafters of the contract, and granted as a hereditary right to his male heirs. Supreme legislative power rested in a senate, whose members had to be at least forty years old. Each parish elected one senator. No family could supply more than three senators in the course of a hundred years "lest any family acquire too great an influence." Senators sat for life, unless they were judged to be incapacitated by senility, "dissolution," "oppression," or "injustice," in which case they could be removed by the Senate itself, or by the governor upon presentation of a petition signed by a majority of the senator's constituents. The senators met infrequently and for a strictly limited number of days, lest they consider themselves "an aristocracy." The Senate's re-

[51]Ibid., pp. iii, 6, 67, 45, 89.

sponsibility was to make new laws, abolish old ones, and levy taxes. The governor's job was to execute the laws and preserve the terms of the original contract. A governor, like a senator, could be removed if a majority of citizens petitioned the Senate. If he were found guilty after a trial by the Senate, the next heir would assume the office. Citizenship in Cessares was reserved for married Protestant men over twenty-one. In addition an applicant for citizenship was required to "bring sufficient proof to the Senate, on the testimony of several citizens, that he is sober, industrious and peaceable."[52]

The most significant office in the Cessarean constitution was that of inspector. Each parish had six inspectors, at least thirty years old, who held office for three years. One-third of the inspectors were elected each year, and a term as inspector was a prerequisite for election to the Senate. The inspectorate and its responsibilities reveal the ideological core of Burgh's utopian vision. Inspectors were the "guardians of the state." Their function was "to watch over the whole community, to take notice of the first beginnings of vice and every irregularity, and to take care that the virtue and innocence of the nation be not corrupted." Burgh's inspectorate might seem, then, to be an institutionalization of Machiavelli's *ridurre ai principii*, providing for the constant elimination of corruption and renewal of public virtue. The inspectors were uninterested, however, in the realization of personal virtue through civic participation. Their responsibility, on the contrary, was "to keep everyone within the bounds of order and decency," which required "masters of families to bring up [their] children to be tractable and orderly, to behave with modesty, civility and courteousness, and to enure them at home to such labour and industry as their ages will admit of, that they may not acquire a habit of sloth and idleness."[53]

Inspectors had quasi-judicial functions as well. They were "obliged to inform against all offenders," so that "no crime could escape its proper punishment." Vice was not a lack of interest in public life; it was "idleness, fraud and oppression." The inspectors were to keep Cessares true to its ideals, whereby "none were allowed to be idle or exempt from labour; even the lame and infirm were not entirely excused; and children of five years of age were employed according to their strengths and capacities and were brought up to be obedient, modest and of an obliging behaviour."[54]

Inspectors were responsible to the Senate and could be removed for abuse of their power. Each inspector was required to report to the Senate at its meetings (held four times a year) "on the state and be-

[52]Ibid., pp. 16, 45, 50.
[53]Ibid., pp. 43, 51, 44.
[54]Ibid., pp. 51, 34, 35.

haviour of the people under his care." Inspectors were to pay particular attention to "the moral character and behaviour of ministers," who were chosen in each parish by a majority of citizens. The inspectors were also required to "have a constant eye upon the schools and on the teachers," for in Cessares education was not left to the parents, lest they be "indolent and effeminate lovers of ease and pleasure and impatient of labour." The Senate built a public school in each parish, appointed masters and mistresses for each, and required all children to attend. The inspectors had to see to it that in the schools the children

> learned religion, virtue, justice, goodness, temperance, moderation, self-government, modesty, due respect, obedience to their superiors and also were early accustomed to labour and industry . . . one half of the day spent learning useful trades and employments, the other half reading, writing and understanding accounts.[55]

Cessares was by no means a Neoclassical republic. Burgh's utopia was a Calvinist republic, complete with all the contradictions of liberation and repression inherent in that ideal. On the side of liberty, Cessareans could not be prosecuted for their religious opinions, nor were they required to subscribe to any article of faith. Duels and usury were not allowed. There were public jury trials and no paid lawyers. All "laws are plain, natural and obvious." No one was tortured. All punishments (fines and community service) were to serve "the reformation of the offender." The death penalty was reserved for treason, murder, and adultery. There were no poaching laws; wild fish, fowl, and animals were fair game for all. As God gives to all "the natural right to liberty, we allow of no slavery among us." Marriage was a freely consensual contractual arrangement involving no financial settlements, and divorce was a civic right freely granted by the Senate "for just reasons."[56]

Alongside these liberating features of Christian freedom was the other side of the nonconformist inheritance in Burgh's Cessares, the dark side of dragooning Protestantism. Any indecent talk or behavior was cause for punishment. "All immoral and obscene books, prints, pictures are ordered to be burnt. Those that have them to be fined as encouragers of vice." All "unnecessary refinements and embellishments of life" which "minister only to idleness and pride" were prohibited. Banquets, plays, horse racing, and card games were forbidden, lest "they encourage indolence and seduce the industrious from their necessary business and employments." Cessareans were allowed to

[55]Ibid., pp. 53, 63, 73.
[56]Ibid., pp. 59, 60, 64, 68, 79, 83.

drink only water; wine and beer were outlawed. The senators "regulated everyone's dress according to their age and sex," so that all would appear "plain, decent and becoming." And over all the citizens of Cessares hovered the specter of "bettering houses," where the inspectors were to send "effeminate fops, idle men, bad husbands, wives or children," to be bettered by the discipline of work. The inspectors of Cessares fulfilled the mission Burgh had demanded of magistrates and the police in his *Britain's Remembrancer;* they were "a terror and a restraint upon evil doers, not a gigantic but harmless bugbear."[57]

Burgh's Puritan utopia offers homage to Rousseau, but not to the Rousseau of the *Social Contract,* reviver of the ancient city and ancient virtue. It is the Rousseau of *The Letter to D'Alembert* and *La Nouvelle Héloïse,* so fancied by English Dissenters in the 1750s and 1760s, whom Burgh cites. It is to Rousseau's Calvinist sensibility, his claustrophobic household ideal, that Burgh points as a European model for the people of Cessares. Rousseau has told us of a people in Switzerland, Burgh reminds us, who, like the Cessareans, are

> free from taxes, imports and oppressions, who cultivate their own lands with all possible care and who employ their leisure hours in many handicraft trades. . . . The snow comes and they are shut up in their own homes with their numerous family in a neat wooden house of his own building where he employs himself in useful and amusing exercises. . . . They also make cranes, spectacles, clocks, pumps, barometers and camera-obscura . . . so that you would take his room to be the shop of a mechanic, or the closet of some experimental philosopher. . . . Their chief enjoyment is to sing psalms with their wives and children.[58]

Burgh's utopian ideal, like that of Rousseau's novels, while egalitarian, is primarily privatistic and apolitical. The proper cultivation of individual character is his concern. The children in Cessares are not brought up for a life of civic responsibility, they "are brought up to be sober and modest, enured to labour and industry and instructed in every branch of useful knowledge." They are brought up "to sing psalms and such moral songs as tend to excite to piety . . . to encourage purity of heart and manners and a wise and regular course of life." As in Rousseau's texts, so in Cessares, women are brought up to be "loving, frugal and industrious wives and good mothers." In a rhapsodic summary of the Cessarean ideal Burgh repeats his debt to the

[57]Ibid., pp. 34, 41, 80, 83, 85.
[58]Ibid., p. 112. For Rousseau's popularity among dissenters, see Staughton Lynd, *The Intellectual Origins of American Radicalism* (New York, 1969), p. 33, and Clinton Rossiter, *Seedtime of the Republic* (New York, 1953), p. 359. Among the dissenting radicals Thomas Day and David Williams were particularly influenced by Rousseau.

domestic, sentimental paradise of Rousseau and adds to it a theme borrowed from another great Calvinist text, Locke's.

> Oh Happy state! Founded upon and conducted by the principles of reason, goodness and equity. Where the equal division of land, and the moderate quantity allowed everyone, without any foreign commerce, restrain pride, ambition and luxury, and establish temperance and industry while everyone is contented and cheerful, crowned with liberty, possessing all the blessings of a calm country life, and peaceably enjoying the fruits of his own labour.[59]

Burgh used the utopian genre once again, more temporally than geographically, in his two-volume *Crito, or Essays on Various Subjects*, published in 1766 and 1767. Volume 2 is dedicated "to the good people of Britain of the twentieth century." In this 120-page dedication, Burgh offers advice "from my age to yours, since I am not much heeded in my own." *Crito*, the first of Burgh's writings to concern itself primarily and overtly with reform and British politics, is the clear forerunner of *Political Disquisitions*. Here, too, Burgh finds many of the same problems that had troubled Bolingbroke and *Cato's Letters*. But much of this continuity is only apparent. At the same time that Burgh uses commonwealth or country rhetoric he subverts its nostalgic antimodernist connotations and redefines its vocabulary. Burgh's joining of his Protestant concerns with Lockean liberal ideals gives his *Crito* an orientation quite different from Bolingbroke's writings. This orientation was picked up in the 1770s by other radical Dissenters in the opposition camp, such as Price and Priestley.

From the first page of the *Crito* Burgh's call for change is differentiated from earlier opposition assumptions. He denies that politics is an inappropriate subject for ordinary tradesmen and uneducated common folk who attend Dissenter chapels. Politics is not a pastime appropriate only for leisured gentlemen and lettered scholars. Anyone, Burgh writes, "can be a judge of political subjects." To write on politics one "need not be master of the sublime geometry or the Newtonian philosophy." All that is necessary "to criticize government," according to Burgh, is "plain sense, common sense, common honesty, and a moderate knowledge of history." Is the brain of a statesman "made of materials different from that of a citizen?" he asks.[60]

To be sure, what such ordinary people as Burgh and his Dissenter friends find wrong with Britain reads very much like the litany of corruption that Bolingbroke and his opposition of leisured indepen-

---

[59]Burgh, *Account of the First Settlement*, pp. 106, 115, 117, 119.
[60]James Burgh, *Crito, or Essays on Various Subjects*, 2 vols. (London, 1766, 1767), 1:1, 2.

dent men of means had complained about. Burgh's list of "the real grievances under which the nation groans" includes

> the hideous incumbrance of a debt of 140 millions; the length of Parliament and the inequality of Parliamentary representation; the enormous power of the Court through places and pensions; the unconstitutional evil of a multitude of placemen in the House of Commons . . . the universal decay of public spirit and prevalency of political corruption.[61]

Burgh proudly presents himself to his twentieth-century readers as an innovative reformer who was labeled in his age a "romantic and a visionary." He denounces the traditionalists of his age, for whom "whatever has been done, may always be done; and whatever is always done, is ipso facto right to be always done."[62] But most of his twentieth-century readers, as we have seen, have agreed with his contemporary critics in labeling him a reactionary reformer who called for a return to the "Gothic constitution" or the idealized balanced constitution of the revolutionary settlement destroyed by Walpole and his corrupt Robinocracy, with its alliance of the court and the new world of financial capitalism and public credit. But is Burgh's response to the "real grievances under which this nation groans" as reactionary as his twentieth-century readers contend?

Take, for example, his important proposal in the *Crito* for reform of the House of Commons. In the dedication Burgh tells the reader that he hopes the House will be different in the twentieth century. In his day Cornwall and Devon had 70 MPs, North Britain 45 MPs, and "meaner boroughs" 200. His proposal is not for increased county representation, however, but for an enlarged representation of industrial centers. Far from using older categories of landed independence, virtue, and public spirit, Burgh speaks in the newer idiom of class. "Would you believe," he asks his future reader of the twentieth century, that in his day "the great interests of the nation are not represented in Parliament at all, viz. the commercial, the manufactural and the monied;" that "a merchant, a manufacturer, or a proprietor in the funds, is not by being such, entitled to one vote for a member to represent his property?"[63]

It is difficult for a twentieth-century reader of Burgh's *Crito* to find him a nostalgic critic of market society. On the list of "real grievances" Burgh included "the enhancing of the price of labour and of manufactures." He appreciated the laws of the market only too well, as he

[61]Ibid., p. 29.
[62]Ibid., 2:21.
[63]Ibid., pp. 14, 23, 24, 35.

insisted that "all manners of machines" and "inventions for reducing the price of labour" should be encouraged. Rivals in trade who have more machines than we "infallibly undersell us at foreign markets." According to Burgh, then, "whatever enhances the prices of labour prejudices our trade." Like Priestley and virtually all the other radical Dissenters, Burgh was a critic of the poor laws, which he saw as inflating the price of labor. The "idle poor should lose their right to public charities," he wrote. They should be sent "to the plantations when they come to want, instead of alms-houses." This same concern about the price of labor leads Burgh to a lengthy attack on "working men having to pay so much for bread." The landed gentry benefit, Burgh writes, while poor workingmen, the manufacturers who must pay their laborers, and, finally, England's trade all suffer. Burgh makes no secret of the fact that his worries over the price of bread are not motivated simply by concern for the poor. He writes, much like a Manchester opponent of the corn laws in the next century, of those evil landlords who take "the opportunity to ingross and monopolize the necessaries of life, to the distressing of the poor, and increasing their numbers, and the enhancing of the price of labour and of manufactures."[64]

The same can be said for the national debt, opposition to which has become for Pocock and others, as we have seen, a litmus test indicating disapproval of the economics of the capitalist market. Burgh is, in fact, much less critical of the new financial order than Bolingbroke was. Burgh does object to the national debt, but his objections are quite compatible with the capitalist market. To begin with, he exhibits the basic Protestant revulsion at debt. "An individual plunged in debt," writes Burgh, "is confessedly in a precarious condition. Why should the case be different with respect to a nation?"

More important even than the curse of debt in general, with its suggestion that one has failed in one's calling, is the symbolic role of the national debt in particular, as exemplifying a corrupt society where idle men acquire great riches through the impersonal operations of the market, not as the fruits of their own labor. The national debt is evil because it produces legions of well-to-do jobbers "employed in a very useless way . . . who would otherwise have been carrying on arts, manufactures, and commerce." The national debt, according to Burgh, hampers commerce and trade by the heavy taxes needed to pay its interest. A contribution of one-tenth of the property of every English subject to end the debt, he suggests, would "set our nation free and put our manufactures on a more nearly equal foot with those of our

[64]Ibid., 1:30, 54; 2:92–93; 1:30.

rivals." If there were no government securities and no national debt "in which persons of property could secure their superlucrations," people would invest "their money in trade and manufactures. How much this would tend to the advancement of commerce needs not to be specified."[65]

The taxes on the debt fall too "directly and immediately on manufactures." Instead, Burgh suggests, the idle and their "useless and dangerous" pastimes should suffer. Dogs, playhouses, opera tickets, saddle horses, rich clergy, landlords, lawyers, placemen, "and all other nuisances" should be severely taxed. Far from being a critic of commerce and the corrupting effect of market society, Burgh is blunt in exhorting England to be more competitive in the international market. "Our tax loaded trade gives our enemies an advantage in peace they had not in war. If we are excluded from markets the more necessary that we look out for new markets and extend our commerce to places yet unfrequented by our merchants, as the interior parts of Africa, behind our settlements, etc."[66]

Burgh calls for an end to all trade monopolies, which "cramp and diminish the national commerce." Instead of maintaining monopolies, governments should offer "public honours and emoluments" to "discoverers of anything useful in arts, manufactures and commerce." Far from honoring virtuous statesmen, lawgivers, or soldiers, the likes of Cato, Brutus, and Cincinnatus, Burgh, the alleged nostalgic republican critic of modernity, would give public honors for "the invention of a richer dye, or a more beautiful, or more convenient cloth, stuff or silk than any now known."

> Manufactures, for which a vent in foreign countries can be found are a more valueable fund of riches to a nation, than mines of gold and silver; inasmuch as it is more to be wished, that the people be industrious than idle. Therefore, every eating mouth, without a pair of working hands to it, is an evil to be avoided in every well-regulated state. As, on the contrary, the greater the number of industrious people in a country, the more flourishing that country.[67]

When Burgh turns to the evil of placemen, his concerns are much more economic and moral than constitutional. He introduces the subject, for example, in his discussion of exorbitant taxation, not in his treatment of parliamentary reform. What's wrong with placemen is their "easy, often affluent circumstances . . . innumerable needless

[65]Ibid., 1:31, 32.
[66]Ibid., pp. 35, 56, 61.
[67]Ibid., pp. 36, 37, 50–51.

posts and places . . . exorbitant salaries." Particularly offensive is public subsidization of the useless and the unproductive, "the enormous national expense to the great encouragement of idleness . . . to the heavy detriment of the arts, manufactures and commerce while the state is almost swallowed up in debt." Every industrious subject is right in complaining, Burgh writes, when he sees "the fruits of his labour" dished out to "a set of overgrown bloodsuckers, such are those placemen and pensioners." Placemen, according to Burgh, are usually idle men of privilege, "tinselled things," "persons of fortune and rank," "persons of high quality and large property." Like his friend Franklin, who would, indeed, make such a suggestion during the Constitutional Convention, Burgh proposed that government officials "should serve the public for nothing." His emphasis, then, is not on the mere presence of placemen in the Commons, as a violation of constitutional balance, but on the violation by this practice of the work ethic as well as of the principle of public careers open to the talented. In Britain, he laments, "the state was looked on, not as the subject of general care, but as a fat carcass for a set of ravenous beasts, called Grandees to worry one another about . . . rewarding [them] with money throws a false glare on worthlessness and disgraces merit."[68]

Burgh expresses here what we have recognized to be a central theme in emerging eighteenth-century liberal social theory, equal opportunity in the race of life. "Give all," Burgh demands in volume 2 of the *Crito*, "an equal chance for rising to honours in the state according to merit." It is an ideal that informs Burgh's assault on placemen as well as his indictment of the onerous Test and Corporation Acts. "Away with all foolish distinctions about religious opinions," he writes; "those with different religious views are both equally fit for being employed in the service of our country."[69]

In his plea for religious toleration, for individual rights "against the cruel restraints on conscience" posed by "clerical subscriptions," as well as in his vision of the industrious man of talent receiving "the fruits of his labour," Burgh in the *Crito* writes very much in the shadow of Locke. As Locke in his *Letter on Toleration* would clearly separate the civil realm of the magistrate from the otherworldly concerns of religion, so Burgh urges his twentieth-century readers (in a passage that could well be the source of Jefferson's metaphoric rendering of Locke's notion) to "build an impenetrable wall of separation between things sacred and civil." Equally significant is Burgh's adoption of the Lockean logic that depicts all social institutions in voluntaristic and contractual

---

[68]Ibid., pp. 59, 61.
[69]Ibid., 2:68.

terms. We see this logic in Burgh's discussion of marriage in the *Crito*. Just as Locke demystified church membership in the *Letter on Toleration* by suggesting that people voluntarily choose to join and to leave a church in accordance with its ability to serve their interests, Burgh takes a wholly nonspiritual contractual view of marriage. He criticizes the process of publishing banns in churches and the celebration of marriage by clergy at high altars, all of which are but "remains of popish superstition." Burgh ridicules the "pretended holiness of the marriage state" with a vivid illustration of the new liberal attitude toward social institutions, complete with an analogy to the practical world of business.

> There is no more of holiness in holy matrimony than in an apprenticeship or partnership in trade. They are alike matters of mere civil concerns, for in the future state there is neither marriage nor giving in marriage; and it would be full as rational to oblige every tradesman to have the banns of apprenticeship published in the church, and the indenture signed at the altar.[70]

Burgh has also absorbed the Lockean voluntaristic and contractual theory of the state. What states do, Burgh contends, is merely serve the interests of those who consent to their creation. They protect well-being and property. Governors are but trustees for the governed and as such can be recalled if they violate their trust. In a wonderfully revealing passage at the beginning of volume 1 of the *Crito*, Burgh expresses this liberal idea of the state, again with an analogy to business. This is not language suggestive of a classical view of politics.

> The subjects in a free country have a right to consider themselves on the same foot with the stockholders in a trading company. If a proprietor of East India stock sees the directors pursuing measures detrimental to the interest of the company, he will not, I believe, hesitate long about his being a competent or incompetent judge of directorial politics. He will soon make ENGLAND ring with his complaints. The same every subject has a right to do, whenever the conduct of the ministry becomes justly suspicious.[71]

But Burgh was by no means consistently a liberal preoccupied with private rights. He was capable, as indeed Locke was, of utter disregard for private rights when idleness was involved. Just as Locke had suggested in *Some Thoughts Concerning Education* that children of the idle should at the age of three "be obliged to come" to "working schools" to

[70]Ibid., 1:30, 2:118, 1:45.
[71]Ibid., 1:2.

be cured of idleness, so Burgh in the *Crito* would give magistrates the power "to insist on every man and every woman giving an account of some useful work, or business, done by them, on pain of a handsome fine." A register, he suggests, should be kept in every parish. If anyone were idle, a complaint would be made to the magistrate, who would enter it in the register. People who were complained of frequently would be sent to workhouses. No one, Burgh writes, "has a right to be totally idle."[72]

The *Crito* has a paradoxical countertheme related to but quite at odds with this vision of repressive magistrates. Hunting down the idle is seen primarily as the civic responsibility of everyone. Burgh calls on neighbors to inform on one another, to form associations to encourage such informing and mutual inspection. With its roots deep in the ancient Anglo-Saxon frankpledge system, Burgh's call is also an interesting anticipation of Godwin's illiberal parish-based anarchism. Godwin's doctrine of mutual supervision and neighborly persuasion would root out evil and culminate in the elimination of the magistrate and law itself. In the *Crito* Burgh would do away with lawyers, juries, and law, using many of the same arguments that Godwin was later to use. It is difficult, Burgh writes, to fix by permanent laws rules for all times and all circumstances. "Your people," Burgh informs his twentieth-century readers, "shall be incomparably better held to their duty, by seeing themselves in the absolute power of their honest neighbors, to be acquitted, or punished, as the matter may on examination appear." Neighbors punishing neighbors will end the horrors of a legal system that treats too many too severely "for trifling offenses."

Like Godwin, Burgh adds to his critique of "the tediousness, uncertainty or expense of the law" its brutality and its injustice. But even on this issue, Burgh cannot resist touching base with the social and ideological heart of his vision. The major consequence of the uncertainty of the law is the "precarious state of property." Only one law will, in fact, persist, and it alone will be the guiding concern of neighborly justice. "Thou shalt not wrong thy neighbor in his property." As for the too great severity of the legal system, here, too, we find a deeper level of moral concern. "The gallows deprive us every year of many hands, which might be usefully employed." Perhaps it is not the dissenting philosopher Godwin but the dissenting prison reformer Howard who is anticipated in Burgh's ultimate indictment of British law—its wastefulness.

[72]For Locke, see his *Some Thoughts Concerning Education* (1693), ed. R. H. Quick (London, 1899), pp. 189–90. Burgh, *Crito*, 2:71, 1:54.

Forty thousand are in all the jails of Britain and Ireland. How ridiculous is it to suffer such a multitude to continue, for many years together, useless to the community. Not useless only, but hurtful. Every prison ought to be a workhouse. Offenders ought to be obliged to work as part of their punishment, for idleness is oftenest the cause of their coming into such places.[73]

"Have I Read My Bible, Sir?": Burgh's *Political Disquisitions*

Despite its dedication to readers of the twentieth century, *Crito* is not the work for which Burgh is best known in this century. That work is, of course, his magnum opus, the three-volume *Political Disquisitions*, which made Burgh's reputation in his own era. Widely read and widely cited in the quarter century after its publication in 1774, it became a veritable sourcebook for the reformers who were to plague George III and his ministers through the era of the American and French revolutions. Wilkes used the text in his famous speech of 1776 advocating parliamentary reform, and Catharine Macaulay, John Jebb, Capel Lofft, John Cartwright, Granville Sharpe, Richard Price, and Joseph Priestley all cited Burgh's three-volume work in their own reform efforts.[74]

A major reason for the success and widespread use of Burgh's last work was its format. It was literally a sourcebook. The three volumes consist primarily of long passages reproduced from the works of other writers and historians, ancient and modern, as well as long exerpts from parliamentary speeches and legal commentary. Notwithstanding Burgh's insistence in the preface that "politics, as observed by Locke . . . are only common sense . . . plain sense . . . applied to national instead of private concerns," he wanted to provide, as he put it, "from authentic history, and the opinions of many of the best politicians of various ages and nations, the true principles according to which the British Empire ought to be governed."[75]

Burgh provided these "true principles" for use by contemporaries who shared his rage at "public ERRORS, DEFECTS, and ABUSES" and his

---

[73]Ibid., 2:76, 81, 101–2; 1:30; 2:102–3; 1:30, 49–50. See also the utopian community planned by Granville Sharpe, the great critic of slavery, for freed Negroes in Sierra Leone, where "the eye of every neighbour" was upon every other: Granville Sharpe, *A Short Sketch of the Temporary Regulation for the Intended Settlement . . . Near Sierra Leone* (London, 1788).

[74]The impact of the *Political Disquisitions* is documented in Hay, *James Burgh*, pp. 40–41.

[75]James Burgh, *Political Disquisitions: An Enquiry into Public Errors, Defects, and Abuses*, 3 vols. (London, 1774), 1:x.

commitment for "REFORMING those ERRORS, DEFECTS, and ABUSES: of RESTORING THE CONSTITUTION and SAVING the STATE." They have been useful also for twentieth-century scholars who wish to reconstruct the ideological cast of late eighteenth-century radical thinking. What modern scholars have tended to find there, as we have seen, is a case for Burgh the transmitter of traditional opposition or country concerns, informed by a nostalgic world view, Neoclassical, civic humanist, or republican in its foundations.[76]

It is not a difficult case to make. Much of the *Political Disquisitions* is devoted to themes closely associated with the country-based or commonwealthman opposition of the early eighteenth century. Balanced parliamentary government is depicted as threatened by pervasive ministerial corruption and the lack of annual parliaments. Bribes and jobs have undermined the independence of the Commons. A standing army, luxury, the national debt, and placemen have brought Britain to the brink of ruin. Numerous pages are devoted, in fact, to reprintings of Bolingbroke and *Cato's Letters* on each of these topics. Large amounts of space are also given to Harrington, Trenchard, Gordon, and Davenant, even to Machiavelli, Livy, and Cicero. Long exerpts from parliamentary assaults on Walpole are included, as are numerous parliamentary speeches on place bills and proposals for annual parliaments, suffrage reform, and measures to fund the national debt.

Many twentieth-century readers have been struck by the mood of gloom and ruin created by the reprinting of so much of Bolingbroke, *Cato,* and Davenant. The *Political Disquisitions* reads in many places like Bolingbroke's *Craftsman,* with long histories of ministerial corruption and repeated comparison of Britain's decline with the fall of Rome. Burgh, to be sure, does add to this mood in his own contributions to the text. Nostalgically comparing his contemporaries with their predecessors, who "had a high relish for patriotism, liberty and glory," he finds that "they defended themselves, we use mercenaries; they served their country disinterestedly, we fill our pockets with spoils of the country; they served the public for honour, we for yellow dirt." To Burgh, indeed, the spread of commerce and luxury suggests that one should "not expect from mankind much disinterested public spirit." This decline of public spirit leads to a corrupt and enslaved England. A return to its true virtuous principles perhaps requires, according to Burgh, a patriot king to awaken the corrupt English, "to insist on laws and regulations for gradually abolishing places and pensions and restoring the nation to the condition it was in." More realistic, however, are the prospects for renewal through Burgh's "plan for retrieving the

[76]Ibid.; the capitalized words are from the subtitle to the work.

nation." "A grand National Association for restoring the Constitution and saving the state" would pit "the body of independent people" against "a designing minister, a mercenary army, and a corrupt parliament." Burgh sees liberty itself as a victim of conspiring forces, an alliance of "a corrupt and corrupting Court . . . blood sucking placemen . . . standing army . . . debauching commerce . . . luxury." The fear he expresses is seemingly basic to the opposition spirit of the eighteenth century.

> Liberty seems, indeed, to be bidding mankind farewell, and, like Astraca, to be taking her flight from the earth. All Europe was once free. Now all Europe is enslaved, excepting what shadow of liberty is left in England, Holland, Switzerland, and a few republics in Italy. And such is the encroaching nature of power and so great the inattention of mankind to their supreme worldly interest, that the states of Europe, which still boast themselves free, are like to be soon in the same condition with the others, which do not even pretend to possess any degree of liberty.[77]

Two years later Tom Paine implored Americans to embrace this freedom "hunted round the globe" and "recently warned to depart from England." How moving, then, Burgh's reading of corrupt England must have appeared to the colonials, whose sense of liberty's and their victimization, Bailyn suggests, lay at the ideological heart of the American Revolution. Here, then, is the crucial link in the transmission of opposition ideas across the Atlantic, for Americans devoured Burgh's *Political Disquisitions.* Colonial newspapers published extracts in 1775 and an American edition was available in the same year. The list of subscribers, as Carla Hay notes, was a veritable "who's who in the American Revolution." Jefferson, as we've seen, included *Political Disquisitions* on a short list of great books on political theory, and John Adams in 1774 described reading the *Disquisitions* as "the best service that a citizen could render to his country at this great and dangerous crisis."[78]

Americans who read Burgh's three volumes in 1775 no doubt saw them as proof of what Bailyn describes as their sense of "a comprehensive conspiracy against liberty throughout the English-speaking world."[79] They could read in them numerous passages describing the struggle of power and liberty, emphasizing always the aggressive and encroaching nature of power, a theme Bailyn depicts as pervasive in prerevolutionary America. The "love of power," Burgh writes, "is nat-

---

[77]Ibid., 2:90, 421, 90, 423, 449, 410, 415.
[78]Hay, *James Burgh*, pp. 42, 44.
[79]Bailyn, *Ideological Origins*, p. ix.

ural; it is insatiable; it is whetted, not cloyed, by possession. All men possessed of power may be expected to endeavor to prolong it beyond the due time, and to increase it beyond the due bounds, neither of which can be attempted without danger to liberty."[80]

The *Disquisitions* appealed to Americans, however, not simply because of its vivid sense of the impending ruin of power-hungry England or its meticulous depiction of ministerial and court corruption, or its moving attack on the unrepresentative Parliament. Equally important was that Burgh wrote directly about the Americans in his text, feeding, in fact, their deepest fears. The object of government ministers in taxing the Americans, Burgh writes, was simply to enlarge the power of the court, by increasing "the number of places, and pensions for their dependents." He sympathized in general with the plight of the colonists, criticizing the government measures that required them to use British ships, to purchase British goods, and, above all other grievances, to pay taxes without representation. Burgh's list of alternatives the government should have undertaken before taxing the Americans fits the general opposition and American sense of thoroughly corrupt England. The government should, he wrote, have "reduced salaries, abolished places, pensions, withheld election expenses and bribes for voters, reduced an odious and devouring army, and taxed vice, luxury, gaming, and public diversions." These measures, Burgh calculates, would have produced ten times more revenue than Grenville did by taxing the colonies. Even more flattering to his American readers, and equally confirming of their deeply held beliefs, was Burgh's suggestion that the example of "the Dissenters retired to America" provided the hope for the renewal and regeneration of virtue in the English-speaking world.[81]

A good deal of material in the *Disquisitions*, then, justifies a reading of Burgh as a nostalgic country theorist operating in the same continuous republican discourse begun by Bolingbroke earlier in the century. Knowing what we now know about Burgh's earlier writings, however, we should be surprised if this civic humanist dimension were all there was in the *Disquisitions*. That, indeed, is not all there is.

Burgh did rely heavily on reprints of earlier works. The enemies of those writers, after all, were also his: a corrupt court, placemen, an ineffectual Commons, the national debt. Since distinguished authorities had already produced extensive attacks on the common enemy, Burgh enlisted their help in his indictment of corrupt England in 1774. The rhetorical attacks on the common enemy were even couched

---

[80]Burgh, *Political Disquisitions*, 1:107. *Cato's Letters* is the preeminent source of this opposition theme.
[81]Ibid., 2:275, 38; 3:30, 219.

in a common vocabulary centering on corruption and virtue. But these core concepts that structured the deeper world views of early and late eighteenth-century oppositions had, as we have seen, changed meaning and been redefined.

Alongside—indeed, overshadowing—republican Burgh in the *Disquisitions* is Burgh the theorist of individualism, of rights, and of market society. His Protestant discourse in the *Disquisitions* is self-consciously linked to older arguments of the juridical rights school, to Locke, and to middle-class economic and social interests. In each of the *Political Disquisitions'* lengthy expositions of Bolingbrokean themes, the earlier ideological reading is, in fact, subverted, the common vocabulary describes quite a different opposition ideology.

The issue to which Burgh devotes almost the entire first volume is the unrepresentative nature of the House of Commons. He is perfectly willing to quote Bolingbroke at great length on this matter, but far from echoing Bolingbroke's plea for greater representation of independent landed gentry, or Wyvill's later demand for greater county representation, Burgh's argument anticipates the middle-class arguments for reform in 1832. The sense of the people, he writes, is grossly misrepresented because no one represents in Parliament "the multitudes who swarm in the cities and great towns of Liverpool, Manchester and Birmingham." As in his earlier writings, Burgh isolates an aggrieved middle class, squeezed between the abuses of the great and those of the lowly. The present unrepresentative House gives too much power to the urban poor, he argues. Many MPs in the boroughs are "elected by a handful of beggars" or by "the most needy and dependent part of the people." British government, Burgh notes, "best may be called a ptochocracy or government of beggars. For a few beggarly boroughs do avowedly elect the most important part of the government." But an unholy alliance is at work, according to Burgh, for "the Court directs the beggars whom to choose." Most of Burgh's anger is directed above, not below. The main problem of representation is a question less of personal independence and lack of civic virtue than of class. Here he sounds not at all like Bolingbroke.

> The landed interest was too much represented to the detriment [in our times] of the mercantile and monied. This is an occasion of various evils, for many of our country gentlemen are but bad judges of the importance of the mercantile interest and do not wisely consult it in their bills and acts. . . . Is not our House of Peers wholly and our House of Commons chiefly filled with men, whose property is land? Is not, therefore, the government of this mercantile and manufacturing country in the hands of the landed interest to the exclusion of the mercantile and manufacture?[82]

[82]Ibid., 1:27, 50, 51.

Burgh rejects the conventional claim that property in land is more easily proved than property "in merchandise, manufactures, or stocks." Anyone who owns a landed estate, he insists, may be in debt for more than the value of his estate; "where then is his qualification?" When Burgh specifies his plan for reforming the representation in Parliament, his concern has to do with class, not at all with moral or civic qualifications. This concern leads him to suggestions that would have appalled Bolingbroke. The interest of merchants, he writes,

> is so much the interest of the nation, that there can hardly be too many merchants in Parliament. The London members almost always vote on the side of liberty. It is proper that the monied interest be in the House, too, or else what security have we that a profligate Court will not shut up the Exchequer, as Charles II did.[83]

The present system, in which "the mercantile, manufactual and monied interests" are grossly underrepresented, has disastrous policy implications, quite familiar to anyone who has read Burgh's earlier works. "It is the overbalance of the power in the hands of the landed men," he writes, "that has produced the bounty on exportation of corn which increases the manufacturer's expense of living, and discourages the exportation of our manufactures."[84]

Burgh turns to Locke as an authority in arguing his case for parliamentary reform—to Locke, the allegedly irrelevant influence on English reform. Two years before Wilkes would invoke Locke as the distinguished authority to legitimize his motion of March 21, 1776, to bring about "a just and equal representation of the people in England in Parliament," Burgh quoted paragraph 157 of Locke's *Second Treatise*, on the people's "interest as well as intention . . . to have a fair and equal representation."[85] If Burgh is, as is often claimed, the father of parliamentary reform, hovering in the background is John Locke, quite alive and well in the late eighteenth century.

Locke's influence is seen most vividly in Burgh's discussion of annual parliaments. Burgh does, of course, repeat the traditional opposition argument in support of this strategy to reduce the court's corrupt influence over the Commons. Annual parliaments, Burgh writes, were part of the Anglo-Saxon constitution long before Magna Carta. He quotes Livy also. "The greater the power . . . the shorter ought to be the time of holding it." Annual parliaments are necessary to prevent the court and government ministers from "bribing, canvassing, elec-

[83]Ibid., pp. 52–53.
[84]Ibid.
[85]Ibid., p. 73.

tioneering, placing, and pensioning."[86] To this point Burgh reads very much like Bolingbroke and the earlier opposition. But he strikes out into new territory when he discusses annual parliaments in the more basic theoretical context of the origin and purpose of government, an area of little interest to the traditional opposition.

The short theoretical description of the origin of government at the beginning of the *Disquisitions* mirrors Locke's contractual image, even to the notion of governors as trustees subject to dismissal if they betray their trust. Every man has natural rights "to what may be called property," writes Burgh, and that "unalienable property" consists of "a life, a personal liberty, a character, a right to his earnings, a right to religious profession and worship according to his conscience." Even poor men have rights in their "lives, their personal liberty, their little property, and the chastity of their wives and daughters." Government is established to protect those rights. Governors are trustees voted on by rights holders. To be sure, "it is commonly received doctrine that servants and those receiving alms do not have the right to vote." Governing and being governed have little to do with moral enhancement; they are parts of a process of protecting rights. This is the much more potentially radical argument that informs Burgh's repeated calls for annual parliaments. He is not simply invoking a Saxon historical precedent; he insists that annual parliaments are a "natural right," and so is "freedom of persons."[87]

Behind the principle of annual parliaments is the even more basic radical principle of legislators as mere agents or delegates of the people, which Burgh also attributes to Locke. When legislators do not strictly serve their constituents' interest, Burgh writes, "Locke sees it as a breach of trust that dissolves government." Burgh cannot believe that anyone questions "the right of constituents to instruct their members and the consequent duties of members to obey instructions." He ridicules Lord Perceval's rebuke to his constituents (he has not yet had the benefit of Burke as an advisary on this issue) for confusing the independence of Commons with the member's independence of his constituents, "who sent you there on purpose to do their business." Blackstone, too, is soundly thrashed for suggesting that MPs need not consult or take the advice of their constituents. Here, too, Burgh marshals the weight of the past, insisting that instructing MPs is an immemorial part of the British Constitution. But Burgh also stresses the crucial relationship of this radical theory of representation to the origin and purpose of popular consensual government. The language,

[86]Ibid., pp. 134, 97, 174.
[87]Ibid., pp. 37, 130.

with its demystification of authority, is Lockean. A legislator who votes against his constituents' instructions is "a wrong-headed agent, who will act according to his own opinion in spite of his master, and ought besides being immediately turned out of office, to be answerable for all danger." "How," Burgh asks of Perceval, "would your lordship take such language from your steward?" Governors are mere agents and stewards temporarily serving the interests of the governed. Theirs is not a responsibility to exercise independent reason and wisdom in a common quest for noble ends sought by a moral community. Burgh's sense of governing and being governed is quite different. If we follow Perceval and Blackstone, Burgh insists, we "elect despots every seven years and are slaves except at election time."[88]

Burgh agrees with Locke in suggesting that "the people may take the power out of the hands of a king, or government when they abuse it." Kings and governments "are in all cases responsible to the people. . . . A majority of the people can at any time change the government." This responsibility of members of Parliament is undermined if they "are not obliged to regard instructions from their constituents."[89] Burgh's concern is clearly less the relationship of the Commons with king and court—Bolingbroke's concern—than the relationship of the Commons with the people. Whereas Bolingbroke criticized the Commons for its sycophantic subservience to the court, Burgh attacks the Commons for its lack of deference to its popular masters.

Blackstone, with his claim that the Commons has unlimited power, is again the foil. Burgh is alarmed that the Commons has "assumed such a superiority over its constituents." The Commons has no power to expel members or to change the fundamental laws; "only the people can," Burgh insists. In his populist assault on Parliament, Burgh invokes unexpected allies. Charles I is quoted on the limits of parliamentary power: "The House of Commons has no more power to administer an oath than to cut off a head."[90]

Note the dramatic radical turn that Burgh has given to opposition thought. The idealized House of Commons is no longer envisioned as a free and independent deliberative branch of a marvelously balanced constitutional edifice; it is now nothing more than an assembly of agents and stewards doing the bidding of their popular masters. Behind Burgh's radical turn is Locke.

> Parliament always answers the call of the Crown and is always deaf to the
> cries of the people. They have waived their privileges in compliment to the

[88]Ibid., pp. 279, 188, 181–85.
[89]Ibid., p. 200.
[90]Ibid., pp. 226, 205, 224.

prerogative, and put them to stretch, to oppress, and subdue the subjects, that instead of redressing grievances, they have authorised them . . . instead of protecting and defending the rights of their constituents they have perfidiously betrayed them. . . . England can never be undone but by a Parliament. . . . Let it then be recollected, that even the authority of Parliament has a bound. That they are not empowered to sell, but to serve their constituents. That whoever accepts of a trust is answerable for the exercise of it. That if the House of Commons should make ever so solemn a surrender of the public liberties into any hand whatever, that surrender would be ipso facto void. That if the people have reason to apprehend any such conspiracy against them, they have a right not only to put in their protest, but renounce the deed and refuse obedience. That in such a case the delegation they had made would return into the hands of those who gave it.[91]

Just as members of Parliament should be instructed and elected annually, they should be paid "to do the business of those who paid them." Their speeches should be published, too. The House of Commons, Burgh writes, "is the people's House, where the people's deputies meet to do the people's business. For the people's deputies, therefore, to shut the people out of their own House is a rebellion of the servants against their masters." For Burgh, it is not simply a change in the quality of men who sit in Parliament that is needed, as it was for Bolingbroke; the representative structure of Commons has to be totally reformed. The principal cause of the conflict between the Commons and the people is, for Burgh, the unrepresentative quality of Commons. Members are chosen "by a handful." The Commons assumes its exorbitant power and privilege to "the disadvantage of the people," imprisons and punishes its constituents, neglects the business of the nation, because "inadequate representation deprives the greatest part of the people, both in number and property, of their weight in legislation and gives it up as a monopoly into the hands of a few."[92] This vision of a reformed Commons is very different from Bolingbroke's.

Burgh is surprisingly blunt in offering what for an opposition writer is a most uncharacteristic dismissal of the venerable ideal of mixed or balanced government. He is less concerned about reasserting the independence of Commons as a counterweight to the Lords and the crown than in asserting the intrinsic power of a reformed Commons as the sole focus of legitimate popular government. He is arguing for a unicameral legislature. There is no danger, he writes, in "unbalancing the power of the estates." If the reformed Commons keeps the "people of property happy," would it make any difference if the King and Lords be

[91]Ibid., pp. 368–69.
[92]Ibid., pp. 186, 259, 256–57, 265.

unhappy?" he asks. This is no mere plea for restoring lost balance. Burgh's oft-noted fear of power seems to apply only to courts, ministers, and grandees. He has no such worries about unchecked popular sovereignty.

> Can we not imagine a very happy state, in which there was neither King nor Lords? What is the necessity of a check on the power of the Commons by King and Lords? Is there any fear that the Commons be too free to consult the general good? Must the representatives of the people be checked and clogged in putting the interests of their constituents? If there be not some necessity for this (which to me seems as rational as to say there ought to be a check to prevent individuals from being too healthy, or too virtuous) I cannot see the solidity of that reasoning, which lays so much stress on the necessity of a balance, or equality of power among the three estates, or indeed (speculatively or theoretically speaking) of a necessity of any more estates than one, viz. an adequate representation of the people, unchecked and uninfluenced by anything, but the common interest; and that they appoint responsible men for the execution of the laws made by them with the general approbation. . . . I can see very clearly the use of a check upon the power of a King or Lords, but I own I have no conception of the advantage of a check upon the power of the people, or their incorrupt and unbiased representatives.[93]

There is, then, a much more radical Burgh to be found in the *Disquisitions* than the one contemporary republican scholarship has described. One can easily imagine such passages as this being of great interest to the drafters of the Pennsylvania Constitution in 1776 or to the host of other state constitution writers who were busily eliminating or seriously limiting the powers of senates and governors in the United States' first decade. At least one distinguished American in the postindependence period had clearly reread his *Disquisitions* and found it full of suggestions he had not seen in 1774 and 1775, when he so fulsomely praised it. John Adams wrote Richard Price in 1789 that it was a desire to respond to the blind advocacy of unicameralism that prompted him to write his *Defense of the Constitution* in 1787. Adams went on:

> It appeared to me that my countrymen were running wild, and into danger, from a too ardent and inconsiderate pursuit of erroneous opinions of government, which had been propagated among them by some of their ill-informed favourites, and by some writings which were very popular among them, such as the pamphlet called *Common Sense*, for one example, among many others; particularly Mrs. Macaulay's *History*, Mr. Burgh's *Political Disquisitions*, Mr. Turgot's *Letters*. These writings are all excellent in

[93]Ibid., pp. 116–17.

some respects, and very useful, but extremely mistaken in the true conception of a free government.[94]

Turning now to Burgh's criticism of standing armies in the *Political Disquisitions,* we find that here, too, his real concerns are by no means the same as those of earlier opposition writers. To be sure, he presents long passages from Bolingbroke, commonwealthman texts, and parliamentary debates on the evils of standing armies. But when Burgh criticizes mercenaries and suggests the value of a militia, he does not argue that the right to bear arms allows ordinary citizens an opportunity to express devotion to the public good. What it does provide, according to Burgh, is an opportunity for "every man of property" to "defend his property," which is "the mark of a free people." Burgh's criticism of a standing army reads much more like general Enlightenment and liberal abhorrence of war and militarism than civic humanist fear of the corrupting influence of standing armies and mercenaries on the polity. Burgh's vision of trading England is incompatible with Harrington's of Oceana, "the most blessed and fortunate of all nations . . . the most martial in the whole world."[95] For Burgh standing armies were expensive and too often used to provide places and jobs for legions of idle and worthless grandees.

To the extent that republicanism can be said to encourage martial values and a militaristic commitment to the glory, strength, and defense of one's *patria,* Burgh reads less like the civic humanist than like the *philosophe* appalled by the barbarism and wastefulness of such monarchic and aristocratic sport. It is "horrible, cruel and hellish," he writes, that so many men live short lives "because a couple of frantic and mischievous fiends in human shape, commonly called kings," have fallen out or disagreed. Those who head countries are more concerned with "the art of war" than with "the improvement of all liberal arts and sciences." Vast fortunes are wasted in costly war; militias, at least, cost little. Like Priestley, Paine, and other fellow Dissenters, Burgh wants more to deglorify and demystify the aristocratic honor and heroism of war than to isolate the evil of standing armies, "those butchers of mankind."

> The whole art of war from beginning to end is at best, but a scene of folly and absurdity. . . . War is not a more proper method of deciding controversies between kings, than single combat between individuals. All that

[94]John Adams to Richard Price, May 2, 1789, in *The Works of John Adams,* ed. Charles Francis Adams (Boston, 1850–1856), 9:558–59.

[95]Burgh, *Political Disquisitions,* 2:401. For Harrington, see Pocock, *Machiavellian Moment,* pp. 390–94.

can be determined by fighting is that the conqueror is the best fighter of the two; not that he has justice on his side.[96]

It is in the *Political Disquisitions'* discussion of placemen, however, that we see most dramatically Burgh's departure from the course taken by earlier opposition writers. Burgh states his position forthrightly in the title to chapter IV of volume 2: "Places and Pensions are not given according to Merit."[97] For Bolingbroke Walpole's placemen represented the triumph of new, upstart, moneyed men in politics over men of breeding and privilege whose natural responsibility it was to govern. For Burgh placemen were symbols of a corrupt society in which public office and public rewards went to the rich and privileged instead of the industrious and talented.

Once again Burgh used the image of a virtuous middle between two corrupt extremes. Why do we deny the right of voting to receivers of alms? he asks. Is it not because we assume that they, "being needy, will of course be dependent, and under undue influence?" Then why do we let men sit in Commons, Burgh asks, who "receive alms," that is, pensions and places? They, too, "are upon the parish, that is the nation." "Half our nobility" is "upon the parish, I mean the nation," and they cost hundreds of thousands of pounds, "while we are sinking in a bottomless sea of debt." By his calculations these "over drenched Court sponges" cost the nation £2 million a year. All the while, of course, the real business of the nation is being done by the placemen's clerks, who receive "but 50 pounds a year."[98]

Burgh's concern is the violation of the principle of equal opportunity. "If the nation is to be plundered," he writes, "it would be some comfort to think that the spoil was divided among the deserving," but alas, "modest merit gets no reward." The present system inhibits ambition, as the talented know full well that they will be excluded. Public service should be a public reward for talent, merit, and hard work, Burgh insists. As Figaro charged that Almaviva had received everything he had merely by having taken the trouble to be born, so Burgh complains in the *Disquisitions* that public offices in Britain go to the "worthless blockheads" who just "take care to be the son of a Duke." Burgh quotes his friend Benjamin Franklin on how irrelevant merit seems to be in England in comparison with the ability to "second views of the Court." Pensions and places go to "men of family and fortune," who, instead of offering their services to the public, act as "greedy sordid hirelings." The "nobility and gentry . . . scramble for the profitable places." They

---

[96]Burgh, *Political Disquisitions*, 2:341–42, 396.
[97]Ibid., p. 401.
[98]Ibid., pp. 60, 97, 99.

serve their country only for hire. Burgh offers an alternative to corrupt placemen and pensioners, and it is a far cry from Bolingbroke's: "If the nobility and gentry decline serving their country in the great offices of the state, without sordid hire, let the honest bourgeoisie be employed. They will think themselves sufficiently rewarded by the honour done them."[99]

These men of the hard working middle class would not demand great salaries, so public expenditures would decline dramatically. They would replace the overpaid "lord who has no necessary business to fatigue him but drinking, whoreing, masquerading and New Marketing." Why shouldn't "the honest bourgeoisie" be employed in the offices of state? Burgh cannot resist the Dissenter's urge to demystify the state. "Public business being all a mere routine," all its offices, even those of the secretary of state, the lord chamberlain, and the lord steward, are "places which any man of common sense and common honesty can fill."[100]

Corruption for Burgh has two meanings, and both are quite different from the Machiavellian concept that informs the arguments of such earlier opposition writers as Bolingbroke. A corrupt system for Burgh involves gross unfairness in the principles of distributive justice. It is, as we have seen, a system in which the prizes in the race of life go to men of no ability (as Paine was to call them) instead of to deserving men of talent. "In a corrupt state," Burgh writes, "that which should give a man the greatest consequences . . . gives him the least."[101]

Burgh also writes of corruption from the perspective of a Protestant moralist, and here, too, his focus is far removed from a republican notion of declining civic virtue. In volume 3 of the *Disquisitions* Burgh returns to concerns that have characterized his writings since *Britain's Remembrancer*. All about him he sees total and "general corruption of manners." It is not a decline of public virtue that concerns him, however, but the insidious spread of personal corruption. The principal source of this all-pervasive corruption, according to Burgh, is the upper classes. These "haughty and insolent" men care little "for religion and virtue" and know "only plays and romances." They spend their money as quickly as they get it, these "nobility and gentry who repeatedly beggar themselves at Mrs. Connoley's and Arthur's." They spend their time at "useless diversions," at lewd theatrical performances of women dancing on the stage. These men of "higher stations" think they can "strike out from the limited path of virtue into the wilds of licentiousness." These "persons of quality" think "they may rebel against

[99]Ibid., pp. 80, 85, 87, 89, 90, 96, 97.
[100]Ibid., pp. 97–98.
[101]Ibid., 3:57.

God's law." Burgh's charges of vice are consistently aimed at personal degeneracy, not at public corruption.

> Our nobility and gentry, so far from attending to these considerations, are the great leaders of the people into this ruinous vice. Besides the example they exhibit of an endless attachment to carding, rooking, cocking, racing, pitting, gambling, jobbing, they have introduced gaming into their system of politics. . . . Our governors are Christians, and live in an improved age. Therefore, they lead their people to laugh at religion and conscience; they play at cards on Sundays instead of countenancing the public worship of their maker; they have made adultery a matter of merriment; they cheat at play whenever they can; they lead their inferiors into extravagance and dissipation by encouraging public diversions more luxurious and more debauched than all that ever the orientals exhibited.[102]

People below Burgh's virtuous middle class are deeply infected by the vices of these "persons of quality" above them. "The inferior rank of men . . . grow lazy, effeminate, impatient of labour, and expensive." Drunkenness, blasphemy, and obscenity are "rife among the common people, because they see the nobility and gentry do it."[103]

Perhaps this indictment of private corruption represents, as it represented for earlier opposition writers, a turning to self, away from the corruption that marks the decline of civic virtue. If this were the case, however, one would expect Burgh's prescription to be a return to civic concern. This is not the case. His proposals for Britain's renewal reflect a vision much more radically Protestant than republican. Manners can be improved and virtue increased, he suggests, "by simple and easy laws," but none that he calls for involves a renewed commitment to public life. On the contrary, all have a virtuous Protestant character.

A virtuous government, for example, would place heavy taxes on saddle horses and carriages. It would prevent the nobility and gentry from traveling abroad, where they spend too much money and meet loose women. Burgh would revive Cromwell's laws against fornication, adultery, cockfighting, and duels. A virtuous government would copy Geneva's law barring the son of an insolvent person from the magistracy until he had paid his father's debts. It would pass laws curbing luxury, though they need not repudiate commerce and trade. It is, after all, "only occasionally and not necessarily that commerce, arts and taste do harm." A people can pursue commerce and riches "and not be ennervated and effeminated." Riches, he concludes, "do not necessarily ennervate a people unless there be a relaxation of disci-

---

[102]Ibid., pp. 1, 66, 31, 98, 112, 173, 179.
[103]Ibid., pp. 31, 204.

pline." Burgh would have laws passed against "exorbitant wealth," which he defines as property worth more than £10,000. Excessive riches are a "thing of ill example, and excite unbounded desires, which lay men open to corruption."[104]

Here again Burgh returns to themes he dealt with in his earlier writings. Magistrates who would "promote virtue . . . propogate what [is] good and suppress vice . . . they should discountenance immoralities of all sorts, should expose them in public." Magistrates should see that Englishmen become more law-abiding, for in "England we have little notion of obeying either our maker, our laws or our parents." Magistrates must encourage "order and regularity," and police must more effectively "keep order." There must be harsher laws against "perjury, adultery, seduction of modest women, insolvency occasioned by overtrading or extravagance, and idleness in the lower people."[105]

A virtuous government would "reward industry." Burgh would revive the law of Anne's reign which gave magistrates the right "to take up idle people for the army." He proposes a press gang to seize "all idle and disorderly persons" who have been complained about three times. Such persons would be "set to work during a certain time for the benefit of great trading or manufacturing companies." By hard work the idle would be made virtuous. Burgh articulates in the *Disquisitions* a theme he shared with virtually all the middle-class Dissenter reformers of the 1770s and 1780s. A virtuous government would repeal the poor laws.

> A benevolent disposition revolts against every encouragement to the exercise of the Godlike virtue of charity. But truth is truth, and it must be acknowledged that the profusion of our charities is hurtful to the manners of our people. . . . All that policy is sound which tends to improve and increase industry and frugality among the working people, and all that economy is hurtful, which tends to produce in the poor people a contrary spirit and which occasions their becoming more burdensome to their richer fellow subjects than is absolutely necessary, because this lays an additional burden upon all our exports, and hurts our trade at foreign markets upon which all depends. Let our innumerable and exorbitant public charities be considered in this light. If the poor are led by them to look upon industry and frugality as unnecessary, they will neither be industrious nor frugal; and the consequence will be that they and their children will come upon the parish, instead of being maintained by labour and industry.[106]

[104]Ibid., pp. 96, 156–57, 190, 63–64, 66, 189.
[105]Ibid., pp. 168, 172, 245, 194.
[106]Ibid., pp. 220, 225.

A little more than twenty years later, Jeremy Bentham, in reply to Pitt's Poor Law Bill of 1796, resurrected some of Burgh's ideas in his own *Outline of a Work Entitled Pauper Management Improvement* (1798). Bentham's National Charity Company would set up a "universal register" of all adults and children, such as Burgh had proposed in his *Crito*. The company would establish some five hundred "industry houses" across England and Wales to teach the work ethic to a million "of the burdensome poor" and particularly to their children. Instead of being apprenticed at the conventional age of fourteen, the children of the poor would start work at the age of four. "Ten years, ten precious years, may be looked upon in the existing state of things as the waste period of human life, the period lost to industry. . . . Ten precious years in which nothing is done! nothing for industry!" In one respect Bentham would go even further than Burgh—or than Priestley and Locke, for that matter—in introducing children and the poor to virtuous industry and triumph over sloth and idleness. Sleep, the last frontier of unproductive activity, came under Bentham's attack. His "industry houses" would provide "the least that can be made sufficient for health and strength . . . sleep is not life, but the cessation of life . . .in so far as it is idleness, pernicious to moral health."[107]

Returning to Burgh's *Disquisitions*, we find in addition to his prototypical workhouses other proposals to encourage a national revival of virtue. The most interesting of these proposals was for the creation of a "National Moral Academy." Its membership would consist of people who had set the highest moral example to their age. Like the Royal Society, it would publish "moral discourses, and examples from history." It would circulate satires and criticisms of the "indecencies and crimes of eminent individuals," as well as praise of "good and moral men." Men would quake with fear of being stigmatized by the Academy, Burgh predicted, and thrilled by the prospect of its approbation. The virtue encouraged—indeed, enshrined in immortality— would clearly be that of private character, not of public service.[108]

But where are such "good and moral men" to be found? In the course of Burgh's long journey through corrupt Britain in volume 3 he singles out several virtuous models for emulation, and they make a fascinating list, all of a piece. What they share is not a republican preoccupation with participation in public life but a Protestant zeal for industry and thrift. He singles out first Americans, and Dissenters in general, as people of virtue, with "their sobriety . . . their thrift and regular manner of living." They have "bounded . . . their riotous appe-

---

[107]Jeremy Bentham, *Outline of a Work Entitled Pauper Management Improvement* (1798), in *The Works of Jeremy Bentham*, ed. J. Bowring (London, 1838–1843), 8:404, 396.

[108]Burgh, *Political Disquisitions*, 3:228.

tites" and their "lust." In New England, Burgh notes, strict laws prevent adultery, blasphemy, drunkenness, and striking or cursing a parent. Other models of virtue that Burgh cites for the edification of corrupt Britain are the Quakers, who "hold frugality and industry for religious duties"; the Dutch, "disciplined and frugal"; and the Swiss, with their "character of simplicity, honesty, frugality, modesty and bravery." The models of virtue, then, are not the public-spirited citizens of ancient Athens and Sparta, of Rome, or even of Elizabethan England; they are modern Protestants all.[109]

Burgh warns Britain that time is running out. The Dissenters, who represent so great a potential for the regeneration of Britain, may well be forced to leave if the Test and Corporation Acts are not repealed. As for Priestley in 1792, the exile of the Huguenots loomed vividly in memory. But Burgh had classical models as well. He invoked Sparta's fall, for as he saw it, one of its causes was that "those among them, who were distinguished by their merit and their morals, were on this very account proscribed by the tyrants, and hated by their creatures, so that they were forced to forsake their country."[110]

It is, then, a very Protestant vision of a reformed Britain that Burgh offers in volume 3 of the *Disquisitions*. It is almost as if Burgh would have the virtuous magistrate stand in place of the omniscient God, forever watching the lonely individual in his solitary pilgrimage forge his character through the trials that Satan throws in his path, watching and forever noting the successes and the failures.

> Did magistrates keep an attentive eye upon the behavior of individuals, and were they to keep a register of the complaints made against the idle and debauched, the register to be inspected upon every individual's applying for the benefit of public charity . . . it might appear whether he lived a life of labour and frugality, or brought himself to want by his own fault.[111]

But what of Burgh's "Grand National Association for the Restoration of the Constitution"? Surely this is where those who read Burgh as backward-looking have their way. Restoring the independence of Parliament is one of the association's objectives, and to its ranks Burgh invites "all men of property, all friends of liberty." An independent Parliament is one free of court management, an evil that Burgh sees as stretching back beyond even Walpole, to the era of Charles II. Though

---

[109]Ibid., pp. 30, 219, 172, 89, 410.
[110]Ibid., p. 81. For Priestley, see his *Appeal to the Public on the Subject of Riots in Birmingham* (Birmingham, 1792), p. 104.
[111]Burgh, *Political Disquisitions*, 3:226.

we get a sure sense of a wish to restore an older, more virtuous mode of government, Burgh's association is by no means a repudiation of modern Britain and market society. Burgh speaks directly to the holders of public funds, urging them to join the Grand National Association, since one of its goals is to put public credit on a sounder footing. He would even give them "certain preferences and other advantages." Who, in fact, does Burgh envision as heading his Grand Association? He rejects the king, who lacks the courage; the nobility are too preoccupied with their "useless diversions." "Let the great, the rich, the independent City of London take the lead." The class assumptions behind what Burgh sees as the potential confrontation between his popular association and the unreformed Parliament are clearly stated. "Members of Parliament would hardly dare to reject the proposed reformation bill, knowing themselves not to be invulnerable and remembering that they could not command a guard of 500 soldiers each at their country houses at all times."[112]

The association, introduced at the end of volume 3, rests at bottom on Lockean, not republican or civic humanist, foundations. It is informed by Burgh's conviction, announced in the opening pages of volume 1 and repeated throughout, that government is a trust created through a voluntary contract revocable by the people should their agents violate the trust. The unreformed Parliament must do the bidding of the Grand National Association, for it will be the people speaking. Governors are but servants, who have no right "to resist the supreme power, the majority of the people. Whoever undertakes to manage any person's or any people's affairs in spite of the proprietors is answerable for all consequences." In describing the association, Burgh once again uses the Lockean language of servants and masters, of stewards, managers, and proprietors, which the Dissenters used so frequently to describe the rather routine, not terribly majestic, relationship between governor and governed. We need not speculate on the theoretical influence of Locke on Burgh's Grand National Association, for as his final argument for the proposal offered in the very last pages of his three-volume work Burgh calls once again upon "Mr. Locke":

> But Mr. Locke, who is never at rest till the subject he is treating of is exhausted, and whose comprehension and precision can never enough be admired, though he sees and acknowledges the danger, distress, and wretchedness of such a case, yet he carries his reader a step farther. Suppose the Parliament do so abuse their trust, exceed their power, and are so many tyrants and leechworms to the people; what then is there no

[112]Ibid., pp. 456, 428, 330, 433, 438.

remedy? Yes, saith he, there remains still inherent in the people, a supreme power to remove or alter the legislature. . . . The power in such cases devolves to the people, who may make such alterations as to them seem meet. Begin again, saith Mr. Locke, according to the original design of government, as instituted by God.[113]

Burgh and His American Readers, Then and Now

In his early embrace of Burgh's republicanism, John Adams urged that the *Political Disquisitions* "ought to be in the hands of every American who has learned to read."[114] By the late 1780s, he feared Burgh's radicalism or what we have seen as Burgh's individualism and Lockean liberalism. Indeed, several decades later Thoreau, the quintessential American individualist, would pore over a copy of Burgh borrowed from the Harvard College library.[115] Here, in fact, may lie part of the explanation for the powerful impact Burgh had on the American mind in the late eighteenth century. He was a transmitter of republican ideals, to be sure. His lamentation on the flight of freedom from corrupt Britain must have appealed to an American readership informed in part by the republican paradigm. But there is much more to Burgh than simply republicanism, as we have seen; his articulation of the Protestant ethic, too, appealed to the American mind.

Central in work-ethic Protestantism, as we have seen, was the vision of a cosmic struggle between the forces of industry and idleness. Its texts vibrated less with the dialectic of civic virtue and self-centered commerce than with the dialectic of productive hardworking energy, on the one hand, and idle unproductive sloth, on the other. Its idiom was more personal and individualistic than public and communal. Work was a test of self-sufficiency and self-reliance, a battleground for personal salvation. All people were "called" to serve God by busying themselves in useful work that served both society and the individual. Daily labor was sanctified and thus was both a specific obligation and a positive moral value. The doctrine of the calling gave each person a sense of a unique self; work appropriate to each individual was imposed by God. After being called to a particular occupation, one was duty-bound to labor diligently and to avoid idleness and sloth.

The fruits of one's labor were justly one's own. Baxter regarded an "honest increase and provision" as "the end of our labour." It was therefore "no sin, but a duty to choose a gainful calling rather than

---

[113]Ibid., pp. 439, 446–47.
[114]Adams, "Novanglus," in *Works of John Adams*, 4:21.
[115]Kenneth Cameron, *Emerson the Essayist* (Raleigh, N.C., 1945), 2:193.

another, that we may be able to do good." Not only was hard work and an effort to prosper the mark of a just and virtuous person and idleness a sign of spiritual corruption; work was also the anodyne for physical corruption. Hard work disciplined the wayward and sinful impulses that lay like Satan's traces within everyone. Baxter wrote that "for want of *bodily* labour a multitude of the idle Gentry, and rich people, and young people that are slothful, do heap up in the secret receptacles of the body a dunghill of unconcocted excrementitious filth . . . and dye by thousands of untimely deaths. . . . It is their own doing, and by their sloth they kill themselves."[116]

Contemporary scholars such as Edmund S. Morgan, J. E. Crowley, Joyce Appleby, and John Patrick Diggins have described this alternative paradigm of Protestantism and the Protestant ethic in eighteenth-century America and with it a language quite congenial to individualistic liberalism and the capitalist spirit.[117] Next to the Bible, the texts of Protestant moralists such as Baxter were the books most likely to be found in the libraries of eighteenth-century Americans.[118] From them Americans came to know the virtuous person as productive, thrifty, and diligent. Morgan and Crowley, especially, have documented how the American response to English taxation centered on a dual policy of self-denial and commitment to industry. Richard Henry Lee, as early as 1764, assumed that the Sugar Act would "introduce a virtuous industry." The subsequent nonconsumption and nonimportation policy of colonial protestors led many a moralist, in fact, to applaud parliamentary taxation as a blessing in disguise, recalling Americans to simplicity and frugality. As Morgan notes, many people saw the boycott movements as not simply negative and reactive. "They were also a positive end in themselves, a way of reaffirming and rehabilitating the virtues of the Puritan Ethic."[119]

From pulpit and pamphlet Americans had long heard praises of industry and denunciations of idleness. For Benjamin Colman, minister of Boston's Brattle Street Church, *"all Nature is Industrious and every Creature about us diligent in their proper Work."* Constant activity was the human telos for Ebenezer Pemberton, an end even after death. He

---

[116]Baxter, *Christian Directory*, pp. 262, 225.

[117]Edmund S. Morgan, "The Puritan Ethic and the American Revolution," *William and Mary Quarterly*, 3d ser., 24 (1967): 3–43; J. E. Crowley, *This Sheba, Self: The Conceptualization of Economic Life in Eighteenth-Century America* (Baltimore, 1974); Joyce Appleby, "Liberalism and the American Revolution," *New England Quarterly* 49 (1976): 3–26, and *Capitalism and a New Social Order: The Republican Vision of the 1790s* (New York, 1984); John Patrick Diggins, *The Lost Soul of American Politics: Virtue, Self-interest, and the Foundation of Liberalism* (New York, 1984).

[118]Crowley, *This Sheba, Self*, p. 50.

[119]Lee to ——, May 31, 1764, in *The Letters of Richard Henry Lee*, ed. James Curtis Ballagh (New York, 1911–1914), 1:7; Morgan, "Puritan Ethic," p. 8.

complained of those who thought that "the happiness of Heaven consisted only in Enjoyment, and a stupid Indolence."[120]

Idleness, then, was a denial of the human essence. To be idle was to neglect "Duty and lawful Employment . . . for Man is by Nature such an active Creature, that he cannot be wholly Idle." Idleness for Americans, as for the English, had specific class referents. It was the sinful mark of the poor and the great, those below and those above the virtuous middle. Cotton Mather made it clear that the idle poor had no claims on society. *"We should let them Starve,"* he wrote. As for the idle rich, Nathaniel Clap expelled them from the very fold of Christendom. "If Persons Live upon the Labours of others," he wrote, "and spend their Time in Idleness, without any Imployment, for the Benefit of others, they cannot be numb[e]red among Christians. YEA, If Persons Labour, to get great Estates, with this design, chiefly, that they and theirs may live in Idleness, They cannot be Acknowledged for Christians."[121]

The widespread importance of the Protestant ethic in America helps explain why Burgh, read in this alternative way, appealed so strongly to Americans in the period from the 1740s to the 1770s. Like Burgh, colonial Americans wrote often of the cyclical historical process by which nations that lost virtue become mired in corruption. But as in Burgh's *Britain's Remembrancer,* so popular in America in the late 1740s and early 1750s, it was the decline of frugality, thrift, and self-denial, not of civic participation, that led the way to corruption. The jeremiad sermon with its lamentation over lost virtue and its invocation of divine retribution was often reinforced by historical references to the nations that rose and fell in accordance with the determination of their inhabitants to live virtuous lives of simplicity and frugality. Rome, according to the *Virginia Gazeteer* of 1771, had fallen from virtue as its "ancient, regular, and laborious life was relaxed and sunk in idleness." In the modern era, the frugal Dutch defeated the indolent and luxurious Spanish. Like Burgh, many an American saw a revival of virtue as an outcome to be attained through encouragement of manufacturing, which "will promote industry" and produce a people "habituated to industry from their childhood."[122]

It was on the issue of placemen, however, that Burgh's writings spoke most perfectly to colonial concerns. His language was theirs. His

---

[120]Benjamin Coleman, *A Sermon at the Lecture in Boston, after the Funeral* (Boston, 1717), p. 14; Ebenezer Pemberton, *A Christian Fix'd at His Post* (Boston, 1704), pp. 6–7.

[121]Cotton Mather quoted in Crowley, *This Sheba, Self,* p. 59; Nathaniel Clap, *The Duty of All Christians* . . . (New London, Conn., 1720), p. 8.

[122]*Virginia Gazetteer* (Williamsburg), Sept. 5, 1771; *New Haven Gazette and Connecticut Magazine,* Nov. 23, 1786.

indictment of corruption rested as much on the violation of basic Protestant values as on threats to constitutional balance. Part of the anger
at the Townshend Acts in the 1760s came from fear that they would
introduce into the colonies new and expensive legions of useless officeholders. The new customs officials were seen as idle placemen fat-
tening themselves on the industry of the colonists. They were vilified
as "parasitical minions" and as "idle, lazy, and to say no worse, altogether useless customs house locusts, catterpillars, flies and lice."
These placemen, according to *The Newport Mercury* in 1773, were "a
parcel of dependent tools of arbitrary power" sent across the sea to
enrich themselves "on the spoil of the honest and industrious of these
colonies." In 1774 the town meeting of Bristol, Rhode Island, complained in a formal resolve (in terms virtually identical to those in
Burgh's *Disquisitions* of the same year) "that so many unnecessary officers are supported by the earnings of honest industry, in a life of
dissipation and ease; who, by being properly employed, might be
useful members of society."[123]

In the very year of the American publication of Burgh's *Political Disquisitions* Franklin wrote from London to Joseph Galloway lamenting
the legions of corrupt, idle, and unproductive dependents of the court
who knew nothing of "virtuous industry." "Here numberless and
needless Places, enormous Salaries, Pensions, Perquisites, Bribes,
groundless quarrels, foolish Expeditions, false accounts or no accounts, Contracts and Jobbs, devour all revenue and produce continual
Necessity in the Midst of natural Plenty."[124]

Burgh's vilification of placemen must have touched a sensitive nerve
in the revolutionary generation of Americans, who, as Edmund Morgan suggests, saw "in their midst, a growing enclave of men whose
lives and values denied the Puritan ethic." Burgh did indeed fuel colonial fears of conspiracy, but the plot was also against Protestant notions
of virtue and justice. For Sam Adams this was the intent of taxation
without representation, which was "against the plain and obvious rule
of equity, whereby the industrious man is entitled to the fruits of his
industry." Such taxes attacked not only property but also the industry
and frugality "for which liberty and property must be the expected
reward." For Jefferson, the purpose of England's oppressive taxes was
"to provide sinecures for the idle or the wicked." Burgh could be read,
then, with utmost interest by colonial Americans convinced that "the

[123]*Newport Mercury*, June 21, 1773, quoted in Morgan, "Puritan Ethic," p. 16.
[124]Franklin to Joseph Galloway, Feb. 25, 1775, in *The Writings of Benjamin Franklin*, ed.
Albert Henry Smyth (New York, 1907), 6:312.

conspirators against our Liberties are employing all their influence to divide the people . . . introducing Levity, Luxury and Indolence."[125]

A final indicator of the appeal to colonial Americans of the Burgh described here requires a discussion, finally, of the one Burgh text I have yet to mention. *The Art of Speaking*, published in 1761, was in fact the most widely read and reissued of Burgh's works in America.[126] The book is a collection of exerpts from well-known classical, continental, and English speeches and essays. The passages chosen do often stress civic commitment and unselfish love of country, to be sure. But it was the volume's stated purpose that recommended it to individualist Americans.

Burgh offers the book, as he did his *Dignity of Human Nature*, to help young men be successful. He writes in a time when "all are aspiring to preferment, worthy and unworthy, qualified and unqualified." He writes for ambitious young men who seek to make it "in Parliament, at the Bar, in the Pulpit, at meetings of merchants."[127] To compete successfully, to make it on one's own, to create oneself, requires training in public speaking. One may use the words of others, but preferment, advancement, and success come to the speaker who has the talent and skill to manipulate words of his own.

Just as Burke intuited the socially subversive role of such training in rhetoric in his complaint that the "age of chivalry" was being replaced by the "age of sophisters," the American Tory Jonathan Boucher had the same fear. In his *View of the Causes and Consequences of the American Revolution* Boucher worried that men of birth and breeding were being replaced in American public life by "the marketable property of a new species of public men, who study the arts of debate, and pursue politics merely as a gainful occupation."[128]

How, then, do we finally assess Burgh's politics and his opposition? Is his radicalism a "fundamentally conservative" quest for lost republican virtue or is it the individualistic politics of Protestant modernity? It is both, and this ability to speak in both languages in no small way helps explain his phenomenal appeal to eighteenth-century Americans, for whom both were relevant and operative. I have emphasized here the Protestant modernist Burgh not only to right the imbalance of

[125]*The Writings of Samuel Adams*, ed. Harry Alonzo Cushing (New York, 1904–1908), 2:271; *The Papers of Thomas Jefferson*, ed. Julian Boyd et al. (Princeton, N.J., 1950–), 1:232.
[126]Hay, *James Burgh*, and Jay Fliegelman, *Prodigals and Pilgrims: The American Revolution against Patriarchal Authority, 1750–1800* (Cambridge, Eng., 1982), pp. 21–22.
[127]James Burgh, *The Art of Speaking*, 4th ed. (Philadelphia, 1775), pp. 264, 7.
[128]Jonathan Boucher, *Views of the Causes and Consequences of the American Revolution* (London, 1797), p. lxxvi.

contemporary scholarship but also to show that Burgh's introduction of Protestant and class themes and interests forever changed the opposition tradition of Bolingbroke and *Cato's Letters.* Opposition writers continued to offer republican arguments; republicanism, after all, had long been the only language of opposition, it still carried tremendous authority and powerful rhetorical and emotive force. Burgh, however, decisively moved the significant center of opposition ideology, and after him Price and Priestley operated even less than he in the republican framework.

As for Burgh himself, how would he like to be remembered by those twentieth-century readers he was so concerned about—as a traditionalist or as a real radical? Fortunately, he has told us in his *Political Disquisitions:*

> I cannot see the use of all this hesitating and mincing the matter. Why cannot we say at once that without any urgency of distress, without any provocation by oppression of government and though the safety of the people should not appear to be in any immediate danger, if the people of a country should think they should be, in any respect, happier under republican government than monarchical or under monarchical than republican, and, find that they can bring about a change of government, without greater inconveniences than the future advantages are likely to balance, why may we not say, that they have a sovereign, absolute, and uncontrolable right to change or new-model their government as they please?[129]

This radical creed must have infuriated Mr. Adams when he read it in 1789. There is no need, Burgh writes, to feel any particular distress or to cite reasons to justify "a people's altering at any time the whole plan of government." Nothing is needed "besides their will and pleasure." Some men, Burgh concedes, are uneasy "about the danger of innovations." They worry lest anyone "depart from the ancient constitution." But to such traditionalists Burgh replies that there is "no power on earth with a right to hinder the majority of a people from making in their form of government what innovations they please." Burgh characteristically frames this innovator–traditionalist opposition in social terms. One need have no fear of the innovations sought by the majority of the people, he writes, for "there is a native generosity in the hearts of ninety-nine in every one hundred Englishmen of the middling and lower ranks of life, which prevents their making a violent or unjustifiable use of power . . . which is not so for the rich and great who are our governors and who have little humanity."[130]

[129]Burgh, *Political Disquisitions*, 3:277.
[130]Ibid., pp. 278, 281, 299.

But Burgh's innovative zeal has limits. He has, after all, always seen the middle rank as the virtuous mean between two extremes, and so he cautions lest he be read as a complete leveler seeking to do away with respect for all ordering in the stations of life. The lower ranks must not think his innovations are those of a "Wat Tyler or a Jack Straw," who wanted "a total demolition of all subordination and all rule." Burgh is to the end a spokesman for bourgeois radicalism. His is the voice of middle-class consciousness as surely as is Figaro's. "The people," Burgh writes,

> may be brought, by inveterate tyranny, to bear patiently to see the most worthless part of mankind (for surely the great by mere birth, in all ages and countries are commonly among the most worthless of mankind) set up above them and themselves obliged to crouch. But sometimes the people grow uneasy under this. And if the people rise to vengeance, woe to those who stand in the way. Let merit be honoured with privilege and prerogative and mankind will be contented.[131]

[131]Ibid., pp. 306, 425.

CHAPTER 8

"The Great National Discussion": The Discourse of Politics in 1787

A MERICANS, Alexander Hamilton wrote on October 27, 1787, in the New York *Independent Journal*, were "called upon to deliberate on a new Constitution." His essay, *The Federalist* no. 1, pointed out that Americans were thus proving that people could create their own governments "from reflection and choice," instead of forever having to depend on "accident and force." These deliberations on the Constitution would by no means be decorous and genteel. Much too much was at stake, and, as Hamilton predicted, "a torrent of angry and malignant passions" was let loose in the "great national discussion." His *Federalist* essays, Hamilton promised, would provide a different voice in the national debate; they would rise above "the loudness of [the opposition's] declamations, and the . . . bitterness of [its] invectives."

How does one read that "great national discussion" more than two centuries later? Most present-day scholars would follow the methodological guidelines offered by J. G. A. Pocock in this respect. The historian of political thought, Pocock suggests, is engaged in a quest for the "languages," "idioms," and "modes of discourse" that characterize an age. Certain "languages" are accredited at various moments in time "to take part" in the public speech of a country. These "distinguishable idioms" are paradigms that selectively encompass all information about politics and delimit appropriate usage. Pocock writes of the "continuum of discourse," which persists over time in paradigms that both constrain and provide opportunities for authors with a language available for their use. To understand texts and "great national discussions," then, is to penetrate the "modes of discourse" and the meanings available to authors and speakers at particular moments in time. The scholar must know what the normal possibilities of language, the capacities for discourse, were. Paradigms change, to be sure, ever so slowly, and we recognize this subtle process through anomalies and innovations. But much more significant is the static and exclusive aspect of "modes of discourse." Pocock cautions that one "cannot get out of a language that which was never in it." People only think "about what they have the means of verbalizing." Anyone studying political texts, then, must use "the languages in which the inhabitants . . . did in fact present their society and cosmos to themselves and to each other."[1]

Problematic in this approach is the assumption that there is but one language—one exclusive or even hegemonic paradigm—that characterizes the political discourse of a particular place or moment in time. This was not the case in 1787. In the "great national discussion" of the Constitution, Federalists and Antifederalists, in fact, tapped several languages of politics, the terms of which they could easily verbalize. Four such "distinguishable idioms" coexisted in the discourse of American politics in 1787–1788. None dominated the field, and the use of one was compatible with the use of another by the same writer or speaker. There was a profusion and confusion of political tongues among the founders. They lived easily with that clatter; it is we, two hundred and more years later, who chafe at their inconsistency. Reading the framers and the critics of the Constitution, one discerns the languages of republicanism, of Lockean liberalism, of work-ethic Protestantism, and of state-centered theories of power and sovereignty.[2]

Civic Humanism and Liberalism in the Constitution and Its Critics

Contemporary scholarship, as we have seen, seems obsessed with forever ridding the college curriculum of the baleful influence of Louis Hartz. In place of the "liberal tradition in America," it posits the omnipresence of Neoclassical civic humanism. Dominating eighteenth-century political thought in Britain and America, it is insisted, was the language of republican virtue. People were political beings who realized their telos only when living in a *vivere civile* with other propertied, arms-bearing citizens, in a republic where they ruled and were ruled in

---

[1] J. G. A. Pocock, *Virtue, Commerce, and History* (Cambridge, Mass., 1985), pp. 7–8, 12–13, 58, 290.

[2] Even this list is not exhaustive. I leave to colleagues the explication of several other, less discernible idioms of politics in the discourse of 1787; for example, the "language of jurisprudence," "scientific whiggism," and the "moral sentiment" schools of the Scottish Enlightenment.

turn. The pursuit of public good is privileged over private interests, and freedom means participation in civic life rather than the protection of individual rights from interference. Central to the scholarly enterprise of republicanism has been the self-proclaimed "dethronement of the paradigm of liberalism and of the Lockean paradigm associated with it."[3]

In response to these republican imperial claims, a group whom Gordon S. Wood has labeled "neo-Lockeans" has insisted that Locke and liberalism were alive and well in Anglo-American thought in the period of the founding.[4] This reading privileges individualism, the moral legitimacy of private interest, and market society over community, public good, and the virtuous pursuit of civic fulfillment. For these "neo-Lockeans" it is not Machiavelli and Montesquieu who set the textual codes that dominated the "great national discussion," but Hobbes and Locke and the assumptions of possessive individualism.

Can we have it both ways? We certainly can if we take Federalist and Anti-Federalist views as representing a single text of political discourse at the founding. A persuasive case can be made for the Federalists as liberal modernists and the Anti-Federalists as nostalgic republican communitarians seeking desperately to hold on to a virtuous moral order threatened by commerce and market society. The Federalist tendency was to depict America in amoral terms as an enlarged nation that transcended local community and moral conviction as the focus of politics. The Federalists seemed to glory in an individualistic and competitive America, which was preoccupied with private rights and personal autonomy. This reading of America is associated with James Madison more than with anyone else, and with his writings in the *Federalist*.

Madison's adulation of heterogeneous factions and interests in an enlarged America, which he introduced into so many of his contributions to the *Federalist*, assumed that the only way to protect the rights of minorities was to enlarge the political sphere and thereby to divide the community as he told the convention, into so great a number of interests and parties that

> in the 1st. place a majority will not be likely at the same moment to have a common interest separate from that of the whole or of the minority; and in

---

[3]J. G. A. Pocock, "An Appeal from the New to the Old Whigs? A Note on Joyce Appleby's Ideology and the History of Political Thought," *Intellectual History Group Newsletter*, Spring 1981, p. 47.

[4]Gordon Wood, "Hellfire Politics," *New York Review of Books* 32, no. 3 (1985): 30. Wood's magisterial *Creation of the American Republic, 1776–1787* (Chapel Hill, N.C., 1969), remains the most brilliant guide to the American founding. The pages that follow should make apparent the debt I (and all who write on this era) owe Wood.

the 2d. place, that in case they shd. have such an interest, they may not be apt to unite in the pursuit of it. It was incumbent on us then to try this remedy, and with that view to frame a republican system on such a scale & in such a form as will controul all the evils wch. have been experienced.[5]

In *Federalist* no. 10 Madison described the multiplication of regional, religious, and economic interests, factions, and parties as the guarantor of American freedom and justice. He put his case somewhat differently in a letter to Thomas Jefferson: "Divide et impera, the reprobated axiom of tyranny, is under certain conditions, the only policy, by which a republic can be administered on just principles."[6] Pride of place among "these clashing interests," so essential for a just order, went to the economic interests inevitable in a complex market society. He described them in the often-quoted passage from *Federalist* no. 10:

The most common and durable source of factions has been the various and unequal distribution of property. Those who hold and those who are without property have ever formed distinct interests in society . . . creditors . . . debtors. . . . A landed interest, a manufacturing interest, a mercantile interest, a moneyed interest. . . . The regulation of these various and interfering interests forms the principal task of modern legislation.

Government for Madison, much as for Locke, was a neutral arbiter among competing interests. Indeed, in *Federalist* no. 43 Madison described the legislative task as providing "umpires"; and in a letter to George Washington he described government's role as a "disinterested & dispassionate umpire in disputes." Sounding much like Locke in chapter 5, "Of Property," of the *Second Treatise*, Madison, in no. 10, attributed the differential possession of property to the "diversity in the faculties of men," to their "different and unequal faculties of acquiring property." It was "the protection of these faculties" that constituted "the first object of government." As it was for Locke—who wrote that *"justice* gives every Man a Title to the product of his honest Industry"—so, too, for Madison and the Federalists: justice effectively meant respect for private rights, especially property rights.[7]

Justice for the Federalists was less a matter of civic virtue, of public participation in politics, as recent American historical scholarship has

---

[5]Max Farrand, ed., *The Records of the Federal Convention of 1787* (New Haven, Conn., 1911), 1:136.

[6]Madison to Jefferson, Oct. 24, 1787, in *The Writings of James Madison . . .* , ed. Gaillard Hunt (New York, 1900–1910), 5:31.

[7]Madison to Washington, Apr. 16, 1787, in ibid., 2:346; John Locke, "First Treatise of Civil Government," in *Two Treatises of Government . . .* (1689), ed. Peter Laslett (Cambridge, Eng., 1960), chap. 4, sec. 42.

emphasized, or of a Neoplatonic ideal of a transcendent moral order, as such scholars as Walter Berns have argued, than it was a reflection of the Lockean liberal world of personal rights, and most dramatically of property rights. It was a substantive, not a procedural or civic, ideal of justice that preoccupied the framers in 1787. It was much more often the content of state legislative actions, not their violation of due process, that condemned them as wicked. With striking frequency the condemnation of state laws that interfered with private contracts or established paper money schemes was cast in the language of "unjust laws." In South Carolina such laws were called "open and outrageous . . . violations of every principle of Justice." New Jersey's debtor relief legislation was criticized as "founded not upon the principles of Justice, but upon the Right of the Sword." The Boston *Independent Chronicle* complained in May 1787 that the Massachusetts legislature lacked "a decided tone . . . in favor of the general principles of justice." A "virtuous legislature," wrote a New Jersey critic in 1786, "cannot listen to any proposition, however popular, that came within the description of being unjust, impolitic or unnecessary." In Massachusetts the legislation sought by the Shaysites was seen to be an "injustice," establishing "iniquity by Law" and violating "the most simple ties of common honesty." The linkage between the procedural and substantive objections to the state legislatures was made clearly by Noah Webster. They were, he wrote, guilty of "so many legal infractions of sacred right—so many public invasions of private property—so many wanton abuses of legislative powers!"[8]

Madison, too, read justice as the substantive protection of rights. In his argument before the convention on behalf of a council of revision he pleaded that the president and judges should have the power to veto "unwise & unjust measures" of the state legislatures "which constituted so great a portion of our calamities."[9] This concern is equally evident in the pages of the *Federalist*. In no. 10, state actions reflecting "a rage for paper money, for an abolition of debts, for an equal division of property" were "schemes of injustice" and "improper or wicked project[s]." The fruit of unjust and wicked laws was the "alarm for private rights" that is "echoed from one end of the continent to the other." In no. 44 Madison equated the "love of justice" with hatred of paper money. Such pestilential laws required, in turn, sacrifices on "the altar of justice." The end of government itself was justice,

---

[8]Walter Berns, *Freedom, Virtue, and the First Amendment* (Baton Rouge, La., 1957); *State Gazette of South-Carolina* (Charleston), Mar. 5, 1787; *Independent Chronicle and Universal Advertiser* (Boston), May 31, 1787; *Political Intelligencer* (Elizabeth Town, N.J.), Jan. 4, 1786; New Jersey and Massachusetts critics and Noah Webster are quoted in Wood, *Creation of the American Republic*, pp. 406, 465, 411.

[9]Farrand, ed., *Records of the Federal Convention*, 2:73–74.

Madison wrote in no. 51, and in no. 54 he refined this concept further by noting that "government is instituted no less for protection of the property than of the persons of individuals." It was the same for Hamilton, who wrote in *Federalist* no. 70 that "the protection of property" constituted "the ordinary course of justice." In no. 78 Hamilton also described the "private rights of particular classes of citizens" injured "by unjust and partial laws."

The commitment in the preamble to the Constitution to "establish justice" meant for the framers that it would protect private rights; that protection would help it achieve the next objective—to "insure domestic tranquility." Should there be doubts about this, we have Madison as our guide to what "establish justice" meant. On June 6 he had risen at the convention to answer Roger Sherman's suggestion that the only objects of union were better relations with foreign powers and the prevention of conflicts and disputes among the states. What about justice? was the thrust of Madison's intervention. To Sherman's list of the Constitution's objectives Madison insisted that there be added "the necessity of providing more effectually for the security of private rights, and the steady dispensation of Justice. Interferences with these were evils which had more perhaps than any thing else produced this convention."[10]

The acceptance of modern liberal society in the Federalist camp went beyond a legitimization of the politics of interest and a conviction that government's purpose was to protect the fruits of honest industry. There was also an unabashed appreciation of modern commercial society. Former Secretary of Education William Bennett was quite right in his reminder that "commerce had a central place in the ideas of the Founders."[11] Hamilton, for example, insisted in *Federalist* no. 12 that

> the prosperity of commerce is now perceived and acknowledged by all enlightened statesmen to be the most useful as well as the most productive source of national wealth, and has accordingly become a primary object of their political cares. By multiplying the means of gratification, by promoting the introduction and circulation of the precious metals, those darling objects of human avarice and enterprise, it serves to vivify and invigorate the channels of industry and to make them flow with greater activity and copiousness.

Hamilton was perfectly aware that his praise of private gratification, avarice, and gain flew in the face of older ideals of civic virtue and public duty, which emphasized the subordination of private interest to

---

[10]Ibid., 1:134.
[11]William Bennett, "How Should Americans Celebrate the Bicentennial of the Constitution?" *National Forum* 44 (1984): 60.

the public good. He turned this very rejection of the republican moral ideal into an argument for the need of a federal standing army. This was a further blow to the ideals of civic virtue, which had always seen professional armies as evil incarnate, undermining the citizen's self-sacrificial participation in the defense of the public realm, which was the premise of the militia. America as a market society could not rely on the militia, according to Hamilton. "The militia," he wrote in *Federalist* no. 24, "would not long, if at all, submit to be dragged from their occupations and families." He was writing of manning garrisons involved in protecting the frontiers: "And if they could be prevailed upon or compelled to do it, the increased expense of a frequent rotation of service, and the loss of labor and disconcertation of the industrious pursuits of individuals, would form conclusive objections to the scheme. It would be as burdensome and injurious to the public as ruinous to private citizens."

In *Federalist* no. 8, another defense of standing armies, Hamilton acknowledged the eclipse of older civic ideals of self-sacrifice and participatory citizenship in commercial America: "The industrious habits of the people of the present day, absorbed in the pursuit of gain and devoted to the improvements of agriculture and commerce, are incompatible with the condition of a nation of soldiers, which was the true condition of the people of those [ancient Greek] republics."

Many of the Anti-Federalists, on the other hand, were still wedded to a republican civic ideal, to the making of America into what Samuel Adams called "a Christian Sparta." The very feature of pluralist diversity in the new constitutional order which Madison saw as its great virtue the Anti-Federalists saw as its major defect. For the Anti-Federalist "Brutus" it was absurd that the legislature "would be composed of such heterogeneous and discordant principles, as would constantly be contending with each other." A chorus of Anti-Federalists insisted that virtuous republican government required a small area and a homogeneous population. Patrick Henry noted that a republican form of government extending across the continent "contradicts all the experience of the world." Richard Henry Lee argued that "a free elective government cannot be extended over large territories." Robert Yates of New York saw liberty "swallowed up" because the new republic was too large.[12]

Montesquieu and others had taught Anti-Federalists "that so extensive a territory as that of the United States, including such a variety of

---

[12]Adams to John Scollay, Dec. 30, 1780, in *The Writings of Samuel Adams*, ed. Harry Alonzo Cushing (New York, 1904–1908), 4:238; "Brutus" quoted in Herbert J. Storing, *What the Anti-Federalists Were For* (Chicago, 1981), p. 47; Henry, Lee, and Yates quoted in *Essays on the Making of the Constitution*, ed. Leonard W. Levy (New York, 1969), p. ix.

climates, productions, interests, and so great differences of manners, habits, and customs," could never constitute a moral republic. This was the crucial issue for the minority members of the Pennsylvania ratifying convention: "We dissent, first, because it is the opinion of the most celebrated writers on government, and confirmed by uniform experience, that a very extensive territory cannot be governed on the principles of freedom, otherwise than by a confederation of republics."[13]

Anti-Federalists' fears over the absence of homogeneity in the enlarged republic were as important as the issue of size. In the course of arguing that a national government could not be trusted if it were to allow open immigration, "Agrippa," the popular Anti-Federalist pamphleteer assumed to be James Winthrop, contrasted the much more desirable situation in "the eastern states" with the sad plight of Pennsylvania, which for years had allowed open immigration and in which religious toleration and diversity flourished:

> Pennsylvania has chosen to receive all that would come there. Let any indifferent person judge whether that state in point of morals, education, energy is equal to any of the eastern states . . . [which,] by keeping separate from the foreign mixtures, [have] acquired their present greatness in the course of a century and a half, and have preserved their religion and morals. . . . Reasons of equal weight may induce other states . . . to keep their blood pure.[14]

Most Anti-Federalists held that a republican system required similarity of religion, manners, sentiments, and interests. They were convinced that no such sense of community could exist in an enlarged republic, that no one set of laws could work within such diversity. "We see plainly that men who come from New England are different from us," wrote Joseph Taylor, a southern Anti-Federalist. "Agrippa," on the other hand, declared that "the inhabitants of warmer climates are more dissolute in their manners, and less industrious, than in colder countries. A degree of severity is, therefore, necessary with one which would cramp the spirit of the other. . . . It is impossible for one code of laws to suit Georgia and Massachusetts."[15]

A just society, for many Anti-Federalists, involved more than simply

---

[13]Montesquieu quoted in Wood, *Creation of the American Republic*, p. 499; Pennsylvania delegate quoted in Levy, *Essays on the Constitution*, p. x.

[14]"Letters of Agrippa," Dec. 28, 1787, in *The Complete Anti-Federalist*, ed. Herbert J. Storing (Chicago, 1981), 4:86.

[15]Jonathan Elliot, ed., *The Debates of the Several State Conventions on the Adoption of the Federal Constitution . . .* , 2d ed. (Philadelphia, 1863), 4:24; "Letters of Agrippa," Dec. 3, 1787, in Storing, *Complete Anti-Federalist*, 4:76.

protecting property rights. Government had more responsibilities than merely to regulate "various and interfering interests." It was expected to promote morality, virtue, and religion. Many Anti-Federalists, for example, were shocked by the Constitution's totally secular tone and its general disregard of religion and morality. Equally upsetting was the lack of any religious content in Federalist arguments for the Constitution.

Some Anti-Federalists were angered that the Constitution, in Article VI, Section 3, prohibited religious tests for officeholders while giving no public support for religious institutions. Amos Singletary of Massachusetts was disturbed that it did not require men in power to be religious: "though he hoped to see Christians, yet, by the Constitution, a Papist, or an Infidel, was as eligible as they." Henry Abbot, an Anti-Federalist in North Carolina, wrote that "the exclusion of religious tests is by many thought dangerous and impolitic. They suppose . . . pagans, deists, and Mahometans might obtain offices among us." For David Caldwell of North Carolina, this prohibition of religious tests constituted "an invitation for Jews and pagans of every kind to come among us." Since Christianity was the best religion for producing "good members of society, . . . those gentlemen who formed this Constitution should not have given this invitation to Jews and heathens."[16]

Anti-Federalists held that religion was a crucial support of government. For Richard Henry Lee, "refiners may weave as fine a web of reason as they please, but the experience of all times shews Religion to be the guardian of morals." The state, according to some Anti-Federalists, had to be concerned with civic and religious education. Several made specific proposals for state-sponsored "seminaries of useful learning" to instill "the principles of free government" and "the science of morality." The state, they urged, should encourage "the people in favour of virtue by affording publick protection to religion." Going a long step further, Charles Turner of Massachusetts insisted that "without the prevalence of *Christian piety and morals,* the best republican Constitution can never save us from slavery and ruin." He urged that the government institute some means of education "as shall be *adequate* to the *divine, patriotick purpose* of training up the children and youth at large, in that solid learning, and in those pious and moral principles, which are the *support,* the *life* and the soul of republican government and liberty, of which a free Constitution is the body."[17]

Not surprisingly, some Anti-Federalists also tended to see the ex-

16Elliot, *Debates,* 2:44; 4:192, 199.
17Lee to Madison, Nov. 26, 1784, in *The Letters of Richard Henry Lee,* ed. James Curtis Ballagh (New York, 1911–1914), 2:304; Storing, *What the Anti-Federalists Were For,* pp. 21, 23.

change principles of commercial society, so praised by the Federalists, as threats to civic and moral virtue. Would not the self-seeking activities "of a commercial society beget luxury, the parent of inequality, the foe to virtue, and the enemy to restraint"? The spread of commerce would undermine republican simplicity, for the more a people succumbed to luxury, the more incapable they became of governing themselves. As one Anti-Federalist put it, speaking critically of the silence of the Constitution on questions of morality, "whatever the refinement of modern politics may inculcate, it still is certain that some degree of virtue must exist, or freedom cannot live." Honest folk like himself, he went on, objected to "Mandevill[e]'s position . . . 'that private vices are public benefits.'" This was not an unfamiliar theme to the men who would oppose the Constitution. Richard Henry Lee singled out the same source of evil, "Mandevilles . . . who laugh at virtue, and with vain ostentatious display of words will deduce from vice, public good!"[18]

The problem with the Federalist position for many Anti-Federalists was the inadequacy of its vision of community based on mere interests and their protection. The Anti-Federalists suspected that such a community could not persist through what Madison called in *Federalist* no. 51 "the policy of supplying, by opposite and rival interests, the defect of better motives." A proper republican community, for these Anti-Federalists, required a moral consensus, which in turn required similarity, familiarity, and fraternity. How, they asked, could one govern oneself and prefer the common good over private interests outside a shared community small enough and homogeneous enough to allow one to know and sympathize with one's neighbors? The republican spirit of Rousseau hovered over these Anti-Federalists as they identified with small, simple, face-to-face, uniform societies.

Madison and Hamilton understood full well that this communitarian sentiment lay at the core of much of the Anti-Federalist critique of the new constitutional order. In *Federalist* no. 35 Hamilton ridiculed the face-to-face politics of the person "whose observation does not travel beyond the circle of his neighbors and his acquaintances." Madison in no. 10 described two alternative ways of eliminating the causes of factions and thus the politics of interest: one by "destroying the liberty which is essential to its existence; the other by giving to every citizen the same opinions, the same passions, and the same interests." Both were unacceptable. To do either would cut out the very heart of the liberal polity he championed.[19]

[18]Storing, *What the Anti-Federalists Were For*, p. 73; Ballagh, *Letters of R. H. Lee*, 2:62–63.
[19]Cf. Walter Berns, "Does the Constitution Secure These Rights?" in *How Democratic Is the Constitution?* ed. Robert A. Goldwin and William A. Schambra (Washington, D.C., 1980), p. 73.

Can one go too far in making the case for the Anti-Federalists as antiliberal communitarians or Rousseauean republicans? Some were, without doubt, but others responded to the enlargement of the federal government and the enhancement of executive power with a call for the protection of private and individual rights through a bill of rights. Even this position, however may be explained by their communitarian bias. If, after all, government was to be run from some city hundreds of miles away, by people superior, more learned, and more deliberative than they, by people with whom they had little in common, then individual rights needed specific protection. The basis for trust present in the small moral community where citizens shared what Madison disparagingly described as "the same opinions, the same passions, and the same interests" was extinguished.

An equally strong case can be made for the Federalists as republican theorists, and here we see full-blown the confusion of idioms, the overlapping of political languages, in 1787. There is, of course, Madison's redefinition of and identification with a republicanism that involved "the delegation of the government . . . to a small number of citizens elected by the rest" as opposed to a democracy "consisting of a small number of citizens who assemble and administer the government in person." But the crucial move that in no. 10 sets Madison firmly within the republican paradigm is his assumption that the representative function in an enlarged republic would produce officeholders who would sacrifice personal, private, and parochial interest to the public good and the public interest. What made the layers of filtration prescribed by the new constitutional order so welcome was their ultimate purpose—producing enlightened public-spirited citizens who found fulfillment in the quest for public good. It is to this feature of Madison's no. 10 that Garry Wills has drawn attention as the crowning inspiration of Madison's moral republicanism.[20] Republican government over a large country would, according to Madison,

> refine and enlarge the public views by passing them through the medium of a chosen body of citizens whose wisdom may best discern the true interest of their country, and whose patriotism and love of justice will be least likely to sacrifice it to temporary or partial considerations. Under such a regulation it may well happen that the public voice pronounced by the representatives of the people will be more consonant to the public good than if pronounced by the people themselves, convened for the purpose.

The greater number of citizens choosing representatives in a larger republic would reject "unworthy candidates" and select "men who

[20]See Garry Wills, *Explaining America: The Federalist* (Garden City, N.Y., 1981).

possess the most attractive merit." A large republic and a national government would lead to "the substitution of representatives whose enlightened views and virtuous sentiments render them superior to local prejudices and to schemes of injustice." We know, given Madison's candor, what this meant.

Working out the mechanisms by which this filtration process would "refine" and "enlarge" public views and enhance the quality of the men chosen to express them preoccupied the delegates at Philadelphia. This explains their lengthy deliberations over how governing officials such as the president and senators should be selected. Indirect processes of selection would, Madison wrote in his notes, "extract from the mass of the Society the purest and noblest characters which it contains."[21] The people involved in choosing the president or senators would be, according to Jay in *Federalist* no. 64, "the most enlightened and respectable." The Senate, Madison wrote in *Federalist* no. 63, would then be made up of "temperate and respectable" men standing for "reason, justice and truth" in the face of the people's "errors and delusions."

Madison privileged public over private elsewhere in the *Federalist* as well. In no. 49 he envisioned a government controlled and regulated by public "reason" and "the true merits of the question," not by particular and private "passions." Similarly, in no. 55 he saw "the public interests" at risk in large legislative assemblies, where "passion" always triumphed over "reason." The smaller House of Representatives constructed by the Federalists would better ensure the victory of public good over self-interest.

The class focus of the Federalists' republicanism is self-evident. Their vision was of an elite corps in whom civic spirit and love of the general good overcame particular and narrow interest: men of substance, independence, and fame who had the leisure to devote their time to public life and the wisdom to seek the true interests of the country as opposed to the wicked projects of local and particular interests. This republicanism of Madison and the Federalists was, of course, quite consistent with the general aristocratic orientation of classical republicanism, which was, after all, the ideal of the independent, propertied, and therefore leisured citizen with time and reason to find fulfillment as *homo civicus*.

For Madison the filtering out of mediocrity went hand in hand with disinterested pursuit of the public good. Many Anti-Federalists, for their part, saw legislatures as most representative when their membership mirrored the complexity and diversity of society—when, in

---

[21]James Madison, "Vices of the Political System of the United States," in *The Papers of James Madison*, ed. William T. Hutchinson et al. (Chicago, 1962–), 4:357.

fact, each geographical unit and social rank was represented. In offering the mirror, not the filter, as the model for representation, Anti-Federalists seemed to be calling for the representation of every particular interest and thus appear to resemble interest-centered liberals. They, as well as Madison in his nonrepublican passages, it can be claimed, articulated the politics of interest, to be sure in a language much more democratic and participatory. The classic expression of this Anti-Federalist interest theory of representation came from Melancton Smith, the great antagonist of Hamilton at the New York ratification convention. He told the delegates that "the idea that naturally suggests itself to our minds, when we speak of representatives, is, that they resemble those they represent. They should be a true picture of the people, possess a knowledge of their circumstances and their wants, sympathize in all their distresses, and be disposed to seek their true interests." Directly refuting the filtration model, Smith insisted that a representative system ought to seek not "brilliant talents" but "a sameness, as to residence and interests, between the representative and his constituents."[22]

Hamilton repudiated the Anti-Federalist interest theory in *Federalist* no. 35. "The idea of an actual representation of all classes of the people, by persons of each class," so that the feelings and interests of all would be expressed, "is altogether visionary," he wrote. The national legislature, Hamilton recommended, should be composed only of "landholders, merchants, and men of the learned professions." Ordinary people, however much confidence "they may justly feel in their own good sense," should realize that "their interests can be more effectually promoted" by men from these three stations in life.

The confusion of paradigms is further evident when one analyzes in more detail these Federalist and Anti-Federalist theories of representation. The interest- and particularistic-oriented Anti-Federalists tended to espouse the traditional republican conviction, dominant in most states under the Articles of Confederation, that representatives should be directly responsible to their constituents and easily removable. This position, of course, tapped a rich eighteenth-century republican tradition of demanding frequent elections. Implicit in the Federalist notion of filtration, however, was a denial of the representative as mere delegate or servant of his constituents. In Madison's republicanism the representative was chosen for his superior ability to discern the public good, not as a mere spokesman for his town or region, or for the

[22]Elliot, *Debates*, 2:245; *Letters from the Federal Farmer*, in Storing, *Complete Anti-Federalist*, 298. For Smith as author of the *Federal Farmer* see Robert H. Webking, "Melancton Smith and the *Letters from the Federal Farmer*," *William and Mary Quarterly*, 3d ser., 44 (1987): 510–28.

farmers or mechanics who elected him. It followed, then, that Federalists rejected the traditional republican ideal of annual or frequent elections, which was so bound to the more democratic ideal of the legislator as delegate. We are not surprised to find Madison, in *Federalist* nos. 37, 52, and 53, critical of frequent elections and offering several arguments against them. The proposed federal government, he insisted, was less powerful than the British government had been; its servants, therefore, were less to be feared. State affairs, he contended, could be mastered in less than a year, but the complexity of national politics was such that more time was needed to grasp its details. More important than these arguments, however, was the basic ideological gulf that here separated Madison's republicanism from that of the Anti-Federalist proponents of annual elections. Madison's legislators of "refined and enlarged public views," seeking "the true interest of their country," ought not to be subject to yearly review by local farmers and small-town tradesmen.

The Language of Virtuous Republicanism

The meaning of virtue in the language of civic humanism is clear. It is the privileging of the public over the private. Samuel Adams persistently evoked the idioms of Aristotle and Cicero. "A Citizen," he wrote, "owes everything to the Commonwealth." He worried that Americans would so "forget their own generous Feelings for the Publick and for each other, as to set private Interest in Competition with that of the great Community." Benjamin Rush went so far in 1786 as to reject the very core belief of what in a later day would come to be called possessive individualism. Every young man in a true republic, he noted, must "be taught that he does not belong to himself, but that he is public property." All his time and effort throughout "his youth—his manhood—his old age—nay more, life, all belong to his country." For John Adams, "public Virtue is the only Foundation of Republics." Republican government required "a positive Passion for the public good, the public interest . . . Superiour to all private Passions."[23]

This is not all that virtue meant. As we have noted, subtle changes were taking place during the founding of the American republic in the

[23]Adams to Caleb Davis, Apr. 3, 1781, in Cushing, *Writings of Samuel Adams*, 4:255; Adams to Scollay, Mar. 20, 1777, in ibid., 3:365; Rush quoted in Wood, *Creation of the American Republic*, p. 427, and Dagobert D. Runes, ed., *Selected Writings of Benjamin Rush* (New York, 1947), p. 31; John Adams, in *Warren-Adams Letters* [ed. Worthington Chauncey Ford], Massachusetts Historical Society Collections, vols. 72–73 (Boston, 1917–1925), 1:201–2, 222.

notion of virtue, and at their core was a transvaluation of public and private. Dramatic witness is given to these changes by Madison's *Federalist* no. 44, where he depicted paper money as a threat to the republican character and spirit of the American people. That spirit, however, was neither civic nor public; the values at risk were apolitical and personal. Madison feared for the sobriety, the prudence, and the industry of Americans. His concern was "the industry and morals of the people." William Livingston expressed a similar concern when he worried that his countrymen "do not exhibit the virtue that is necessary to support a republican government." John Jay agreed. "Too much," he wrote, "has been expected from the Virtue and good Sense of the People." But when Americans became specific about exactly what the decline of virtue meant, their language, like Madison's, was often noncivic and instead self-referential. Writing to Jefferson in 1787, friends told of "symptoms . . . truly alarming, which have tainted the faith of the most orthodox republicans." Americans lacked "industry, economy, temperance, and other republican virtues." Their fall from virtue was marked not by a turning from public life (was there not, indeed, too much of that very republican value in the overheated state legislatures?) but by a tendency to become "a Luxurious Voluptuous indolent expensive people without Economy or Industry." Virtuous republican people could, in fact, be described in noncivic, personal terms by the very same men who used the language of civic humanism. John Adams could see the foundation of virtuous government in men who are "sober, industrious and frugal."[24]

One of the most striking aspects of political discourse in this era is the formulaic frequency with which this different sense of virtue is heard. For Joel Barlow in a 1787 Fourth of July oration at Hartford, the "noble republican virtues which constitute the chief excellency" of government were "industry, frugality, and economy." Richard Henry Lee described a virtuous people as a "wise, attentive, sober, diligent & frugal" people—such people as those who had established "the independence of America." A Virginian who wondered whether America could sustain republican government asked, "Have we that Industry, Frugality, Economy, that Virtue which is necessary to constitute it?" The constitutions of Pennsylvania and Vermont actually enlisted the Machiavellian republican notion of the return to original principles for their noncivic definition of a virtuous people. They specified that "a

---

[24]Theodore Sedgwick, *A Memoir of the Life of William Livingston* . . . (New York, 1833), p. 403; Jay to Jefferson, Feb. 9, 1787, in *The Papers of Thomas Jefferson*, ed. Julian Boyd et al. (Princeton, N.J., 1950–), 11:129; letters to Jefferson quoted in Wood, *Creation of the American Republic*, p. 424; John Adams, "Thoughts on Government," in *The Works of John Adams*, ed. Charles Francis Adams, vol. 4 (Boston, 1851), p. 199.

frequent recurrence to fundamental principles, and a firm adherence to justice, moderation, temperance, industry, and frugality are absolutely necessary to preserve the blessings of liberty and keep a government free."[25]

The Anti-Federalists, ostensible communitarian and public-oriented foils to Madisonian interest-based liberalism, could also use this more personal idiomatic notion of virtue. The Articles were not at fault, according to John Williams of New York. The great problem was the decline of virtue in the middle 1780s, "banishing all that economy, frugality, and industry, which had been exhibited during the war." For the Anti-Federalist pamphleteer "Candidus," it was not a new constitution that America needed but a return to the virtues of "industry and frugality."[26]

The republican tradition had, to be sure, always extolled economy over luxury. From Aristotle and Cicero through Harrington and the eighteenth-century opposition to Walpole, republican rhetoric linked a virtuous republican order to frugal abstention from extravagance and luxury. But more than the all-pervasive paradigm of republicanism is at work here. The inclusion of industry in the litany of virtues directs us to another inheritance, to another language in which Americans in the late eighteenth century conceptualized their personal and political universe. Americans, as we have seen, also spoke the language of work-ethic Protestantism derived from Richard Baxter, John Bunyan, and the literature of the calling and of "industry." It was this discourse that monopolized the texts of the English Dissenters whose writings were so influential in the founding generation.[27]

The Protestant language of work and the calling is, of course, complementary to the liberal language of Locke, with its similar voluntaristic and individualistic emphasis. Locke's *Second Treatise* and its chapter "Of Property," with its very Protestant God enjoining industrious man to subdue the earth through work and thus to realize himself, is, as Quentin Skinner insists, "the classical text of radical Calvinist politics."[28] The kinship of work-ethic Protestant discourse to Locke has less to do with the juristic discourse of rights than with the Protestant theme of work. "Virtue" and "corruption" are prominent in

[25]Joel Barlow and Virginian quoted in Wood, *Creation of the American Republic*, pp. 418, 95; Lee to Arthur Lee, Feb. 11, 1779, in Ballagh, *Letters of R. H. Lee*, 2:33; Pennsylvania and Vermont constitutions quoted in O. G. Hatch, "Civic Virtue: Wellspring of Liberty," *National Forum* 64 (1984): 35.

[26]Elliot, *Debates*, 2:240; "Essays by Candidus," in Storing, *Complete Anti-Federalist*, 4:129.

[27]Burgh, indeed, is cited in *Federalist* no. 56.

[28]Quentin Skinner, *The Foundations of Modern Political Thought* (Cambridge, Eng., 1978), 2:239.

the Protestant vocabulary, as we have seen, but they have primarily nonclassical referents. The virtuous man is solitary and private, realizing himself and his talents through labor and achievement; the corrupt man is unproductive, indolent, and in the devil's camp. He fails the test of individual responsibility. Few have captured the compatibility of the liberal and work-ethic Protestant paradigms as well as Tocqueville, albeit unintentionally. In *Democracy in America* he wrote of the American character in noncivic, individualistic terms that are central to both liberal and Protestant discourse. Americans, Tocqueville wrote, "owe nothing to any man, they expect nothing from any man; they acquire the habit of always considering themselves as standing alone, and they are apt to imagine that their whole destiny is in their own hands."[29]

In this Protestant work-ethic vocabulary, industry, simplicity, and frugality were the signs not only of a virtuous people but also of a free people. As one Rhode Island writer put it, "the industrious and the frugal only will be free." The Boston *Evening-Post* of November 16, 1767, noted that "by consuming *less* of what we are not really in want of, and by industriously cultivating and improving the natural advantages of our own country, we might save our *substance, even our lands,* from becoming the property of others, and we might effectually preserve our *virtue* and our *liberty,* to the latest posterity." Three weeks later the *Pennsylvania Journal* proclaimed: "SAVE YOUR MONEY AND YOU WILL SAVE YOUR COUNTRY." In one of her famous letters to her husband, John, away at the Continental Congress, Abigail Adams revealed how salient the Protestant virtues were in the political context of her day. Would, she wrote, that Americans "return a little more to their primitive Simplicity of Manners, and not sink into inglorious ease." They must "retrench their expenses. . . . Indeed their [*sic*] is occasion for all our industry and economy."[30]

America in the 1780s, Drew R. McCoy tells us, may well have had one of the highest rates of population growth in its history. For many Americans this growth conjured up fears of vast increases in the numbers of the poor and idle. Only a cultivation of domestic manufactures would keep these idle hordes from the devil's hands. Once again the marriage of necessity and virtue led Americans to turn from foreign imports to local manufacture and domestic hard work. As Morgan noted of the prewar boycott of the British, so McCoy characterizes similar promotion of native production in the 1780s "as the necessary

[29]Alexis de Tocqueville, *Democracy in America* (1835), ed. Richard D. Heffner (New York, 1956), p. 194.

[30]*Newport Mercury,* Feb. 28, 1774; *Pennsylvania Journal* (Philadelphia), Dec. 10, 1767; Abigail Adams to John Adams, Oct. 16, 1774, in *Adams Family Correspondence,* ed. L. H. Butterfield et al. (Cambridge, Mass., 1963), 1:173.

means of making Americans into an active, industrious, republican people." Indeed, in February 1787 one observer noted how absurd it was for Americans to support manufactures "at several thousand miles distance, while a great part of our own people are idle." American manufactures would "deliver them from the curse of idleness. We shall hold out . . . a new stimulus and encouragement to industry and every useful art."[31]

Communitarian critics of an individualistic, interest-based politics could speak the Protestant language of sobriety, frugality, and industry and also locate these virtues in the particularly virtuous middle ranks of life. The Anti-Federalists were in good company, then, when they enlisted that language to condemn what they saw as the aristocratic character of the new constitutional order. To the Federal Farmer, the new Constitution resulted from the conflict between leveling debtors "who want a share of the property of others" and men "called aristocrats" who "grasp at all power and property." Uninvolved and victimized were the larger number of "men of middling property" who worked hard and made up the "solid, free, and independent part of the community." It was Melancton Smith, the bearer of a proud Protestant name, who best made the Protestant case for the virtuous middle against Hamilton's aristocratic constitution at the New York ratifying convention. It was an evil constitution, Smith claimed, because it restricted representation to the idle few, excluding those who were morally superior. Note that virtue here is apolitical and noncivic:

> Those in middling circumstances, have less temptation—they are inclined by habit and the company with whom they associate, to set bounds to their passions and appetites—if this is not sufficient, the want of means to gratify them will be a restraint—they are obliged to employ their time in their respective callings—hence the substantial yeomanry of the country are more temperate, of better morals and less ambitious than the great.[32]

J. G. A. Pocock has noted that in the eighteenth century "virtue was redefined," but he is wide of the mark in suggesting that "there are signs of an inclination to abandon the word" and in claiming that it was simply redefined "as the practice and refinement of manners." Virtue had for some time been part of the Protestant discourse, with its nonrepublican image of the virtuous person as productive, thrifty, and frugal. By the second half of the century this noncivic personal reading

---

[31]Drew R. McCoy, *The Elusive Republic: Political Economy in Jeffersonian America* (Chapel Hill, N.C., 1980), p. 116; *American Museum* 1 (1787): 116, 119.

[32]*Letters from the Federal Farmer*, in Storing, *Complete Anti-Federalist*, 2:253; Melancton Smith in ibid., 6:158.

of virtue became secularized, as in Adam Smith's negative assessment of the aristocrat who "shudders with horror at the thought of any situation which demands the continual and long exertion of patience, industry, fortitude, and application of thought. These virtues are hardly ever to be met with in men who are born to those high stations."[33]

Virtue was becoming privatized in the latter part of the eighteenth century. It was being moved from the realm of public activity to the sphere of personal character. The virtuous man partook less and less of that republican ideal which held sway from Aristotle to Harrington— the man whose landed property gave him the leisure necessary for civic commitment in the public arena, be its manifestations political or martial. Property was still important in the Protestant paradigm—not, however, as grantor of leisure but as the rightful fruit of industrious work.

Gordon Wood has noted that Carter Braxton more than any other in the founding generation of Americans sensed the tension between a republicanism based on public virtue—the "disinterested attachment to the public good, exclusive and independent of all private and selfish interest"—and an American polity where in reality most people practiced a private virtue, each man "act[ing] for himself, and with a view of promoting his own particular welfare." Republican esteem of the public over the private had never been, according to Braxton, the politics of "the mass of the people in any state." In this observation lay Braxton's real insight. Republican virtue was historically the ideal of a circumscribed, privileged citizenry with an independent propertied base that provided the leisure and time for fulfillment in public life through moral involvement in the public business, the *res publica*. Americans, on the other hand, Braxton wrote, "inhabit a country to which Providence has been more bountiful"; they live lives of hard work and private virtue, and their industry, frugality, and economy produce the fruits of honest labor. From our perspective, we can credit Braxton with perceiving the decline of republican hegemony in the face of the alternative worlds of Lockean liberalism and the Protestant ethic. We now know that one hears more and more in the course of the late eighteenth century a different language of virtue. At the heart of this shift from republican to Protestant notions of virtue was also the transvaluation of work and leisure. Many Americans in 1787 would have dissented vigorously from the centuries-old republican paradigm set forth in Aristotle's *Politics:* "Citizens must not live a mechanical or commercial life. Such a life is not noble, and it militates against virtue.

---

[33]Pocock, *Virtue, Commerce, and History,* pp. 48, 50; Adam Smith, *The Theory of Moral Sentiments* (1759), ed. D. D. Raphael and A. L. Macfie (Oxford, 1976), 1:24.

Nor must those who are to be citizens be agricultural workers, for they must have leisure to develop their virtue, and for the activities of a citizen."[34]

The Language of Power and the State

Lost today in the legitimate characterization of the Constitution as bent on setting limits to the power exercised by less than angelic men is the extent to which the Constitution is a grant of power to a centralized nation-state. This loss reflects a persistent privileging of Madison over Hamilton in reading the text. While posterity emphasizes the Constitution's complex web of checks and balances and the many institutionalized separations of powers, the participants in the "great national discussion," on whichever side they stood, agreed with Hamilton that the Constitution intended a victory for power, for the "principle of *strength* and *stability* in the organization of our government, and *vigor* in its operations."[35]

A pro-Constitution newspaper, the *Pennsylvania Packet*, declared in September 1787: "The year 1776 is celebrated . . . for a revolution in favor of liberty. The year 1787, it is expected, will be celebrated with equal joy, for a revolution in favor of Government." The theme was repeated by Benjamin Rush, also a defender of the Constitution. Rush wrote in June 1787 to his English friend Richard Price that "the same enthusiasm *now* pervades all classes in favor of *government* that actuated us in favor of *liberty* in the years 1774 and 1775."[36]

Critics of the Constitution saw the same forces at work. For Patrick Henry, "the tyranny of Philadelphia" was little different from "the tyranny of George III." An Anti-Federalist told the Virginia ratification convention that "had the Constitution been presented to our view ten years ago, . . . it would have been considered as containing principles incompatible with republican liberty, and, therefore, doomed to infamy." But the real foil to Hamilton, using the very same Whig language, was Richard Henry Lee, who wrote in 1788: "It will be considered, I believe, as a most extraordinary epoch in the history of mankind, that in a few years there should be so essential a change in

---

[34][Carter Braxton], *An Address to the Convention of . . . Virginia, on the Subject of Government . . .* (Philadelphia, 1776), pp. 15, 17 (Wood discusses this text in *Creation of the American Republic*, pp. 96–97); Aristotle, *Politics*, bk. 7, chap. 9.

[35]Elliot, *Debates*, 2:301.

[36]*Pennsylvania Packet and Daily Advertiser* (Philadelphia), Sept. 6, 1787; Rush to Price, June 2, 1787, in *Letters of Benjamin Rush*, ed. L. H. Butterfield (Princeton, N.J., 1951), 1:418–19.

the minds of men. 'Tis really astonishing that the same people, who have just emerged from a long and cruel war in defense of liberty, should now agree to fix an elective despotism upon themselves and their posterity."[37]

But always other and louder voices were using this same language in defense of the Constitution. Benjamin Franklin wrote that "we have been guarding against an evil that old States are most liable to, *excess of power* in the rulers; but our present danger seems to be *defect of obedience* in the subjects." For the *Connecticut Courant* it was all quite simple. The principles of 1776 had produced a glaring problem, "a want of energy in the administration of government."[38]

Thus in the political discourse of 1787 a fourth paradigm was at work, the state-centered language of power. It, too, reached back into the classical world, to the great lawgivers and founders Solon and Lycurgus, and to the imperial ideal of Alexander and Julius Caesar. Its institutional units were not republican city-states but empire and, much later, the nation-state. Its doctrines and commitments were captured less by *zöon politikon, vivere civilere, res publica,* and *virtú* than by *imperium, potestas, gubernaculum,* prerogative, and sovereignty. Its prophets were Dante, Marsilio, Bodin, Richelieu, Hobbes, Machiavelli (of *The Prince,* not the *Discourses*), and James I. This language of politics focused on the moral, heroic, and self-realizing dimensions of the exercise and use of power.

For Charles Howard McIlwain the recurring answer to this power-centered language of politics was the discourse of *jurisdictio;* for contemporary scholars it would be the law-centered paradigm or the language of jurisprudence and rights.[39] For our purposes, it is important to recognize how the discourse of power and sovereignty renders problematic the reading of the "great national discussion" as simply a dialogue between republicanism and liberalism. To be sure, as the language of Protestantism was complementary to and supportive of liberalism, so the state-centered language of power was closer to and more easily compatible with the discourse of republicanism. Hamilton was fascinated by the nation-state builders in early modern Europe, but his power-centered politics still touched base with much of the

---

[37]Elliot, *Debates,* 3:436, 607; Lee to John Lamb, June 27, 1788, in Ballagh, *Letters of R. H. Lee,* 2:475.

[38]Franklin to Charles Carroll, May 25, 1789, in *The Writings of Benjamin Franklin,* ed. Albert Henry Smyth (New York, 1907), 10:7; *Connecticut Courant* quoted in Wood, *Creation of the American Republic,* p. 432.

[39]Charles Howard McIlwain, *Constitutionalism: Ancient and Modern* (Ithaca, N.Y., 1947). For a discussion of these other paradigms and languages, see the essays in *Wealth and Virtue: The Shaping of Political Economy in the Scottish Enlightenment,* ed. Istvan Hont and Michael Ignatieff (Cambridge, Eng., 1983), and Pocock, *Virtue, Commerce, and History.*

older republican ideal. It shared the reading of human beings as political animals as community-building creatures. It, too, stressed public life and public pursuits over the self-regarding lives of private individuals. It did not, however, share the participatory ideals of moral citizenship, basic to much of the republican tradition, and this difference dramatically sets it off as a separate discourse.

In *Federalist* no. 1 Hamilton proclaimed his "enlightened zeal" for "the energy" and "vigor of government." His achievement, and that of the other young men at Philadelphia, was the creation of the American state. Some decades later, Hegel could find nothing in America that he recognized as the "state."[40] But his standard of comparison was the typical established European state, and in that sense he was quite right. What little there was of an American state, however, was crafted by Hamilton, Madison, and the framers of the Constitution, who began their work *de nouveau*, from nothing. There was no royal household whose offices would become state bureaus, no royal army from a feudal past to be transformed into an expression of the state's reality.

It was the experience of war that shaped the vision of America's state-builders. The war against Britain provided them with a continental and national experience that replaced the states-centered focus of the pre-1776 generation. A remarkable number of framers of the Constitution either served in the Continental Army or were diplomats or administrative officials for the Confederation or members of the Continental Congress. Indeed, thirty-nine of the fifty-five delegates to the Constitutional Convention had sat in the Congress. This is where the generational issue, so brilliantly described by Stanley Elkins and Eric McKitrick, was so crucial.[41] Most of the principal Federalists had forged their identity in service to the war and the national cause and in dealing with the individual states' reluctance to assist that continental effort. Washington, Henry Knox, and Hamilton were key figures in military affairs. Robert Morris was superintendent of finance, whose unhappy task it was to try to finance the war. John Jay had been president of the Confederation Congress for a short while and a central actor in trying to implement a common foreign policy for the thirteen states. Whereas most of the Anti-Federalists were states-centered politicians whose heroics took place before 1776, most of the Federalists were shaped by the need to realize the national interest in an international war. Their common bond was an experience that transcended and dissolved state boundaries.

[40]Georg Wilhelm Friedrich Hegel, *The Philosophy of History*, trans. J. Sibree (New York, 1956), pp. 84–87.
[41]Stanley Elkins and Eric McKitrick, "The Founding Fathers: Young Men of the Revolution," *Political Science Quarterly* 76 (1961): 181–216.

Madison and Hamilton had sat on the same committee of the Continental Congress in 1782–1783, working on the funding of the war and the maintenance of the French alliance. Such experiences led them and their state-building colleagues to view the thirteen states collectively as a "country," a country among countries. If their country were going to live in a world of nation-states, it needed to become, like the others, a centralized nation-state with sovereign power to tax, regulate trade, coin money, fund a debt, conduct a foreign policy, and organize a standing army.

The lack of such an American state was profoundly dispiriting to Hamilton. In *Federalist* no. 85 he declared that "a nation without a national government is, in my view, a sad spectacle." In no. 15 he was even more distraught: "We have neither troops, nor treasury, nor government for the Union . . . our ambassadors abroad are the mere pageants of mimic sovereignty." One can, in fact, construct a theory of the origin and development of the state in *The Federalist*, all from Hamilton's contributions. The state is defined in no. 15 as a coercive agent having the power to make laws. To perform this function, a state requires a stable and predictable system of taxation (nos. 30, 36) and agencies of force; that is, armies and police (nos. 6, 34). Especially important for Hamilton's theory of state development are nos. 16 and 17. In the former he insisted that "the majesty of the national authority" cannot work if it is impeded by intermediate bodies: "It must carry its agency to the persons of the citizens." Independent and sovereign nations do not govern or coerce states; they rule over individuals.

Hamilton's preoccupation with money and arms as essential for state-building and his zeal to push aside any intermediate bodies between the state and individuals, while directly relevant for the case he was making on behalf of the Constitution, were also heavily influenced by his perceptive reading of the pattern of state-building in Europe. In the all-important *Federalist* no. 17 Hamilton compares America under the Articles of Confederation with the "feudal anarchy" of medieval Europe. Clearly, for Hamilton, the separate American states were intermediate "political bodies" like "principal vassals" and "feudal baronies," each "a kind of sovereign within . . . particular demesnes." Equally evident is his sense that the pattern of European development, with the triumph of coercive centralized nation-states, should be reproduced in America under the Constitution. On both sides of the Atlantic, then, the state would have "subdued" the "fierce and ungovernable spirit and reduced it within those rules of subordination" that characterize "a more rational and more energetic system of civil polity." Nor is this state-building scenario unrelated to liberal ideological concerns. Hamilton in *Federalist* no. 26 sounds very much like the liberal theorists of state, Hobbes and Locke, when he writes of the role that the "energy of government" plays in ensuring "the security of private rights." However, Hamilton was interested less in the limited liberal state than in the heroic state; heroic state-builders such as he cannot fear power, for power is the essence of the state. The fact that power is so often abused does not rule out its creative and useful role. This was the message of a Hamilton speech to the New York legislature in early 1787:

> We are told it is dangerous to trust power any where; that *power* is liable to *abuse* with a variety of trite maxims of the same kind. General propositions of this nature are easily framed, the truth of which cannot be denied, but they rarely convey any precise idea. To these we might oppose other propositions equally true and equally indefinite. It might be said that too little power is as dangerous as too much, that it leads to anarchy, and from anarchy to despotism. . . . Powers must be granted, or civil Society cannot exist; the possibility of abuse is no argument against the *thing*.[42]

All of the power-centered paradigm's euphemisms for power— "strength," "vigor," "energy"—come together in Hamilton's conception of the presidential office. The presidency was the heart of the new American state for Hamilton, just as the monarch or chief magistrate was for older European nation-states. In Hamilton's president could be heard the echoes of *potestas* and *gubernaculum*. Had he not argued at Philadelphia for a life term for presidents? Short of that, in *Federalist* no. 72 he supported the president's eligibility for indefinite reelection. How else, he asked, would a president be able to "plan and undertake extensive and arduous enterprises for the public benefit"? The president was the energetic builder of an energetic state. In *Federalist* no. 70 Hamilton argued: "Energy in the executive is a leading character in the definition of good government. . . . A feeble executive implies a feeble execution of the government. A feeble execution is but another phrase for a bad execution; and a government ill executed, whatever it may be in theory, must be in practice, a bad government."

Hamilton saw a close relationship between a state with energy and power at home and a powerful state in the world of states. At the Constitutional Convention he angrily replied to Charles Pinckney's suggestion that a republican government should be uninterested in being respected abroad and concerned only with achieving domestic happiness: "It had been said that respectability in the eyes of foreign Nations was not the object at which we aimed; that the proper object of

---

[42]Harold C. Syrett et al., eds., *The Papers of Alexander Hamilton* (New York, 1961–1979), 4:11.

republican government was domestic tranquillity & happiness. This was an ideal distinction. No governmt. could give us tranquillity & happiness at home, which did not possess sufficient stability and strength to make us respectable abroad."[43]

Hamilton was preoccupied with the interrelationship of commerce, state power, and international politics. A powerful state in his vision was a commercial state. In the competitive international system, nation-states sought to improve or protect their commercial strength, and such efforts led inevitably to wars. Powerful states therefore needed standing armies and strong navies. In *Federalist* no. 24 Hamilton insisted that "if we mean to be a commercial people, it must form a part of our policy, to be able to defend that commerce." In contrast to Paine and many isolationist Anti-Federalists, he rejected the notion that wars were fought only "by ambitious princes" or that republican government necessarily led to peace. Hamilton, the realist, ridiculed in *Federalist* no. 6 "visionary or designing men" who thought republics or trading nations immune to the natural conflicts of nation-states, who talked "of perpetual peace between the states," or who claimed that "the genius of republics is pacific."

> Have republics in practice been less addicted to war than monarchies? Are not the former administered by men as well as the latter? Are there not aversions, predilections, rivalships and desires of unjust acquisitions that affect nations as well as kings? Are not popular assemblies frequently subject to the impulses of rage, resentment, jealousy, avarice and of other irregular and violent propensities?

But Hamilton did not want to build an American state with all that statehood required—a financial and commercial infrastructure, energetic leadership, and powerful military forces—merely to allow America to hold its own in a world system characterized by conflict, competition, and clashing powers. He had a grander vision for the American state, a call to greatness. In *Federalist* no. 11 Hamilton wrote of "what this country is capable of becoming," of a future glory for America of "a striking and animating kind." Under a properly "vigorous national government, the natural strength and resources of the country, directed to a common interest, would baffle all the combinations of European jealousy to restrain our growth." If Americans would only "concur in erecting one great American system," the American state would be "superior to the control of all transatlantic force or influence, and able to dictate the terms of the connection between the old and the new world." In the face of a vigorous American state

[43]Farrand, *Records of the Federal Convention*, 1:466–67.

Europe would cease to be "mistress of the world." America would become ascendant in the Western Hemisphere.

Hamilton's horizons were dazzling. His internationalism transcended the cosmopolitan vision of his fellow Federalists as it transcended the localism of the Anti-Federalists. The victory of the state center over the American periphery would in Hamilton's fertile imagination catapult America from the periphery of nations to the center of the world system.

It would be a heroic achievement for Hamilton and his colleagues in Philadelphia to create such a powerful American state. It would bring them everlasting fame, and, as Douglass Adair has told us, that may well have been the ultimate motive that prompted their state-building. In *Federalist* no. 72 Hamilton suggested that political leaders who undertake "extensive and arduous enterprises for the public benefit" are activated by "the love of fame, the ruling passion of the noblest minds." He was describing his ideal of an energetic president and the heroic enterprise of constitutional state-building on which he and his fellow Federalists were embarked. That enterprise, as Madison described it in *Federalist* no. 38, would bring them the fame and immortality of a Lycurgus. The classical and Renaissance discourse of power was replete with praise for creative wielders of *potestas*. Literate men in the eighteenth century, such as Hamilton and Madison, knew that Plutarch in his *Lives of the Noble Greeks and Romans* reserved the greatest historical glory for the "lawgiver" and the "founder of commonwealth." In a text equally well known in this period, Francis Bacon's *Essays*, the top of a five-tier hierarchy of "fame and honour" was occupied by "Conditores Imperium, Founders of States and Commonwealths." David Hume, who was well read by both Hamilton and Madison, echoed this theme. He wrote that "of all men that distinguish themselves by memorable achievements, the first place of honour seems due to legislators and founders of states who transmit a system of laws and institutions to secure the peace, happiness and liberty of future generations.[44]

Hamilton must have seen himself and his fellow state-builders as achieving such everlasting fame. Ten years earlier, in a pamphlet attacking congressmen for not better realizing the potential of their position, he had written of true greatness and fame. He signed the pamphlet with the pseudonym "Publius," the name of a fabled figure in

---

[44]*Plutarch's Lives in Six Volumes* (London, 1758), 1:96; Francis Bacon, "Of Honour and Reputation," in *Bacon's Essays, with Annotations,* ed. Richard Whatley (London, 1886); David Hume, "Of Parties in General," in *The Philosophical Works of David Hume* (Edinburgh, 1826), 3:57. For Douglas Adair, see *Fame and the Founding Fathers,* ed. Trevor Colbourn (New York, 1974).

Plutarch's *Lives* and one later used by the authors of the *Federalist*. Hamilton's vision transcended the walls of Congress in the infant nation and spoke to the historic discourse of power.

> The station of a member of C——ss, is the most illustrious and important of any I am able to conceive. He is to be regarded not only as a legislator, but as the founder of an empire. A man of virtue and ability, dignified with so precious a trust, would rejoice that fortune had given him birth at a time, and placed him in circumstances so favourable for promoting human happiness. He would esteem it not more the duty, than the privilege and ornament of his office, to do good to mankind.[45]

We must not lose sight of the other side in the "great national discussion," however. Hamilton's discourse of power with its vision of an imperial American state attracted the fire of Anti-Federalists like one of Franklin's lightning rods. It was Patrick Henry who most angrily and most movingly repudiated the Federalist state. Henry's American spirit was Tom Paine's. With the Federalist state America would lose its innocence and "splendid government" would become its badge, its dress. On the ruins of paradise would be built, if not the palaces of kings, then armies and navies and mighty empires. At the Virginia ratifying convention Henry evoked a different language of politics.

> The American spirit has fled from hence; it has gone to regions where it has never been expected; it has gone to the people of France, in search of a splendid government, a strong, energetic government. Shall we imitate the example of those nations who have gone from a simple to a splendid government? Are those nations more worthy of our imitation? What can make an adequate satisfaction to them for the loss they have suffered in attaining such a government, for the loss of their liberty? If we admit this consolidated government, it will be because we like a great, splendid one. Some way or other we must be a great and mighty empire; we must have an army, and a navy, and a number of things. When the American spirit was in its youth, the language of America was different; liberty, sir, was then the primary object.[46]

What was Madison's relation to the discourse of power and the Hamiltonian state? Madison was a state-builder, too, but his state was quite different from Hamilton's, and upon these differences a good deal of American politics in the next two decades, and to this day, was to turn. Madison and Hamilton were in agreement on many things. They agreed on the need to establish an effective unified national govern-

[45]"Publius Letter, III," in Syrett et al., *Hamilton Papers*, 1:580–81.
[46]Elliot, *Debates*, 3:53.

ment. They agreed on the serious threats to personal property rights posed by the state legislatures and on the role that a central government would play in protecting these rights. They agreed on the need to have the central government run by worthy, enlightened, and deliberative men. They agreed on the Constitution as necessary to provide the essential framework for commercial development through the creation of a national market, public credit, uniform currency, and the protection of contract. To be sure, Madison's vision tilted toward agrarian capitalism and Hamilton's toward manufactures and commerce. Where they markedly disagreed, however, was in giving positive, assertive power, "energy," and "vigor" to the state.

Hamilton held the new American state to be valuable for its own sake as assertive power. He saw the nation-state, with its historic and heroic goals, as seeking power in a competitive international system of other power-hungry states. Madison saw the nation-state as necessary only to protect private rights and thus to ensure justice. Like Locke, he saw the need for a grant of power to the state, but a grant of limited power. Madison saw the central government as providing an arena for competitive power, where free individuals, groups, and interests would bargain among themselves; the state would define no goals of its own other than ensuring the framework for orderly economic life. All the state would do was regulate "the various and interfering interests," or, as Madison put it to Washington in straightforward Lockean terms, be an impartial umpire in disputes. Energy in politics for Madison would come from individuals and groups in pursuit of their own immediate goals, not from an energetic state in pursuit of its own heroic ends.

What about Madison's governing elite of "enlightened views and virtuous sentiments," "whose wisdom may best discern the true interest of their country," of which he wrote in *Federalist* no. 10? Madison's "true interest" was not the "national interest" of Hamilton's realism. Nor was it some ideal transcending purpose or goal to which wise leadership would lead the state and those still in the shadows. Madison's enlightened leaders would demonstrate their wisdom and virtue more by what they did not do than by what they did. Being men of cool and deliberate judgment, they would not pass unjust laws that interfered with private rights. They would respect liberty, justice, and property, and run a limited government that did little else than preside over and adjudicate conflicts in a basically self-regulating social order. Did not Madison criticize in *Federalist* no. 62 the "excess of law-making" and the voluminousness of laws as the twin "diseases to which our governments are most liable"?

If the state legislators of the Confederation period had acted with self-restraint, there would have been no need for the institutions of the central state, but among generally fallen men they were an even more inferior lot, fired by local prejudices and warm passions. Should the unexpected happen and cooler men of enlightened views seek to do too much—that is, undertake what *Federalist* no. 10 describes as "improper or wicked projects"—Madison's new constitutional government would rapidly cut them down as its multiplicity of built-in checks and balances preserved the Lockean limited state.

Madison's limited Federalist state may well have appeared meek and tame set next to Hamilton's energetic and vigorous state, but it was a matter of perspective. To the Anti-Federalists, even Madison's state, limited as it was by checks and balances and its cool men resisting the temptations of lawmaking, seemed a monstrous betrayal of the Revolution and its spirit. The Constitution could be seen, then, as the last, albeit Thermidorean, act of the American Revolution. Like most revolutions, the American began as a repudiation of the state, of power, and of authority in the name of liberty. Like most revolutions, it ended with a stronger state, the revival of authority, and the taming of liberty's excesses.

The American state would never be quite so bad, however, as the Anti-Federalists feared. They assumed, for example, that "Congress will be vested with more extensive powers than ever Great Britain exercised over us." They worried that "after we have given them all our money, established them in a federal town, given them the power of coining money and raising a standing *army* . . . what resources have the people left?"[47] The reason the results would not be quite that bad is that the new American state created by that "triple headed monster" of a Constitution was much closer to Madison's state than to Hamilton's—at least, that is, for the rest of the eighteenth century and through most of the nineteenth. The twentieth century would be another matter and another story.

[47]Ibid., 2:159, 62.

CHAPTER 9

"Then All the World Would Be Upside Down"

B URKE, more than anyone else, understood and despised the nature of bourgeois radicalism in England. The ideas subversive of the English Constitution and English life were, he wrote, "imported from France and disseminated in this country from dissenting pulpits." Writing to the French émigré Charles Alexandre de Calonne in 1790 of his *Reflections on the Revolution in France*, Burke insisted that "in reality, my object was not France, in the first instance, but this country." The book was written, as we know, in response to the Reverend Richard Price's sermon praising the principles of the French Revolution. It was Price and his fellow English Dissenters, then, who were the real threat, and it was against them that Burke penned his *Reflections*. In a letter to Philip Francis in February 1790 describing his forthcoming book, Burke pledged "to set in a full view the danger from their wicked principles and their black hearts." In response to the subversive Dissenters he would "state the true principles of our constitution." His mission was "to expose them to the hatred, ridicule, and contempt of the whole world."[1]

The Dissenters' great sin, according to Burke, was their "selfish and mischievous ambition." This striving of upstarts to improve their situation, a tendency that Smith described as inherent in the human condition from the womb to the grave, was particularly frightening for Burke when it was linked to talent and merit. It would lead to political revolu-

[1]Edmund Burke, *An Appeal from the New to the Old Whigs*, in *The Works of the Right Honourable Edmund Burke*, ed. Henry Bohn (London, 1877–1884), 3:44; Burke to Charles Alexandre de Calonne, October 25, 1790, in *The Correspondence of Edmund Burke*, ed. Alfred Cobban and Robert A. Smith, 9 vols. (Chicago and Cambridge, 1958–1971), 6:41; Burke to Philip Francis, February 20, 1790, in ibid., p. 92.

tion. Radicalism for Burke was an assault on the aristocracy's political control of the state by self-made talented people excluded from political power. "Jacobinism," he wrote, "is the revolt of the enterprising talents of a country against its property."

> This [French] system has very many partisans in every country in Europe, but particularly in England, where they are already formed into a body, comprehending most of the dissenters of the three leading denominations; to those are readily aggregated all who are dissenters in character, temper, and disposition, though not belonging to any of their congregations . . . all the atheists, deists and Socinians . . . a good many among the monied people . . . who cannot bear to find that their present importance does not bear a proportion to their wealth.[2]

Burke had not always detested the Dissenters. In the 1770s and 1780s he had, in fact, supported parliamentary moves to lift the civil disabilities that weighed down Dissenters and Catholics alike. In 1789, however, he switched, opposing Fox's effort to repeal the Test and Corporations Acts, and throughout the 1790s he thundered against repeal, suggesting that Dissenters sought not religious freedom but political and social revolution. He conjured up in 1793 a picture of them "burning down . . . London, after the massacre of half its inhabitants." The previous year, when he pleaded with the Commons not to remove the legal prescriptions against the Unitarians, he offered an equally nightmarish vision.

> This is not a question of theology, but of legislative prudence. Unitarians were associated for the expressed purpose of proselytism, aiming to collect a multitude sufficient by force and violence to overthrow the church. And this concurrent with a design to subvert the state. . . . The House should not wait till the conspirators, met to commemorate the 14th of July, should seize the Tower of London and the magazines it contains, murder the governor and the Mayor of London, seize upon the King's person, drive out the House of Lords, occupy your gallery and thence as from a high tribunal, dictate to you.[3]

No doubt Burke exaggerated, but he was not alone in reading bourgeois radical consciousness and ambition in apocalyptic terms. Burke's assessment was shared by George Canning, who several decades later saw rampant individualism replacing the corporate world of depen-

---

[2]Edmund Burke, *Reflections on the Revolution in France*, in *Works of Burke*, 2:320; *Regicide Peace*, in ibid., 5:332; *Thoughts on the French Affairs*, in ibid., 4:558–59.
[3]Burke to William Windham, August 23, 1793, in *Correspondence of Burke*, 7:56; *Parliamentary History* 29 (1791–1792): 1382 (May 11, 1792).

dence and patronage: "The first work of the Reformers was to loosen every established political relation, every legal holding of man to man, to destroy every corporation, to destroy every subsisting class of society, and to reduce the nation into individuals, in order, afterwards to congregate them into mobs." Wellington, as befits his calling, was even blunter in his rendering of the changes he thought he had seen in his lifetime: "The revolution is made; that is to say that power is transferred from one class of society, the gentlemen of England, professing the faith of The Church of England, to another class of society, the shopkeepers, being dissenters from the Church, many of them Socinians, others atheists."[4] Burke, Canning, and Wellington distort, of course. Their language is too simplified, too suggestive. But their exaggeration and their anger provide a vivid sense of how bourgeois radicalism appeared to contemporaries.

For Burke the striving of ambitious self-made men was evidence of the sin of pride. The idea of life as a race broke asunder the divine chain by which the "author of our being is the author of our place in the order of existence." It inverted the natural order of things "to set up on high in the air what is required to be on the ground." Ingenious upstarts were driven with "the poisoned talents of a vulgar low bred insolence" to seek to "get above their natural size."[5]

In the replacement of the chain of being by the race of life lay the seeds of anarchy and chaos. God had assigned humankind two basic "places," according to Burke: the rank of people and the rank of "their proper chieftains," the "governing part." Part of God's plan is the establishment of certain people, the aristocracy, in a particular relation of authority above other people, "the common sort." The people assigned to a superior place were "bred in a place of estimation." They were bred "to see nothing low and sordid" from early childhood. They stood "upon such elevated ground" that they had a broad view of the many and complex affairs of individuals and of society. They had "leisure to read, to reflect." Such persons were formed by nature to have "the leading, guiding and governing part."[6] Misery was the fate of any society that did not assign particular importance to such natural aristocrats.

The Protestant Dissenters were, then, the principal enemies of the hierarchical ideal. When Burke spoke in the Commons in 1792 to op-

---

[4]George Canning, "Speech at Liverpool" (January 1820), *Blackwood's* 7 (1820): 13–15; Wellington to John Wilson Croker, March 6, 1833, in *The Correspondence and Diaries of J. W. Croker from 1809 to 1830*, ed. L. J. Jennings (London, 1884), 2:205–6.

[5]Burke, *Appeal from New to Old Whigs*, p. 79; *Reflections*, p. 322; *Parliamentary History* 29 (1791–1792): 1389.

[6]Burke, *Appeal from New to Old Whigs*, pp. 86–87.

pose the motion decriminalizing Unitarianism, he used a Swiftian metaphor to condemn Dissenters for their failure to keep to their natural station, their refusal "to act the part which belongs to the place assigned." They transcended their God-given size, their place in God's creation. Their monstrosity was the defilement of nature. It was the ambition of the bourgeois radicals that Burke indicted.

> These insect reptiles, whilst they go on only caballing and toasting, only fill us with disgust; if they go above their natural size, and increase the quantity, whilst they keep the quality, of their venom, they become the objects of the greatest terror. A spider in his natural size is only a spider, ugly and loathsome; and his flimsy net is only fit for catching flies. But, good God! Suppose a spider as large as an ox, and that he spread cables about us; all the wilds of Africa would not produce anything so dreadful.[7]

America was a living repudiation of the Burkean ideal: a place for everyone and everyone in the place assigned. As Price noted, in America there were no "haughty grandees." There, he and Thomas Cooper claimed, only merit was the path to distinction. Even God, as Franklin noted, was worshiped in America more "for the variety, ingenuity and utility of his handiworks, than for the antiquity of his family."[8] In the late eighteenth century, America embodied the inversion of social order, the shattering of the great chain of being, the violation of political and social principles that for centuries had appeared natural and God-given. It seemed to be the realization of the seventeenth-century radical Puritan quest for "the world turned upside down."

A perceptive General Cornwallis intuited this outcome in 1781. That a ragtag army of farmers and tradesmen could defeat the great imperial power of Britain; that the ambitious, ingenious, and upstart child could topple the parent, the "proper chieftain"; that Mr. Washington could humble Milord Cornwallis—this was indeed the reign of social inversion, the world turned upside down. So it was that when the English general, preparing to surrender his troops at Yorktown, ordered his band to play melancholy tunes, according to the military custom of the day, he insisted that one particular English nursery rhyme be played:

> If buttercups buzz
> after the bee;
> if boats were on land,
> churches on sea;

---

[7]Edmund Burke, "Speech on the Petition of the Unitarians," in *Works of Burke*, 6:121.
[8]Richard Price, *Observations on the American Revolution* (London, 1784). For Cooper and Franklin see Cooper's *Some Information Respecting America* (London, 1794), pp. 53, 55, 57, 230.

If ponies rode men,
and grass ate the cow;
If cats should be chased
into holes by the mouse;
If mammas sold their babies
to gypsies for half a crown;
If summer were spring
and the other way round;
Then all the world would be upside down.[9]

The independence of upstart America, its Declaration proclaims, is legitimized by a theory of rights and the discourse of social contract, a discourse of the origins and purposes of government. Garry Wills notwithstanding, Locke lurks behind its every phrase. Protestant dissent and the American founding generation were both preoccupied, as we have seen, with fundamental questions of political obligation and legitimacy. One of Burke's many complaints against the Dissenters (and for that matter against the colonists, with whom he sympathized) was, in fact, that they loved "to discuss the foundations on which all government is founded," a subject best left alone.[10] This preoccupation led them to use the ridiculously abstract and metaphysical language of natural rights. It was, indeed, their quest for religious freedom that led Protestant Dissenters back to Locke and his seminal arguments about the magistrate's function in a secular polity whose origins rested on the protection of civil rights in matters of this world. Their political writings were grounded in Lockean texts and Lockean concerns. So, too, one cannot fully understand the Framers' constitutional prohibition of religious tests for public office without reference to the Dissenters' crusade against the Test and Corporations Acts and its theoretical grounding in Locke's writings on the nature and purpose of the state.

Republican revisionists must reconsider their judgment that late eighteenth-century political thought was engaged less by "Locke's concern with questions of obligation, original contract and natural rights than was originally thought to be the case."[11] The revisionist assumption that ideas of mixed government, a balanced constitution, and separation of powers monopolized political discourse in the last half of the century at the expense of concern with the state of nature or the doctrine of consent must be revisited. The language of politics in late eighteenth-century England and America was about the origins of government as well as about the forms of government. It was about

[9]An account of this incident is found in Samuel Elliot Morrison's *Oxford History of the American People* (New York, 1965), p. 265.
[10]Burke, "Speech on the Petition," p. 120.
[11]Donald Winch, *Adam Smith's Politics* (Cambridge, Eng., 1985), p. 36.

consent as well as civic virtue. It was about the social roots of magistrates as well as about the moral duties of magistrates.

Eighteenth-century witnesses tell us as much. That a concern with social questions should be wedded to an inquiry into the foundations of the state, that an ambitious preoccupation with talent and merit might lead inexorably to a Lockean world view, would not surprise the astute observer of the Anglo-American scene in the late eighteenth century. Thus it was apparent to Samuel Johnson that "he who thinks his merit underrated . . begins soon to talk of natural equality, the absurdity of many made for one, the original compact, the foundation of authority, and the majority of the people."[12]

Better for the cosmic Toryism of both Burke and Johnson that the naturalness and givenness of hierarchy implicit in the notion of the great chain of being never be subjected to abstract questions about authority and the origins of government. The people who asked such questions were ambitious and ingenious, and with them came the dreaded world of Locke and liberal competitive individualism.

In America that very dreaded world view of Locke and competitive liberalism flourished, however, not only in 1776 but in 1787 and 1788 as well. Madison and the Federalists presume a Lockean polity, and of course they triumphed in the "great national discussion" that was the debate over the ratification of the Constitution. But posterity has not remembered simply the victorious liberal advocates of the Constitution. The Anti-Federalists, too, have lived on in the American imagination. Their republican values lived on in America, as they themselves did, and have been absorbed into the larger pattern of American political culture.

Just as there ultimately was no decisive victor in the political and pamphlet battle, so there was none in the paradigm battle. No one paradigm cleared the field in 1788 and obtained exclusive dominance in the American political discourse. Liberalism scored no watershed victory over republicanism. Both languages were heard during the "great national discussion." Other paradigms as well were available to the Framers' generation, such as the Protestant ethic and the ideals of sovereignty and power. So it has remained. American political discourse to this day tends, more often than not, to be articulated in all of these distinguishable idioms, however discordant they may seem to professors of history or political thought.

The generations of Americans who lived through the founding and the framing have left us proof positive of their paradigmatic pluralism.

---

[12]Samuel Johnson, *The Patriot: Addressed to the Electors of Great Britain* (London, 1774), pp. 4–5.

They imprinted on the landscape of their experience place names by which future generations would know them and their frames of reference. They took the physical world as their text and wrote on it with the conceptual structures of their political language. My corner of the American text, upstate New York, was settled by Revolutionary War veterans in the last decades of the eighteenth century. When they named their parcels of American landscape, they knew in what tongues to speak.

There is a Rome, New York, and an Ithaca and a Syracuse. For state builders fascinated with founders of states, there is a Romulus, New York. There is a Geneva, New York, at the foot of Seneca Lake and ten miles from Ithaca there is even a Locke, New York. Such is the archaeology of paradigms far above Cayuga's waters.

Index

Library of Congress Cataloging-in-Publication Data

Kramnick, Isaac.
  Republicanism and bourgeois radicalism : political ideology in late eighteenth-century England and America / Isaac Kramnick.
    p. cm.
  Includes index.
  ISBN 0-8014-2337-6 (alk. paper). —ISBN 0-8014-9589-X (pbk. : alk. paper)
    1. Political science—Great Britain—History—18th century.   2. Political science—United States—History—18th century.   I. Title.
JA84.G7K73 1990
320.5'09'033—dc20   90-55133